LOND
PLAQUES

Derek Sumeray and John Sheppard

SHIRE PUBLICATIONS

To the memory of John Sheppard and Derek Sumeray.

'Go where we may – rest where we will,
Eternal London haunts us still.'

Thomas Moore (1779–1852).

Published in Great Britain in 2010 by Shire Publications Ltd, Midland House, West Way, Botley, Oxford OX2 0PH, United Kingdom.
44-02 23rd Street, Suite 219, Long Island, NY 11101, USA.

E-mail: shire@shirebooks.co.uk   www.shirebooks.co.uk

Every attempt has been made by the Publishers to secure the appropriate permissions for materials reproduced in this book. If there has been any oversight we will be happy to rectify the situation and a written submission should be made to the Publishers.

A CIP catalogue record for this book is available from the British Library.

Shire Library no. 568   •   ISBN-13: 978 0 74780 735 3

John Sheppard and Derek Sumeray have asserted their right under the Copyright, Designs and Patents Act, 1988, to be identified as the authors of this book.

Designed by Tony Truscott Designs, West Sussex, UK and typeset in Perpetua and Gill Sans.
Printed in China through Worldprint Ltd.

10 11 12 13 14   10 9 8 7 6 5 4 3 2 1

CONTENTS

INTRODUCTION

THIS BOOK contains entries for just over 1,800 plaques across the metropolis. It is the most comprehensive gazetteer available, aspiring to, but not claiming, completeness. It amounts to a collage history of London, each entry a keystroke confirming the unrivalled depth and variety of London's past. In these pages scientists jostle with cricketers, long-gone tollgates with vanished churches, physicians with novelists, botanists with composers, reformers with reactionaries, VCs with suffragettes – each contributing a residual vibration to the ensemble. Taken together, these plaques are a chorus, belting out a confirmation that London is the greatest city on earth.

Derek Sumeray (1933–2003) was the original begetter of this book in 1999 and the majority of the contents remains his. He had been a successful manufacturer of jewellery, with a custom-built factory in Milton Keynes, but, having sold the business, he turned to indulging his hobby of photography, and in particular to documenting the plaques of his native London. His widow estimates he devoted five years to the initial trawl, along with countless days in the British Museum Newspaper Library at Colindale. The effort, in pre-internet times, is awesome. Just as *The Buildings of England* series is known in short as 'Pevsner', in tribute to its founder and original author, so should *London Plaques*, whoever comes along to do further revisions in another ten years time, forever be known as 'Sumeray'.

Due tribute to Derek Sumeray having been paid, we have thought it right to make some alterations in the structure and remit of the book. He styled the collection 'A Guide to Commemorative Plaques within the M25', whereas we have preferred to make our boundary Greater London. This means farewell, for example, to the vigorous programme of plaque erection carried out by Loughton Town Council in Essex, such as those illustrated below.

Similarly, other plaques within the M25, but in Surrey or Hertfordshire, have gone.

Another fundamental change from Derek Sumeray's first edition is that we have divided the entries by borough; it is thought the book will be more useful for a reader out walking if the plaques of particular areas are grouped together. Otherwise, the criteria remain the same: the plaque must be exterior and readily visible to a passer-by, and it must evoke something historic about the place of its erection – words like 'was born here', 'lived here', 'died here', 'in a house on this site' and 'near this spot' mean that as you read the plaque you are invited to summon to mind a presence from the past right where you are standing. So, for example, a plaque which simply said 'This is an eighteenth-century warehouse' would not qualify, but if it said 'This is an eighteenth-century warehouse where Lord Greymatter conducted experiments with early hydraulic lifts' it would be included. Even with these restrictions, Derek Sumeray mustered some fourteen hundred plaques in 1999, a total now swollen by well over four hundred additions ten years later.

The first mention of memorial plaques came in the House of Commons on Friday 17 July 1863, when William Ewart (q.v.), the reforming Liberal MP for Dumfries, rose to ask:

> whether, through the agency of the Metropolitan Board of Works, it may be practicable to have inscribed on those houses in London which have been inhabited by celebrated persons, the names of such persons. The places which have been the residences of the ornaments of their history could not but be precious to all thinking Englishmen and when he reminded the House how rich the metropolis was in such associations, he thought they would agree with him that it was desirable some record should be placed upon the respective localities.

In the event, the Metropolitan Board of Works was not to be the agency, but, after further discussions in *The Builder* and in *The Journal of the Royal Society of Arts*, it was the RSA that undertook the scheme, putting up its first plaque, to Lord Byron, in Holles Street, W1, in 1867. That plaque does not survive, but sixteen of the thirty-five erected by the RSA do. In 1901 the scheme was taken over by the London County Council, and 253 of its plaques are recorded here. The LCC was replaced by the Greater London Council in 1965 and from its twenty-year management we find 246 plaques surviving. Then, in 1985, when Mrs Thatcher temporarily dispatched London local government to oblivion, the baton passed to English Heritage, which to date has put up 309, while also taking responsibility for the conservation of its predecessors' plaques. This continuous strand, from the Royal Society of Arts to English Heritage, has produced 824 surviving plaques, over 40 per cent of the total recorded here. Many people casually think English Heritage is responsible for all plaques in London, but there are numerous other schemes, most notably those of the City Corporation and the City of Westminster. And, aside from formally organised programmes, there are 271 plaques recorded here that have been privately erected; indeed anyone may put up a plaque anywhere, so long as they have the building owner's permission and, where necessary, Listed Building consent.

Briefly to continue the statistical vein, the man with the most plaques in his honour is Charles Dickens, who musters ten. The silver medal goes to William Morris, with eight, and the bronze to William Wilberforce with seven. Tied for fourth place are Charles Lamb and George Orwell, with six plaques each, followed by a veritable pile-up of notables with four or five plaques each, including Churchill and Chaplin, Dr Johnson and Pepys, along with the most-plaqued females, Sylvia Pankhurst and Jacqueline Du Pré. Men outnumber women by roughly seven to one, and the English outnumber the next largest nationality by roughly fifteen to one. The other nations most represented are the Scots, Irish, Americans, French, Germans and Welsh.

Any claim to completeness in a guide such as this would be the height of folly. In the ten months that I have worked on this revision, nineteen further plaques have been put up *that I know about*. I feel sure there have been more, just as I feel sure there are many more that have been up for years undiscovered by Derek Sumeray or me. Similarly, there will be plaques recorded here that have regrettably been removed. Shire Publications will be maintaining an open file in anticipation of a third edition in some years time and will be grateful to receive information on any new plaques going up, and indeed corrections to any mistakes that surely lurk, despite my best efforts, herein. All suggestions, additions, deletions and amendments should be sent to plaques@shirebooks.co.uk

This is one of those books where the index is a major contribution to the fun; I commend to you any list that throws up shoulder to shoulder partnerships such as Captain Cook and Peter Cook, Jimi Hendrix and Henry VIII, Bobby and Henry Moore, Bob Hope and Gerard Manley Hopkins, Joe Orton and George Orwell, Monty Python and Queen Mary, Madame Tussaud and Mark Twain, Johann Zoffany and Émile Zola. There are bogus plaques, spoof plaques, inaccurate plaques, and there is a plaque to a cat – overall a pot-pourri that surely no other city in the world could muster.

In preparing this revised edition I have been greatly helped by local archives and local history societies, too numerous to mention individually, but to them all a collective heartfelt thank-you. To my editor at Shire, Nick Wright, particular gratitude for thinking I could do the job and then for keeping me on the straight and narrow while doing it. Finally, to my wife, Olga, who has tolerated my hogging the computer, sorted out various computer mysteries for me, and chauffeured me on several photographic forays, my love and thanks.

John Sheppard
Fulham, March 2009

John Sheppard photographs a plaque.

THE CITY OF LONDON

THE CITY is London's ancient core, its boundaries not significantly changed since the Middle Ages. It is the smallest of Greater London's administrative districts, known also as 'the Square Mile', which is indeed its rough extent. It has its own Lord Mayor and its own police force. It is Britain's financial centre and vies with New York as the world's financial centre. It is a place of work for some 350,000 people, who commute in daily, while the City's resident population was a mere 7,800 in 2006, compared with its peak of 208,000 in 1700.

Topographically, the two big events in the City's history are the Great Fire of 1666 and the Blitz of 1940–1, which both wrought widespread damage. These events are reflected in the many plaques recording some ancient building 'destroyed in the Great Fire' or in the Blitz.

The principal erector of plaques is the Corporation of the City of London, which has been putting them up since 1923. Ninety-eight of their distinctive blue ceramic rectangular plaques are recorded here, out of the total of 152 plaques found in the City. Sadly, several of those noted by Derek Sumeray have not survived redevelopments in the subsequent decade; the lame-brained property developers who had not the wit to remove the plaques before demolition and reinstate them after rebuilding should in my view have their severed heads stuck up on London Bridge.

ALDERSGATE
1 Aldersgate Street, EC1.
Corporation of the City of London
This is the site of Aldersgate, the main northern entrance to London. There were eight gates in the wall surrounding the old City, all demolished by the end of the eighteenth century, with the exception of Temple Bar. Aldersgate was first built in Roman times, but its name is Saxon, meaning originally 'Ealdred's gate'. It was rebuilt in 1617, damaged in the Great Fire, repaired, and finally demolished in 1761.

ALDGATE
89 Aldgate High Street, EC3.
Corporation of the City of London
This is the site of Aldgate, the eastern entrance to London. One of the six gates dating back to Roman

times, its name is the Saxon 'Ealdgate' ('old gate'). Chaucer (q.v.) lived in the room over the gate from 1374 to 1385. Rebuilt in the early twelfth century and again at the beginning of the seventeenth century, it was demolished in 1760.

ANTI-CORN LAW LEAGUE
69 Fleet Street, EC4. *Private*
This was the site of the London offices of the Anti-Corn Law League from 1844 to 1846. Founded in Manchester in 1838, the League sought the abolition of the protectionist Corn Laws, which inflated the price of basic foodstuffs. The Corn Laws were

repealed in 1846, and the League turned to a general campaign for free trade.

ASTLEY, Dame Joanna (*c*.1388–1452), English, courtier
St Bartholomew's Hospital, West Smithfield, EC1. *Dove Brothers*
Dame Joanna (or Joan) Astley (or Asteley) lived in a house formerly on this site. In January 1424 she was appointed principal nurse to the two-year-old Henry VI, at an annual salary of £20. In 1433 she was granted an annuity, presumably because the twelve-year-old king no longer needed a nurse. The plaque is incorporated in a 1907 foundation stone on a building of St Bartholomew's Hospital.

AUTOMOBILE ASSOCIATION
18 Fleet Street, EC4.
Automobile Association
The Automobile Association was formed by a group of motoring enthusiasts at a meeting at the Trocadero restaurant on 29 June 1905 and opened its first office in this building the same year. The initial aim was to help motorists avoid police speed traps, but they also began erecting the first useful road signs.

BECKET, St Thomas à (?1118–70), English, prelate
90 Cheapside, EC2. *Private*
86 Cheapside, EC2. *Corporation of the City of London*
Both plaques tell of Becket's birth here or nearby. He became chancellor to Henry II in 1155 and was for a time the king's most intimate courtier, being made Archbishop of Canterbury in 1162. Thereafter relations with the king went downhill and Becket was murdered in his cathedral by four knights seeking Henry's favour. His shrine became the most famous place of pilgrimage in Christendom until the Reformation.

BETHLEHEM HOSPITAL, First
Great Eastern Hotel, Liverpool Street, EC2.
Corporation of the City of London
This was the site of the first Bethlehem Hospital, 1247–1676. It was built by Simon FitzMary and by the late fourteenth century had come to specialise in 'distracted' cases. It moved in 1676.

BETHLEHEM HOSPITAL, Second
145–149 London Wall, EC2.
Corporation of the City of London
This was the site of the second Bethlehem Hospital, 1676–1815. Designed by Robert Hooke, the gates were adorned with Cibber's statues of *Melancholy* and *Madness*, two giant figures modelled on inmates (which can still be seen in the Bethlem Royal Hospital Museum at Beckenham). The patients here were one of the sights of London, arranged in galleries like a zoo. The hospital moved to Lambeth in 1815, to the building that is now the Imperial War Museum.

BETJEMAN, Sir John
(1906–84), English, poet, conservationist
43 Cloth Court, Cloth Fair, EC1.
Private
Sir John lived here. A founder member of the Victorian Society in 1958, he was a passionate conservationist, leading the successful campaign to save the St Pancras Hotel, but failing to save the Euston Arch. He was made Poet Laureate in 1972 and enjoyed a popularity unusual for modern poets, not least through his jolly, whimsical television documentaries.
(See also page 99.)

BINNEY, Captain Ralph (1888–1944), English, naval officer
22 Birchin Lane, EC3. *Royal Navy*
Binney had joined the Royal Navy in 1903 and retired in 1933, but with the outbreak of the Second World War he was back in uniform serving as chief staff officer to Admiral Nasmith. At noon on 8 December 1944 he was among a large crowd of shoppers in Birchin Lane when a smash and grab raid took place. Fifty-six-year-old Captain Binney, alone among the onlookers, attempted to stop the thieves and was dragged under their speeding car across the river as far as Tooley Street, Southwark, where he was thrown clear. He died three hours later in Guy's Hospital.

BLACKFRIARS PRIORY
7 Ludgate Broadway, Ludgate Hill, EC4.
Corporation of the City of London
The Priory existed on this site from 1278 until dissolution in 1538, with grounds extending to the river.

The priory was sold to Sir Thomas Cawarden, Master of the Revels, who demolished most of the buildings. Parts survived, being used for various purposes, including a playhouse, until the whole was destroyed in the Great Fire of 1666.

BLACKSMITHS' HALL
Queen Victoria Street, EC4.
Corporation of the City of London
This was the site of the second hall of the company, 1668–1785. Its first hall, on the site of today's Salvation Army headquarters, had been built in 1494 and was destroyed in the Great Fire.

BOMB, First of the Second World War
Fore Street, EC2.
Private
The first bomb of the Second World War on the City fell here at 12.15 a.m. on 25 August 1940. The 'first' Blitz would last till May 1941, killing 43,000 civilians, half of them in London, and destroying or damaging over a million houses in London alone. It had no significant effect on the British war effort. (For other Second World War bomb damage sites, see Tower Hamlets, Southwark, Newham, Kingston and Lewisham.)

BRADFORD, John (?1510–55), English, cleric, martyr
St Bartholomew's Hospital, West Smithfield, EC1. *Protestant Alliance London*
Burnt near this spot in 1555, Bradford was a very popular preacher. Imprisoned on a charge of preaching seditious sermons, he wrote to Cranmer, Latimer and Ridley as his execution approached: 'God forgive me mine unthankfulness for this exceeding great mercy, that, amongst so many thousands, it pleaseth His mercy to choose me to be one, in whom He will suffer.'

BRAY, John (*fl.*1738–42), English, brazier
13 Little Britain, EC1.
Corporation of the City of London
Bray has a walk-on part in history. This was the site of his home; he was a layman, 'a pious brazier', whose house was used for early Methodist/Moravian meetings until the Fetter Lane Meeting Room was formed. It was here that Charles Wesley (see page 22)

experienced his evangelical conversion on 21 May 1738. Bray quarrelled with the Wesleys in 1740 and with the Moravians in 1742 and thereafter disappears from the records.

BRIDEWELL PALACE
14 New Bridge Street, EC4. *Private*
This was the site of the Bridewell Palace, erected by Henry VIII in 1515–20 and granted to the City by Edward VI in 1553 to house the Bridewell Royal Hospital. It continued as a hospital, prison and orphanage until 1855. The buildings were demolished in 1863–4, apart from the 1802 gateway, which survives.

BRIGHT, John (1811–89), English, reformer
69 Fleet Street, EC4. *Private*
This plaque commemorates the Anti-Corn Law League (see page 6), of which Bright and Richard Cobden (see opposite) were the leading lights. Bright was one of the greatest orators of the nineteenth century, campaigning not only for free trade but also against the Crimean War. He coined the phrase 'England is the Mother of Parliaments' in 1865.

BRODERERS' HALL
Priest Court, 32 Gutter Lane, EC2.
Corporation of the City of London
This was the site of the hall of the Broderers' Company from 1515 to 1940. The company is recorded from 1376 and English embroidery was famous throughout Europe. The hall was rebuilt after the Great Fire of 1666, but by the nineteenth century had fallen into disuse and was used as a warehouse until destroyed by enemy action in 1940.

BROOKING, Charles (1723–59), English, marine artist
Tokenhouse Yard, EC2. *Corporation of the City of London*
Brooking lived near here in 1754. It is suggested that he was brought up near the dockyard at Deptford and that his father worked at Greenwich Naval Hospital. He is considered the finest marine artist of his era, and his attention to detail shows clear understanding of the sea and ships. Most of his extant work dates from the last six years of his career, and

the National Maritime Museum has twenty of his paintings.

BUCKINGHAM, second Duke of (1628–87), English, courtier
Newcastle Court, College Hill, EC4.
Corporation of the City of London
Politician and courtier, the second Duke of Buckingham, whose house was here, was brought up with Charles I's children, escaped the country during the Civil War and returned with Charles II, afterwards spending many years in Parliament. He also wrote several comedies.

BULL AND MOUTH INN
Nomura House, St Martin's-le-Grand, EC1.
Corporation of the City of London

This was the site of the Bull and Mouth inn, first recorded as 'The Mouth' in 1661. The inn was a regular meeting place of the Quakers and, before the coming of the railways, a coaching office. It was demolished in 1888 to make way for the General Post Office.

CHRIST'S HOSPITAL
Former Post Office Building, Newgate Street, EC1. *Corporation of the City of London*
This was the site of Christ's Hospital from 1552 to 1902. It was founded by Edward VI as a hospital (school) for orphans. Severely damaged in the Great Fire of 1666, it was rebuilt under the supervision of Sir Christopher Wren. The school moved to Horsham, Sussex, in 1902.

CITY OF LONDON GIRLS' SCHOOL
Carmelite Street, EC4.
Corporation of the City of London

This was the site of the school from 1894 to 1969. It was founded with a bequest from William Ward, a philanthropist and City freeman, who, although he had no daughters himself, believed that girls were just as entitled to a proper education as boys. The school moved to the Barbican in 1969.

CITY OF LONDON SCHOOL
3 Milk Street, EC2. *Corporation of the City of London*
This was the site of the school from 1835 to 1882. Warren Stormes Hale, chairman of the Corporation's Schools Committee, led the drive for an Act of Parliament establishing the school, which grew so rapidly that it moved to the Embankment in 1882. It has moved again since, in 1986, to new buildings by the Millennium Bridge.

CLAYTON, Reverend 'Tubby' (1885–1972), English, cleric
43 Trinity Square, EC3.
English Heritage

'Tubby' Clayton lived here. He founded Talbot House (in signals parlance 'Toc H') in Belgium in 1915 as a rest house for soldiers. This has now grown into a worldwide organisation promoting especially racial harmony – 'to love widely, to build bravely, to think fairly, to witness humbly'.

CLEARY, Fred (1905–84), English, property developer
Cleary Gardens, Huggin Hill, EC4.
Corporation of the City of London
A chartered surveyor, Cleary founded and chaired a property company noted for restoring old buildings and responsible for some of the largest developments in the City. A City councillor, he was, as the plaque says, 'tireless in his wish to increase open space'. This garden is named in his honour.

COBDEN, Richard (1804–65), English, statesman
69 Fleet Street, EC4. *Private*
The plaque commemorates the Anti-Corn Law League

(see page 6), with which Cobden and John Bright (see pages 8–9) are always associated. Cobden spent his life promoting free trade, based on the high moral purpose of seeking peace and goodwill among all men. Disinterested and modest, he declined all honours from both Britain and France after his work had brought reconciliation between the perennial enemies.

COFFEE HOUSE, First in London
Jamaica Wine House, St Michael's Alley, EC3.
Corporation of the City of London
This was the site of the first London coffee house, 'At the Sign of Pasqua Rosee's Head', established in 1652. Pasqua Rosee was a Turk from Smyrna, brought to England as the servant of a Levant merchant, Daniel Edwards, whose friends were so taken with Rosee's brew that Edwards helped him set up a coffee house. He produced a handbill, 'The Vertue of the Coffee Drink', and the vogue began.

COLET, Dean John (?1467–1519), English, cleric
New Change, EC4. *Corporation of the City of London*
The plaque records that near this spot stood St Paul's School from 1512 to 1884, founded by Dean Colet. Colet wrote a Latin grammar for the school and endowed it with the fortune he inherited from his father. The school moved to Hammersmith in 1884.

COOKS' HALL
10 Aldersgate Street, EC1.
Corporation of the City of London
This was the site of the hall of the Cooks' Company, founded in 1311 and given its first charter in 1482. The hall was built in 1500, survived the Great Fire, was extended in 1674, burnt down and rebuilt in 1764, finally burnt down (and not rebuilt) in 1771.

CORDWAINERS' HALL
Festival Garden, Cannon Street, EC4.
Corporation of the City of London
This was the site of six successive halls of the Cordwainers' Company from 1440 until the sixth was destroyed by enemy action in 1941. 'Cordwainer' originally meant a worker in Cordovan goatskin leather, producing shoes, bottles and harnesses, but came to mean a shoemaker.

CRIPPLEGATE
Roman House, Wood Street, EC2.
Corporation of the City of London

This is the site of Cripplegate, first built by the Romans and rebuilt in 1490 for use as a prison and gateway. The gate was destroyed in the reign of Charles II and the building finally demolished in 1760.

CROSSKEYS INN
Bell Yard, Gracechurch Street, EC3.
Corporation of the City of London
The crossed keys of St Peter were the arms of the papal see, and the inn on this site was in the shadow of a church dedicated to St Peter. First recorded in 1552, it was destroyed in the Great Fire and not rebuilt.

CURTIS, William (1746–99), English, botanist
51 Gracechurch Street, EC3.
Corporation of the City of London
Curtis lived in a house on this site. He translated Linnaeus's *Fundamenta Entomologiciae* (1772), published the six-volume *Flora Londiniensis* (1777–98) and founded the *Botanical Magazine* (1781). He also set up public botanical gardens at Bermondsey and Lambeth, which were frequented by students.

CUTLERS' HALL
College Hill Chambers, Cloak Lane, EC4.
Corporation of the City of London
The Cutlers' first hall was built in 1285 in Poultry but they moved to Cloak Lane in 1416. The hall was rebuilt in 1451, again in 1660 and yet again in 1671. It was demolished to make way for the railway. The present Cutlers' Hall is in Warwick Lane.

DAILY COURANT
12 Ludgate Circus, EC4.
Corporation of the City of London
Near this site was published in 1702 the *Daily Courant*, London's first daily newspaper. It was produced by Edward Mallet and consisted of a single sheet with two columns. It merged with the *Daily Gazetteer* in 1735.

DE ROKESLEY, Gregory
(d.1292), English, wool merchant
72 Lombard Street, EC3.
Corporation of the City of London
De Rokesley lived in a house on this site. Eight times mayor of London

(1274–81 and 1285), he was a prominent wool merchant, member of the Goldsmiths' Company, alderman of Dowgate ward, chief saymaster of all the King's Mints, keeper of the King's Exchange, and evidently a favourite of Edward I.

DEVIL TAVERN
1 Fleet Street, EC4.
Corporation of the City of London
This is the site of the Devil Tavern, first recorded around 1563; it was demolished in 1787. It was first called the St Dunstan Tavern owing to its proximity to the church of that name; but it became known as the Devil, or the Devil and Dunstan, because its sign illustrated the story of St Dunstan and the Devil:

> Saynct Dunstane, as ye storie goes,
> Once seized ye Deville by ye nose,
> Hee tugged soe harde and made hym rore
> That he was heerd thre myles and more.

DISRAELI, Benjamin (1804–81), English, Prime Minister, novelist
6 Frederick's Place, EC2.
Corporation of the City of London
Disraeli was an articled clerk to Messrs Swain, Stevens, Maples, Pearse & Hunt, solicitors, in this building from 1821 to 1824. (See also Waltham Forest, Westminster 3, and Camden 2.)

DOCKWRA, William (d.1716), English, merchant
Lloyd's Building, Lime Street, EC3.
Corporation of the City of London
Dockwra founded a Penny Post system for London near this spot in 1680. He was comptroller of the Penny Post from 1697 to 1700 but was dismissed on charges of maladministration.

DOCTORS' COMMONS
Faraday Building, Queen Victoria Street, EC4.
Corporation of the City of London
This is the site of Doctors' Commons, demolished in 1867. This was the colloquial name for the College of Advocates and Doctors of Law, from 1572 housing the Ecclesiastical and Admiralty courts. Steerforth, in Dickens's *David Copperfield*, described it as 'a lazy old

nook near St Paul's … where they play all kinds of tricks with obsolete old monsters of Acts of Parliament, which three-fourths of the world know nothing about'.

FARYNER, Thomas (*fl.*1666), English, baker
Pudding Lane, EC3. *Worshipful Company of Bakers*
Faryner, the king's baker, had his shop near this spot. Because he failed to damp down his oven kindling for

the weekend, this is where the Great Fire of London of 1666 started. It began at 1.30 a.m. on Saturday 1 September and burned till 6 September, destroying 13,200 houses, St Paul's Cathedral and eighty-seven other churches, fifty-two livery company halls, two prisons, three city gates, four bridges etc. – and the Bakers' Company has never been allowed to forget it.

FOUNDERS' HALL
Founders' Court, Lothbury, EC2.
Corporation of the City of London
In this court stood the Founders' Hall from 1531 to 1845. The Founders' Company, dating from at least 1365, received its first charter in 1614. Its members made brass and bronze candlesticks, water bowls and the like. Their hall was destroyed in the Great Fire and rebuilt on the same spot. In the 1790s it was a meeting place for people sympathetic to the French Revolution and was known as 'the cauldron of sedition'.

FREEMASONS, First meeting of English Grand Lodge
Juxon House, St Paul's Churchyard, EC4.
Corporation of the City of London
English Masonic historians attach great significance to 24 June 1717 (St John the Baptist's Day), when four London lodges came together at the Goose and Gridiron alehouse on this spot in St Paul's Churchyard and formed what they called the 'Grand Lodge of England'. Although Freemasonry had existed in

England since at least the mid-seventeenth century, this founding of the Grand Lodge is taken as the formation of organised Freemasonry in its modern sense.

FRENCH PROTESTANT CHURCH
Nomura House, St Martin's-le-Grand, EC1.
Corporation of the City of London
This is the site of the first French Protestant church, built in the sixteenth century for French refugees from persecution at home. It was demolished in 1888, and the present French Protestant church (built 1891–3) is in Soho Square, W1.

FRY, Elizabeth (1780–1845), English, prison reformer
St Mildred's Court, Poultry, EC2.
Corporation of the City of London
Mrs Fry lived here from 1800 to 1809. A Quaker, she devoted her life to prison and asylum reform, having discovered the appalling conditions in Newgate jail. Her face appears on the reverse side of the current £5 note. (See also Hackney.)

GENERAL LETTER OFFICE
Princes Street, EC2. *Corporation of the City of London*
Near this spot, in Post House Yard, stood the General Letter Office from 1653 to 1666. The first postmarks in the world were introduced here in 1661. They indicated the date of receipt of the letter in the London office. At that time all British mail had to pass through London.

GILTSPUR STREET COMPTER
2 Giltspur Street, EC1.
Corporation of the City of London
This was the site of the Giltspur Street Compter, a small prison holding mainly debtors, but also felons, vagrants and other overnight charges such as recalcitrant drunks. Designed by George Dance the Younger (q.v.), it opened in 1791 and was demolished in 1854.

GLOVERS' HALL
Silk Street entrance, Barbican, EC2.
Corporation of the City of London
The hall of the Glovers' Company stood near here from the seventeenth century until the company gave it up in 1882.

GRAHAM, George (1673–1751), English, clockmaker

69 Fleet Street, EC4. *Private*
'Honest George', a Quaker like his mentor Tompion (see below), made improvements to the pendulum clock, invented the mercury pendulum and the Graham or dead-beat escapement. He was master of the Clockmakers' Company in 1722.

GRAY, Thomas (1716–71), English, poet
39 Cornhill, EC3. *Private*
Gray was the leading poet of his day. His *Elegy Written in a Country Churchyard* (1751), quoted on the plaque, was composed in Stoke Poges churchyard, Buckinghamshire, and remains one of the most popular poems in the English language.

GRESHAM, Sir Thomas (1519–79), English, financier
International Finance Centre, Old Broad Street, EC2. *Corporation of the City of London*
Sir Thomas lived in a house on this site. Besides acting

as a royal agent in Spain and the Low Countries, he was an important source of political intelligence to William Cecil, Elizabeth I's principal adviser. He founded the first English paper mills at Osterley in 1565, founded and built at his own expense the first Royal Exchange in 1566–8 and bequeathed his house in Bishopsgate for the foundation of Gresham College. Sir Thomas's plaque is currently almost entirely hidden by the insensitive location of a portable sandwich kiosk.

GREY FRIARS' MONASTERY
106 Newgate Street, EC1.
Corporation of the City of London
This was the site of the Grey Friars' monastery from 1225 to 1538, built on land given to the monks by a mercer, John Ewin. After the dissolution of the monasteries, the buildings continued in various uses until the last of them were demolished at the end of the nineteenth century to make way for the General Post Office.

GUY, Thomas (c.1644–1724), English, bookseller
1 Cornhill, EC3. *Private*
Guy's home and bookselling business were here from
1668 until his death. In addition to founding Guy's
Hospital, he also built and furnished three wards at
St Thomas's Hospital (1707) and founded several
almshouses. His fortune was based on shrewd stock
speculation, especially with the South Sea Company.

THOMAS GUY (1644/5–1724)
Who founded and endowed
Guy's Hospital had his home &
his bookshop on this site from
1668 until his death in 1724

HAZLITT, William (1778–1830), English, essayist
6 Bouverie Street, EC4.
Corporation of the City of London
Hazlitt lived here in 1829. A prolific journalist, critic,
essayist and lecturer, heavily influenced by Coleridge
(q.v.), his work is characterised by invective, irony and
a gift for epigram. His *Lectures on the English Comic
Writers* (1819) and *The Spirit of the Age* (1825) are
among his enduring works. (See also Westminster 3.)

HOOD, Thomas (1799–1845), English, poet
Midland Bank, Poultry, EC2.
Corporation of the City of London
Hood was born in a house on this site on 23 May
1799. 'Next to being a citizen of the world', he wrote
in his *Literary Reminiscences*, 'it must be the best thing
to be born a citizen of the world's greatest city.'
(See also Westminster 1, Westminster 4 and Enfield.)

HOWARD, Sir Ebenezer (1850–1928), English,
garden city pioneer
Moor House, London Wall, EC2.
Corporation of the City of London
The plaque records that Sir Ebenezer was born near
this spot on 29 January 1850 at 62 Fore Street.
(See also Hackney.)

JOHNSON, Dr Samuel (1709–84), English,
lexicographer, critic, conversationalist
17 Gough Square, EC4. *Royal Society of Arts*
Johnson's Court, Fleet Street, EC4. *Corporation of
the City of London*

Dr Johnson lived at
the first address
from 1748 to
1759, and at the
second from
1765 to 1776.
In Gough
Square he
compiled his
celebrated *Dictionary
of the English Language*
(1755), which included such cherishable definitions as
'Oats: a grain, which in England is generally given to
horses, but in Scotland supports the people'. The
Gough Square house is now a shrine to the doctor,
open six days a week.

JONATHAN'S COFFEE HOUSE
Change Alley, EC3. *Corporation of the City of London*
This was where the 'South Sea Bubble', the great
speculation scandal of the early eighteenth century,
was fomented. The house was destroyed by fire in
1748, rebuilt, destroyed again by fire in 1778 and not
rebuilt.

KEATS, John (1795–1821), English, poet
87 Moorgate, EC2. *Corporation of the City of London*
The plaque records that Keats was born in the 'Swan
& Hoop', livery stables run by his father, on this site
in 1795. (See also Enfield and Camden 1.)

**KING WILLIAM STREET UNDERGROUND
STATION**
Monument Street, EC3.
Corporation of the City of London
This was the site of the City's first Underground
terminus from 1890 to 1900. The City & South
London line from Stockwell was the world's first
electric tube, but problems with the gradients and an
awkward curve into the station led to closure after ten
years. It had a revival as an air-raid shelter in the
Second World War.

KING'S ARMS TAVERN
Change Alley, EC3. *Private*
Originally 'The Swan', built in 1681, the tavern was
destroyed in the Cornhill fire of 1748, rebuilt as the
King's Arms and survived till the 1790s. 'King's Arms'
was and is one of the most ubiquitous pub names;
there are over fifty in Greater London today.

KING'S WARDROBE 5 Wardrobe Place, EC4. *Corporation of the City of London* This was the site of the King's Wardrobe, built in the fourteenth century as a private house and sold to Edward III to house his ceremonial robes. After its destruction in the Great Fire of 1666, the Wardrobe was moved to the Savoy and later to Buckingham Street.

LAMB, Charles (1775–1834), English, essayist
2 Crown Office Row, Temple, EC2. *Private*
10 Giltspur Street, EC1. *Private*
Lamb was born in chambers formerly on the first site and attended the Bluecoat School near the second site. (See Enfield and Islington.)

LAURENCE POUNTNEY CHURCH and CORPUS CHRISTI COLLEGE Laurence Pountney Hill, EC4.
Corporation of the City of London
This was the site of the church and college, destroyed in the Great Fire of 1666. Sir John de Poultney (died 1349), four times mayor of London, endowed the college of priests. He lived nearby and his house, too, was destroyed in the fire. After the fire the parish was united with St Mary Abchurch.

LINACRE, Thomas (1460–1524), English, physician
Rear wall of Faraday Building, Knightrider Street, EC4. *Corporation of the City of London*
Linacre lived in a house on this site. Physician to Henry VII and Henry VIII, he was the founder and first president of the Royal College of Physicians (1518), as well as founding lectureships in medicine at both Oxford and Cambridge. He was also a noted classical scholar, tutoring the future Queen Mary. The plaque, in a poor condition, is not easily accessible.

LLOYD'S COFFEE HOUSE 15 Lombard Street, EC3.
Corporation of the City of London
This was the site of Lloyd's Coffee House from 1691 to 1785. Established by Edward Lloyd, it became a meeting place for businessmen, some of whom

developed an insurance business devoted to shipping. Over the years this grew into the present Lloyd's insurance company.

LONDON HOUSE 172 Aldersgate Street, EC1.
Corporation of the City of London
This was the site of London House, home of the bishops of London from the Reformation until its destruction by fire in 1766.

LONDON PENNY POST Lloyd's Building, Lime Street, EC3.
Corporation of the City of London
See the entry for William Dockwra (page 11).

LONDON SALVAGE CORPS 61 Watling Street, EC4. *Private*
Founded in 1866, when firefighting was the responsibility of the Metropolitan Board of Works, which gave insurance companies the right to set up a separate salvage force to attend fires. After leaving here, the Corps continued till 1984, when its duties were taken over by the London Fire Brigade.

LORINERS' HALL London Wall, EC2. *Corporation of the City of London*
The Loriners' Hall stood near this spot, at the northern end of Basinghall Street, from 1711 to 1759.

LORINERS' TRADE
1 Poultry, EC2. *Corporation of the City of London*
This was the site where Loriners traded from the
eleventh century to the thirteenth. Loriners made bits
and metal mountings for horses' bridles, spurs,
stirrups and other harness parts. They were initially
inferior to the Saddlers, but their own livery company
was chartered in 1711.

LUDGATE
Ludgate Hill, EC4. *Corporation of the City of London*
The original Lud Gate was supposedly built by King
Lud in pre-Roman times but, since his very existence is
open to question, it is more plausible to attribute it to
the Romans. Rebuilt in 1215, again in 1586, and
repaired after the Great Fire, it was demolished in
1760. Statues of Queen Elizabeth I and of King Lud and
his sons, which formerly adorned the gate, are
preserved outside the church of St Dunstan in the West.

MARCONI, Guglielmo (1874–1937), Italian,
physicist, inventor
British Telecom Building, Newgate Street, EC1.
Private
Marconi's first successful transmission had been in
Italy in 1895, but there was not much interest there,
so he came to England and gave his first public
demonstration here on 27 July 1896. By 1901 he had
achieved transatlantic radio communication. He
shared the 1909 Nobel Prize for Physics.
(See also Westminster 2.)

MARINE SOCIETY
Change Alley, EC3. *Private*
The society, now operating from Lambeth, was
formed at the King's Arms Tavern here on 25 June
1756 to promote careers at sea for boys, especially
those living in needy circumstances. It is now the
world's oldest seafarers' charity, providing advice,
training and support to merchant sailors.

MILTON, John
(1608–74), English, poet,
essayist
**Bow Bells House,
Bread Street, EC4.**
*Corporation of the City of
London*
Born near here, Milton's reputation as England's
greatest poet – which some dispute – rests mainly

on his epic *Paradise Lost* (1667), but his merits are
equally demonstrated by his pamphleteering in the
Parliamentary cause, especially in *Areopagitica*
(1644), a ringing defence of press freedom that
should be compulsory reading for any would-be
censors to this day.

MITRE TAVERN
37 Fleet Street, EC4. *Corporation of the City of London*
This was a favourite watering hole for Shakespeare
(q.v.) and Ben Jonson (q.v.). Dr Johnson (q.v.) and
James Boswell (q.v.) had their first long evening
together here in June 1763. 'Give me your hand,
I have taken a liking to you,' said the Doctor.

MOOR GATE
72 Moorgate, EC2. *Corporation of the City of London*
This was the site of Moor Gate, demolished in 1761.
Originally a postern, a minor gate, leading to
Moorfields, the marshy open land to the north, it was
rebuilt twice in the fifteenth century, again in 1511,
and again in 1672 after damage in the Great Fire. The
stones from its demolition were sold to the
Corporation for £166 and used to support the newly
widened central arch of London Bridge.

MORE, St Thomas (1478–1535), English, cleric,
statesman
20 Milk Street, EC2. *Corporation of the City of London*
More was born in a house on this site. (See fuller
entry in Kensington & Chelsea 2.)

NEWBERY, John (1713–67), English, publisher
St Paul's Churchyard, EC4.
Pennsylvania Library Association
Newbery lived, published and sold books on this site.
His most notable publications were *Goody Two Shoes*
(possibly by Oliver Goldsmith [q.v.]) and *Mother Goose*.
His memory is particularly alive in the United States,
where the annual prize for best children's book is
named in his honour.

NEWGATE
Newgate Street, EC1.
Corporation of the City of London
This was the site of Newgate, possibly in existence as
early as 857, rebuilt in the reign of Henry I, rebuilt by
Sir Richard Whittington (q.v.), destroyed by fire and
rebuilt in 1555–6, destroyed again in the Great Fire of
1666, rebuilt in 1672, and finally demolished in 1777.

NEWMAN, Cardinal John Henry (1801–90),
English, prelate
Old Broad Street, EC2. *Private*
Cardinal Newman was born near this spot.
(See fuller entries in Richmond and Camden 2.)

NORTHUMBERLAND HOUSE
Nomura House, St Martin's-le-Grand, EC1.
Corporation of the City of London
This was the site of Northumberland House. Dating
from 1352, the house was owned by Henry Percy,
Earl of Northumberland, descended from William de
Percy, who came over with William the Conqueror.
The second earl, known as Harry Hotspur, who lived
here, was killed at the battle of Shrewsbury in 1403.
By the early eighteenth century the house is recorded
as having become a tavern.

HERE LIVED IN 1784
DOSITEY OBRADOVICH
1742~1811
Eminent Serbian man of letters
First Minister of Education
in Serbia

OBRADOVICH,
Dositey (1742–1811),
Serbian, man of letters
27 Clement's Lane,
EC4. *Private*
Before Obradovich,
Serbian literature was
written in Russian-
Slavonic, a language known only to the educated
classes. Obradovich said books should be in the
language people spoke, and his works were a huge
success. He was made Minister of Education in 1807.

O'CONNOR, T. P.
(1848–1929), Irish,
journalist, politician
78 Fleet Street, EC4.
Private
O'Connor was a notably
popular public figure,
widely called 'the Tribune
of the People', who
founded various radical
journals. He entered
Parliament in 1880, the
only Irish Nationalist
ever elected by an
English constituency,
eventually becoming
'Father of the House',
and from 1924 he was a
privy councillor.

OLD LONDON BRIDGE, Approach
St Magnus the Martyr, Lower Thames Street,
EC3.
Corporation of the City of London
This churchyard formed part of the approach to Old
London Bridge from 1176 to 1831. This was the first
stone bridge, replacing previous wooden bridges dating
from Roman times. The 1831 replacement was built
upstream but now stands at Lake Havasu, Arizona.

OLD SERJEANTS' INN
5 Chancery Lane, EC4.
Corporation of the City of London
The serjeants, a branch of the legal profession,
occupied various premises in this area from the
fifteenth century. This one stood from 1415 to 1910,
though the serjeants had sold it in 1877.

PARISH CLERKS' COMPANY, First hall
Clerks Place, EC2. *Corporation of the City of London*
This was the site of the first hall of the Parish Clerks'
Company. Originally the Fraternity of St Nicholas,
dating from at least 1274, they are not strictly a livery
company, on the grounds that the surplice has
precedence over the livery. This hall was confiscated
during the Reformation under the Act of 1547 for
suppressing chantries.

PARISH CLERKS' COMPANY, Third hall
88 Wood Street, EC2.
Corporation of the City of London
Their second hall having been destroyed in the Great
Fire, the Parish Clerks occupied a hall on this site
from 1671 until it was destroyed by fire in the Blitz,
December 1940.

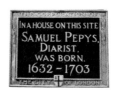

IN A HOUSE ON THIS SITE
SAMUEL PEPYS,
DIARIST.
WAS BORN.
1632 – 1703

PEPYS, Samuel
(1632–1703), English,
diarist, civil servant
Salisbury Court, EC4.
Corporation of the City of
London
Seething Lane Garden,
EC3. *Corporation of the City of London*
Pepys was born in a house on the first site and worked
in the Navy Office on the second site until its
destruction by fire in 1671. His *Diary*, now regarded
as a priceless window on Restoration London, was
written between 1660 and 1669 in a private
shorthand that was not deciphered until 1825. After

his death Pepys was remembered by John Evelyn as 'universally beloved, hospitable, generous, learned in many things, skilled in music, a very great cherisher of learned men'. (See also Westminster 4.)

PHILPOT, John (1516–55), English, cleric, martyr
St Bartholomew's Hospital, West Smithfield, EC1. *Protestant Alliance London*
Philpot was burnt near this spot on 18 December 1555. He had been constantly engaged in controversy and was imprisoned as a heretic after Queen Mary's accession. Condemned to death, he replied: 'I thank God that I am a heretic out of your cursed church; I am no heretic before God.'

POPE, Alexander (1688–1744), English, poet, essayist
Plough Court, 32 Lombard Street, EC3.
Corporation of the City of London
Pope was born in a house in this court. He was the only child of his elderly parents (his mother was in her forties when he was born), and they were Catholics, which meant that his father had to retire from his successful linen business at the time of Pope's birth under anti-Catholic laws introduced with the coming of William III. When Pope was seven they moved to Hammersmith. (See also Hounslow.)

POULTERS' HALL
King Edward Street, EC1.
Corporation of the City of London
Near this spot stood the hall of the Poulters' Company from 1630 to 1666, destroyed in the Great Fire. The Poulters' (i.e. poulterers') Company was in existence as early as 1345 but did not receive its royal charter until the reign of Henry VII in 1504. The hall was originally sited at Leadenhall Market.

ROGERS, John (?1500–55), English, cleric, martyr
St Bartholomew's Hospital, West Smithfield, EC1. *Protestant Alliance London*
Burnt at the stake near this spot in 1555, Rogers became the first Protestant martyr in the reign of 'Bloody Mary'. An intimate of William Tyndale, he was responsible for the clandestine production of the first Bible in English in 1537 (see Southwark). Foxe, in his *Book of Martyrs*, describes his death: 'When the fire had taken hold both upon his legs and shoulders, he, as one feeling no smart, washed his hands in the flame, as though it had been in cold water.'

ROMAN BASILICA
Gracechurch Street and Leadenhall Street, EC3. *Private*
On this site stood the Roman basilica, AD c. 120. Its remains were uncovered during excavations by the Museum of London in 1986. The basilica was the north range of the Roman forum. A pier from its south arcade is preserved in the basement of 90 Gracechurch Street, in a hairdressing salon.

ROYAL COLLEGE OF PHYSICIANS
Warwick Lane, EC4. *Corporation of the City of London*
This was the site of the College of Physicians from 1674 to 1825. Founded by Henry VIII's physician, Thomas Linacre (see page 14), in 1518, the college had leased premises from St Paul's in Paternoster Row. When they were destroyed in the Great Fire, this building was erected to designs by Christopher Wren (q.v.). The college moved to Pall Mall in 1825, and again in 1964 to its present site in the south-east corner of Regent's Park, a building designed by Sir Denys Lasdun.

ST ANTHONY'S HOSPITAL and FRENCH PROTESTANT CHURCH
53 Threadneedle Street, EC2.
Corporation of the City of London
This was the site of the Hospital of St Anthony and the French Protestant church, which was demolished in 1840. Started by brothers from France, who received the building from Henry III in 1242, it was subsequently developed to include a chapel and grammar school. By the mid-sixteenth century the school had declined and the chapel became the French Protestant church. The buildings were destroyed in the Great Fire.

ST BENET FINK
1 Threadneedle Street, EC2.
Corporation of the City of London
This was the site of St Benet Fink, first recorded in 1216. It was repaired in 1633, destroyed in the Great Fire, and replaced in 1670–3 by a Wren church. It was demolished in 1844, to make way for the new Royal Exchange.

ST BENET GRACECHURCH
60 Gracechurch Street, EC3.
Corporation of the City of London
This was the site of St Benet Gracechurch, first

mentioned in 1181, repaired in 1630–3, destroyed in the Great Fire, and rebuilt by Wren in 1681–7. Declining congregations led to a union with All Hallows, Lombard Street, in 1864, and the disused church was demolished three years later. The site was sold for £24,000 and Mile End Road was built with the proceeds.

ST BENET SHEREHOG
Pancras Lane, EC4.
Private / Corporation of the City of London
The church was built in the early twelfth century in the centre of the City's wool trading area and destroyed in the Great Fire. (A sherehog is a ram that

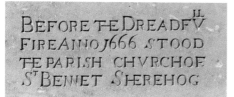

has been castrated after its first shearing.) The parish was merged with St Stephen Walbrook in 1670.

ST GABRIEL FENCHURCH
Plantation House, Fenchurch Street, EC3.
Corporation of the City of London
In the middle of the road here stood St Gabriel Fenchurch, first recorded in 1315, destroyed in the Great Fire. The parish merged with St Margaret Pattens in 1670.

ST JOHN THE EVANGELIST, FRIDAY STREET
1 Watling Street, EC4.
Corporation of the City of London
Dedicated in the mid-thirteenth century to St Werburga, a seventh-century abbess, it was known from the fourteenth century onwards as St John the Evangelist. It had the smallest parish in the city, measuring only four-fifths of an acre. It was repaired and improved in 1626, only to perish in the Great Fire. The churchyard survived until 1954, when it was covered by the extension to the Bank of England.

ST JOHN ZACHARY
Goldsmiths' Garden, Gresham Street, EC2.
Corporation of the City of London

Originally called St John the Baptist, this church was given to a man named Zacharie in 1180 by the canons of St Paul's. It was rebuilt several times before its eventual destruction in the Great Fire, after which the parish was united with St Anne and St Agnes, Gresham Street. Goldsmiths' Garden is the original churchyard.

ST KATHERINE COLEMAN
St Katherine's Row, Fenchurch Street, EC3.
Corporation of the City of London
The first church on this site was of fourteenth-century origin with seventeenth-century alterations but by the 1730s it was almost buried in the surrounding ground that had risen around it. It was rebuilt by James Horne in 1739, very plainly, and by the late nineteenth century was home to a dwindling congregation and it was closed to worship for months at a time. It was demolished in 1926 and the parish merged with St Olave, Hart Street.

ST LEONARD
St Martin's-le-Grand, EC1.
Corporation of the City of London
When recorded for the first edition of this book, this plaque was at 35 Foster Lane. After a massive office rebuild, it has been reinstated in St Martin's-le-Grand. Dating from at least the thirteenth century, the church was destroyed in the Great Fire, but its ruins were not finally cleared away until the early nineteenth century.

ST LEONARD, EASTCHEAP
2a Eastcheap, EC3. *Corporation of the City of London*
Also sometimes referred to as St Leonard Milkchurch, probably in honour of a benefactor, Robert Melker, this church was first recorded in 1214. Burned out in 1618, it was repaired and enlarged, only to be burned down again in the Great Fire. This time it was not rebuilt and the parish was merged with St Benet Gracechurch. The churchyard was retained as a burial ground until 1882.

ST MARGARET, FISH STREET HILL
Monument Street, EC3.
Corporation of the City of London

Being the nearest church to Thomas Faryner's bakery (see page 11), this was probably the first to be consumed in the Great Fire. The Monument stands on its site and its parish was joined to St Magnus the Martyr.

ST MARTIN ORGAR

Martin Lane, EC4. *Corporation of the City of London*
First mentioned in the twelfth century when it was granted by the deacon Orgar to the canons of St Paul's, this church was badly damaged in the Great Fire, and the parish was united with St Clement, Eastcheap. The tower, however, was restored and used by a congregation of Episcopalian French Protestants until it was demolished in 1820.

ST MARTIN OUTWICH

39 Threadneedle Street, EC2.
Corporation of the City of London
St Martin Outwich was founded in 1403. It escaped the Great Fire but was burnt down in 1765 in a fire that swept through Cornhill. Rebuilt in 1796 by Samuel Pepys Cockerell, but serving a declining congregation, it was demolished in 1874, and the parish united with St Helen, Bishopsgate.

ST MARY BOTHAW

Cannon Street Station, EC4.
Corporation of the City of London
The name of this church was explained by the historian John Stow as meaning there was a 'boat haw' (boatyard) nearby. When it was destroyed in the Great Fire, some of its stones were reused in building the new St Swithin, London Stone, with which its parish was merged.

ST MARY COLE

82 Poultry, EC2. *Corporation of the City of London*
According to Stow, St Mary Cole, on this site, is named after its founder, one Cole, who built it 'upon a wall above ground, so that men are forced to go to ascend up thereunto by certain steps'. Henry IV granted it the right to maintain a chantry brotherhood because, reputedly, the martyrs St Edmund and St Thomas à Becket (see page 7) were baptised here. It was destroyed in the Great Fire and the parish united with St Mildred, Poultry.

ST MARY MOORFIELDS

Blomfield Street, EC2. *Corporation of the City of London*
The plaque says this is the site of St Mary Moorfields, 'Pro-Cathedral of the Roman Catholic Church 1852–1870'. However, all other references have it built in 1820 by John Newman, and remaining in use until 1902, when a new St Mary's was built round the corner in Eldon Street.

ST MARY WOOLCHURCH HAW

Walbrook, EC4. *Corporation of the City of London*
First mentioned in the eleventh century, this church got its name, according to Stow, because wool was weighed in the churchyard (*haw* being an Old English word for 'yard'). It was not rebuilt after the Great Fire, and the parish was amalgamated with St Mary Woolnoth. The Mansion House now stands on the site.

ST MILDRED

HSBC Bank, Poultry, EC2.
Corporation of the City of London
First recorded in 1175, rebuilt in 1475, the church was burnt down in the Great Fire and rebuilt by Wren. The baptismal records for 1610 show an entry for the son of a chief from 'the Cuntrey of Guinny'. It was pulled down in 1872 under the Union of Benefices Act, and the parish united with St Margaret Lothbury.

ST NICHOLAS ACONS, Parsonage of

Nicholas Lane, EC4. *Corporation of the City of London*
The twelfth-century church was not rebuilt after the Great Fire, but the parsonage survived and was the first headquarters of the Society for Equitable Assurances on Lives and Survivorships (later the Equitable Life Assurance Society), which was based on formulae developed by mathematician James Dodson (1710–57) to calculate fair annual premiums from research into mortality figures and probability studies.

ST PANCRAS

Pancras Lane, EC4. *Corporation of the City of London*
The church of St Pancras, on this site, belonged to the monastery of Christchurch, Canterbury, and is first mentioned in 1257. It was not rebuilt after the Great Fire, and the parish was united with St Mary le Bow. A part of the churchyard remains as a garden.

ST PAUL'S SCHOOL

New Change, EC4.
Corporation of the City of London
Near this spot from 1512 until 1884 stood St Paul's School, founded by Dean Colet (see page 10) in 1509. The school, *alma mater* to Milton (q.v.), Pepys (q.v.), Thomas Clarkson, the anti-slavery campaigner, G. K. Chesterton (q.v.) and Field Marshal Montgomery (q.v.), moved to Hammersmith in 1884, and on to Barnes in 1968.

SALISBURY COURT PLAYHOUSE

8 Salisbury Square, EC4.
Corporation of the City of London
The Salisbury Court Playhouse was a private theatre built by Richard Gunnell and William Blagrove for £1,000. Its interior was destroyed by soldiers in 1649, at the height of the Puritan repression of all kinds of fun. It was repaired at the Restoration, but destroyed in the Great Fire.

SARACEN'S HEAD INN

Snow Hill, EC1. *Corporation of the City of London*
This was the site of the well-known coaching inn, demolished in 1868. Known from at least the sixteenth century, it was the departure point for coaches to Yorkshire, described by Dickens (q.v.) in *Nicholas Nickleby* as having 'a portal guarded by two Saracens' heads and shoulders, which it was once the pride and glory of the choice spirits of this metropolis to pull down at night, but which have for some time remained in undisturbed tranquillity'.

THE STANDARD IN CORNHILL

59–60 Cornhill, EC3. *Corporation of the City of London*
The Standard, which stood at the middle of the
crossroads with Gracechurch Street, supplied water
from the Thames to the vicinity by means of a system
of lead pipes until about 1603. It was used as a
measuring point until its demolition in 1674, and
many mileposts around London still tell of a distance
'to the Standard in Cornhill'. The plaque is at the first
floor on the Gracechurch Street elevation.

STOCKS MARKET

Mansion House, EC4.
Corporation of the City of London
Near this spot stood the Stocks Market from 1282
to 1737. Until the Great Fire it was a meat and fish
market, but when rebuilt it was used for fruit and
vegetables, relocating to Covent Garden in 1737
to make way for the building of the present
Mansion House.

THE *SUNDAY TIMES*

4 Salisbury Court, EC4. *Private*
The plaque records that the first issue of the *Sunday
Times* was edited on this site by Henry White on
20 October 1822. It was intended to be a rival to the
Observer, and both papers were mildly liberal, though
that can no longer be said of the *Sunday Times*.

SYNAGOGUE, First after the Resettlement

**Corner of Bury Street and Creechurch Lane,
EC3.** *Corporation of the City of London*
This was the site of the first synagogue after the
Resettlement (1657–1701). In 1701 the congregation
moved to the splendid new synagogue in Bevis Marks.

SYNAGOGUE, Great

Old Jewry, EC2. *Corporation of the City of London*
The Great Synagogue stood at the north-west corner
of Old Jewry. This area had been the centre of the
medieval Jewish population, subject to regular
pogroms and extortionate taxes. The synagogue
was ransacked and destroyed in 1272, and the Jews
were expelled by Edward I in 1291. They were not
re-admitted to London until the seventeenth century.

TAXATION, Chartered Institute of

Pancras Lane, EC4. *Corporation of the City of London*
The professional body for Chartered Tax Advisers was
founded on this site in 1930. Its original headquarters

here were destroyed in the Blitz, and the Institute is
now found at Upper Belgrave Street, SW1.

TOMPION, Thomas

(1638–1713),
English, clockmaker
**69 Fleet Street,
EC4.** *Private*
Tompion, who lived
on this site, was a
Quaker, known as
'the Father of English
Clockmaking', and is
reckoned to have
made about 5,500 watches and 650 clocks in his
career. He invented the balance spring regulator and
the cylinder escapement. Two of his clocks are in
Buckingham Palace. He was master of the
Clockmakers' Company in 1703.

TURNERS' HALL

22 College Hill, EC4.
Corporation of the City of London
Turners made cups, platters, furniture and other
items using a lathe. Their original hall was in Philpot
Lane from 1591 until destroyed in the Great Fire.
Rebuilt there in 1670, it came to this site in 1736.
Sold in 1766, it was not replaced.

UPHOLDERS' HALL

Peters Hill, Queen Victoria Street, EC4.
Corporation of the City of London
The Upholders were associated with upholstery and
bedding. They were granted a petition in 1474 and
received their charter in 1626. Their hall was not
rebuilt after the Great Fire.

WAKEFIELD, Viscount (1859–1941), English,

industrialist, philanthropist
41 Trinity Square, EC3. *Private*
Viscount Wakefield of Hythe, who had led the
restoration of the Trinity Square area, gave this house
to the local church and people in 1937. He was
founder of Castrol Oil in 1899, Lord Mayor of
London in 1915–16, and made a freeman of the City
in 1935. He was involved in numerous charitable
causes and known in Hythe, Kent, as the town's
greatest benefactor. The Wakefield Trust continues to
operate in this part of the City.

WALLACE, Edgar (1875–1932), English, novelist, journalist
Ludgate Circus, EC4. *Private*
The plaque celebrates the journalism of Wallace, but undoubtedly he is today best remembered, and still read, for his prolific output of thrillers and adventure stories, including *The Four Just Men* (1905), *Sanders of the River* (1911) and *The Mind of Mr J. G. Reeder* (1925). He died in Hollywood while working on the screenplay for *King Kong*. (See also Lewisham.)

WALLACE, Sir William (*c.*1270–1305), Scottish, patriot, hero
St Bartholomew's Hospital, West Smithfield, EC1. *Private*
Sir William was put to death near this spot on 23 August 1305 after being betrayed at the end of a nine-year war against the English in Scotland. His story has perennially been the stuff of Scots romance,

from the fifteenth-century minstrel Blind Harry's *Acts and Deeds of Sir William Wallace* to the Mel Gibson film *Braveheart* (1995).

WATERHOUSE, Edwin (1841–1917), English, accountant
3 Frederick's Place, EC2.
Corporation of the City of London
Sir Edwin worked in this building from 1899 to 1905. He was head of Price, Waterhouse & Company from 1887 to 1906, and President of the Institute of Chartered Accountants of England and Wales from 1892 to 1894. He was the brother of the architect Alfred Waterhouse (q.v.).

WESLEY, Charles (1707–88), English, Methodist, hymn writer
13 Little Britain, EC1.
Corporation of the City of London
In a house adjoining this spot belonging to John Bray (see page 8), Charles Wesley experienced an evangelical awakening on 21 May 1738. He wrote in his diary: 'I found myself at peace with God, and rejoiced in hope of loving Christ … I saw that by faith I stood; by the continual support of faith, which kept me from falling, though of myself I am ever sinking into sin.' (See also Westminster 2 and Westminster 4.)

WESLEY, John (1703–91), English, Methodist
Aldersgate Street, EC1.
Drew Theological Seminary, Madison, New Jersey

Three days after his brother Charles's experience (see page 22), John wrote in his diary of listening to someone 'reading Luther's preface to the Epistle to the Romans. About a quarter before nine, while he was describing the change which God works in the heart through faith in Christ, I felt my heart strangely warmed. I felt I did trust in Christ, Christ alone, for salvation; and an assurance was given me that He had taken away my sins, even mine, and saved me from the law of sin and death.' (See also Islington, Tower Hamlets and Westminster 4.)

WHITE, Henry (*fl.*1822), English, newspaper editor
4 Salisbury Court, EC4. *Private*
On this site Henry White edited and published the first number of the *Sunday Times* on 20 October 1822, in hopes of rivalling the *Observer*.

WHITTINGTON, Richard (d.1423), English, financier, philanthropist
20 College Hill, EC4.
Corporation of the City of London
St Michael Paternoster Church, College Hill, EC4. *Corporation of the City of London*
Whittington's house stood on the first site, and he is buried in the church, which he rebuilt in 1409. He advanced loans to Richard II, Henry IV and Henry V, and left money for rebuilding Newgate prison, building almshouses and the foundation of Whittington College. The legend of Dick Whittington and his cat is not known before 1605, and the story of a cat helping its owner to fortune is found in many countries around Europe.

WILLIAMS, Sir George (1821–1905), English, Christian reformer
Juxon House, St Paul's Churchyard, EC4. *Private*
Williams was working here for Messrs Hitchcock & Rogers, drapers; he and some of his fellows were appalled at the situation for young men in London and wanted to found a place that would 'win souls to Christ'; the foundation of the Young Men's Christian Association is dated from this spot on 6 June 1844. (See also Camden 2.)

WORDE, Wynkyn de (d.1534), Alsatian, printer
Stationers' Hall, Ave Maria Lane, EC4. *Private*
'The Father of Fleet Street' was brought to London by Caxton in 1476 and carried on the business in Westminster after Caxton's death in 1491. He came

to Fleet Street in 1500 and opened a shop in St Paul's churchyard in 1509, and his press put out numerous important books, often several editions in one year, including the third edition of *The Canterbury Tales* and the second edition of Malory's *Mort d'Arthur*.

THE CITY OF
WESTMINSTER

WESTMINSTER, though styling itself a city, is in fact a borough and extends far further than the area one traditionally thinks of as 'Westminster': the Abbey, the Houses of Parliament and Whitehall. Having swallowed the Metropolitan Boroughs of St Marylebone and Paddington, it now reaches as far west as the Albert Hall and as far north as Lord's Cricket Ground, takes in most of Regent's Park, and to the east includes the Royal Courts of Justice up against the boundary with the City of London. With 485 plaques recorded here, it is by far the biggest contributing borough to this book, and I have accordingly divided its entries into four separate areas, the boundaries readily marked by three arterial east–west roads.

Westminster City Council inaugurated its own green plaque scheme in 1991 and has so far erected eighty-seven. Having a slightly more unbuttoned set of criteria than English Heritage, its plaques include the likes of Don Arden and the Small Faces, the Bee Gees, Keith Moon, Ken Colyer and the 2i's Coffee Bar – all adding to the gaiety and worthy of remembrance, however louche. English Heritage remains, however, the major source, with eighty-six of its plaques entered here, plus of course their inherited responsibility for the earlier erections of the Greater London Council (eighty-two), the London County Council (114) and the Royal Society of Arts (nine). The richness and diversity of Westminster is further augmented by sixty-two privately erected plaques, as well as one-off contributions by organisations as various as the Ancient Order of Druids, the Colonial Dames of America, Bentley Motor Cars, the Leopold Stokowski Society, the Britain Vietnam Association, the Dead Comics Society, the British Puppet and Model Theatre Guild, the Anglo-Texan Society, the Serbian Council of Great Britain and La Société d'Études Staëliennes.

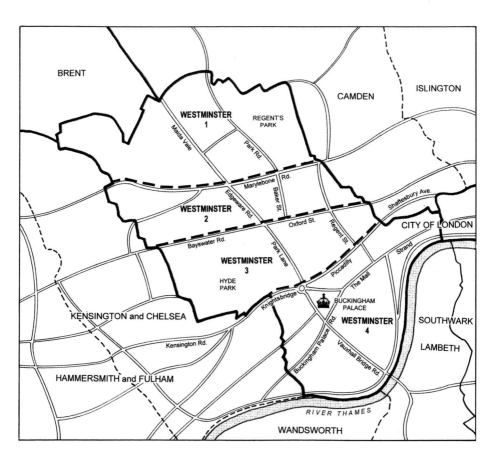

Westminster 1:
Lisson Grove, Maida Vale and St John's Wood
North of the Marylebone Road

ACHESON, Edward Goodrich (1856–1931),
American, inventor, chemist, industrialist
31 Prince Albert Road, NW8. *Private*
Acheson worked for Thomas Edison from 1880 to
1884, during which period he helped install electric
lighting at La Scala, Milan. Leaving Edison, he took out
a patent for his invention carborundum in 1893 and
established his own Carborundum Company in 1894.
He was also the inventor of artificially prepared
graphite and, in a lifetime of discoveries, took out
seventy patents.

ADAMS-ACTON, John (1831–1910), English,
sculptor
14 Langford Place, NW8. *Westminster City Council*
Adams-Acton lived here from 1882 to 1906. Born
John Adams, he added Acton (his birthplace) to
distinguish himself from another artist called John
Adams. Primarily a portrait sculptor, his subjects
included John Wesley (q.v.), W. E. Gladstone (q.v.),
Cardinal Manning, Edward VII and Queen Victoria.

ALLINGHAM, Margery
(1904–66), English,
novelist
**1 Westbourne Terrace
Road, W2.**
City of Westminster
Allingham, who lived here
from 1916 to 1926, wrote
superior detective fiction.
Albert Campion is her most
recurring character, first appearing in *The Crime at
Black Dudley* (1929), and featuring in a further
seventeen novels and twenty short stories. He flits
between aristocratic and criminal milieux, part
detective, part adventurer.

ALMA-TADEMA, Sir Lawrence (1836–1912),
Dutch, painter
44 Grove End Road, NW8. *Greater London Council*
Sir Lawrence, who lived and worked here from 1886

until his death, settled in
Britain in 1870, received
his papers of denization
in 1873, was elected a
Royal Academician in
1879 and awarded the
Order of Merit in 1907.
His works (totalling
408) chiefly depict
scenes in ancient Egypt,
Greece and Rome and show profound archaeological
knowledge.

ARDIZZONE, Edward (1900–79), French, artist,
illustrator
130 Elgin Avenue, W9. *English Heritage*
Ardizzone lived and worked in this house from 1920
to 1972. Among his vast output is the *Tim* series,
beginning with *Little Tim and the Brave Sea Captain*
(1936), which he both wrote and illustrated. *Tim All
Alone* (1956) won him the Kate Greenaway (q.v.)
Medal. He also illustrated Trollope (q.v.), Betjeman
(q.v.) and Graham Greene's children's books. An
official war artist in the Second World War, he was
once arrested for sketching in the East End during the
Blitz.

BANNISTER, Sir Roger
(b.1929), English, athlete
**Paddington
Recreation Ground,
Randolph Avenue,
W9.** *City of Westminster*
There are two plaques,
both unveiled by Bannister
himself, recording that it was
on the cinder track here, while a
medical student at St Mary's Hospital between 1951
and 1954, that Bannister trained in preparation for the
attempt to run the first four-minute mile with his
friends Chris Brasher and Chris Chataway. The feat
was achieved at Oxford on 6 May 1954, with a time of

3 minutes 59.4 seconds. Famously, the stadium announcer, Norris McWhirter, teased the crowd in announcing the result, saying Bannister had won with 'a time which is a new meeting and track record, and which – subject to ratification – will be a new English Native, British National, All-Comers, European, British Empire, and World Record. The time was 3 … [crowd erupts]'.

BAZALGETTE, Sir Joseph (1819–91), English, civil engineer
17 Hamilton Terrace, NW8. *Greater London Council*
Sir Joseph, who lived here, was a notable pioneer of public health engineering. As chief engineer of the Metropolitan Board of Works from 1856 to 1889, he designed London's sewerage system (completed in 1865), with 83 miles of brick main sewers and 1,100 miles of street sewers, and four great pumping stations, thus beginning the long slow process of cleaning up the Thames. He also designed the Albert, Victoria and Chelsea embankments, as well as four of London's bridges.

BEATTY, David, first Earl (1871–1936), English, naval officer
Hanover Lodge, Outer Circle, NW1.
Greater London Council
The house, originally designed by John Nash, was altered by Lutyens (q.v.) in 1909 and Beatty lived here from 1910 to 1925. He commanded the British fleet at the battle of Jutland in 1916, the major naval engagement of the First World War, which has been the subject of controversy ever since, with Beatty himself sponsoring a version of the battle highly critical of Jellicoe, his commander-in-chief, and others making a damning case against Beatty's handling of his fleet.

BEECHAM, Sir Thomas (1879–1961), English, conductor
31 Grove End Road, NW8. *Greater London Council*
Scion of the 'Beecham's Pills' dynasty, Sir Thomas, who lived here, began with the New Symphony Orchestra in 1906, became principal conductor at Covent Garden in 1932, conductor of the New York Metropolitan Opera in 1943, and in 1947 founded the Royal Philharmonic Orchestra. He was a noted after-dinner speaker, offering thoughts such as: 'There are two golden rules for an orchestra: start together and finish together. The public doesn't give a damn what goes on in between.'

BEN-GURION, David (1886–1973), Israeli, prime minister of Israel
75 Warrington Crescent, Maida Vale, W9.
Greater London Council
Born David Grun in Poland, he settled in Palestine in 1906 and became a leader of the Zionist movement. He lived here in London at the time of volunteering for the British Army in the First World War after the Balfour Declaration of 1917. He oversaw the military operations during the war of 1948 and was twice prime minister of Israel (1948–53 and 1955–63).

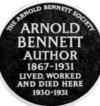

BENNETT, Arnold (1867–1931), English, novelist
Chiltern Court, Baker Street, NW1.
Arnold Bennett Society
Bennett lived the last year of his life here. In his early career he had been a journalist, and his first novel was published in 1898. His works, mostly set in the Potteries, where he was born, include *Anna of the Five Towns* (1902), *The Old Wives' Tale* (1908) and the *Clayhanger* series (1910–16). He also had a strand of lighter fiction, including *The Card* (1911) and *Mr Prohack* (1922).

BERKELEY, Sir Lennox (1903–89), English, composer
8 Warwick Avenue, W9. *City of Westminster*
Sir Lennox, who lived here from 1947 until his death, was a pupil of Nadia Boulanger in Paris from 1926 to 1932, giving his music a French complexion and setting him a little aside from the mainstream of British music in the twentieth century. His most productive period was the late 1930s and 1940s, in which he produced his *Serenade for Strings* (1939), Symphony No. 1 (1940), *Divertimento in Bb* (1943) and piano concertos (1947–8). He was professor of composition at the Royal Academy of Music from 1946 to 1968

BRITTAIN, Vera (1893–1970), English, writer, feminist
11 Wymering Mansions, Wymering Road, W9.
Westminster City Council

Brittain's most famous book, the poignant *Testament of Youth* (1933), recounted her First World War experiences, when she lost both her brother and her fiancé, and developed thereafter a philosophy of Christian pacifism. It brought her immediate fame. She was the mother of the Labour (later Liberal Democrat) politician Shirley Williams. (See also Camden 2.)

BRITTEN, Benjamin (1913–76), English, composer
45a St John's Wood High Street, NW8.
City of Westminster / The Britten-Pears Foundation
Britten and his partner Peter Pears (see page 32) lived and worked here from 1943 to 1946. During this period, Britten, a pacifist, secured conscientious objector status and completed his opera *Peter Grimes*, which opened at Sadler's Wells in 1945 and was his biggest success to date. He also wrote his most familiar work, *The Young Person's Guide to the Orchestra*, which debuted in a Crown Film Unit production in 1946 with the London Symphony Orchestra under Malcolm Sargent (q.v.), who conducted and narrated. (See also Islington and Kensington & Chelsea 2.)

BROWNING, Robert (1812–89), English, poet
Warwick Crescent, Little Venice, W2.
City of Westminster
After the early death of his wife, Elizabeth (q.v.), in Italy, he returned to England, living here between 1862 and 1887, and came at last to be regarded as one of the leading poets of the age, along with Tennyson. (See also Southwark and Kensington & Chelsea 1.)

CHAPLIN, Charlie (1889–1977), English, music-hall and film star
71 Church Street, NW8. *City of Westminster*
This was the site of the Royal Marylebone Theatre from 1837 to 1868, and the Royal West London Theatre from 1896 to 1913, where Chaplin appeared as 'Billy' in a dramatisation of *Sherlock Holmes* in 1904. He was by this time quite an experienced performer, having first appeared on stage in Aldershot at the age of five. (See also Lambeth and Southwark.)

COCHRANE, Thomas (1775–1860), English, naval officer
Hanover Lodge, Outer Circle, NW1.
Greater London Council
Cochrane, who lived here, entered the Navy in 1793 and had an eventful career, often plundering the French, who called him '*le loup des mers*', the 'sea wolf',

and gaining rapid promotion. He was imprisoned for a year on charges of involvement in the Great Stock Exchange Fraud of 1814, though probably innocent, and was thrown out of the Navy in disgrace. He then served as naval commander for Chile and Peru (1818–22), Brazil (1823–5) and Greece (1827–8), before eventually being reinstated as an admiral in the Royal Navy, pardoned by Queen Victoria. His life and exploits inspired the Hornblower stories of C. S. Forester (q.v.) and the Jack Aubrey character in Patrick O'Brien's novels.

DAVIES, Emily (1830–1921), English, feminist, reformer
17 Cunningham Place, St John's Wood, NW8.
Greater London Council
Davies, who lived here from 1862 to 1886, was associated in the women's movement with Elizabeth Garrett Anderson (q.v.) and Frances Mary Buss (q.v.). She founded Girton College, Cambridge, in 1873, but the women undergraduates there were not admitted to full university membership till 1948.

ELGAR, Sir Edward (1857–1934), English, composer
Abbey Road Studios, Abbey Road, NW8.
Westminster City Council / EMI Records
The plaque records that Sir Edward opened and recorded in these studios on 12 November 1931. Pathétone filmed the event, with Sir Edward conducting *Land of Hope and Glory*, having asked the London Symphony Orchestra to: 'Please play this tune as though you've never heard it before.' (See also Hammersmith & Fulham, Camden 1 and Westminster 2.)

FINZI, Gerald (1901–1956), English, composer
93 Hamilton Terrace, NW8. *City of Westminster*
Finzi lived here from 1930 to 1933 while teaching at the Royal Academy of Music. Though an agnostic, he wrote a number of sacred choral works and was particularly noted for his musical settings of poems by Traherne, Thomas Hardy (q.v.) and Christina Rossetti (q.v.).

His most popular composition is the Clarinet Concerto (1949), and his last major work, the Cello Concerto (1955), is remarkably serene, considering that he composed it knowing that he had little time left to live.

FLEISCHMANN, Arthur (1896–1990), Czech, sculptor, physician
92 Carlton Hill, NW8. *City of Westminster*
Fleischmann lived and worked here from 1958 until his death. Primarily a maker of portrait busts, his subjects included Kathleen Ferrier (q.v.), Lord Robens, Trevor Howard, and four popes: Pius XII, John XXIII, Paul VI and John Paul II. In the 1950s he was a pioneer in the use of Perspex in sculpture, and his last piece, *A Tribute to the Discovery of DNA*, now in the State Library, Sydney, Australia, represents his greatest achievement in that medium.

FLEMING, Sir Ambrose (1849–1945), English, physicist, electrical engineer
9 Clifton Gardens, Maida Vale, W9.
Greater London Council
Sir Ambrose lived here. In 1904 he invented the thermionic valve, the first vacuum tube, known as the Kenotron, which may be said to be the beginning of electronics, a major step forward in the 'wireless revolution'. His insights on radar and electronic communications were of great significance in the winning of the Second World War.

FRAMPTON, Sir George (1860–1928), English, sculptor
32 Queen's Grove, St John's Wood, NW8.
Greater London Council
Sir George lived and worked here from 1894 to 1908. A leading figure in the 'New Sculpture' movement, his works include *Peter Pan* in Kensington Gardens, commissioned by J. M. Barrie (q.v.), and the Edith Cavell (q.v.) memorial in St Martin's Place. He was joint first principal with William Lethaby (q.v.) of the Central School of Arts and Crafts.

FRITH, William Powell (1819–1909), English, painter
114 Clifton Hill, St John's Wood, NW8.
Greater London Council
Frith, who lived, worked and died here, was noted for his large, densely populated canvases of contemporary scenes, such as *Ramsgate Sands* (1851), bought by Queen Victoria for Buckingham Palace and now in Tate

Britain, *Derby Day* (1856–8) and *The Railway Station* (1862).

FURY, Billy (1940–83), English, pop star
1 Cavendish Avenue, NW8. *Musical Heritage*
Born Ronnie Wycherley, Fury had eleven top ten hits from 1960 to 1965, without ever reaching number one. His career was bedevilled by Decca's attempts to mould him as a teen idol, when he was truly an adult sexy rocker, and by recurrent heart disease, which ultimately caused his early death.

GIBSON, Guy, VC (1918–44), English, air force officer
32 Aberdeen Place, NW8. *English Heritage*
Wing Commander Gibson lived here briefly in 1943. Already awarded the DFC and Bar and the DSO, he was selected to command a new squadron, No. 617, to attack the strategic German dams in the Ruhr using the 'bouncing bombs' designed by Barnes Wallis (q.v.). The 'Dam Busters' raid on 16 May 1943 succeeded in breaching the Moehne and Eder dams, with the loss of eight out of the nineteen Lancasters on the mission. Gibson was awarded the VC for his leadership. He was killed a year later on operations over Germany.

GOMME, Sir Laurence (1853–1916), English, folklorist, historian
24 Dorset Square, NW1. *English Heritage*
Sir Laurence lived here from 1895 to 1909. He was clerk to the London County Council, founded the London Museum, the Folklore Society and the Victoria County History series, and edited successively *The Antiquary*, *The Archaeological Review* and *The Folklore Journal*. Among his many books are *Folklore as a Historical Science* (1908) and *The Making of London* (1911). He was a keen pioneer of the blue plaque scheme, and his plaque here was the eight hundredth to be erected.

GROSSMITH, George, Senior (1847–1912), English, actor
28 Dorset Square, NW1. *London County Council*
Grossmith, who lived here, created leading parts in Gilbert and Sullivan (1877–89) and was a noted performer of solo piano sketches, but is today remembered for writing, with his brother Weedon, *The Diary of a Nobody* (1892), in which Charles Pooter, of Brickfield Terrace, Holloway, records fifteen months of minor humiliations.

GUZMÁN, Juan Pablo Viscardo y (1748–98), Peruvian, Jesuit, agitator
185 Baker Street, NW1. *City of Westminster / Consulate General of Peru*
Guzmán lived the last nine years of his life in London. As the third centenary of the Spanish arrival in Latin America approached, he was the author in 1791 of the celebrated *Carta a los Españoles Americanos*, the incendiary first call for Latin Americans to throw off the Spanish yoke and fight for self-determination. He was in London when the English version appeared in 1791 and hoped for British assistance, but was disappointed.

HALL, Henry (1898–1989), English, dance-band leader
8 Randolph Mews, W9. *City of Westminster*
Hall lived here from 1959 to 1981. His popular *Henry Hall's Guest Night* broadcasts started on the BBC in 1932, with the signature tune 'Here's to the Next Time', which he had composed. In the 1950s he hosted the television show *Face the Music* and is remembered for his catchphrase 'This *is* Henry Hall speaking'.

HAYDON, Benjamin (1786–1846), English, painter
116 Lisson Grove, NW1. *London County Council*
Haydon lived here from 1817 to 1822. He specialised in historical subjects, painting vast canvases such as *Christ's Entry into Jerusalem* (1820). Unfortunately, he had a higher estimation of his abilities than the public or the critics. Perpetually in debt, twice in debtors' prison, he shot himself in despair, his last diary entry being 'Stretch me no longer on the rack of this rough world' (from *King Lear*).

HERTZ, Dr J. H. (1872–1946), Hungarian, rabbi
103 Hamilton Terrace, St John's Wood, NW8.
City of Westminster / The United Synagogue
Dr Hertz, Chief Rabbi of the British Empire, lived here from 1913 until his death. A combative conservative, he was opposed to reform and liberal Judaism. He favoured, he said, calm discussion, when all other ways had failed. His *Commentary on the Torah* (1937) is still found in most Orthodox synagogues and

Jewish homes. He was made a Companion of Honour in 1943.

HOLMES, Sherlock (*fl.*1881–1904), English, detective
237 Baker Street, NW1. *Private*
Holmes, a fictional independent detective created by Sir Arthur Conan Doyle (q.v.), lived and worked from this area. Noted for his cerebral approach, he was much consulted by Scotland Yard in the late nineteenth and early twentieth centuries.

HOOD, Thomas (1799–1845), English, poet
28 Finchley Road, NW8. *English Heritage*
Hood lived here from 1840 until his death, after his return from living on the Continent since 1835. During his time here he succeeded Theodore Hook, with great success, as editor of the *New Monthly Magazine*, and produced his most famous poem, 'The Song of the Shirt', for the Christmas 1843 edition of *Punch*. (See also City, Enfield and Westminster 4.)

HUXLEY, Thomas Henry (1825–95), English, biologist, physician
38 Marlborough Place, St John's Wood, NW8.
London County Council
Huxley, one of the pre-eminent scientists of the Victorian age, lived here from 1872 to 1890. He was professor of natural history at the Royal School of Mines (1854–85) and was the principal staunch defender of Charles Darwin (q.v.) against his 'creationist' opponents. He coined the word 'agnostic' to describe his own religious attitude. He was father of Leonard (q.v.) and grandfather of Julian and Aldous (q.v.).

INMAN, John (1935–2007), English, comic actor
4 Robert Close, W9. *Comic Heritage*
Best remembered for his role as the very camp shop assistant Mr Humphries in the BBC television sitcom *Are You Being Served?* (1972–85), which earned him the BBC TV Personality of the Year Award in 1976, but which was unpopular with sections of the gay community, who objected to what they saw as stereotyping. Inman also had a very successful career as a pantomime dame.

JONES, Dr Ernest (1879–1958), Welsh, psychoanalyst
19 York Terrace East, Regent's Park, NW1.
Greater London Council
Jones, who lived here, was a disciple, friend and biographer of Sigmund Freud (q.v.). He organised the world's first psychiatric conference at Salzburg in 1908 with Carl Jung, and founded the British Psycho-Analytical Society in 1913. Thanks to him, the British Medical Association, after some humming and harring, recognised psychiatry as a medical discipline in 1929.

JONES, Philip (1928–2000), English, trumpet player
14 Hamilton Terrace, NW8. *City of Westminster*
Jones, who lived here, was born into a family of trumpeters and was successively the principal trumpeter of six of the great London orchestras between 1956 and 1971. He formed the Philip Jones Brass Ensemble in 1951, which varied in size from five to ten players, made over thirty recordings and toured the world to great acclaim. In 1986 he accidentally drove his car over his trumpet case and took this as a cue for retirement.

KALVOS, Andreas (1792–1869), Greek, poet
182 Sutherland Avenue, Maida Vale, W9.
English Heritage
Accounted one of the great Greek writers of the nineteenth century, Kalvos, who lived here, spent most of his life outside Greece. Secretary for a time to Ugo Foscolo (q.v.), who greatly influenced his writings, he published twenty patriotic odes. His last years were spent in England.

KLEIN, Melanie (1882–1960), Austrian, psychoanalyst
42 Clifton Hill, St John's Wood, NW8.
Greater London Council
Klein lived here. Invited to England in 1921 by Ernest Jones (see above), her contribution to psychoanalysis was pioneering work with children, even as young as two, especially using toys to bring out hidden conflicts. She was involved in prolonged clashes with Anna Freud (q.v.) about how to treat children, a schism in the world of psychoanalysis that is only now beginning to heal, decades after the women's deaths.

KNIGHT, Harold (1874–1961), English, painter
16 Langford Place, St John's Wood, NW8.
Greater London Council
Harold Knight, who lived here, was a quiet man, a conscientious objector in the First World War, who suffers by comparison with his more flamboyant wife, Dame Laura (see below). But his portraiture is to be found in the collections of the Royal Academy, Tate Britain and the National Portrait Gallery.

KNIGHT, Dame Laura (1877–1970), English, painter
16 Langford Place, St John's Wood, NW8.
Greater London Council
Dame Laura lived here with her husband, Harold (see above). An Impressionist, and a member of the Newlyn School of artists, she found her milieu in the world of the theatre, ballet and circus. She was the first woman artist to be made a dame and the first elected to the Royal Academy. She was an official artist at the Nuremberg War Crimes Trials.

KOKOSCHKA, Oskar (1886–1980), Austrian, painter
Eyre Court, Finchley Road, St John's Wood, NW8. *English Heritage*
Kokoschka, who lived here, came to Britain in 1938 to escape Nazism and was naturalised in 1946. The most famous of his intensely expressionist paintings is *Bride in the Wind* (1913), a memorial to his doomed affair with Alma, Mahler's widow.

LAWRENCE, Philip (1947–95), English, headmaster
St George's School, Maida Vale, W9. *Private*
The plaque commemorates the school's former head, who was stabbed to death at this gate on 8 December 1995 while trying to defend a pupil who was being attacked by a gang.

LORD, Thomas (1755–1832), English, sportsman
Dorset Square, Marylebone, NW1.
Marylebone Cricket Club
This is the site of the original Lord's cricket ground. Bankrolled by the future Duke of Richmond,

Lord acquired 7 acres off Dorset Square and played for Middlesex in the first match against Essex on 31 May 1787. This ground survived till 1810, a second till 1813, and the present Lord's was opened in 1814.

LOWE, Arthur (1915–82), English, actor
2 Maida Avenue, Little Venice, W2.
Dead Comics Society
Lowe lived here from 1969 until his death. He was one of the very few actors to escape from a leading role in a television soap opera and continue working successfully. After being one of the founding stars of *Coronation Street* (1960–5), he went on to immortality as Captain Mainwaring in *Dad's Army* (1968–77).

MACFARREN, George Alexander (1813–87), English, composer
20 Hamilton Terrace, St John's Wood, NW8.
Incorporated Society of Musicians
Macfarren lived and died in this house. Professor at the Royal Academy of Music from 1837, and principal from 1876, he was a prolific composer of oratorios, operas, overtures and symphonies, mostly now forgotten. His best-remembered piece is the overture *Chevy Chace* (1836).

MASEFIELD, John (1878–1967), English, poet
30 Maida Avenue, W2. *English Heritage*
While living here, Masefield was working for the *Manchester Guardian* and published *Ballads and Poems* (1910), which contained his most famous poem, *Cargoes* ('Quinquireme of Nineveh from distant Ophir …'). He was Poet Laureate from 1930 to 1967. His old-fashioned sturdy rhythms have been derided by modernists, but his reputation is intact.

MAURICE, Frederick Denison (1805–72), English, cleric
2 Brunswick Place, NW1. *Greater London Council*
Maurice was the first clergyman to call himself a 'Christian socialist'. He co-founded Queen's College for Women (1848), founded the Working Men's College in 1854, and was hugely influential on many nineteenth-century social reformers, including Canon Barnett (q.v.),

founder of Toynbee Hall, Charles Kingsley (q.v.), and later socialists such as R. H. Tawney (q.v.).

McMILLAN, William (1887–1977), Scottish, sculptor
20 Hamilton Terrace, St John's Wood, NW8.
Private
McMillan was elected a Royal Academician in 1933 and was master of sculpture at the Academy School from 1929 to 1941. Among his works are the East Fountain in Trafalgar Square (1948), the Goetz Memorial Fountain in Regent's Park (1950), George VI on Carlton House Terrace (1955), Raleigh in Whitehall (1959), and Alcock and Brown at Heathrow (1966).

MOST, Mickie (1938–2003), English, record producer
RAK Studios, 42–48 Charlbert Street, NW8.
Musical Heritage
Born Michael Hayes, Most, who founded and owned these studios, was the most successful individual British record producer of the 1960s and 1970s, masterminding an endless string of hits with the Animals, Herman's Hermits, Brenda Lee, Donovan, Lulu, the Seekers, Jeff Beck and Suzi Quatro, among others. He was one of the first producers to own the rights to his records, and his house in Totteridge was reputedly the largest private dwelling in England.

PALGRAVE, Francis Turner (1824–97), English, poet, anthologist
5 York Gate, Regent's Park, NW1.
Greater London Council
Palgrave lived here from 1862 to 1875. His *The Golden Treasury of Best Songs and Lyrical Poems in the English Language* (1861) was compiled with advice from Tennyson (q.v.). It reflected the taste of its age, including no works by living poets, no Donne, no Blake. It was revised and reprinted many times, with new entries (including Donne and Blake); the most recent edition was in 1965.

PEARS, Sir Peter (1910–86), English, tenor
45a St John's Wood High Street, NW8.
City of Westminster / The Britten-Pears Foundation
Pears lived here with Benjamin Britten (see page 28)

32

from 1943 to 1946. They had met in 1936, and they became lifelong companions, with Pears best remembered for his interpretations of Britten compositions, especially *Peter Grimes*. It was said that he had 'one good note' – E natural a third above middle C.

REID DICK, Sir William (1878–1961), Scottish, sculptor
Clifton Hill Studios, 95a Clifton Hill, NW8.
English Heritage
Sir William worked here in Studio 3 from 1910 to 1914. Among his many public works are the equestrian group at Unilever House, Blackfriars, the statue of Sir John Soane at the Bank of England, the *Boy with a Frog* in Regent's Park, and President Roosevelt in Grosvenor Square. President of the Royal Society of British Sculptors from 1933 to 1938, he was sculptor in ordinary for Scotland to George VI from 1938 until his death.

ROSSI, Charles (1762–1839), English, sculptor
116 Lisson Grove, NW1. *London County Council*
Rossi lived here. Elected a Royal Academician in 1802, he was sculptor in ordinary to the Prince Regent and William IV. Among his public works in London are memorials in St Paul's to heroes of the wars with France, including Cornwallis and Rodney, *Thalia* and *Melpomene* on the frontage of the Royal Opera House, and the caryatids on St Pancras church, Marylebone Road.

ROYAL MARYLEBONE THEATRE
71 Church Street, NW8. *City of Westminster*
The Royal Marylebone Theatre stood on this site from 1837 to 1868. Originally the Royal Sussex, knocked together out of two old stable blocks in 1831, it had a very long list of managers, who all failed, with the exception of Nelson Lee (q.v.). He, unlike the others, seems to have understood that the locals wanted strong, broad melodrama, with plenty of gore, whereas they were being offered 'culture'.

ROYAL WEST LONDON THEATRE
71 Church Street, NW8. *City of Westminster*
The Royal Marylebone Theatre (see above), renamed the Royal Albert, staggered on through the late nineteenth century, until another refurbishment saw it become the Royal West London Theatre (1896–1913), where, most famously, Chaplin (see page 28) appeared

in 1904. By 1913, movies were the thing, and it became the Royal West London Cinema. Damaged in the Blitz in 1941, it became a storehouse and was eventually destroyed by fire in 1962.

SALVIN, Anthony (1799–1881), English, architect
11 Hanover Terrace, Regent's Park, NW1.
English Heritage
Salvin lived here from 1858 to 1879. A pupil of John Nash, he was an authority on the restoration of old castles and churches and worked on the Tower of London and the castles at Windsor, Caernarfon and Warwick. His own style favoured the Tudor, and his best-known design is Harlaxton Manor, Lincolnshire (1835–43).

SAN MARTÍN, José de (1778–1850), Argentinian, soldier, politician
23 Park Road, Regent's Park, NW1.
London County Council
San Martín stayed here in 1824. He was centrally involved from 1812 to 1822 in the liberation of Argentina, Chile and Peru and earned the title 'the Liberator'. He retired to Europe in 1824, refusing to be involved in the civil wars that were tearing Argentina apart. The Order of the Liberator General San Martín is Argentina's highest honour.

SANTLEY, Sir Charles (1834–1922), English, baritone
13 Blenheim Road, St John's Wood, NW8.
London County Council
Sir Charles, who lived and died here, was the greatest English baritone of his day and starred in the first Wagner opera presented in London, *Der Fliegender Holländer*, in 1870. He gave up opera in 1876 to concentrate on concerts and in 1907, after a fifty-year career, he was the first singer to be knighted.

SHEPARD, E. H. (1879–1976), English, painter, illustrator
10 Kent Terrace, Regent's Park, NW1.
English Heritage
Shepard lived here. His most notable works were the original illustrations to A. A. Milne's (q.v.) *Winnie the Pooh* (1926) and Kenneth Grahame's (q.v.) *Wind in the Willows* (1931). He eventually became rather tired of Winnie, claiming the bear overshadowed all his other work.

SOYER, Alexis (1810–58), French, chef
28 Marlborough Place, St John's Wood, NW8.
City of Westminster
Soyer, who lived here, was the most famous chef in
Victorian London. He fled France in the upheaval of
1830 and became chef at the Reform Club in 1837.
He took a soup kitchen to Ireland in the Great Famine
of 1847–8 and travelled at his own expense to the
Crimea and tried to reform army catering. In 1854 he
published *A Shilling Cookery for the People*, the first
popular book on the subject.

SPILSBURY, Sir Bernard (1877–1947), English,
forensic pathologist
31 Marlborough Hill, NW8. *English Heritage*
The most famous forensic pathologist of the twentieth
century, Sir Bernard lived here from 1912 to 1940.
His evidence was crucial in several sensational cases at
the Old Bailey, including Dr Crippen, the Brides in the
Bath and the Brighton Trunk Murders. He became
more dogmatic and modern researches have suggested
that his evidence may have contributed to some
miscarriages of justice. His belief in his own
infallibility led to problems towards the end of his
career and he committed suicide.

STRANG, William (1859–1921), Scottish, painter,
illustrator
20 Hamilton Terrace, St John's Wood, NW8.
London County Council
Strang lived here from 1900 until his death. He was an
original member of the Royal Society of Painter-
Etchers and featured in their first exhibition in 1881.
Among his over seven hundred etching plates are
illustrations for Bunyan, Cervantes, Coleridge and
Kipling.

TEMPEST, Dame Marie (1864–1942), English,
soprano, comedy actress
24 Park Crescent, Regent's Park, W1.
Greater London Council
Dame Marie lived here from 1899 to 1902. Her
hugely successful early career was in operetta, but
while living here she was persuaded to move to light
comedy, a field in which she became known as 'the
queen of her profession'. In 1927 she created the role
of Judith Bliss in Nöel Coward's (q.v.) *Hay Fever*. In
1934 she was a co-founder of the actors' union,
Equity.

TILAK, Lokamanya
(1856–1920), Indian,
politician, agitator
**10 Howley Place,
Little Venice, W2.**
English Heritage
Tilak stayed here in
1918–19. He had come to
England to press a suit for libel
against Sir Valentine Chirol, foreign editor of *The Times*,
who had made defamatory comments about him in a
book, *Indian Unrest*. Needless to say, Tilak lost the case,
the judge saying in his summing up: 'a man twice
convicted of sedition has no character to lose.' Tilak
was one of the first proponents of the idea of *Swaraj*
(complete independence) for India, and he was a
leader of the *Garam Dal* (the 'Hot Faction'), which got
him in prison more than once. Chirol dubbed him
'the Father of the Indian Unrest'.

TURING, Alan (1912–54), English, mathematician
2 Warrington Crescent, Maida Vale, W9.
English Heritage
Turing was born here. His title as 'the Father of
Modern Computer Science' dates from his 1936 paper
on the *Entscheidungsproblem*. He is known also as a key
member of the Second World War code-breaking team
at Bletchley Park, which successfully broke the
German Enigma codes.

TUSSAUD, Madame Marie (1761–1850), French,
artist in wax
24 Wellington Road, NW8. *English Heritage*
Madame Tussaud lived here in 1838–9. She was taught
wax modelling by her guardian, Dr Philippe Curtius,
and made her first model, of Voltaire (q.v.), in 1777.
During the French Revolution she modelled from the
severed heads of prominent people. She came to
England in 1802 and set up her first permanent show
in 1835.

VAUGHAN WILLIAMS, Ralph (1872–1958),
English, composer
10 Hanover Terrace, Regent's Park, NW1.
Greater London Council
Vaughan Williams lived here from 1953 until his death.
He studied at Cambridge, the Royal College of Music,
and in Berlin under Bruch and in Paris with Ravel.
Influenced by Holst (q.v.), he was a key figure in
reviving English folk music. He produced nine

symphonies, concertos, operas, choral works and the themes for several films, including *Scott of the Antarctic* (1948), which he later developed into his Seventh Symphony.

VOYSEY, C. F. A.

(1857–1941), English, architect, designer
6c Carlton Hill, St John's Wood, NW8.
English Heritage
Voysey lived here. He had a distinctive architectural style all of his own, featuring white rough-cast walls, buttresses, horizontal ribbon windows and huge pitched roofs. 'His best house in London', according to Pevsner (q.v.), is 8 Platts Lane, NW3, designed for his father in 1896.

WATERHOUSE, John William (1849–1917),
English, painter
10 Hall Road, NW8. *English Heritage*
Waterhouse lived here from 1900 until his death. His work was steeped in romance and mythology, and painted in the Pre-Raphaelite style. Among his best-known works are *The Lady of Shalott* (1888), *The Danaides* (1906), *Penelope and the Suitors* (1912) and another *Lady of Shalott* (1915). He was elected a Royal Academician in 1895.

WELLS, H. G. (1866–1946),

English, novelist
Chiltern Court, Baker Street, NW1.
H. G. Wells Society
13 Hanover Terrace, NW1.
Greater London Council
Wells lived at the first address from 1930 to 1936, and at the second from 1936 until his death. In these last years he was increasingly pessimistic about the future; in 1934 he predicted another world war would break out in 1940, and his novel *The Shape of Things to Come* (1933) foresaw the horrors of aerial bombing. His last book, *Mind at the End of Its Tether* (1945), argued that it might be a good idea to replace human beings with another species altogether.

WHEATSTONE, Sir Charles (1802–75),
English, scientist, inventor
19 Park Crescent, Regent's Park, W1.
Greater London Council
Sir Charles, who lived here, was a prolific inventor. He patented a railway telegraph in 1837, developed the 'Wheatstone bridge', a device to measure electrical resistance, and also invented the concertina, the stereoscope, the harmonica, the Playfair cipher (an encryption device) and an early microphone.

WILLIAMS, Henry Sylvester
(1867–1911), Trinidadian, lawyer, politician
38 Church Street, NW8. *City of Westminster*
This building was the Church Street ward office of the Labour Party when Williams was elected the first black councillor in Westminster in 1906. A remarkable early figure in the struggle for racial equality, Williams organised the first Pan-African Conference in 1900, saying: 'The time has come when the voice of Black men should be heard independently in their own affairs.'

WYNDHAM, Sir Charles (1837–1919), English,
actor-manager
20 York Terrace East, Regent's Park, NW1.
Greater London Council
Sir Charles, who lived and died here, initially trained and practised as a surgeon but could not resist the lure of the stage, making his London debut in 1866. He became successful in light comedy and melodrama, rather than Shakespeare, taking over the Criterion Theatre in 1876, opening his own Wyndham's Theatre in 1899, and adding the New Theatre in 1903.

Westminster 2:
Bayswater, Marylebone, Fitzrovia
South of Marylebone Road, north of Bayswater Road–Oxford Street

ADAMS, Henry Brooks (1838–1918), American, historian
98 Portland Place, W1. *Greater London Council*
Adams lived here when his father was American ambassador, and this was his embassy (see page 52). His most celebrated book is his autobiography, *The Education of Henry Adams*, which was awarded the Pulitzer Prize in 1919.

ARNOLD, Benedict (1741–1801), American, soldier
62 Gloucester Place, W1. *Private* Arnold lived here from 1796 until his death. Distinguished in battle with the colonial forces, he was made commandant of West Point but plotted to betray it to the British. He then fled to the British and was a given a command, coming to England in 1781. He died here in poverty. The plaque describes him as an 'American patriot', which might be disputed by his contemporaries.

ASQUITH, Herbert Henry (1852–1928), English, Prime Minister
20 Cavendish Square, W1. *London County Council* Asquith lived here from 1894 until he moved into 10 Downing Street in 1908. The house was a wedding present from his father-in-law. It was sold to the Royal College of Nursing in 1920. (See also Camden 1.)

AUXILIARY AMBULANCE STATION No. 39
Weymouth Mews, W1. *City of Westminster*
This was the site of one of nearly a hundred volunteer ambulance stations set up in London during the Second World War. It was opened in August 1939 Josephine Butler, who worked here in 1940–2, was later acclaimed as a war heroine after her book *Cyanide in My Shoe* was published, detailing numerous

undercover missions in occupied France at the personal orders of Churchill.
Unfortunately, her book was complete fantasy, and she was in Holloway Prison for theft in 1944.

AYER, Professor Sir Alfred (1910–89), English, philosopher
51 York Street, W1. *Westminster City Council* Ayer, who lived the last nine years of his life here, was professor of logic at Oxford from 1959 to 1978. His many publications include *Language, Truth and Logic* (1936), *Probability and Evidence* (1972) and *Philosophy in the Twentieth Century* (1982). A notable populariser, he was known to a wide public through television.

AYRTON, Hertha (1854–1923), English, electrical engineer, physicist
41 Norfolk Square, W2. *English Heritage*
Ayrton lived here from 1903 until her death. Her experiments on the electric arc, excluding air, saw her elected in 1899 as the first woman member of the Institute of Electrical Engineers. Her book *The Electric Arc* (1902) became a standard work. She was also the first woman to read a paper to the Royal Society.

BABBAGE, Charles (1791–1871), English, mathematician
1a Dorset Street, W1.
City of Westminster / St Marylebone Society
Babbage lived in a house on this site from 1829 until his death. He devised a calculating machine, the Difference Engine, and another, the Analytical Engine, neither built in his lifetime, which were forerunners of the modern computer. In 1991 the Science Museum built a Difference Engine to his exact plans and showed it worked. (See also Southwark.)

BALFE, Michael William (1808–70), Irish, composer
12 Seymour Street, W1.
London County Council
Balfe, who lived here, was a child prodigy violinist and singer, studied under Rossini in Italy in 1825–6, returned to England in 1833 and was appointed conductor of the London Italian Opera at Her Majesty's Theatre in 1846. Among his compositions is the opera *The Bohemian Girl* (1843).

BARING, Evelyn (1841–1917), English, colonial administrator
36 Wimpole Street, W1. *English Heritage*
Baring, who lived and died in this house, was British Consul-General in Egypt from 1883 to 1907. Although notionally he was advising the Egyptian king, it was understood that in practice his advice would always be accepted. Reviewing his portrait by Sargent (q.v.), the *Spectator* called him 'the greatest ruler Egypt has had since the days of the Pharaohs'.

BARRIE, Sir James (1860–1937), Scottish, playwright
100 Bayswater Road, W2. *London County Council*
Sir James lived here from 1902 to 1909. Although he wrote a number of successful straight plays, including *Dear Brutus*, *Quality Street* and *The Admirable Crichton*, as well as a handful of novels, his fame rests on his creation of *Peter Pan, or The Boy Who Wouldn't Grow Up*, first performed in 1904, which remains a perennial success with every new generation. He was awarded the Order of Merit in 1922.

BARRY, James (1741–1806), Irish, painter
36 Eastcastle Street, W1. *City of Westminster*
Barry lived here from 1786 until his death. A notoriously belligerent personality, he is the only Royal Academician in history to have been expelled from the Academy. He is best remembered for his massive series of murals *The Progress of Human Knowledge and Culture* (1777–83) at the Royal Society of Arts.

BEAUFORT, Sir Francis (1774–1857), English, naval officer, hydrographer
51 Manchester Street, W1. *London County Council*

Beaufort lived here. He is most famous for his development of the Beaufort Scale, a standardised order of different wind strengths. From 1829 he was head of the Hydrographic Office at the Admiralty, converting a dusty chart store into the finest survey institute in the world.

BENEDICT, Sir Julius (1804–85), German, composer
2 Manchester Square, W1. *London County Council*
Sir Julius, who lived and died in this house, had settled in London in 1836 and composed several operas, of which the most successful was *Lily of Killarney* (1862). He was also a conductor and accompanist, notably of Jenny Lind's (q.v.) London debut and her first American tour.

BENNETT, Sir William Sterndale (1816–75), English, composer
38 Queensborough Terrace, Bayswater, W2.
English Heritage
Sir William, who lived here, was the founder of the Bach Society (1849), Professor of Music at Cambridge (1856) and Principal of the Royal Academy of Music (1866). These tasks curbed the volume of his compositions. His most frequently performed work is the oratorio *The Woman of Samaria* (1867).

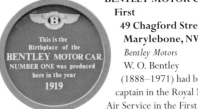

BENTLEY MOTOR CAR, First
49 Chagford Street, Marylebone, NW1.
Bentley Motors
W. O. Bentley (1888–1971) had been a captain in the Royal Naval Air Service in the First World War, where he significantly improved the Clerget engine on the Sopwith Camel, for which he was awarded £8,000.

Bentley No. 1 led to legendary successes in the Le Mans Twenty-Four Hour Race.

BERLIOZ, Hector (1803–69), French, composer
58 Queen Anne Street, W1. *Greater London Council*
Berlioz stayed here in 1851. The greatest musical figure of the French romantics, he formed, according to Gautier, a Trinity with Hugo and Delacroix. Among his many enduring compositions are the *Symphonie Fantastique* (1830), *Romeo and Juliet* (1838) and *The Damnation of Faust* (1846).

BODLEY, George Frederick (1827–1907), English, architect
109 Harley Street, W1. *English Heritage*
Bodley lived here from 1862 to 1873. A leading church architect in the Gothic Revival style, he designed the cathedrals at Washington DC, San Francisco and Hobart. He was a friend of the Pre-Raphaelites (q.v.) and William Morris (q.v.), and his own most important pupil was C. R. Ashbee (q.v.).

BONHAM-CARTER, Lady Violet (1887–1969), English, politician
43 Gloucester Square, Bayswater, W2. *English Heritage*
Lady Violet, who lived here, was a daughter of the Prime Minister Herbert Asquith (q.v.). She was president of the Liberal Party from 1945 to 1947, a governor of the BBC from 1941 to 1946, and a governor of the Old Vic from 1945 to 1969. Her voluminous diaries are a valuable record of British politics in the first half of the twentieth century.

BOSWELL, James (1740–1795), Scottish, biographer
122 Great Portland Street, W1.
London County Council
Boswell lived and died in a house on this site. He is remembered above all for his *Life of Samuel Johnson* (1791), based on their friendship from 1763 until Johnson's death. It is justly regarded as the liveliest biography in British literature. Boswell held himself in high esteem: 'I think there is a blossom about me of something more distinguished than the generality of mankind.' (See also Westminster 4.)

BROOKE, Sir Charles Vyner (1874–1963), English, Rajah of Sarawak
13 Albion Street, Bayswater, W2.
Greater London Council
Brooke reigned from 1917 to 1946, the third Brooke to do so, abdicating when Sarawak was incorporated into the British Empire. His reign was a benevolent despotism; Christian missionaries were banned and indigenous culture fostered, though headhunting was outlawed. The *Daily Telegraph* wrote of him: 'He is one of the few monarchs left in the world who can say: "*L'État, c'est moi*".'

BROWNING, Elizabeth Barrett (1806–61), English, poet
99 Gloucester Place, Marylebone, W1.
London County Council
50 Wimpole Street, W1. *Royal Society of Arts*
Browning lived at the first address from 1835 to 1838, and at the second, largely a housebound invalid, from 1838 to 1846. It was from Wimpole Street that Robert Browning (q.v.) stole her away to marriage, against her father's wishes. Her most famous poems, *Sonnets from the Portuguese* (1850), include one of the great openings in English poetry: 'How do I love thee? Let me count the ways...'

BURNETT, Frances Hodgson (1849–1924), English, children's writer
63 Portland Place, W1. *Greater London Council*
Burnett, who lived here, was a prolific writer of books for both adults and children, but she is remembered for the latter, especially *Little Lord Fauntleroy* (1886), which provoked some derision, and the classic *The Secret Garden* (1909), which remains a popular read to this day.

CATO STREET CONSPIRACY
1a Cato Street, Marylebone, W1.
Greater London Council
The conspiracy, twenty-seven strong, planned to murder the entire British cabinet at a dinner in Lord

38

Harrowby's house in Grosvenor Square in 1820. They were betrayed and arrested by the Bow Street Runners. Five were hanged and the rest transported to Australia.

CAVAFY, Constantine
(1863–1933), Greek, poet
14–15 Queensborough Terrace, Bayswater, W2.
London Hellenic Society
Cavafy lived here from 1873 to 1876 while at school in England. He published only two slim privately printed books of verse, in 1904 and 1910, and recognition in the English-speaking world came only from the steady support of E. M. Forster (q.v.), who met him in 1917 and maintained a long friendship.

CHATEAUBRIAND, François-René,
Viscomte de (1768–1848), French, writer, diplomat
Paddington Street Gardens, Marylebone, W1.
Private
Chateaubriand lived here in a nearby garret from 1793 to 1800, after being left for dead at the siege of Thionville in 1792. A major figure in early French Romanticism, he made ends meet by giving French lessons here. His reputation now rests mainly on the brilliance of his posthumously published autobiography, *Mémoires d'Outre-Tombe* (1849–50), which recounts his life in an age of uncommon political upheaval.

CHURCHILL, Lord Randolph (1849–95),
English, politician
2 Connaught Place, Bayswater, W2.
London County Council
Lord Randolph, who lived here from 1883 to 1892, had entered Parliament as a Tory in 1874 and was Secretary of State for India (1885–6) and Chancellor of the Exchequer (1886). He was a difficult colleague and when he resigned from the cabinet in 1886 his career was over. He was the father of Winston Churchill (see below).

CHURCHILL, Sir Winston (1874–1965), English,
Prime Minister
3 Sussex Square, W2. *Private*
Churchill lived in a house on this site from 1921 to

1924. During this period he was Secretary of the Colonies (1921–2), then out of Parliament from the 1922 election to 1924, when he rejoined the Conservative Party and became Chancellor of the Exchequer. (See also Kensington & Chelsea 1 and Westminster 4.)

CLOVER, Dr Joseph (1825–82), English, physician
3 Cavendish Place, W1.
Westminster City Council / History of Anaesthesia Society
Dr Clover lived in a house on this site from 1853 until his death. One of the first physicians to specialise in anaesthesia, he invented an apparatus in 1862, the first to give chloroform in a controlled dosage, and also in 1877 he invented the 'portable regulating ether-inhaler'.

COLERIDGE, Samuel Taylor (1772–1834),
English, poet, critic
71 Berners Street, W1. *London County Council*
Coleridge lived in a house on this site in 1812–13. Although at this time his opium addiction was becoming a major problem, he was able to give a series of lectures on Shakespeare and Milton, of which the talk on *Hamlet*, delivered on 2 January 1812, is considered the most important; it has influenced Shakespeare scholarship ever since. (See also Camden 1 and Hammersmith & Fulham.)

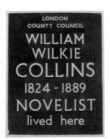

COLLINS, Wilkie
(1824–89), English, novelist
65 Gloucester Place, Marylebone, W1.
London County Council
Collins, who lived here, was one of the earliest writers to specialise in crime, mystery and suspense. His works include *The Woman in White* (1860) and *The Moonstone* (1868), the last being widely regarded as 'the first detective story', built round the character of Sergeant Cuff.

CONS, Emma (1837–1912), English, philanthropist
136 Seymour Place, Marylebone, W1.
Greater London Council
Cons lived and worked here. She started as a rent collector with Octavia Hill (q.v.) in 1864, then in 1879

formed her own South London Dwellings Company in Lambeth, run along the same lines as Hill's. She is most famous for taking over the Royal Victoria Hall in 1880, formerly a typical boozy, raucous music hall, and re-founding it as the Old Vic, run along strict temperance lines, with its presentations 'purged of innuendo in word and action'.

CRNJANSKI, Milos (1893–1977), Serbian, poet, novelist
Queen's Court, Queensway, W2.
Serbian Council of Great Britain
Crnjanski lived and worked here from 1953 to 1965. A prolific key figure in twentieth-century Serbian literature, his writings were hugely influenced by his grim experiences in the First World War. His novel *Migrations* (1929) is the only one of his works translated into English, but with his name rendered as 'Milos Tsernianski'.

DANNREUTHER, Edward (1844–1905), German, musician
12 Orme Square, W2. *City of Westminster*
Dannreuther lived here from 1873 to 1894 and hosted a five-week visit by Richard Wagner (see page 53) in 1877. He had settled in England from 1863. A pianist and writer of music, he was a champion of Wagner and founded the London Wagner Society in 1872.

DEARMER, Percy (1867–1936), English, cleric
107 Sussex Gardens, W2. *Hyde Park Estate*
Dearmer lived here from 1919 to 1923. A lifelong socialist, he was secretary of the Christian Social Union from 1891 to 1912 and was an early advocate of the ordination of women. He wrote *The Parson's*

Handbook (1899) and is credited, with Vaughan Williams (q.v.), with the revival of traditional English musical forms. With Vaughan Williams and Martin Shaw (q.v.) he edited *Songs of Praise* (1925) and *The Oxford Book of Carols* (1928).

DICK-READ, Dr Grantly (1890–1959), English, physician
25 Harley Street, Marylebone, W1.
Westminster City Council / The Natural Childbirth Trust
Dick-Read practised here from 1935 to 1941. The father of the Natural Childbirth movement, he believed in minimum medical interference in the birth process. His ideas were anathema to the medical profession, and he was expelled from the London Clinic. His book *Childbirth without Fear* (1942) remains the movement's bible.

DICKENS, Charles (1812–70), English, novelist
15–17 Marylebone Road, NW1. *Private*
Dickens lived at 1 Devonshire Place on this site from 1839 to 1851. During that time he produced six novels – *The Old Curiosity Shop*, *Barnaby Rudge*, *Martin Chuzzlewit*, *A Christmas Carol*, *Dombey and Son* and *David Copperfield*. Some of the characters from these books are depicted in the relief panel by the plaque. (See also Camden 2, Southwark, Haringey and Westminster 4.)

DOYLE, Sir Arthur Conan (1859–1930), Scottish, novelist
2 Upper Wimpole Street, W1. *City of Westminster*
Doyle set up an ophthalmic practice here in 1891. It was short-lived; he claimed in his autobiography that not a single patient came through the door. This gave him ample time to write, and in his brief time here he produced *The White Company*, one of his historical adventures, set in the Hundred Years War. (See also Croydon.)

DU PRÉ, Jacqueline (1945–87), English, cellist
27 Upper Montagu Street, W1. *Private*
Du Pré lived here from 1967 to 1971. These were the first four years of her marriage to Daniel Barenboim, a partnership whose musical fruitfulness has drawn comparisons with the Schumanns. In 1971 she began to lose sensitivity in her

fingers, and in 1973 this was diagnosed as multiple sclerosis. (See also Croydon, Westminster 4 and Camden 1.)

DUKE-ELDER, Sir Stewart (1898–1978), Scottish, physician
63 Harley Street, W1. *English Heritage*
Sir Stewart lived and worked here from 1934 to 1976. The leading ophthalmologist in the world of his generation, he was an authority on eye diseases and eye surgery and produced the definitive fifteen-volume *System of Ophthalmology*. He was eye doctor to Edward VIII, George VI and Elizabeth II.

ELIOT, T. S. (1888–1965), English, poet, critic, playwright
Crawford Mansions, 62–66 Crawford Street, Marylebone, W1. *City of Westminster*
Eliot lived in Flat 18 here from 1916 to 1920. To earn money, he taught at Highgate School, where the young John Betjeman (q.v.) was among his pupils, and worked in a bank. While here, he published his first two books of poetry, *Prufrock and Other Observations* (1917) and *Ara Vos Sec* (1920). (See also Camden 2 and Kensington & Chelsea 2.)

EQUIANO, Olaudah (1745–97), Nigerian, writer
73 Riding House Street, W1. *City of Westminster*
Equiano was living here in 1789 when he completed his autobiography, *The Interesting Narrative of the Life of Olaudah Equiano, or Gustavus Vassa, the African*.
The book was an immediate sensation, shocking readers with its account of the horrors of the passage of slaves from Africa to America, and it contributed significantly to the anti-slavery movement then gathering momentum, led by Wilberforce (q.v.) in Parliament.

FARADAY, Michael (1791–1867), English, scientist
48 Blandford Street, W1. *Royal Society of Arts*
Faraday lived and worked here from 1805 to 1812 as apprentice to a bookbinder, George Riebau. One of Riebau's customers, William Dance, gave Faraday tickets to hear lectures by Humphry Davy at the Royal Institution, and within a year he began a second apprenticeship, in science. (See also Southwark and Richmond.)

FENWICK, Ethel Gordon (1857–1947), Scottish, nursing reformer
20 Upper Wimpole Street, W1. *English Heritage*
Fenwick lived here from 1887 to 1924. She was a sister at the London Hospital from 1879 to 1881, matron at St Bartholomew's Hospital from 1881 to 1887, and Director of the Gordon Home Hospital from 1889 to 1896. She founded the British Nurses' Association, edited the *British Journal of Nursing*, and from 1926 was president of the British College of Nurses.

FLAXMAN, John (1755–1826), English, sculptor
7 Greenwell Street, W1. *Royal Society of Arts*
Flaxman lived and died here. He was a designer for Wedgwood from 1775 to 1794, and he became the first Professor of Sculpture at the Royal Academy in 1810. His work, in serene neo-classical style, includes the monuments to Robert Burns in Westminster Abbey and to Nelson (q.v.) in St Paul's.

FLEMING, Sir Alexander (1881–1955), Scottish, physician, bacteriologist
St Mary's Hospital, Praed Street, Paddington, W2. *Private*
It was in his laboratory here that Fleming discovered penicillin, more or less by accident, in 1928. This is recognised as the beginning of modern antibiotics. Subsequently Florey and Chain (q.v.) developed the method of mass-producing it, and they shared the

Nobel Prize for Medicine with Fleming in 1945. Fleming's laboratory is now a small museum in his honour. (See also Kensington & Chelsea 2.)

FUSELI, Henry (1741–1825), Swiss, painter
37 Foley Street, W1. *London County Council*
Fuseli lived here from 1788 to 1803. He was encouraged towards art by Reynolds (q.v.) and his work had a visionary romanticism that inspired Blake (q.v.). *The Nightmare* (1781) is his most famous work, thought to anticipate Freud in its sexuality.

GAGE, Thomas (1721–87), English, soldier
41 Portland Place, W1. *English Heritage*
Gage, who lived here, had charge of all British forces in North America from 1763 to 1775. In a situation of mounting tension, unable to deal effectively with Paul Revere and the Sons of Liberty, after the pyrrhic victories of Concord and Bunker Hill in 1775, he was relieved of command.

GIBBON, Edward (1737–94), English, historian
7 Bentinck Street, Marylebone, W1.
London County Council
Gibbon lived in a house on this site from 1773 to 1783. He was the author of the greatest work of history in English, the six-volume *Decline and Fall of the Roman Empire* (1776–88), which he had first conceived in October 1764 'as I sat musing amidst the ruins of the Capitol', and which he completed twenty-four years later with a sense of sadness at taking 'an everlasting leave of an old and agreeable companion'.

GLADSTONE, William Ewart (1809–98), English, Prime Minister
73 Harley Street, W1. *London County Council*
Gladstone lived here from 1876 to 1882. He had 'retired' from politics in 1875, after his first stint as Prime Minister, and actually spent more time at Hawarden Castle than here. During this time he

maintained a steady output of pamphlets and articles as well as a couple of books on Homer. He had three more premierships still to come, and when he began the next, in 1880, he moved into 10 Downing Street. (See also Greenwich and Westminster 4.)

GODLEY, John Robert (1814–61), Irish, colonial pioneer
48 Gloucester Place, Marylebone, W1.
London County Council
Godley, who lived and died here, is remembered as the founder of Canterbury, New Zealand. He arrived in New Zealand in 1850 under the auspices of the Canterbury Association, whose object was to create an Anglican church settlement. He successfully negotiated the pastoral basis of the community and returned to England in 1852, his job done.

GREEN, Benny (1927–98), English, jazz musician, critic
Howard House, 161 Cleveland Street, W1.
Private
Green lived in a house on this site from 1932 to 1962. He began his career as a bass saxophonist but later became better known as a writer and broadcaster. In 1964 he wrote the book and lyrics of the opera-ballet *Lysistrata*.

GREEN, John Richard (1837–83), English, cleric, historian
4 Beaumont Street, W1. *London County Council*
Green lived here from 1869 to 1876. He had just completed a period as the vicar of St Philip's, Stepney, which had broken his health, and was recovering in the relative peace of the library at Lambeth Palace. His works *A Short History of the English People* (1874), *A History of the English People* (1877–80), *The Making of England* (1881) and *The Conquest of England* (1883) established him as the most gifted popular historian of his day. (See also Tower Hamlets.)

GROSSMITH, George, Junior (1874–1935), English, actor-manager
3 Spanish Place, Marylebone, W1.
London County Council
Grossmith, who lived here, was pre-eminent in the field of Edwardian musical comedy, known for 'speaking' a song and deploying his gangling physique to comic effect. An innovator in bringing cabaret and revue on to the London stage, he managed the Gaiety

Theatre and Drury Lane. He was the son of George Grossmith Senior (q.v.).

HALLAM, Henry (1777–1859), English, historian
67 Wimpole Street, Marylebone, W1.
London County Council
Hallam lived here. His fame rests on three works:
A View of Europe in the Middle Ages (1818),
A Constitutional History of England from Henry VII to George II (1827) and *The Literature of Europe during the Fifteenth, Sixteenth and Seventeenth Centuries* (1837–9). His son Arthur was Tennyson's (q.v.) best friend at Cambridge, whose sudden early death in 1833 inspired Tennyson's *In Memoriam.*

HANDLEY, Tommy (1892–1949), English, radio comedian
34 Craven Road, Paddington, W2.
Greater London Council
Handley lived here. He is remembered above all for his much-loved weekly wartime radio series *ITMA* ('It's That Man Again'). At his memorial service in St Paul's, the bishop of London said: 'He transmuted the copper of our common experience into the gold of exquisite foolery.'

HARDY, Thomas (1840–1928), English, novelist, poet
16 Westbourne Park Villas, W2. *Private*
Hardy lived here from 1863 to 1874. His Dorset origins provided the background to his novels, which he began to produce here: *Desperate Remedies* (1871), *Under the Greenwood Tree* (1872), *A Pair of Blue Eyes* (1873) and *Far from the Madding Crowd* (1874). The big success of the last title enabled him to give up his work in architecture and concentrate on writing. (See also Wandsworth and Westminster 4.)

HARTE, Francis Bret (1836–1902), American, novelist, poet
74 Lancaster Gate, Bayswater, W2.
Greater London Council
Harte lived here from 1895 until his death. His reputation rests on his early short stories, mainly deriving from his youthful experiences in California.

He founded the *Overland Monthly* in 1868 and contributed many stories, including *The Luck of Roaring Camp* (1868) and *The Outcasts of Poker Flats* (1870).

HERZEN, Alexander (1812–70), Russian, political thinker
1 Orsett Terrace, Paddington, W2.
Greater London Council
'The Father of Russian Socialism', Herzen lived here from 1860 to 1863. Sent into internal exile in Russia in 1834, he left for Paris in 1847 and was in London from 1851 to 1864. He founded the Free Russian Press, publishing the *Polar Star* and the *Bell*, periodicals that were smuggled into Russia.

HILL, Octavia (1838–1912), English, social housing pioneer
2 Garbutt Place, Marylebone, W1. *English Heritage*
Greatly influenced by the Christian socialist F. D. Maurice (q.v.), she put her energies into social housing and sought to raise living standards by getting her tenants actively involved in the upkeep of their homes. These premises, originally 1–3 Paradise Place, were purchased for Hill in 1864 by John Ruskin (q.v.), who paid £750 for fifty-six year leases. Within ten years she had fifteen schemes around London, with three thousand tenants. She was also a co-founder of the National Trust in 1894. (See also Southwark.)

HILL, Sir Rowland (1795–1879), English, postal reformer
1 Orme Square, W2. *London County Council*
Sir Rowland, reformer of the postal system, lived here. He is not to be confused with Rowland Hill the preacher (see Southwark). (See also Camden 1 and Camden 2.)

HINDOOSTANE COFFEE HOUSE
102 George Street, Marylebone, W1.
City of Westminster
This was the site, in 1810, of London's first Indian restaurant, owned by Sake Dean Mahomed (see page 46). Aimed at Anglo-Indians, it offered hookahs with 'real chilm tobacco' and Indian cuisine, 'allowed by the greatest epicures to be unequalled'. Despite these attractions, it was not a success and closed in 1812.

HOGG, Quintin (1845–1903), English, philanthropist
5 Cavendish Square, W1. *London County Council*
Having made a fortune in the tea and sugar trades, Hogg turned to Christian philanthropy, founding a Ragged School in 1864, and a Young Men's Christian Institute in 1882, later called the Regent Street Polytechnic, now the University of Westminster.

HUGHES, David Edward (1831–1900), English, scientist, inventor
4 Great Portland Street, W1. *English Heritage*
Hughes, who lived and worked here, invented the microphone and the induction balance, and patented his system of telegraphy in 1855, which became the worldwide standard. He was one of the first to transmit using radio waves, years before Hertz or Marconi (q.v.).

HUTCHINSON, Sir Jonathan (1828–1913), English, physician
15 Cavendish Square, W1. *Greater London Council*
Sir Jonathan, who lived here, was an expert in many fields: neuropathogenesis, gout, leprosy, diseases of the tongue, and syphilis. His name is given to thirteen different medical conditions. He was the founder and sole author of the quarterly *Archives of Surgery* (1890–1900).

IRVING, Sir Henry (1838–1905), English, actor
15a Grafton Street, W1. *London County Council*
Sir Henry Irving (stage-name of John Henry Brodribb) lived here from 1872 to 1899. He first appeared on stage at Sunderland in 1856, reaching London ten years later. At the Lyceum Theatre, which he managed from 1878 onwards, he staged many Shakespeare plays with Ellen Terry (q.v.) as his co-star. He was the first actor to be knighted. (See also Hammersmith & Fulham.)

JACKSON, John Hughlings (1835–1911), English, physician
3 Manchester Square, Marylebone, W1. *London County Council*
Jackson, who lived here, was a neurologist. He is particularly remembered for his contribution to the understanding of epilepsy. He was a co-founder of the journal *Brain* in 1878, and a co-founder of the National Society for Epilepsy in 1892.

KELLY, Sir Gerald (1879–1972), English, painter
117 Gloucester Place, Marylebone, W1. *English Heritage*
Sir Gerald, a portrait painter, lived here from 1916 until his death. Among his subjects were T. S. Eliot (q.v.), Somerset Maugham (q.v.) several times, various members of the Royal Family (with whom he was a favourite), and a celebrated series of his wife, Lilian. He was president of the Royal Academy from 1949 to 1954.

KEMPE, Charles Eamer (1837–1907), English, stained-glass designer
37 Nottingham Place, Marylebone, W1. *English Heritage*
Kempe lived and worked here. After studying in the office of the architect G. F. Bodley (q.v.), Kempe set up his stained-glass company in 1866 (it survived till 1934). His work was often in fifteenth-century style, with a distinct attention to facial drawing, intricate detailing and sparkling colours, particularly pale and dark greens.

LAWRENCE, Susan (1871–1947), English, social reformer
44 Westbourne Terrace, Bayswater, W2. *English Heritage*
Lawrence lived here. Influenced by the Webbs (q.v.), she converted from Conservative to Labour in 1913. As a Poplar councillor, she was imprisoned in 1921 with George Lansbury (q.v.) for taking part in the Poplar 'Rates Revolt'. She worked tirelessly to the end of her life, latterly in particular with the blind.

LEAR, Edward (1812–88), English, poet, painter, travel writer
30 Seymour Street, Marylebone, W1. *London County Council*

Lear, who lived here, is best remembered for his nonsense verse, first published anonymously in 1846 as *A Book of Nonsense*, followed by others. *The Yonghy-Bonghy-Bó, The Chankly Bore, The Dong with the Luminous Nose* and *The Owl and the Pussy Cat* all continue to delight. Sadly, his landscape and ornithological painting and his vivid travel writing are more or less forgotten. (See also Islington.)

LENNON, John (1940–80), English, rock star
94 Baker Street, W1. *Musical Heritage*
This was the site of the legendary, fabulously decorated Apple Boutique, opened on 5 December 1967, in the final flush of the 'Summer of Love', and closed seven months later owing to a hopelessly unworldly approach to business. Lennon and the Beatles had another two years of hits, then split, and he went on to a successful solo career.

LISTER, Lord (1827–1912), English, physician
12 Park Crescent, W1. *London County Council*
Lord Lister lived here. He is principally remembered for pioneering antiseptic surgery; his series of articles for *The Lancet* in 1867 on 'The Antiseptic Principle of the Practice of Surgery' conclusively blew away the old beliefs in 'miasma'. He was president of the Royal Society from 1895 to 1900.

LOUDON, Jane (1807–58), English, novelist, horticulturalist
3 Porchester Terrace, Bayswater, W2.
London County Council
Jane Webb wrote a futuristic novel in 1827 called *The Mummy* (using a masculine pen-name), which imagined, among many future inventions, a steam plough. This brought her to the attention of John Loudon (see below); they married seven months later and lived here. She became a prolific writer on gardening for women, feeling that gardening literature up to then had not been accessible for beginners, and was the first editor of *The Ladies' Companion*.

LOUDON, John (1783–1843), Scottish, horticulturalist, writer
3 Porchester Terrace, Bayswater, W2.
London County Council
Loudon lived here with his wife, Jane (see above). He was the founder of *Gardener's Magazine* (1826) and *Architectural Magazine* (1834), and compiler of the *Encyclopaedia of Gardening* (1822) and an *Encyclopaedia of Cottage, Farm and Villa Architecture and Furniture* (1833). He originated the 'gardenesque' theory, which stresses the individual character of all trees and plants in any planting.

LUTYENS, Sir Edwin (1869–1944), English, architect
13 Mansfield Street, Marylebone, W1.
London County Council
Sir Edwin lived here. He is regarded as the greatest British architect of the twentieth century, designing numerous country houses (many with gardens by Gertrude Jekyll), the government buildings of New Delhi, the Cenotaph in Whitehall and the Memorial to the Missing of the Somme at Thiepval.

LYELL, Sir Charles (1797–1875), Scottish, geologist
73 Harley Street, W1. *London County Council*
Sir Charles lived here from 1854 until his death. His most important work was his three-volume *Principles of Geology* (1830–3), which was hugely influential on Darwin (q.v.), Wallace (q.v.) and Huxley (q.v.). Craters on the moon and on Mars are named in his honour.

MACAULAY, Rose (1881–1958), English, novelist
Hinde House, 11–14 Hinde Street, Marylebone, W1. *English Heritage*
Macaulay lived and died here. Her thirty-five books, mostly novels, but also biography and travel, culminated in a strongly autobiographical masterpiece, *The Towers of Trebizond* (1956), which treats of the conflict between adultery and Christianity, and for which she was awarded the James Tait Black Memorial Prize.

MACKENZIE, Sir James (1853–1925), Scottish, physician
17 Bentinck Street, Marylebone, W1.
College of General Practitioners
Sir James lived and worked here

from 1907 to 1911. As a general practitioner in Burnley between 1879 and 1907, he made a careful study of heart conditions among his patients, and his book *Diseases of the Heart* (1908) is regarded as ground-breaking. He was a consultant at West London and Mount Vernon Hospitals.

MAHOMED, Sake Dean (1759–1851), Indian, entrepreneur, traveller
102 George Street, Marylebone, W1.
City of Westminster
Mahomed opened the Hindoostane Coffee House (see page 43) on this site in 1810; it closed after two years. He had previously written *The Travels of Dean Mahomet* (1794), the first book to be written and published in English by an Indian. In 1814 he set up the Indian Vapour Baths and Shampooing Establishment in Brighton, and claimed to have introduced shampoo into Britain. He retired in 1834, a well-known citizen of Brighton, often seen at the races.

MALONE, Edmond (1741–1812), Irish, Shakespearean scholar
40 Langham Street, W1. *London County Council*
Malone lived here from 1779 until his death. His study of the chronology of Shakespeare's works (1778) is still largely accepted. He published a critical *Collected Shakespeare* in 1790, and a *Collected Dryden* in 1800. He helped Boswell (q.v.) in revising his *Life of Samuel Johnson* (q.v.).

MANBY, Charles (1804–84), English, civil engineer
60 Westbourne Terrace, Bayswater, W2.
London County Council
Manby lived here from 1870 to 1876. He and his father, Aaron, designed and built the first iron steamship to go to sea (1822). He settled in London in 1835, and among his achievements were the planning of the Suez Canal and preparing the Great Exhibition of 1851. He was secretary of the Institute of Civil Engineers from 1839 to 1856 and was made a Fellow of the Royal Society in 1853.

MANSON, Sir Patrick (1844–1922), Scottish, physician
50 Welbeck Street, Marylebone, W1.
Greater London Council
Sir Patrick, who lived here, is described on the plaque as 'the Father of Modern Tropical Medicine'. He was noted for his pioneering work with Ross (q.v.),

especially the discovery that malaria is mosquito-borne (1877). He worked for many years in China and Hong Kong, where he founded a school of medicine, and he co-founded the London School of Tropical Medicine (1899).

MARCONI, Guglielmo (1874–1937), Italian, physicist, inventor
71 Hereford Road, Westbourne Green, W2.
London County Council
Marconi lived here in 1896–7.

MARRYAT, Captain Frederick (1792–1848), English, novelist
3 Spanish Place, W1. *London County Council*
Marryat lived here from 1841 to 1843, publishing four novels in that time, including *Masterman Ready, or the Wreck in the Pacific* (1841), one of his still popular naval adventures. (See also Enfield and Merton.)

MAYER, Sir Robert (1879–1985), British, businessman, music patron
2 Mansfield Street, Marylebone, W1.
English Heritage
Sir Robert, who lived here in Flat 31, was naturalised as British in 1902. He founded the Robert Mayer Concerts for Children in 1923, co-founded the London Philharmonic in 1932, and founded the London Schools Symphony Orchestra in 1951. He is the oldest person ever to be knighted, on his hundredth birthday.

MEYNELL, Alice (1847–1922), English, poet, essayist, suffragist
47 Palace Court, Bayswater, W2.
London County Council
Meynell (née Thompson) lived here from 1890 to 1905. She converted to Catholicism in 1868, and her poetry was invariably religious and reads rather heavily today. She is better remembered for her sensitive essays in literary criticism, and the compilation of anthologies. She married Wilfrid Meynell in 1877 and they jointly owned and edited several magazines, including *The Pen*, *The Weekly Register* and *Merry England*. She was a prominent member of the Women Writers' Suffrage League.

MILLIGAN, Spike (1918–2002), Irish, actor, writer, comedian
9 Orme Court, W2. *Comic Heritage*
This was the site of Milligan's office from 1962 until his death. The building also housed Eric Sykes, Tony Hancock (q.v.) and Frankie Howerd (q.v.), so there is unlikely to have been a dull moment. (See also Barnet.)

MILNER, Alfred, Lord (1854–1925), English, colonial administrator
14 Manchester Square, Marylebone, W1.
Greater London Council
Milner, who lived here, was employed by successive British governments as a troubleshooter in various sensitive colonial fields, notably South Africa from 1897 to 1905. Milner saw himself as a 'British race patriot'; his political ideal was a global parliament with the delegates all of British descent.

MOORE, Thomas 'Tom' (1779–1852), Irish, poet
85 George Street, Marylebone, W1.
London County Council
Moore lived here. His best-known poem is *Lalla Rookh* (1817). He was also an accomplished musician and set many of his patriotic Irish poems to old Irish tunes, becoming the National Bard. The best-loved of these works are 'The Harp that Once through Tara's Halls', 'The Minstrel Boy' and 'The Last Rose of Summer'.

MORSE, Samuel (1791–1872), American, inventor, painter
141 Cleveland Street, Fitzrovia, W1.
London County Council
Morse stayed here from 1812 to 1815 while studying at the Royal Academy, and painting was his main activity until 1832. Then, returning to the United States after a painting tour of Europe, he saw early attempts at electromagnetic communication and conceived the idea of a single-wire telegraph system. Eventually, after much lobbying, he was able to link Baltimore and Washington in 1844 and send his famous inaugural message in Morse code: 'What hath God wrought?'

MUNRO, Hector Hugh ('Saki') (1870–1916), English, short-story writer
97 Mortimer Street, W1. *English Heritage*
Munro lived here from 1908. His short stories are noted for their macabre wit and satirical depiction of Edwardian society, and he is routinely compared to O. Henry and Dorothy Parker. Although forty-three at the outbreak of the First World War, he immediately volunteered for the Royal Fusiliers and was killed by a German sniper at Beaumont Hamel on 13 November 1916, his last words being 'Put that damned cigarette out'.

MURROW, Edward R. (1908–65), American, reporter
Weymouth House, 84–94 Hallam Street, W1. *English Heritage*
Murrow lived here in Flat 5 from 1938 to 1946. He is regarded as one of the greatest broadcasters ever. As Chief European Reporter for CBS, his radio broadcasts to North America, particularly during the Blitz, played a significant role in getting American sympathies on the British side. He always began his reports with 'This … is London' and ended them 'Goodnight … and good luck'.

NIGHTINGALE, Florence (1820–1910), English, nurse, reformer
90 Harley Street, Marylebone, W1. *Private*
Florence Nightingale's fame rests on her work in the Crimean War (1854–7), when she earned the title 'the Lady with the Lamp'; her hospital at Scutari in Turkey brought order to the previously ghastly and chaotic treatment of the wounded. She returned to England a national heroine, said to be second only to Queen Victoria in the public mind. (See also Westminster 3.)

NOLLEKENS, Joseph (1737–1823), English, sculptor
44 Mortimer Street, W1. *London County Council*

Nollekens lived and died in a house on this site. He is considered the best English sculptor of the late eighteenth century and was elected a Royal Academician in 1772. He enjoyed royal patronage and made busts of George III (q.v.), Pitt the Younger (q.v.), Charles James Fox (q.v.) and Dr Johnson (q.v.). A notorious miser, he left £200,000.

ORANJEHAVEN
23 Hyde Park Place, W2. *Private*

Over 1,700 Dutchmen successfully escaped occupied territory in the Second World War between the Dutch surrender and the D-Day invasion. They were all carefully interrogated here to check that they were not double agents before being welcomed.

PATEL, Sardar Vallabhbhai Javerbhai (1875–1950), Indian, politician
23 Aldridge Road Villas, Westbourne Green, W11. *Greater London Council*

Patel lived here from 1912 to 1914, while studying law at the Middle Temple. Influenced by Gandhi (q.v.), he went on to organise the peasants in his native Gujarat to non-violent civil disobedience in the 1930s and was a leader of the Quit India movement. Later he was the first Home Minister and deputy Prime Minister after independence, where he is remembered as the 'patron saint' of Indian civil servants for his establishment of all-India services.

PEARCE, Stephen (1819–1904), English, painter
54 Queen Anne Street, Marylebone, W1. *Private*

Pearce lived here from 1856 to 1884. A portrait and equestrian painter, his most famous work, *Coursing at Ashdown Park* (1869), was 10 feet long and contained sixty equestrian portraits, for which he was paid 1,000 guineas, plus 200 guineas for the copyright. Forty-nine portraits by him are in the National Portrait Gallery.

PEARSON, John Loughborough (1817–97), English, architect
13 Mansfield Street, Marylebone, W1. *London County Council*

Pearson, who lived and died here, is mainly known for his prolific church work, including St Augustine's, Kilburn (1870–7), described by Pevsner as 'a proud, honest, upright achievement', and Truro Cathedral (1880). But see also his exquisite Astor Estate Offices (1894) at 2 Temple Place.

PINERO, Sir Arthur Wing (1855–1934), English, playwright
115a Harley Street, Marylebone, W1. *Greater London Council*

Sir Arthur lived here from 1909 until his death. He wrote several plays about society's double standards for men and women, most notably *The Second Mrs Tanqueray* (1893). He was also a consummate farceur, his best-known farce being *The Magistrate* (1885), last revived in London in 1969, starring Alastair Sim (q.v.).

PITT, William, the Younger (1759–1806), English, Prime Minister
120 Baker Street, W1. *London County Council*

Pitt lived here in 1803–4. This was between his two stints as Prime Minister. When he began the first, in 1783, he was aged twenty-four, making him the youngest premier ever. This ministry lasted till 1801, the second longest ever; during it he was sustained in office by the support of George III, who could not stand the Fox/North opposition. His second ministry ran from 1804 until his death, when his reported famous last words were: 'I think I could eat one of Bellamy's veal pies.'

QUEEN'S HALL
Henry Wood House, Langham Place, W1. *City of Westminster/British Broadcasting Corporation*

This is the site of the Queen's Hall (1893–1941). It was here that Sir Henry Wood (see page 54) inaugurated the Promenade Concerts in 1895. They were the brainchild of the impresario Robert Newman, who explained to Sir Henry: 'I am going to run nightly concerts to train the public in easy stages. Popular at first, gradually raising the standard until I have created a public for classical and modern music.' On 10 May 1941 the hall was destroyed in a bombing raid, and the Proms moved to the Albert Hall thereafter.

RAY-JONES, Tony (1941–72), English, photographer
102 Gloucester Place, Marylebone, W1.
City of Westminster / Royal Photographic Society
Ray-Jones lived and worked here. A graduate of the London College of Printing and Yale School of Art, he sought to document the English way of life at leisure from 1966 to 1969, 'before', he said, 'it becomes too Americanised'. His posthumous book, *A Day Off* (1974), shows the results.

REES, Sir John Milsom (1866–1952), Welsh, surgeon
18 Upper Wimpole Street, Marylebone, W1.
City of Westminster
Sir John lived here from 1914 to 1939. A specialist in the throat, he was consultant laryngologist to the Royal Family from 1910 to 1936, and to the Royal Opera House, where he treated Nellie Melba (q.v.), Adelina Patti and Kirsten Flagstad, among others.

RESCHID PASHA, Mustapha (1800–58), Turkish, diplomat, reformer
1 Bryanston Square, Marylebone, W1.
Greater London Council
Reschid Pasha lived here as ambassador from the Sublime Porte in 1839. An ardent reformer, he was a foremost activist in the *Tanzimat* ('reorganisation', 1839–76) movement, a prolonged attempt by westernised Turks like himself to haul the Ottoman Empire into the nineteenth century. He was also a key player in the settlement after the Crimean War.

RICHMOND, George (1809–96), English, painter
20 York Street, Marylebone, W1.
London County Council
Richmond lived here from 1843 until his death. Much influenced by Blake (q.v.) in his youth, he formed 'The Ancients' group with Samuel Palmer (q.v.). After

1830 he turned more to conventional portrait painting. His father, Thomas Richmond, was a miniaturist, and his son, William Blake Richmond, was a well-known portrait painter.

RIE, Dame Lucie (1902–95), Austrian-English, potter
18 Albion Mews, W2. *English Heritage*
A refugee from Nazism in Austria, Dame Lucie lived and worked here from 1939 until her death. Her work ranged from ceramic buttons and jewellery to bowls and bottle forms, brightly glazed and functional. Her studio here, which did not change in her fifty-year occupancy, has been moved and reconstructed in the new Ceramics Gallery at the Victoria and Albert Museum, opened in 2009.

ROBERTS, Earl, VC (1832–1914), Anglo-Irish, soldier
47 Portland Place, W1.
London County Council
Roberts, who lived here, won his VC as a Lieutenant in 1858 at Khudaganj, India, when he single-handedly recaptured a standard from two sepoys. He was commander-in-chief, India, from 1885 to 1893, and commander-in-chief of the British Army from 1900 to 1904. He was very popular with the troops, who nicknamed him 'Bobs'.

ROSS, Sir Ronald (1857–1932), English, physician
18 Cavendish Square, W1. *Greater London Council*
Sir Ronald, who lived here, studied malaria in various postings round India between 1881 and 1899. His breakthrough was the discovery of the life cycle of the malarial parasite *Plasmodium*, from which he demonstrated that malaria was mosquito-borne. He was awarded the Nobel Prize for Medicine in 1902.

ROSSETTI, Dante Gabriel (1828–82), English, painter, poet
110 Hallam Street, W1. *London County Council*
Rossetti was born in a house on this site. The plaque was originally installed in 1906, but another plaque below notes, with typical LCC thoroughness, 'Premises rebuilt and tablet refixed 1928'. (See also Kensington & Chelsea 2 and Camden 2.)

SCHREINER, Olive
(1855–1920), South African, novelist
16 Portsea Place, Bayswater, W2.
London County Council
Her best-known novel is her first, *The Story of an African Farm* (1883), published under the pseudonym Ralph Iron, which introduced a 'new woman' character, Lyndall. Bold and unconventional, Schreiner was close to Havelock Ellis (q.v.) and Karl Pearson (q.v.) and was an early champion of the rights of women and blacks.

SCOTT, Sir Giles Gilbert
(1880–1960), English, architect
Chester House, Clarendon Place, Bayswater, W2.
English Heritage
Sir Giles designed this house and lived here from 1926 until his death. Grandson of George Gilbert Scott (q.v.), he designed Liverpool Anglican Cathedral (1904), Cambridge University Library (1931–4), the new Bodleian Library at Oxford (1936–46), Waterloo Bridge (1939–45), and the red telephone box. He also supervised the rebuilding of the Houses of Parliament after bomb damage in the Second World War.

SEACOLE, Mary
(1805–81), Jamaican, nurse
147 George Street, W1.
City of Westminster / The Portman Estate
Seacole, who lived in a house on this site in the 1870s, famously went to the Crimea at her own expense and set up a rest station, hotel and hospital much nearer the action than Florence Nightingale's (see page 47) at Scutari. Immensely popular with the troops, she was twice rescued from financial difficulties after the Crimean War by huge public events in her honour. She was voted the 'Greatest Black Briton' in an online poll in 2004. (See also Westminster 3.)

SMITH, W. H. (1825–91), English, entrepreneur, politician
12 Hyde Park Street, Bayswater, W2.
London County Council
Smith lived here. Joining his father in business in 1846, he procured an exclusive contract with the London & North Western Railway to sell papers at Euston station and around their network. By the 1850s W. H. Smith & Son had exclusive contracts at all London railway stations. An MP from 1868 to 1891, he was First Lord of the Admiralty from 1877 to 1880, Secretary of State for War in 1885 and Leader of the House from 1886 to 1891.

SMITHSON, James (1764–1829), English, mineralogist, chemist
9 Bentinck Street, W1. *English Heritage*
Smithson, whose bequest to the United States led to the foundation of the Smithsonian Institute, lived here. We know less about him than we would like because a fire at the Smithsonian in 1865 destroyed his collections, notebooks, diaries and letters. He made a number of mineralogical discoveries, and a zinc ore was posthumously named Smithsonite in his honour. He also produced numerous scientific papers on topics including the chemical contents of a lady's teardrop, the crystalline form of ice and a superior method of coffee-making.

STANHOPE, Charles, third Earl (1753–1816), English, scientist, inventor, politician
20 Mansfield Street, Marylebone, W1.
London County Council

Stanhope lived here. Sympathetic to the French Revolution, he was nicknamed 'the minority of one' in Parliament. His inventions include the Stanhope press, the Stanhope lens, a monochord for tuning musical instruments, and two calculating machines.

STEPHENSON, Robert (1803–59), English, engineer
35 Gloucester Square, Bayswater, W2.
London County Council
Stephenson lived and died in a house on this site. He founded, with his father, George, the first railway works in the world at Newcastle in 1823, and designed and built the steam locomotive *Rocket* for the Rainhill Trials (1829). Among his civil engineering works, he built Kilsby Tunnel (1838), the Newcastle High Level Bridge (1849) and the Menai railway bridge (1850).

STILL, Sir George Frederic (1868–1941), English, physician
28 Queen Anne Street, Marylebone, W1.
English Heritage
Sir George lived here. His 1897 doctoral thesis described a form of childhood febrile arthritis known today as Still's disease. He was also the first to pick out the symptoms of ADHD (attention deficit hyperactivity disorder).

STOKOWSKI, Leopold (1882–1977), English, conductor
63 Marylebone High Street, W1.
Leopold Stokowski Society – London
Stokowski went to school here. Born in England, but half Polish and half Irish, he made his career as a conductor in America. He conducted all the great American orchestras, revised the standard orchestral seating arrangements, appeared with Mickey Mouse in *Fantasia* (1939) and had an affair with Greta Garbo.

STOTHARD, Thomas (1755–1834), English, painter, illustrator
28 Newman Street, W1. *London County Council*
Stothard, who lived here from 1794 and died here, produced over five thousand illustrations, of which about three thousand have been engraved, of works by

Shakespeare, Cervantes, Bunyan, Goldsmith, Richardson, Smollett, Pope and others. His *Canterbury Pilgrims* was one of the most popular engravings of the nineteenth century.

STREET, George Edmund (1824–81), English, architect
14 Cavendish Place, W1. *Greater London Council*
Street lived here. After five years in Sir George Gilbert Scott's (q.v.) office, he set up on his own in 1849. He was a Gothicist and his 1865 book *The Gothic Architecture of Spain* inspired the 'Streaky Bacon style'. His most famous work is the Royal Courts of Justice in the Strand (1871–82).

TAGLIONI, Marie (1804–84), Italian, ballerina
14 Connaught Square, Bayswater, W2.
London County Council
Taglioni lived here in 1875–6. She came to fame when her father created *La Sylphide* for her in 1832, the first ballet in which the ballerina danced *en pointe* throughout. She retired in 1847 and taught social dance to society ladies. The plaque wrongly dates her birth to 1809.

TAUBER, Richard (1891–1948), Austrian, tenor
Park West, Kendal Street, Bayswater, W2.
English Heritage
One of the greatest singers of the twentieth century, Tauber lived the last year of his life in Flat 297 here. Franz Lehar wrote many operettas specially for him. He left Austria for England after the Anschluss in 1938 and became a British citizen in 1940. His lyric tenor was the epitome of Viennese charm; according to the critics, 'his heart felt every word he sang'.

THACKERAY, William Makepeace (1811–63), English, novelist, journalist
18 Albion Street, Bayswater, W2. *Private*
Thackeray lived here in 1837, after returning from a period studying art in Paris. He was newly married and determined to make a living as a journalist writing for magazines such as *Fraser's*, which published his early story *The History of Samuel Titmarsh and the Great Hoggarty Diamond* (1837–8), considered a great success. (See also Kensington & Chelsea 1 and Kensington & Chelsea 2.)

TOSTI, Sir Francesco Paolo (1846–1916), Italian, composer
12 Mandeville Place, Marylebone, W1. *City of Westminster / Association Abruzzo-Molise GB*
Sir Francesco lived here from 1886 to 1910. He was a composer of light songs, known as salon music, very popular in the *Belle Époque*. In 1880 he was appointed singing master to the Royal Family, and in 1894 Professor of Singing at the Royal College of Music. Knighted by his friend Edward VII in 1908, he retired to Italy in 1910.

TREVES, Sir Frederick (1853–1923), English, physician
6 Wimpole Street, W1. *English Heritage*
Sir Frederick lived here from 1886 to 1907. He was a professor at the Royal College of Surgeons and a co-founder of the Red Cross Society but is best remembered for his humanity towards Joseph Merrick, the 'Elephant Man', whom he rescued from a freak show and installed at the London Hospital in 1886.

TROLLOPE, Anthony (1815–82), English, novelist
39 Montagu Square, Marylebone, W1.
London County Council
Trollope lived here from 1872 to 1880. Working to a strict daily writing schedule, he was producing a least a book a year, including *The Eustace Diamonds* (1873), *Phineas Redux* (1874), *The Way We Live Now* (1875), which some account his masterpiece, *The Prime Minister* (1876) and *The Duke's Children* (1879). The onset of asthma made him remove to the country. (See also Barnet.)

TURNER, Joseph Mallord William (1775–1851), English, painter
23 Queen Anne Street, W1. *Portman Estate Trustees*
This was Turner's town house and gallery from 1820 until his death. In the last years of his life, when he was a recluse in Cheyne Walk, the gallery was said to be in

a very dilapidated state. After his death in Chelsea, his body was brought here and then conveyed to the crypt of St Paul's for burial. (See also Richmond, Kensington & Chelsea 2 and Westminster 4.)

TYBURN MARTYRS
Tyburn Shrine, Bayswater Road, W2.
City of Westminster / Friends of Tyburn
The plaque memorialises 105 Catholic martyrs who were hanged at the Tyburn gallows near this site between 1538 and 1681. The plaque is in the front wall of the Convent of the Adorers of the Sacred Heart of Jesus, a French order forced out of Paris in 1903. Their settling here fulfils a prophecy made back in the days of the persecution that one day a religious house would stand near Tyburn and venerate the martyrs.

TYBURN TREE
Junction of Edgware and Bayswater Roads, W2. *London County Council*
The circular plaque is not readily accessible, set flat amid the traffic island at a busy junction. This was the site of public hangings, the first recorded in 1196, and continuing until 1783. Prisoners were brought from Newgate prison, the popular ones being given drinks along the way, and grandstands were erected round the gallows. Among the notables executed here were Edmund Campion, St Oliver Plunkett, Jack Sheppard and Jonathan Wild.

UNITED STATES EMBASSY
98 Portland Place, W1. *Greater London Council*
This was the United States Embassy from 1863 to 1866. Henry Brooks Adams (see page 36), the distinguished historian, stayed here when his father

was ambassador. The building now houses the Gulbenkian Foundation.

VAN BUREN, Martin (1782–1862), American, President
7 Stratford Place, W1. *Greater London Council*
Van Buren was the eighth President of the United States, and the first to be born an American citizen. A key early organiser of the Democratic Party, he was Secretary of State from 1829 to 1831, and briefly ambassador to London, when he lived here, vice-president (1833–7), and a one-term president (1837–41).

WAGNER, Richard (1813–83), German, composer
12 Orme Square, W2. *City of Westminster*
Richard Wagner, who stayed here with his friend Edward Dannreuther (see page 40) for five weeks in 1877, was the embodiment of nineteenth-century German Romanticism, feeding intensely off Teutonic myth and legend. His *Ring* cycle has established him as the sacred monster of German culture, the object of an abiding cult.

WATERHOUSE, Alfred (1830–1905), English, architect
61 New Cavendish Street, Marylebone, W1.
English Heritage
Waterhouse lived here. A leading exponent of the Victorian Gothic revival, his buildings include Manchester Town Hall (1869–77), the Natural History Museum (1873–81) and the Prudential Headquarters in Holborn (1899). He was president of the Royal Institute of British Architects from 1888 to 1891. His brother was the accountant Edwin Waterhouse (q.v.).

WEBER, Carl Maria von (1786–1826), German, composer
103 Great Portland Street, W1.
Incorporated Society of Musicians
His works, especially his operas *Der Freischütz* (1821), *Euryanthe* (1823) and *Oberon* (1826), were influential in the development of the nineteenth-century German romantic school. He died here two months after overseeing the première of *Oberon* at Covent Garden.

WEISZ, Victor (1913–66), German, cartoonist
Welbeck Mansions, 35 Welbeck Street, Marylebone, W1. *English Heritage*
Weisz lived in a flat here. He came to the United

Kingdom in 1935 to escape Nazism and worked variously for the *News Chronicle*, *Daily Mirror* and *Evening Standard* as 'Vicky'. In the 1950s he famously caricatured Harold Macmillan as 'Supermac', but it did the Prime Minister a good turn and he increased his majority at the next election.

WESLEY, Charles (1707–88), English, Methodist, hymn writer
1 Wheatley Street, W1. *London County Council*
Wesley lived in a house on this site from 1771 until his death. The house was the scene of subscription concerts given by his children (see below), which were attended by Dr Johnson (q.v.) and members of fashionable society. Wesley himself composed over six thousand hymns, many of which are still sung today, the best-known being 'Hark! The Herald Angels Sing'. (See also City and Westminster 4.)

WESLEY, Charles, Junior (1757–1834), English, musician
1 Wheatley Street, W1. *London County Council*
A musical prodigy, and the eldest son of Charles Wesley (see above), he was playing the organ before the age of three. He played in various London churches and was for a time private organist to the Prince Regent.

WESLEY, Samuel (1766–1837), English, musician, composer
1 Wheatley Street, W1. *London County Council*
A younger son of Charles Wesley (see above), like his brother, he played the organ, but he also played the violin, was a conductor, lectured on music and composed. Among his pieces that still get the occasional airing are the motet *In Exitu Israel* and his madrigal setting of the Chatterton poem 'O singe unto mie roundelaie'.

WILHEMINA, Queen of the Netherlands (1880–1962), Dutch, monarch
23 Hyde Park Place, W2. *Private*
Queen Wilhelmina endowed this building as a club (see Oranjehaven, page 48) for Dutchmen escaping Nazi occupation during the Second World War.

She reigned longer than any other Dutch monarch, from 1890 to 1948, when her abdication in favour of her daughter was precipitated by revolt in the Dutch East Indies, now Indonesia. Her wartime broadcasts to Holland were very popular. (See also Westminster 4.)

WOOD, Sir Henry (1869–1944), English, conductor
Henry Wood House, Langham Place, W1.
City of Westminster / British Broadcasting Corporation
This was the site of the Queen's Hall (see page 48), where Sir Henry conducted the Promenade Concerts from their inception in 1895 until the building was destroyed in the Blitz in 1941. (See also Camden 1.)

WOOLNER, Thomas (1825–92), English, sculptor, poet
29 Welbeck Street, Marylebone, W1. *Private*
Woolner lived here from 1860 until his death. He was a founder member of the Pre-Raphaelite Brotherhood, known in his day for his poetry as much as his sculpture, but it is for the latter that posterity holds him in higher esteem; see, for example, his John Stuart Mill (q.v.) on the Victoria Embankment, Palmerston (q.v.) in Parliament Square, and memorial busts of Cobden (q.v.), Tennyson (q.v.), F. D. Maurice (q.v.), Kingsley (q.v.) and Lord Lawrence (q.v.) in Westminster Abbey.

YOUNG, Thomas
(1773–1829), English,
physician, scientist
**48 Welbeck Street,
Marylebone, W1.**
London County Council
Young lived here. While practising as a doctor, he found time to contribute to the understanding of vision, the wave theory of light, solid mechanics, energy, physiology and, in Egyptology, to make a significant breakthrough in the decipherment of the Rosetta Stone.

ZYGIELBOJM, Szmul 'Artur' (1895–1943), Polish, politician
Corner of Porchester Road and Porchester Square, W2.
City of Westminster / Szmul Zygielbojm Memorial Committee
Zygielbojm lived near this spot in 1942–3. A Polish trade union official and councillor in the 1930s, he joined the government in exile in 1940 and lobbied tirelessly but fruitlessly to save European Jewry. He committed suicide in despair at the world's apparent indifference to the Holocaust.

Westminster 3:
Mayfair and Soho
South of Oxford Street, north of Knightsbridge–Piccadilly–Shaftesbury Avenue

ADAMS, John (1735–1826), American, President
9 Grosvenor Square, W1. *Colonial Dames of America*
Adams lived here in 1785–8 while he was the first American ambassador to the Court of St James. Subsequently he was the second President of the United States (1797–1801). Earlier, while he was George Washington's vice-president (1789–97), he was the first holder of that position to notice its status: 'My country has in its wisdom contrived for me the most insignificant office that ever the invention of man contrived or his imagination conceived.'

AMBROSE, Bert (*c.*1896–1971), English, dance-band leader
May Fair Hotel, Stratton Street, W1.
English Heritage
Ambrose had previously played at the Embassy Club but the club had a policy of not allowing radio broadcasts from its premises, so he moved to the May Fair in 1927. When the May Fair asked him to take a pay cut in 1933, he moved back to the Embassy, but he returned to the hotel in 1936. During this second stint he discovered and promoted two young singers, Vera Lynn and Anne Shelton (q.v.), who both went on to be 'forces' sweethearts' in the Second World War.

ARDEN, Don (1926–2007), English, agent, promoter
52–55 Carnaby Street, W1.
City of Westminster
This was the site of Don Arden's offices in the 1960s. Born Harry Levy, he changed his name and had a brief career as a singer, comedian and impressionist before realising in the mid-1950s that he could make more money as an agent. His management style earned him the nickname 'the Al Capone of Pop', and he never denied his fearsome reputation. The Small Faces (see page 68), whom he signed up here in

1965, had their first hit as a result of Arden's 'chart fixing' at a cost of £12,000. He was the father of Sharon Osbourne, the television personality.

ARTISTS RIFLES
8 St George Street, W1. *Private*
Part of a widespread volunteer movement that sprang up in 1859–60 in the face of a perceived threat of French invasion, the Artists Rifles were organised in London by Edward Sterling, an art student, and were made up of painters, musicians, actors, architects and others involved in the creative professions. The first meeting was here on 28 February 1860 and the regiment was formally known as the 38th Middlesex (Artists) Rifle Volunteers, with Wyndham Phillips (see page 66) as its first commanding officer. A memorial at the entrance to the Royal Academy recalls the 2,003 members of the regiment killed in First World War.

ASHFIELD, Lord (1874–1948), English, transport manager
43 South Street, W1. *Greater London Council*
Lord Ashfield lived here. After experience running transport in Detroit and New Jersey, he was hired in 1907 to manage the precursor of London Underground. During his forty years' service, London Transport changed from a scrappy set of competitors to the envy of the world.

BAGEHOT, Walter (1826–77), English, writer, banker, economist
12 Upper Belgrave Street, SW1.
Greater London Council
Bagehot lived here. He was editor of *The Economist* from 1860 until his death, and his books include *The English Constitution* (1867), which remains the best

introduction to Britain's political system, and *Lombard Street* (1873). He delivered a particularly apt verdict on Dickens (q.v.): 'He describes London like a special correspondent for posterity.'

BAIRD, John Logie (1888–1946), Scottish, television pioneer
22 Frith Street, W1. *London County Council*
Baird hired two attic rooms in this house in 1924 and demonstrated his television system to members of the Royal Institution here on 27 January 1926. His system was adopted by the BBC in 1929, and improvements led to the first regular public transmissions in 1936 (see Haringey). (See also Westminster 4 and Lewisham.)

BANKS, Sir Joseph (1743–1820), English, botanist
32 Soho Square, W1. *London County Council*
Sir Joseph lived in a house on this site from 1777. Most famously, he travelled round the world with Captain Cook (1768–71), collecting plants. He introduced the eucalyptus, acacia and mimosa to Europe. President of the Royal Society from 1778 to 1819, he was a founder of Kew Gardens and of the Africa Association. He shares this plaque with Robert Brown and David Don (see pages 57 and 59).

BASEVI, George (1794–1845), English, architect
17 Savile Row, W1. *London County Council*
Basevi, who lived here from 1829 until his death, was the designer of the Fitzwilliam Museum in Cambridge and of many country mansions and Gothic churches. He also designed the layout of part of Belgravia. He was killed when he fell from a height while surveying Ely Cathedral.

BEE GEES
67 Brook Street, W1. *City of Westminster / Heritage Foundation*
This house was the residence of the group's manager, Robert Stigwood. Their *Saturday Night Fever* is the world's biggest-selling soundtrack album. In the period when they were working here, they had eight consecutive number one hits in the United States.

BEVIN, Ernest (1881–1951), English, politician
Stratford Mansions, 34 South Molton Street, W1. *English Heritage*
Bevin lived here in Flat 8 from 1931 to 1939. His career as a trade unionist began in 1910, and he swiftly became leader of the Dockers' Union. In 1921 he united fifty unions into the Transport & General Workers Union, the largest union in the world. In the Second World War he was Minister of Labour in the coalition government. Finally, he was Foreign Secretary from 1945 to 1950.

BLAKE, William (1757–1827), English, poet, painter
8 Marshall Street, Soho, W1. *Private*
17 South Molton Street, Mayfair, W1. *Corporation of the City of London*
Blake was born in a house on the site of the first address and lodged at the second from 1803 to 1820. During his time in South Molton Street he wrote and illustrated his most ambitious work, *Jerusalem*, as well as producing illustrations for Milton's (q.v.) *Paradise Lost* and *The Book of Job*. The latter was compared by Ruskin (q.v.) to Rembrandt and inspired Vaughan Williams's (q.v.) ballet *Job*. (See also Lewisham, Camden 1 and Lambeth.)

BONN, Leo (1850–1929), Austrian, banker
22 Upper Brook Street, W1. *City of Westminster*
Bonn, a merchant banker and himself deaf, founded the National Bureau for Promoting the General Welfare of the Deaf in his house here on 9 June 1911. In 1924 the Bureau became the Royal National Institute for Deaf People (RNID).

BRIDGEMAN, Charles (1690–1738), English, gardener
54 Broadwick Street, Soho, W1. *Greater London Council*
Bridgeman lived here from 1723 until his death. Gardener to Queen Anne, George II and Queen

Caroline, he was a key figure in the transition from the formal Anglo-Dutch style to the more 'natural' landscapes of the *jardin anglais* in the eighteenth century. His reputation has sadly been eclipsed by his successors, Kent and Brown.

BRIGHT, Richard

(1789–1858), English, physician
11 Savile Row, W1.
Greater London Council
Known as 'the Father of Nephrology', Dr Bright lived here from 1830 until his death. His researches at Guy's Hospital in the 1820s and 1830s into the causes and symptoms of kidney disorders led to his discovering what is today called Bright's disease.

BROAD STREET PUMP
The John Snow, 39 Broadwick Street, Soho, W1.
Private
The plaque records that the red granite kerbstone nearby is the site of the Broad Street pump, from which local citizens drew their water supplies. In researching the 1854 cholera outbreak, Dr John Snow (see page 68), after whom the nearby pub is named, had to overcome the weight of conventional wisdom that cholera was caused by 'miasma' in the air. When he showed that all the victims had got their water from this pump, he was at last listened to.

BROUGHAM, Lord
(1778–1868), Scottish, politician, lawyer
5 Grafton Street, Mayfair, W1. *City Lands Committee*
Lord Brougham lived here from 1838 until his death. He was a founder of the *Edinburgh Review*, a campaigner against slavery, head of the legal team that defended Queen Caroline against George IV, founder of London University, Lord Chancellor from 1830 to 1834, and discoverer for the English of Cannes. The brougham carriage was named after him.

BROWN, Robert (1773–1858), Scottish, botanist
32 Soho Square, W1. *London County Council*

Brown lived in a house on this site. He went to Australia with Matthew Flinders (q.v.) and is regarded as the leading botanist to collect in Australia in the first half of the nineteenth century. Sir Joseph Banks (see page 56), with whom this plaque is shared, left his library and collection to Brown.

BRUMMELL, Beau

(1778–1840), English, leader of fashion
4 Chesterfield Street, Mayfair, W1. *Greater London Council*
Brummell lived here.
He was fastidious not only in his clothing but in such novel ideas as bathing, shaving and cleaning his teeth. At one time he was an intimate of the Prince Regent, but they quarrelled in 1813, and Brummell lost any chance of reconciliation by remarking of the Prince, in his hearing: 'Who's your fat friend?' Debt forced him to flee to France, where he died penniless in an asylum. The house also has a plaque to Anthony Eden (see page 59).

BUCHANAN, Jack (1890–1957), Scottish, actor-manager
44 Mount Street, Mayfair, W1. *Private*
Epitomising a certain 'white tie' British suavity, Buchanan, who lived here, was one of the most popular entertainers of the 1930s and 1940s, appearing in many light comedy roles, in pantomime and in a number of films, on both sides of the Atlantic. A famously generous man, he was one of John Logie Baird's (see page 56) backers.

BURGOYNE, General John (1722–92), English, soldier, politician, playwright
10 Hertford Street, Mayfair, W1.
London County Council
Burgoyne, who lived and died here, is remembered (and blamed) for the surrender of British forces at Saratoga in 1777, precipitating the loss of the American colonies. He was also a popular dramatist at the time, his plays being produced by Garrick, as well as being a politician, sitting at different times as a Tory and as a Whig.

BURKE, Edmund (1729–97), Irish, politician
37 Gerrard Street, Soho, W1. *Royal Society of Arts*
The finest Parliamentary orator of his day, Burke,

who lived here, sat for the Whigs from 1765 to 1794, denouncing the French Revolution but defending the American colonists. He is regarded as one of the greatest of Conservative theorists.

BURNEY, Fanny (1752–1840), English, novelist, diarist
11 Bolton Street, Mayfair, W1.
Royal Society of Arts
Burney, known also by her married name of Madame D'Arblay, lived here from 1818 until her death. She was from childhood familiar with London literary circles and her first novel, *Evelina* (1778), was an immediate success. Later works included *Cecelia* (1782) and *Camilla* (1796), all three treating acutely of young women arriving in eighteenth-century society. Her posthumously published *Diaries*, with finely drawn characterisations of her friends, such as Dr Johnson (q.v.), are regarded as a valuable source for understanding London life in her time.

CAMPBELL, Colen (1676–1729), Scottish, architect
76 Brook Street, Mayfair, W1.
Greater London Council
Credited as a founder of the Georgian style, Campbell lived and died here. His most famous commission was Burlington House (1718–19). His *Vitruvius Britannicus* (three volumes, 1715–25) was a hugely influential catalogue of British architecture to date.

CANALETTO (1697–1768), Italian, painter
41 Beak Street, Soho, W1. *London County Council*
Antonio Canal, known as Canaletto, lived here from 1746 to 1755. From the 1720s his paintings became popular among Englishmen making the grand tour, and he moved to London to be nearer his market. Noted for his topographical accuracy, his work is a valuable record of mid-eighteenth century London.

CANNING, George (1770–1827), English, Prime Minister
50 Berkeley Square, Mayfair, W1.
Greater London Council
Canning lived here. He is probably best known for fighting a duel with another member of the cabinet, Castlereagh (q.v.), in 1809. Considered to be a precursor of the 'one nation' Toryism of the later nineteenth century, Canning was the shortest-serving British Prime Minister to date, dying in office after a mere 119 days.

CAYLEY, Sir George (1773–1857), English, engineer, inventor
20 Hertford Street, Mayfair, W1.
London County Council
Sir George lived here from 1840 to 1848. He constructed and piloted the first glider in 1853, invented the caterpillar tractor and worked in railway engineering. With Quintin Hogg (q.v.), he was a founder of the Regent Street Polytechnic.

CHARLES X of France (1757–1836), French, royalty
72 South Audley Street, W1. *English Heritage*
Charles, the last Bourbon king of France, lived here from 1805 to 1814. In exile during the French Revolution and Napoleon's reign, he returned to France after Waterloo. When he came to the throne in 1824, his régime proved so reactionary that he was forced to abdicate in 1830.

CLARENCE, Duke of (1765–1837), English, royalty
22 Charles Street, Mayfair, W1. *Private*
The duke lived here in 1826. Having served in the Royal Navy for twelve years (1778–90), he was known as 'the Sailor King' when he succeeded to the throne as William IV in 1830 at the age of sixty-four. He was the last monarch to appoint a Prime Minister contrary to the wishes of Parliament. (See also Lewisham.)

CLARKSON, Willy (1861–1934), English, theatrical wigmaker
41–43 Wardour Street, Soho, W1.
London County Council
Clarkson lived, worked and died here. He has been

described as 'the man who probably knew more about costumes and disguises than any other individual in the early twentieth century'. When the murderer Dr Crippen and his mistress fled the country in 1910, they were wearing Clarkson wigs.

CLIVE, Robert (1725–74), English, soldier, colonial administrator
45 Berkeley Square, Mayfair, W1.
London County Council
Clive lived here from 1761 till his death. His defeat of the French in India in 1751 and of the nawab of Bengal in 1757 established British supremacy in the sub-continent. After a final visit to India in 1765–6, he returned home in shattered health, had to endure a Parliamentary inquiry, became a victim of opium and committed suicide.

COOK, Peter (1937–95), English, satirist
18 Greek Street, W1. *City of Westminster*
This was the site of the legendary Establishment Club, a venue for satirical humour founded by Cook which ran from 1961 to 1964. Cook was a member of the cast of *Beyond the Fringe* (1960–4), the ground-breaking satirical revue, and went on to star with Dudley Moore in three series of *Not Only ... But Also* (1965–70) on BBC television, which introduced the nation to Dud and Pete and their 'Dagenham Dialogues', as well as treasurable Cook creations such as E. L. Wisty and Mr Justice Cocklecarrot. He was also the principal financial support of the magazine *Private Eye* through many years of rough times in the libel courts.

DISRAELI, Benjamin (1804–81), English, Prime Minister, novelist
93 Park Lane, W1.
Private
19 Curzon Street, W1.
London County Council
Disraeli lived at the sumptuous Park Lane address from 1839 to 1873, and, after his wife's death, at the relatively modest Curzon Street house from 1873 until his death. He was Queen Victoria's favourite prime minister and famously declined a visit from her on his

deathbed, saying: 'She'll only want me to take a message to Albert.' (See also Waltham Forest, Camden 2 and City.)

DON, David (1800–41), English, botanist
32 Soho Square, W1. *London County Council*
Don was the third botanist to live in a house on this site (see Banks and Brown, pages 56–7). He was professor of botany at King's College, London, from 1836 to 1841, and he systematised the description of several newly discovered conifers. His main publication was *Prodromus Floræ Nepalensis* in 1825.

DONOVAN, Terence (1936–96), English, photographer
30 Bourdon Street, W1.
City of Westminster / Olympus Cameras
This was Donovan's studio from 1978 until his death. With David Bailey, he was one of the lions of 'swinging London' in the 1960s, photographing for *Vogue* or *Harper's Bazaar*, invariably in gritty 'documentary' settings, and being accorded equal celebrity status with the pop stars, film stars and models. He also directed numerous pop videos, of which Robert Palmer's *Addicted to Love* is routinely voted high in any all-time list.

DRUIDS, Ancient Order of
The King's Arms, 23 Poland Street, Soho, W1.
Ancient Order of Druids
Initially organised here by Henry Hurle, a builder and surveyor, as a secret society along similar lines to the Masons, but nowadays somewhat more open, the AOD initiates new members with rituals at Stonehenge and is dedicated 'to preserve and practise the main principles attributed to the early Druids, particularly those of justice, benevolence and friendship'.

EDEN, Sir Anthony (1897–1977), English, Prime Minister
4 Chesterfield Street, Mayfair, W1. *Private*
Eden lived here. He was three times Foreign Secretary between 1935 and 1955, marshalling an urbane British diplomacy, speaking fluent French, and popular for his belief in 'peace first'. He was made to wait too long

for the top job by an increasingly senile Churchill, and by the time he moved into 10 Downing Street in 1955 he was hopelessly addicted to Benzedrine, which was prescribed after a bungled operation in 1953. This is thought to have contributed to his bad judgement in the Suez Affair of 1956, after which he was forced to resign. The house also has a plaque to Beau Brummell (see page 57).

EISENHOWER, Dwight D.
(1890–1969), American, soldier, President
20 Grosvenor Square, Mayfair, W1. *US Department of Defense*
This building was Eisenhower's headquarters from 1942 to 1944. (See also Westminster 4 and Kingston.)

ELIZABETH II (b.1926), English, royalty
17 Bruton Street, Mayfair, W1. *Private*
The plaque was erected in the Queen's Silver Jubilee year, 1977, and records her birth here on 21 April 1926. This was her parents' home at the time; they moved to 145 Piccadilly shortly after Elizabeth Alexandra May was born. Elizabeth II is the fortieth British monarch since William the Conqueror.

FOX, Charles James (1749–1806), English, politician
46 Clarges Street, Mayfair, W1.
London County Council
Fox lived here from 1782. This was the house of Elizabeth Armistead, a famous courtesan, whom Fox took over and married in 1795. He had entered Parliament aged nineteen and rose to be Foreign Secretary twice. Arch-rival of Pitt the Younger (q.v.), he is remembered as an eloquent speaker, with a colourful and notorious private life. This house is now the Fox Club, with rooms named after various of Armistead's lovers.

GARRETT ANDERSON, Elizabeth (1836–1917), English, physician
20 Upper Berkeley Street, W1.
London County Council
Anderson, the first woman in Britain to qualify as a doctor, lived here from 1860 to 1874, when she was struggling to be allowed to study medicine. She later founded the first hospital for women in London, in the Euston Road, which was renamed the Elizabeth Garrett Anderson Hospital after her death. (See also Tower Hamlets.)

GROTE, George
(1794–1871), English, historian, politician
12 Savile Row, Mayfair, W1. *London County Council*
Grote lived here from 1848 until his death. As MP for the City of London from 1832 to 1841, he was a leading campaigner in the reform movement. He retired from politics to concentrate on history, producing his *magnum opus*, an eight-volume *History of Greece* (1846–56), which remains a standard work. His wife was a notable hostess of concerts here by Jenny Lind (q.v.), Chopin (q.v.) and others.

HALL, Keith Clifford (1910–64), English, optometrist
140 Park Lane, Mayfair, W1.
City of Westminster / British Contact Lens Association
Hall practised here from 1945 until his death. His was the first practice in the United Kingdom to specialise in contact lenses; his technique used scleral fitting shells modified with wax before machining, and he also worked with the original Tuohy corneal lens. He predicted the coming of soft lenses but died too soon to be involved.

HANDEL, George Frederick (1685–1759), German, composer
25 Brook Street, W1. *English Heritage*
Handel lived in this house from 1723 and died here. Settling in England in 1712, he enjoyed royal patronage, composing the *Water Music* for George I, and *Zadok the Priest* for George II's coronation in 1727; it has been played at every coronation since. His masterpiece, *Messiah*, was first performed in Dublin in 1742. He is buried in Poets' Corner in Westminster Abbey. (See also Harrow.)

HARTNELL, Sir Norman (1901–79), English, court dressmaker
26 Bruton Street, W1. *English Heritage*
Sir Norman lived and worked here from 1935 until his death. Appointed dressmaker to the Royal Family in

1938, he designed Queen Elizabeth II's wedding and coronation gowns, as well as whole wardrobes for Queen Elizabeth the Queen Mother and Queen Mary.

HAZLITT, William (1778–1830), English, essayist
6 Frith Street, W1. *London County Council*
Hazlitt lodged here in the last year of his life and died here in poverty. His reputation as one of the greatest English critics, worthy to be ranked with Johnson (q.v.) and Orwell (q.v.), has revived recently. His grave in St Anne's churchyard, Soho, has been refurbished and a Hazlitt Society formed to rescue his name and his works from unmerited neglect. (See also City.)

HEARNE, Thomas (1744–1817), English, painter
6 Meard Street, Soho, W1. *Private*
Hearne, who lived here, is best known for his fifty-two drawings for *The Antiquities of Great Britain* (1777–81) by the engraver William Byrne. He also drew extensively during a stay in the Leeward Islands (1771–5). His drawings were copied by Girtin and Turner (q.v.).

HENDRIX, Jimi
(1942–70), American, guitarist
23 Brook Street, Mayfair, W1.
English Heritage
Hendrix lived here in 1968–9. Discovered in New York by Chas Chandler of the Animals, he was brought to London in 1966 and quickly became an icon as the most casually and spectacularly accomplished guitar player of his or any other time. Unfortunately, in the way of those days, his various excesses rapidly caught up with him.

HMV
363 Oxford Street, W1. *Private*
This was the site of the original HMV shop, opened by Sir Edward Elgar in July 1921. The plaque was unveiled by Sir George Martin on 26 April 2000. According to HMV's publicity, 'The launch signalled a transforming moment in popular culture, not least because the new store was the first to catch the burgeoning demand for recorded music. The store, which featured state-of-the-art interior design and merchandising, was lavish entertainment itself, embellished by the most striking illuminated electric motion sign yet seen in London.'

HUNTER, Dr John
(1728–93), Scottish, surgeon
31 Golden Square, Soho, W1. *London County Council*
Hunter lived here from 1765 to 1768. He founded his anatomy school in London in 1764, was surgeon to George III (1776), and surgeon general of the Army (1789). His collection of fourteen thousand preparations of over five hundred species of plants and animals was purchased by the government after his death. The Hunterian Society of London was founded in 1819 to honour the memory of 'the Father of Scientific Surgery'. His older brother was William Hunter (see page 62).

HUNTER, Dr William (1718–83), Scottish, anatomist
Rear of Lyric Theatre, Great Windmill Street, W1. *London County Council*
This was the site of Dr Hunter's home, anatomy theatre and museum, built by him in 1768. He was physician to Queen Charlotte (from 1764), the first professor of anatomy to the Royal Academy (1768–72), and published *Anatomia Uteri Umani Gravidi* in 1774. He bequeathed his collection of books, manuscripts, coins, medals, paintings, mineral and medical specimens to Glasgow University. His younger brother was John Hunter (see page 61).

IRVING, Washington (1783–1859), American, short-story writer, essayist, historian
8 Argyll Street, Soho, W1.
Greater London Council
Irving lived here. He was the first American 'man of letters', and the first American to be recognised by European literary circles. His collection *The Sketch Book* (1819–20) contains such stories as *Rip Van Winkle* and *The Legend of Sleepy Hollow*. He travelled extensively in Europe and was for a short time secretary to the United States legation in London.

ISAACS, Rufus (1860–1935), English, lawyer, politician
32 Curzon Street, Mayfair, W1.
Greater London Council
Isaacs lived and died here. He entered Parliament in 1904, was Solicitor-General (1910), Attorney General (1910–13), Lord Chief Justice (1913–21), British ambassador to the United States (1918–19), Viceroy of India (1921–6), and finally Foreign Secretary (1931). Retiring from politics, he went into business, serving as president of ICI and chairman of United Newspapers.

IVES, Charles Edward (1874–1954), American, composer
17 Half Moon Street, Mayfair, W1. *Private*
Ives stayed here in 1934. He was largely ignored as a composer in his lifetime, but his reputation has

continued to grow. He did not compose anything new after 1926, reportedly saying with tears in his eyes: 'Nothing sounds right.' He was belatedly awarded the Pulitzer Prize in 1947.

KORDA, Sir Alexander (1893–1956), Hungarian, film maker
21–22 Grosvenor Street, W1. *English Heritage*
These were Korda's offices from 1932 to 1936. He set up Denham film studios in 1932 and among his successes during this time were *The Scarlet Pimpernel*, *Catherine the Great* and *The Private Life of Henry VIII* (1934), *Sanders of the River* and *The Ghost Goes West* (1935) and *Things To Come* and *Elephant Boy* (1936).

LANE, Sir Allen (1902–70), English, publisher
8 Vigo Street, W1.
Penguin Books
It was from here, then the offices of Bodley Head, that Allen Lane launched the first Penguin paperbacks. They were sold for sixpence each. 'We believe in the existence in this country of a vast reading public for intelligent books at a low price,' said Lane, in the face of initial scepticism.

LINNAEAN SOCIETY
32 Soho Square, W1. *London County Council*
The Linnaean Society held its meetings in a house on this site, inhabited by three great botanists in succession (see Banks, Brown and Don on pages 56–7 and 59), from 1821 to 1857. The world's oldest botanical society, founded by Sir James Edward Smith in 1788, it takes its name from Carl Linnaeus (1707–78), the Swedish botanist whose collections have been in the society's care since 1829. The society is now based at Burlington House, Piccadilly.

LISZT, Ferenc (1811–86), Hungarian, composer, musician
18 Great Marlborough Street, Soho, W1.
Liszt Society
Liszt stayed in a house on this site in 1840 and 1841. A child prodigy on the piano, he was constantly

touring Europe, the first 'superstar', hailed by many as the greatest pianist who ever lived. Women threw themselves at him. Meanwhile he was also a prolific composer across all musical genres.

MACKENZIE, Sir Morell (1837–92), English, physician
32 Golden Square, W1.
City of Westminster / Royal Society of Medicine
Sir Morell founded the world's first hospital for diseases of the throat in a building on this site in 1865. His three books are the founding texts of laryngology: *The Use of the Laryngoscope in Diseases of the Throat* (1865), *Growths in the Larynx* (1871) and *Diseases of the Nose and Throat* (1880 and 1884). (See also Waltham Forest.)

MARX, Karl (1818–83), German, political theorist
28 Dean Street, Soho, W1. *Greater London Council*
Marx lived here from 1851 to 1856. 'The Father of Communism' came to London in 1849, a year after publishing *The Communist Manifesto*, co-written with

Engels (q.v.). He produced volume 1 of *Das Kapital* in 1867, volumes 2 and 3 being edited and published posthumously by his daughter Eleanor (q.v.) and Engels. (See also Camden 1.)

MATTHEWS, Jessie (1907–81), English, actress, dancer, singer
22 Berwick Street, Soho, W1.
Westminster City Council
Matthews was born in Berwick Street, one of eleven children of a market-stall holder. She became a huge star of musical comedy in the 1920s and 1930s, known in America as 'the Dancing Divinity'. Her private life was not without scandal, including an affair with the Duke of Kent. After a period of eclipse, she took the lead in the long-running BBC radio serial *Mrs Dale's Diary* (1963–9).

MAUGHAM, W. Somerset (1874–1965), English, novelist, playwright
6 Chesterfield Street, Mayfair, W1. *Greater London Council*
Maugham lived here from 1911 to 1919. He was a prolific novelist and playwright, who in 1908 had four plays running simultaneously in London. His best-known novels are *Of Human Bondage* (1915), *Cakes and Ale* (1930) and *The Razor's Edge* (1945). He sadly described himself as being 'in the very first row of the second-raters'.

MAY FAIR
17 Trebeck Street, Mayfair, W1. *Private*
This was the site of the May Fair, which ran annually for two weeks at the beginning of May. It moved here from Haymarket in 1686 and was suppressed in 1764 after complaints from rich and respectable citizens who were moving into the area.

MAYFAIR'S OLDEST HOUSE
Hilton Mews Hotel, Stanhope Row, Mayfair, W1. *Westminster City Council / Shepherd Street (Mayfair) Residents' Association*
Until it was destroyed in the Blitz in 1940, here stood 'The Cottage 1618 AD', from which a shepherd tended his flock. It is a reminder, in this crowded smart modern quarter of the West End, of how recently this was still a rural area.

MERYON, Edward (1807–80), English, physician
17 Clarges Street, W1. *City of Westminster*
Meryon lived in a house on this site from 1846 until his death. Of Huguenot stock, he was the first physician to make a systematic study of muscular dystrophy. The Meryon Society was formed in his memory to study neuromuscular disorders.

MITFORD, Nancy (1904–73), English, novelist, essayist
Heywood Hill Bookshop, 10 Curzon Street, Mayfair, W1.
English Heritage
Mitford worked here in the

bookshop from 1942 to 1945. The oldest of the six Mitford sisters, she was a moderate socialist, and her novels include *The Pursuit of Love* (1945), *Love in a Cold Climate* (1949) and *The Blessing* (1951). A prolific letter-writer, essayist and biographer, she is wrongly credited with coining the terms 'U' and 'non-U'.

MONTEFIORE, Sir Moses (1784–1885), Italian, financier, philanthropist
99 Park Lane, Mayfair, W1. *Greater London Council*

Sir Moses lived here for sixty years. He retired from the City at the age of forty and devoted his remaining years to philanthropy, especially the support of Jewish communities around the world. His hundredth birthday was celebrated as a British national event and by Jews worldwide.

MOON, Keith (1946–78), English, rock star
90 Wardour Street, Soho, W1.
City of Westminster / Musical Heritage
'Moon the Loon' is honoured here at the site of the Marquee Club (1964–88), where his extravagant antics both on and off the stage made an indelible contribution to the club's ambience. Moon was the first rock star to perceive the natural affinity between a Cadillac and a swimming pool, and his record of exploding toilets with incendiary devices is unlikely to be surpassed. His companion in much of the mayhem was Vivian Stanshall (q.v.) and inevitably they both came to a premature end. Underneath all the lunacy, he was one of the very greatest of rock drummers.

MORRIS, William (1834–96), English, poet, designer, socialist
17 St George Street, W1. *Private*
The plaque states that William Morris started his company in 1861 to manufacture a range of designs from wallpaper to stained glass, etc., and might be understood to mean that the business began here and that Morris himself worked here. In fact, these premises were the last showrooms of Morris & Company, from 1917 until its closure in 1940, by which time Morris was long dead. (See also Hammersmith & Fulham, Camden 2, Hackney, Bexley, Waltham Forest and Redbridge.)

MOZART, Wolfgang Amadeus (1756–91), Austrian, composer
20 Frith Street, Soho, W1. *Royal Musical Association*
Mozart lived in a house on this site, playing and composing, in 1764–5. A child prodigy, he was on a grand tour of Europe when he passed through Soho. Returning to Vienna, he was never in good health and died impoverished aged thirty-five, leaving some of the most magical music, across all genres of the classical canon. (See also Westminster 4.)

NEAGLE, Dame Anna (1904–86), English, actress
63–4 Park Lane, Mayfair, W1. *City of Westminster*
Dame Anna lived here from 1950 to 1964. Anna Neagle was the stage-name of Marjorie Robertson, who made her film debut in 1930, and, under the direction of Herbert Wilcox (see page 70), whom she married in 1943, starred in a number of successful films as various British heroines, including Odette Hallowes, Florence Nightingale and Queen Victoria.

NELSON, Horatio, Lord (1758–1805), English, naval officer
147 New Bond Street, W1.
Royal Society of Arts
103 New Bond Street, W1.
London County Council
Nelson lived at the first address in 1797 and at the second in 1798. He is renowned for a succession of daring victories against the French, during which he lost his right eye and right arm, culminating in his most famous triumph, against the combined French and Spanish fleets at Trafalgar on

21 October 1805, where the French and Spanish lost twenty-two out of thirty-three ships, while the British lost not one. Nelson was mortally wounded but lived long enough to be assured of victory. (See also Merton.)

NEVILL, Lady Dorothy (1826–1913), English, horticulturalist, hostess
45 Charles Street, W1. *City of Westminster*
Lady Dorothy lived here from 1873 until her death. Her fame rests on her salon, which played host to everybody from Edward VII to Gladstone, Disraeli, Tennyson and Whistler, and through which she wielded great influence. The *New York Times*, in its obituary, said: 'No French heroine of the revolution had a more important salon.' Additionally, at her estate in Sussex she had a landmark collection of flora, some of which she lent Darwin (q.v.) for his researches.

NIGHTINGALE, Florence (1820–1910), English, nurse
10 South Street, Mayfair, W1.
London County Council
Returning from the Crimean War as a national heroine, Nightingale lived here from 1865 until her death. Although as a woman she was not allowed to sit on the Royal Commission on the Health of the Army, she wrote the Commission's thousand-page report. She also established proper training for nurses and wrote *Notes on Nursing* (1860), which is still regarded as a useful general introduction. Bedridden from 1896 onwards, she is thought to have had chronic fatigue syndrome, a condition not recognised in her day. She was in 1907 the first woman to be awarded the Order of Merit. (See also Westminster 2.)

OLDFIELD, Ann (1683–1730), English, actress
60 Grosvenor Street, Mayfair, W1. *English Heritage*
Oldfield was the first occupant of this house, living here from 1725 until her death. She was acclaimed the best actress of her day, for either comedy or tragedy.

Pope (q.v.) wrote: 'Engaging Oldfield who, with grace and ease, Could join the arts to ruin and to please.' Lady Dorothy Nevill (see above) was proud to trace some of her blood back to Oldfield.

ONSLOW, Arthur (1691–1768), English, politician
20 Soho Square, Soho, W1. *London County Council*
Onslow lived in a house on this site. Noted for his integrity in an age of bribery and corruption, he was the longest-serving Speaker of the House of Commons (1728–61) in Parliamentary history, retiring only because of ill health, and he was the first Speaker to be granted a pension in recognition of his honourable service.

PAGE, Sir Frederick Handley (1885–1962), English, aircraft designer
18 Grosvenor Square, W1. *English Heritage*
Sir Frederick's company, Handley Page, founded in 1909, was the first publicly traded aircraft company, producing bombers in both world wars. The Halifax was his most famous Second World War plane, and after the war the Victor continued in service long after the company went into liquidation.

PAGE, Walter Hines (1855–1918), American, journalist, diplomat
6 Grosvenor Square, Mayfair, W1.
English Speaking Union
Page lived here while he was ambassador to the Court of St James (1913–18). After a successful career as editor and publisher, Page was appointed to London by President Wilson. He was a key figure in getting the United States to join in the First World War on Britain's side, attracting criticism for representing Britain to America instead of the other way round, which should have been his job.

PALMERSTON, Lord (1784–1865), English, Prime Minister
94 Piccadilly, W1. *London County Council*
This was Palmerston's town house from 1855 until his death, where his wife gave famous parties almost every night. He started as a Tory but switched to the Whigs in 1828. Foreign Secretary for much of the time between 1830 and 1851, he was known as 'Lord Pumice Stone' for his abrasive style and for the invention of gunboat diplomacy. He was Prime Minister twice, in 1855–8 and 1859–65. (See also Westminster 4.)

PAOLI, General Pasquale (1725–1807), Corsican, soldier, statesman
77 South Audley Street, W1.
City of Westminster
General Paoli, known as 'the Father of the Corsican Nation', stayed in a house on this site. He created the first modern democracy in Europe, when he led Corsica to independence from the kingdom of Genoa in 1755. Subsequently the Genoese did a secret deal with the French and Paoli's Corsica became a department of France. He was much admired in America, where four towns are named in his honour.

PECZENIK, Charles Edmund (1877–1967), French, architect
48 Grosvenor Square, Mayfair, W1. *Private*
Peczenik lived here. A native of Paris, he was an engineer turned architect and property developer, responsible for several inter-war buildings in Grosvenor Square, including the Canadian High Commission (1936–8). He also designed the Kensington Close Hotel (1937). His work was dismissed as 'sterile' by Pevsner.

PEEL, Sir Robert, the Elder (1750–1830), English, industrialist, politician
16 Upper Grosvenor Street, Mayfair, W1.
English Heritage
Sir Robert, who lived here, was a wealthy, paternalistic mill-owner from Bury. As a Tory MP from 1790 to 1820, he was responsible for the Health and Morals of Apprentices Act, which sought to limit working hours for children and obliged employers to make some provision for their education.

PEEL, Sir Robert, the Younger (1788–1850), English, Prime Minister
16 Upper Grosvenor Street, Mayfair, W1.
English Heritage
Sir Robert, whose family home was here, was Prime Minister twice (1834–5 and 1841–6) but is best remembered for founding the Metropolitan Police Force in 1829 when Home Secretary. The nicknames

for policemen, 'bobbies' and 'peelers' (both now obsolete), came from his name.

PENGUIN BOOKS
8 Vigo Street, W1. *Penguin Books*
Penguin Books, founded here in 1935, was the brainchild of Sir Allen Lane (see above). Lane wanted a 'dignified but flippant' symbol for his new books, and his secretary suggested a penguin. These were not the world's first paperbacks, but they were the world's first quality paperbacks, in terms both of contents and production.

PHILLIPS, Henry Wyndham (1820–68), English, painter
8 St George Street, W1. *Private*
The plaque records the founding of the Artists Rifles (see page 55) at Phillips's studio here in 1860. Son of the portrait painter Thomas Phillips, Phillips exhibited prolifically at the Royal Academy from 1839 onwards and was developing a reputation as a portraitist in his own right when he died suddenly, aged only forty-eight.

POLIDORI, John William (1795–1821), Anglo-Italian, physician, novelist
38 Great Pulteney Street, Soho, W1.
Westminster City Council
Polidori was born and died here. Engaged as Lord Byron's personal physician, he was with Byron and the Shelleys on a night in June 1816 in Switzerland when Byron suggested they each write a ghost story. Byron quickly abandoned his effort, but Mary Shelley (q.v.) wrote *Frankenstein* and Polidori wrote *The Vampyre*, establishing a genre.

POMBAL, Sebastião José, Marquês de (1699–1782), Portuguese, politician
23–24 Golden Square, Soho, W1.
Greater London Council
Pombal was Portuguese ambassador to the Court of St James, being based in these two houses from 1739 to 1744. After his service in London, he went on to run Portugal under King Joseph (1750–77). He reorganised education, finance, the army and the navy, built new industries, developed Brazil and Macao, and rebuilt Lisbon after the 1755 earthquake.

PURDEY, James, the Younger (1828–1909),
English, gunmaker
57–58 South Audley Street, W1.
City of Westminster / James Purdey & Sons Ltd
Established by James Purdey the Elder in 1814, the
firm of Purdey is synonymous with the finest bespoke
sporting guns. James Purdey the Younger built these
premises in 1880 to be his showrooms and workshop.
The firm has held warrants from various members of
the Royal Family since 1868, as well as making guns
for Ernest Hemingway.

RAGLAN, Lord (1788–1855), English, soldier
5 Stanhope Gate, Mayfair, W1.
London County Council
Raglan, who lived here, was commander of the British
Army in the Crimean War. However gallant his earlier
military career had been, including the loss of an arm
at Waterloo, his promotion to general was clearly a
step too far. In the Crimea, he presided over a sea of
incompetence, displayed a total lack of tactical nous,
issued vague orders, failed to notice the personality
clash between lords Lucan and Cardigan, and is
therefore ultimately responsible for the disastrous
Charge of the Light Brigade.

ROGERS, Dr Joseph (1820–89), English, health-
care reformer
33 Dean Street, Soho, W1. *English Heritage*
Dr Rogers, who lived and practised here, was medical
officer to the Strand Workhouse from 1856 to 1868,
and consulting surgeon at Westminster Infirmary for
twenty-three years. He was founder and first president
of the Poor Law Medical Officers' Association. His
obituary in *The Lancet* said of him: 'If Howard was the
Hercules of prison reform, Rogers was the Hercules of
workhouse reform.'

ROSEBERY, Earl of (1847–1929), English, Prime
Minister
20 Charles Street, Mayfair, W1.
London County Council
Rosebery, who was born here, is supposed to have had
three aims in life: to win the Derby (he did it three
times, in 1894, 1895 and 1905), to marry an heiress
(in 1878 he married Hannah Rothschild), and to
become Prime Minister (he headed the brief Liberal
government of 1894–5).

ROY, Major-General William (1726–90), Scottish,
soldier, cartographer
10 Argyll Street, Soho, W1. *Greater London Council*
Roy, who lived here, mapped the Highlands in 1747
for the Army, and in 1756 he mapped the southern
counties. In 1765 he was made Surveyor General of
the Coasts and in 1783 began the major triangulation
of Britain with a baseline on Hounslow Heath. He
founded the Ordnance Survey but did not live to see it
formally come into existence.

SEACOLE, Mary (1805–81),
Jamaican, nurse
14 Soho Square, W1.
English Heritage
Mrs Seacole, 'Heroine of the
Crimea' as the plaque says,
lived here in 1857, the year
she published *The Wonderful
Adventures of Mrs Seacole in Many Lands*. Also in 1857 she
was the beneficiary of the Seacole Fund Grand Military
Festival, organised in her honour and to help her out
of financial difficulties. (See also Westminster 2.)

SEFERIS, George (1900–71), Greek, poet, diplomat
51 Upper Brook Street, W1. *English Heritage*
Seferis, the pen-name of Georgios Seferiades, lived
here from 1957 to 1962, while serving as Greek
ambassador to the Court of St James. He was awarded
the Nobel Prize for Literature in 1963, the citation
speaking of 'his eminent lyrical writing, inspired by a
deep feeling for the Hellenic world of culture'. His
Complete Poems were published in translation in 1995.
(See also Kensington & Chelsea 2.)

SELFRIDGE, Harry Gordon (1858–1947),
American, magnate
The Lansdowne Club, 9 Fitzmaurice Place, W1.
English Heritage
Selfridge lived here from 1921 to 1929. He coined the
slogan 'Only … shopping days till Christmas' while
working at Marshal Fields department store in
Chicago. When he came to England in 1906 he was
unimpressed by English stores, so he opened Selfridges
in Oxford Street in 1909.

SHELBURNE, second Earl of (1737–1805), Irish,
Prime Minister
The Lansdowne Club, 9 Fitzmaurice Place, W1.
English Heritage

Shelburne lived in a house on this site. It was during his short time as Prime Minister, from July 1782 to April 1783, that American Independence was conceded. This was a cause he had supported, but it led to his forced resignation under pressure from the Fox/North coalition.

SHELLEY, Percy Bysshe (1792–1822), English, poet

15 Poland Street, Soho, W1. *English Heritage* Shelley lived here in 1811. His was a stormy life; he left his first wife (who later committed suicide) for Mary Godwin (q.v.), whom he married. He amassed large debts and was drowned while sailing off the Italian coast. He is a major figure among the English Romantics. (See also Southwark.)

SHERATON, Thomas (1751–1806), English, furniture designer

163 Wardour Street, Soho, W1.

London County Council Sheraton, who lived here, was one of the three great eighteenth-century furniture designers, the others being Chippendale (q.v.) and Hepplewhite. He was especially influential because of his published works, subscribed to by at least six hundred cabinet makers, including *The Cabinet Directory* (1805). There are no known extant pieces actually by him.

SHERIDAN, Richard Brinsley (1751–1816), Irish, playwright, politician

10 Hertford Street, Mayfair, W1. *London County Council*

14 Savile Row, Mayfair, W1. *Royal Society of Arts* Sheridan, who lived at the first address from 1795 to 1802 and subsequently at the second, where he died, was an MP from 1780 to 1812, a noted orator and a strong supporter of Fox (q.v.). But he is best remembered as a playwright; his works, still regularly revived, include *The Rivals* (1775), *The School for Scandal* (1777) and *The Critic* (1779). He took over the Drury Lane Theatre from Garrick (q.v.) and became its manager. When the theatre burned down in 1809, he suffered financial hardship and died in poverty.

SMALL FACES

52–55 Carnaby Street, W1. *City of Westminster* Here at the offices of Don Arden (see page 55), the Small Faces were launched and worked from 1965 to 1967. Perceived as the East End's answer to the West End's The Who, the band contributed a cheerful cockney humour to the psychedelic era, managing to avoid the pretensions of many of their contemporaries, while making it quite plain that they too were busy exploring inner space: 'Here we all are sittin' in a rainbow, Gor blimey hello Mrs Jones, how's old Bert's lumbago?'

SMITH, John Christopher (1712–95), English, musician, composer

6 Carlisle Street, Soho, W1. *Private* Smith lived and died here. A composer in his own right, his works alas long unplayed, he is remembered as Handel's (q.v.) principal copyist, friend, confidant and amanuensis. For many years after Handel's death he continued the annual performance of *Messiah* in aid of the Foundling Hospital. The plaque wrongly states that he died in 1763.

SNOW, Dr John (1813–58), English, physician

53 Frith Street, Soho, W1. *Association of Anaesthetists of Great Britain and Ireland*

The John Snow, 39 Broadwick Street, Soho, W1. *Private* Dr Snow lived in a house on the first site and crucially removed the handle of the Broad Street pump (see page 57) at the second site. Until his researches into the 1854 cholera outbreak in Soho, it was conventionally believed that the disease was caused by 'miasma'. He was able to prove that all the victims had drunk water from this pump and thus that cholera was a water-borne disease. He was also a pioneer developer of anaesthesia, assisting Queen Victoria at the birth of Prince Leopold.

SOPWITH, Sir Tommy (1888–1989), English, aviator, aircraft designer

46 Green Street, Mayfair, W1. *English Heritage* Sir Tommy lived here from 1934 to 1940. He founded Sopwith Aviation in 1912 and in the First World War produced several aircraft for the Royal Flying Corps, including the legendary Sopwith Camel (flown famously by Snoopy in his duels with the Red Baron). He also challenged twice for the America's Cup.

STAËL, Madame de (1766–1817), French-Swiss, literary critic, salon hostess
Argyll Street, Soho, W1.
La Société d'Études Staëliennes
Madame de Staël lived in a house on this site in 1813–14. Daughter of Louis XVI's finance minister, Necker, and mistress of, among others, Benjamin Constant, she held a central place in French intellectual life. She was a forerunner of the French romantic movement, lionised in her time in Britain for her friction with Napoleon. Her two novels *Delphine* (1802) and *Corinne* (1807) present a ground-breaking image of woman: 'A man can brave opinion, a woman must submit to it.'

STANLEY, Lord (1841–1908), English, politician, colonial governor
130 Regent Street, W1. *City of Westminster*
Lord Stanley was governor general of Canada from 1888 to 1893 and developed a passion for ice hockey. He paid 10 guineas at a goldsmith's shop on this site in 1892 for the silver bowl that bears his name and is presented annually to the leading Canadian ice hockey team. Sadly Lord Stanley never saw the inauguration of the competition; his brother died and he returned to England to assume the title Earl of Derby.

STEPHEN, John (1934–2004), Scottish, fashion designer
1 Carnaby Street, W1.
City of Westminster
Stephen, the 'founder of Carnaby Street as a world centre for men's fashion', opened his first boutique in the street, 'His Clothes', at No. 5 in 1958. His empire expanded to fifteen outlets in the area, all servicing the new 'Mod' style, later joined by the likes of 'I Was Lord Kitchener's Valet', which catered for the alternative hippie look.

SUNLEY, Bernard (1910–64), English, property developer
24 Berkeley Square, W1. *City of Westminster*
Sunley, who lived here for many years, was one of the most dynamic and successful property developers of the 1950s, buildings shops, flats, hotels and offices in the City, the West End and the West Indies. He founded the Bernard Sunley Trust, which continues to support a number of charitable causes.

TALLEYRAND, Prince (1754–1838), French, politician, diplomat
21 Hanover Square, Mayfair, W1.
Greater London Council
Talleyrand, who lived here from 1830 to 1834, worked for, and survived, Louis XVI, the French Revolution, Napoleon, Louis XVIII, Charles X and Louis-Philippe. Known as 'the Prince of Diplomats', he could equally well be called 'the Prince of Survivors'. 'Regimes may fall and fail, but I do not,' he said.

2i's COFFEE BAR
59 Old Compton Street, W1. *City of Westminster / Robert Mandry*
This was the site of the 2i's Coffee Bar from 1956 to 1970. Owned by a genial wrestler and promoter called Paul Lincoln, it was in the late 1950s a live basement venue for practically all the earliest British rock 'n' rollers: Tommy Steele (q.v.), Cliff Richard, Adam Faith, Hank Marvin, Marty Wilde, Joe Brown, Jet Harris and Screaming Lord Sutch all bashed out three chords in joyous revolt against whatever their parents were listening to.

WALTERS, Catherine (1839–1920), English, courtesan
15 South Street, Mayfair, W1. *Private*
Catherine Walters, known as 'Skittles', lived here from 1872 until her death. Among her lovers was the heir to the dukedom of Devonshire, who set her up with a life annuity, which enabled her to be a fashion trend-setter. Other conquests included Napoleon III (q.v.), the future Edward VII and Wilfrid Scawen Blunt

(q.v.). Her discretion was highly prized by her various patrons and she was able to retire comfortably from *la vie horizontale* in 1890.

WESTMACOTT, Sir Richard (1775–1856), English, sculptor
14 South Audley Street, Mayfair, W1.
London County Council
Sir Richard, who lived and died here, was well known for his many public monuments, including Pitt the Younger (q.v.), Fox (q.v.) and Addison in Westminster Abbey, and the huge *Achilles* monument (1822) to Wellington in Hyde Park, cast from captured French guns. He was Professor of Sculpture at the Royal Academy from 1827 to 1854.

WILCOX, Herbert (1890–1977), English, film producer/director
63–64 Park Lane, Mayfair, W1. *City of Westminster*
Wilcox, who lived here from 1950 to 1964, began producing and directing films at the end of the silent era, but from 1932 onwards his career was entwined with that of Anna Neagle (see page 64), whom he married in 1943. He produced and directed almost all her films, most notably *Odette* (1950).

WINANT, John Gilbert (1889–1947), American, diplomat
7 Aldford Street, Mayfair, W1.
Greater London Council
Winant lived here while serving as American ambassador to the Court of St James from 1941 to 1946. Twice Republican Governor of New Hampshire, he was appointed by Roosevelt to the London embassy partly because of his friendship with Churchill (q.v.), who loaned him this house for his stay. They were together when the news of Pearl Harbour came through.

WODEHOUSE, P. G.
(1881–1975), English, novelist
17 Dunraven Street, W1. *English Heritage*
Wodehouse, who lived here from 1927 to 1934, was a comic novelist whose main recurring characters, especially Bertie Wooster and his valet, Jeeves, have entered a national literary pantheon.

He rather naively broadcast from Germany during the war, causing considerable resentment in Britain, but the popularity of his books has conquered that unhappy memory, and this plaque was unveiled by the Queen Mother. (See also Kensington & Chelsea 2.)

WYATVILLE, Sir Jeffry (1766–1840), English, architect, garden designer
39 Brook Street, Mayfair, W1.
Greater London Council
Sir Jeffry lived and died here. Slightly out of the blue, he was summoned to Windsor Castle by George IV, who wanted some alterations made. These works then occupied him from 1824 until his death. He was also a prolific garden designer at places such as Badminton, Longleat and Chatsworth.

YEARSLEY, Dr James (1805–69), English, physician
32 Sackville Street, Piccadilly, W1.
Westminster City Council/Mr Ronnie Yearsley
Dr Yearsley was the first physician to recognise the interconnection of ear, nose and throat, and the Metropolitan Ear Institute, which he founded here in 1838, was the world's first hospital devoted to hearing. He was also a co-founder in 1846 of the *Medical Directory*, the public's first protection against quacks.

Westminster 4:
Belgravia, St James's, Pimlico and Westminster
South of Knightsbridge–Piccadilly–Shaftesbury Avenue

ADAM, Robert (1728–92), Scottish, architect
1–3 Robert Street, WC2. *London County Council*
The New Adelphi, WC2. *London County Council*
Adam lived at No. 3 at the first address from 1778 to
1785 and designed and built the Adelphi Terrace
(1768–74) (see below)
on the second site.
Architect to George III
from 1762 to 1768, he
was responsible for many
important mansions in
different parts of the
country, including Luton
Hoo, Osterley House and Compton Verney. He also
improved street architecture in London. He shares
the first plaque with other distinguished former
residents.

THE ADELPHI
The New Adelphi, WC2. *London County Council*
Designed and built in 1768–74 by the Adam brothers,
the Adelphi Terrace was the first great Georgian
riverside development in London, in the Palladian
style that characterised all the Adams' work. Largely
destroyed in 1936, it was replaced by the New
Adelphi office block. Its loss continues to be
regretted to this day. The plaque lists several former
residents.

**ARKWRIGHT, Sir
Richard** (1732–92),
English, industrialist,
inventor
8 Adam Street, WC2.
Greater London Council
Sir Richard, who had his
London base here from
1788 until his death, is known
as 'the Father of the Industrial
Revolution'. His spinning frame of 1769 was an
advance on the 'spinning jenny' of Hargreaves, and he
founded the world's first water-powered cotton mill at

Cromford, Derbyshire, in 1771. He died one of the
richest men in England.

ARNE, Thomas (1710–78), English, composer
31 King Street, WC2. *English Heritage*
Arne, who lived here, is chiefly remembered for 'Rule,
Britannia!', though whether or not the whole English
character can be expressed in eight notes, as Wagner
said of the opening, remains debatable. Arne is
remembered also for charming settings of Shakespeare
songs, such as 'Where the Bee Sucks'.

ARNOLD, Matthew (1822–88), English, poet,
critic
2 Chester Square, SW1. *London County Council*
Arnold lived here. As an inspector of schools from
1851 to 1886, he was involved in trying to improve
English education. He was also Professor of Poetry at
Oxford from 1857 to 1867, but his prolific poetry is
today rather eclipsed by his prose writings, which
established him as the leading literary critic of the day.

ASHLEY, Laura
(1925–85), English, textile
designer
**83 Cambridge Street,
SW1.** *Westminster City
Council / George Hay & Co*
This is where, in 1954–6,
Laura Ashley began printing
fabrics with her husband,
Bernard. From these small
beginnings 'Laura Ashley' rose to being an
internationally famous chain of shops, marketing her
distinctive range of Victorian-style furnishings, fabrics,
clothing and wallpapers.

ASTOR, Nancy (1879–1964), Anglo-American,
politician
4 St James's Square, SW1. *English Heritage*
This was the London home of Nancy and her husband,
William Waldorf Astor. When he became Viscount

Astor, she succeeded him as Conservative MP for Plymouth in 1919 and was the first woman to take her seat in the House of Commons (Countess Markiewitz had been elected in 1918, but, as an Irish Nationalist, refused to take her seat). Many of her attitudes are repellent, notably her anti-semitism and support for the Nazis. On the other hand, she financed and fought a campaign in support of nursery schools in an unlikely alliance with the socialist Margaret McMillan (q.v.), and her wit was widely treasured; she said, for instance: 'I married beneath me, all women do.'

AUSTEN, Jane (1775–1817), English, novelist
10 Henrietta Street, WC2.
City of Westminster / Jane Austen Society
The plaque records that Austen stayed here when in London in 1813–14. These were the London offices of her brother Henry, a banker, who had rooms above, and also acted as her literary agent. In fact, she stayed here over a longer period, until 1816, and in this time produced three of her best-known works, *Pride and Prejudice* (1813), *Mansfield Park* (1814) and *Emma* (1815). (See also Kensington & Chelsea 2.)

BAIRD, John Logie (1888–1946), Scottish, inventor
132–135 Long Acre, WC2. *Royal Television Society*
The plaque records that from this site, on 30 September 1929, Baird broadcast the first television programme in Britain, which led to his system being adopted by the BBC. (See also Westminster 3 and Lewisham.)

BALCON, Sir Michael (1896–1977), English, film producer
57a Tufton Street, SW1. *City of Westminster*
Sir Michael lived here from 1927 to 1939. One of the giants of British cinema history, he was during his time here running Gainsborough Film Studios, until he was briefly seduced to Hollywood (1936–8), after which he returned to England and took over Ealing Studios. (See also Hackney and Ealing.)

BALDWIN, Stanley (1867–1947), English, Prime Minister
93 Eaton Square, SW1. *Greater London Council*

Baldwin, who lived here, entered Parliament in 1908 and was three times Prime Minister (1923–4, 1924–9, 1935–7). His times at No. 10 coincided with the General Strike (1926) and the Abdication Crisis (1936). Supposedly it was his fault, as much as that of Chamberlain and Macdonald, that Britain was unready for the Second World War, since his watchword was 'Wait and see'.

BARBON, Nicholas (*c*.1640–98), entrepreneur, speculator
Essex Hall, Essex Street, WC2.
London County Council
Nicholas Unless-Jesus-Christ-Had-Died-For-Thee-Thou-Hadst-Been-Damned Barbon (to give him his full name) was a man of parts. Essex Street was one of several property schemes in which he bought up tracts of land west of the City, from the 1670s to the 1690s, and built housing, pioneering the terrace to cut building costs. Condemned as 'dubious' and 'Machiavellian' by Pevsner (q.v.), he has nonetheless left London with some handsome streets. The plaque lists several distinguished former residents of the street.

BARRIE, Sir James (1860–1937), Scottish, playwright
1–3 Robert Street, WC2. *London County Council*
Sir James is listed among a number of distinguished former residents at this address. He lived at No. 2 from 1909 until his death. For his main entry see Westminster 2.

BEARDSLEY, Aubrey (1872–98), English, artist
114 Cambridge Street, SW1. *London County Council*
Beardsley lived here with his actress sister, Mabel, from 1893 to 1895. He had the rooms designed in orange and black by Aymer Vallance and he worked in a semi-darkened room at a table flanked by two large candles. He is famous for his black and white Art Nouveau drawings, often darkly erotic, epitomising *fin de siècle* decadence, especially his illustrations for Wilde's *Salome* (1894), Pope's *Rape of the Lock* (1896) and in the *Yellow Book* magazine (1894–5).

BEAUCLERK, Lady Diana (1734–1808), English, illustrator
The New Adelphi, WC2. *London County Council*
Lady Diana is one of the many distinguished former residents of the Adelphi Terrace (see page 71) listed on

the plaque. She and her husband (see below) lived at No. 3 from 1772 to 1776, and she nursed him through a near-fatal illness here. For her main entry see Camden 2.

BEAUCLERK, Topham (1739–80), English, dandy, courtier
The New Adelphi, WC2. *London County Council*
Topham Beauclerk was one of the many distinguished former residents of the Adelphi Terrace (see page 71) on this site. He lived at No. 3 from 1772 to 1776, holding his own in badinage with his friend Dr Johnson (q.v.). For his main entry see Camden 2.

BELGIAN VOLUNTEERS
103 Eaton Square, Belgravia, SW1. *Belgian Embassy*
This building was formerly the Belgian Embassy, to which volunteers flocked during the Second World War. The plaque was unveiled by the Queen Mother in June 1964.

BENTHAM, George (1800–84), English, botanist
25 Wilton Place, Belgravia, SW1. *Greater London Council*
Bentham lived here from 1864 until his death. He was secretary of the Horticultural Society of London from 1828 to 1840 and compiled many important botanical works, of which the greatest was *Genera Plantarum* (1862–83), and the most popular was *Handbook of the British Flora* (1858).

BENTHAM, Jeremy (1748–1832), English, philosopher
50 Queen Anne's Gate, SW1. *City of Westminster*
Bentham, 'the Hermit of Queen Square Place', lived in a house on this site from 1792 until his death. A philosophical radical, he was in advance of contemporary thought in every direction but is best remembered for his concept of Utility, summed up in the phrase: 'the greatest happiness of the greatest number is the foundation of morals and legislation.' A reluctant publisher, his *Complete Works* are still being assembled by the Bentham Project.

BLUNT, Wilfrid Scawen (1840–1922), English, poet, diplomat, traveller
15 Buckingham Gate, SW1. *Greater London Council*
This was Blunt's London home. A notorious womaniser, he married Byron's granddaughter after an affair with Catherine Walters (q.v.). Extensive travels in India and the Middle East led him to an anti-imperialist stance, campaigning for Egyptian, Indian and Irish independence, which gained him the approval of G. B. Shaw (q.v.) and a brief spell in prison in 1888.

BOLÍVAR, Simón (1783–1830), Venezuelan, politician
4 Duke Street, W1. *English Heritage*
Bolívar, *El Libertador*, lodged here in 1810 while on a diplomatic mission from the movement seeking independence. An admirer of the American Revolution, he has been called the 'George Washington of South America'. He led the revolution against Spanish colonial rule, freeing Venezuela in 1821, Colombia and Ecuador in 1822, Peru in 1824 and Upper Peru (renamed Bolivia in his honour) in 1825.

BOOTHBY, Robert, Lord (1900–86), Scottish, politician
1 Eaton Square, Belgravia, SW1. *Private*
Boothby, who lived here from 1946 until his death, was a Conservative MP from 1924 to 1958. He was noted for his colourful private life, which included a long affair with Lady Dorothy Macmillan, as well as a dalliance with the gangster Ronnie Kray. He was described by the Queen Mother as 'a bounder but not a cad'.

BOSWELL, James (1740–95), Scottish, biographer
8 Russell Street, WC2. *Greater London Council*
Boswell met Dr Johnson (q.v.) for the first time here on 16 May 1763 and recalled: 'I had, for a part of the evening, been left alone with him, and had ventured to make an observation now and then, which he received very civilly; so that I was satisfied that though there was a roughness in his manner, there was no ill-nature in his disposition.' From this meeting a friendship developed that led eventually to *The Life of Samuel Johnson* (1791). (See also Westminster 2.)

BOW STREET

19–20 Bow Street, WC2. *London County Council*
The plaque records that Bow Street was formed about 1637 and lists a number of former residents. The street, so named because its curve resembles a bow, is famous also for its former Magistrates' Court at No. 4 (now a boutique hotel), first instituted in 1739, where Henry Fielding (q.v.) founded the Bow Street Runners, precursors of the Metropolitan Police, in the 1740s. Curiously, one of the most famous residents of Bow Street is not mentioned on the plaque: Oliver Cromwell lived here in 1645.

BOW STREET
WAS FORMED ABOUT 1637.
IT HAS BEEN THE RESIDENCE
OF MANY NOTABLE MEN
AMONG WHOM WERE
HENRY FIELDING (NOVELIST),
SIR JOHN FIELDING (MAGISTRATE),
GRINLING GIBBONS (WOODCARVER),
CHARLES MACKLIN (ACTOR),—
JOHN RADCLIFFE (PHYSICIAN),
CHARLES SACKVILLE EARL OF
DORSET (POET),—— WILLIAM
WYCHERLEY (DRAMATIST).

L C C

BRIDGEMAN, Sir Orlando (1606–74), English, lawyer
Essex Hall, Essex Street, WC2.
London County Council
Sir Orlando is listed as one of the former residents of Essex Street, although there is a contradiction: the street was laid out in 1675, but Sir Orlando died in 1674. He presided at the trial of the Regicides, was Lord Chief Justice from 1660 to 1668, and Lord Keeper of the Great Seal from 1667 to 1672.

CAMPBELL, Thomas (1777–1844), Scottish, poet
8 Victoria Square, SW1.
Duke of Westminster

Campbell lived here from 1840 until his death. Very popular in his day, he is now chiefly remembered for his martial poetry, including 'The Battle of Hohenlinden' and 'Ye Mariners of England'. He was also closely associated with the foundation of London University in the 1820s.

CAMPBELL-BANNERMAN, Henry (1836–1908), Scottish, Prime Minister
6 Grosvenor Place, Belgravia, SW1.
London County Council
Campbell-Bannerman, whose London home this was from 1877 until he became Prime Minister, launched the last Liberal government (1905–8), introducing major reforms, designed, he said, to make Britain 'less of a pleasure ground for the few and more of a treasure house for the nation'. He resigned on grounds of ill health in April 1908 and died at No. 10 later that month.

CARTE, Richard D'Oyly (1844–1901), English, impresario
The New Adelphi, WC2. *London County Council*
D'Oyly Carte is listed among the residents of the Adelphi Terrace, formerly on this site. He lived at No. 4 from 1888 until his death. He brought Gilbert and Sullivan together and produced all their operas. He built and ran the Savoy Hotel and Savoy Theatre, the first public building in England lit by electricity, in 1881. He also built an opera house at Cambridge Circus in 1891, which failed, but then prospered as the Palace of Varieties from 1892 onwards.

CECIL, Viscount (1864–1958), English, statesman
16 South Eaton Place, Belgravia, SW1.
Greater London Council
Viscount Cecil of Chelwood, 'the Creator of the League of Nations', lived here from 1923 until his death. He entered Parliament in 1903, and as Under-Secretary for Foreign Affairs in 1918 he helped draft the League of Nations covenant. He was President of the League from 1923 to 1945 and received the Nobel Peace Prize in 1937.

CHAMBERLAIN, Neville (1869–1940) English, Prime Minister
37 Eaton Square, Belgravia, SW1.
London County Council
Chamberlain lived here from 1923 to 1935 and was Prime Minister from 1937 to 1940. His policy of

appeasing Hitler signally failed to stop the Second World War and, when war broke out, he was famously told in the House of Commons 'In the name of God, go!', and was replaced by Churchill. He died six months later.

CHICHESTER, Sir Francis (1901–72), English, yachtsman
9 St James's Place, St James's, SW1.
Westminster City Council / Royal Institute of Navigation
Sir Francis lived here from 1944 until his death. He is remembered for being the first person to circumnavigate the world single-handed, in nine months and a day, in his yacht *Gypsy Moth IV*, in 1966–7. For this feat he was knighted by the Queen, using the same sword with which Queen Elizabeth I had knighted Drake. *Gypsy Moth IV* is now on permanent display near the *Cutty Sark* in Greenwich.

CHIPPENDALE, Thomas (1718–79), English, furniture designer
61 St Martin's Lane, Strand, WC2. *London County Council*
The workshop of Thomas Chippendale & Son stood near this spot from 1753 to 1813. With Sheraton and Hepplewhite, Chippendale was one of the three great furniture designers of the eighteenth century. He was the first to publish a book of his designs and is among the cultural heroes of England, having a statue on the façade of the Victoria and Albert Museum.

CHOPIN, Fryderyk (1810–49), Polish, composer, musician
99 Eaton Place, Belgravia, SW1. *Private*
4 St James's Place, St James's, SW1. *Greater London Council*
Chopin gave his first London concert at the first address and went from the second address to give his last public performance. He had made his debut as a virtuoso pianist at the age of eight. In Paris he was introduced by Liszt (q.v.) to George Sand and they formed a close relationship, she nursing

him through tuberculosis in Majorca. His compositions are mainly for the piano.

CHURCHILL, Sir Winston (1874–1965), English, Prime Minister, historian
34 Eccleston Square, SW1. *Private*
1–12 Morpeth Mansions, Morpeth Terrace, SW1. *Private*
Caxton Hall, Caxton Street, SW1.
Westminster City Council
Churchill lived at the first address from 1909 to 1913, at the second from 1930 to 1939, and spoke regularly at Caxton Hall between 1937 and 1942. He was Prime Minister twice (1940–5 and 1951–5), the second time arguably clinging on to office when he should have gone into honourable retirement. In an eventful life, he took part in the last British cavalry charge (at Omdurman in 1898), oversaw the armed siege of anarchists at Sidney Street (1911), painted some decent watercolours, learnt the skills of bricklaying, wrote some majestic history (his version), and inspired Britain through its 'finest hour' in 1940. (See also Kensington & Chelsea 1 and Westminster 2.)

COBDEN, Richard (1804–65), English, politician
23 Suffolk Street, SW1. *London County Council*
Long a sufferer from bronchial infection, Cobden, the great pillar of the Anti-Corn Law League (q.v.), died in his rooms here on 2 April 1865. He was, the next day, the subject of prolonged eulogies in the House of Commons, led by Palmerston (q.v.) and Disraeli (q.v.), who called him 'an honour to Britain'. (See also City.)

COLYER, Ken (1928–88), English, jazz trumpeter
11–12 Great Newport Street, WC2.
Westminster City Council
Colyer played trumpet here in the basement 'Studio 51' between 1950 and 1973. With Chris Barber, Acker Bilk and Humphrey Lyttleton, Colyer, in various combos, was at the heart of the trad jazz boom in England in the 1950s and is fondly remembered by anyone who wore a duffle coat and tried to grow a beard in those pre-rock days.

CONRAD, Joseph (1857–1924), Polish, novelist
17 Gillingham Street, Pimlico, SW1.
Greater London Council
Conrad, the anglicised pen-name of Józef Teodor Konrad Korzeniowski, rented two rooms here from 1891 to 1896. During this time he gave up his

seafaring life and published his first two novels, *Almayer's Folly* (1895) and *An Outcast of the Islands* (1896). He is regarded as one of the finest prose stylists in English literature, remarkable because he did not learn English until he was in his twenties. His *Heart of Darkness* (1899) inspired Coppola's film *Apocalypse Now* (1979).

COSTA, Sir Michael (1808–84), Italian, conductor
59 Eccleston Square, SW1. *English Heritage*
Sir Michael lived here from 1857 to 1883. Becoming a British citizen, he was the first conductor to be knighted. He is credited with raising the standards of British musical performance by revising the layout of orchestras, introducing systematic use of the baton, and establishing the control of the conductor, rather than the lead violin. His own compositions are long since unplayed; when he sent his oratorio *Eli* to Rossini in 1855, Rossini commented: 'The good Costa has sent me an oratorio and a Stilton cheese. The cheese was very good.'

COWARD, Sir Noël (1899–1973), English, playwright, actor
17 Gerald Road, Belgravia, SW1. *Private*
Sir Noël lived here from 1930 to 1956. He was hugely successful in the 1930s and 1940s, and among his successes were *Private Lives* (1930), *Cavalcade* (1931), *Blithe Spirit* (1941) and *This Happy Breed* (1943). He also produced films, including *In Which We Serve* (1942) and *Brief Encounter* (1945). (See also Sutton and Richmond.)

CRIBB, Tom (1781–1848), English, boxer
36 Panton Street, SW1. *English Heritage*
Cribb lived here. Boxing was still a bare-knuckle affair when he became British champion in 1810 and was titled World Champion by virtue of two defeats of a black American, the former slave Tom Molineaux, in 1810 and 1811. He retired to become a coal merchant, part-time boxing trainer and publican of the Union Arms in Panton Street. The pub has long since disappeared and should not be confused with the present Tom Cribb pub, named in his honour, where the plaque is.

CRICK, Francis (1916–2004), English, scientist
56 St George's Square, SW1. *City of Westminster*
Crick, who lived here from 1945 to 1947, was co-discoverer of the structure of DNA with Watson

and Wilkins in 1953, and they were subsequently jointly awarded the Nobel Prize for Science in 1962. The contribution of Rosalind Franklin (q.v.) was recognised somewhat belatedly.

CROSBY, Brass (1725–93), English, lawyer, politician
Essex Hall, Essex Street, WC2.
London County Council
Crosby is listed on the plaque as one of several distinguished former residents of Essex Street. Between 1772 and his death, he and his wife spent half the year here and the other half at Court Lodge in Bromley, where he was lord of the manor. As Lord Mayor of London, one of his first acts was to suppress the activities of the press gangs by stationing constables to prevent the seizure of men. (See also Bromley.)

CUBITT, Thomas (1788–1855), English, property developer
3 Lyall Street, Belgravia, SW1.
London County Council
Cubitt lived here the last few years of his life. He built swathes of Bloomsbury and most of Belgravia and Pimlico, as well as rebuilding the east front of Buckingham Palace. Queen Victoria said after he died: 'A better, kindhearted or more simple, unassuming man never breathed.'

CURZON, Lord (1859–1925), English, statesman
1 Carlton House Terrace, St James's, SW1.
Greater London Council
Curzon, who lived and died here, was one of the grandest grandees of his day – viceroy of India (1899–1905), member of the War Cabinet (1916) and Foreign Secretary (1919–24). 'Gentlemen do not take soup at luncheon,' he said – so now we know.

DADD, Richard (1817–86), English, painter
15 Suffolk Street, SW1.
Greater London Council
This was Richard Dadd's family home from 1834 until, in a mental

breakdown (thought now to be bipolar disorder), he murdered his father in 1843 and spent the rest of his life in asylums. His talent for art, which had gained him entry to the Royal Academy at twenty, sustained him throughout his life and he produced a stream of paintings of fairies, the supernatural and oriental scenes, characterised by obsessive detail. His most famous work, *The Fairy Feller's Master-Stroke* (1855–64), is in Tate Britain.

DAVIES, Thomas (*c.*1712–85), Scottish, bookseller
8 Russell Street, WC2. *Greater London Council*
This was Davies's house and shop, where he introduced Boswell (q.v.) to Dr Johnson (q.v.) in 1763. Davies, described by Boswell as 'friendly and very hospitable', had previously been an actor and apparently did a very good impersonation of Dr Johnson. When his bookselling business fell into difficulties, Johnson obtained a benefit night for him at Drury Lane, and Davies was one of only a handful of people Johnson received in his last illness.

DE GAULLE, Charles (1890–1970), French, soldier, President
4 Carlton Gardens, St James's, SW1.
Greater London Council
De Gaulle set up the headquarters of the Free French forces here in 1940 and made his famous broadcast: '*La France a perdu une bataille! Mais la France n'a pas perdu la guerre!*' He headed the provisional government after liberation (1944–6) and returned as President of the Fifth Republic (1959–69), vetoing British entry to the Common Market. (See also Camden 1.)

DE LAMERIE, Paul (1688–1751), Dutch, silversmith
40 Gerrard Street, Soho, W1.
Westminster City Council / Worshipful Company of Goldsmiths
De Lamerie lived and worked in a house on this site from 1738 until his death. He was the pre-eminent supplier in his day of gold and silverware to the wealthiest patrons, including the British and Russian royal families and most of the British aristocracy. An obituary said that he was 'instrumental in bringing that branch of trade to the perfection it is now in'.

DE QUINCEY, Thomas (1785–1859), English, journalist, critic
36 Tavistock Street, WC2. *Greater London Council*
De Quincey, misspelt on the plaque, wrote the work for which he is most famous, *Confessions of an English Opium Eater* (1822), while lodging here in the autumn of 1821. His writing is notable for high style, wide learning and often black humour, as in *On Murder Considered as One of the Fine Arts*. He was hugely influential on later writers such as Poe (q.v.) and Baudelaire, and Berlioz (q.v.) said that his *Symphonie Fantastique* was partly based on *Confessions*, with its recurrent theme of internal struggle with oneself.

DELFONT, Bernard (1909–94), English, impresario
Prince of Wales Theatre, Coventry Street, W1.
Comic Heritage
Born Boris Winogradsky in Russia, Delfont was brought to England in 1912 with his brothers Lew and Leslie Grade. They went on to dominate British show business, initially as dancers, then as agents, and later as impresarios. Delfont owned and managed many theatres, including this one.

DERBY, Edward, fourteenth Earl of
(1799–1869), English, Prime Minister
10 St James's Square, SW1. *London County Council*
The earl lived here from 1837 to 1854. He was Prime
Minister three times, in 1852, 1858–9 and 1866–8,
after which he retired from political life. A great
orator, he was criticised for a rather languid style of
leadership but nonetheless led the Conservative party
for twenty-two years, thus far a record.

DICKENS, Charles (1812–70), English, novelist
6 Chandos Place, WC2. *Private*
26 Wellington Street, WC2. *Private*
The first address is the site of Warren's blacking factory,
where a miserable twelve-year-old Dickens worked for
30p a week, labelling shoe-blacking bottles. A fellow
worker, who showed him some kindness, was called
Fagin, and Dickens later rather ungratefully used his
name for the villain in *Oliver Twist*. The second address
housed the offices of Dickens's magazine, *All The Year
Round*, and was also Dickens's London *pied à terre* from
1859 until his death. (See also Haringey, Westminster
2, Southwark and Camden 2.)

DRYDEN, John
(1631–1700),
English, poet, critic
**43 Gerrard Street,
W1.**
Royal Society of Arts
Dryden lived in a
house on this site
from 1686 until his
death. Seen as the
greatest of the Restoration poets, he wrote verse in
support of both Parliamentarians and the Stuarts. He
was appointed Poet Laureate in 1668, holding the post
for twenty years. His work as a critic sometimes got
him into trouble and in 1679 he was assaulted by
hired bravos, it is thought at the instigation of Lord
Rochester. This is one of the oldest extant plaques,
erected by the Royal Society of Arts in 1870, and now
somewhat battered.

DU PRÉ, Jacqueline (1945–87), English, cellist
2 Rutland Garden Mews, SW7. *Private*
Du Pré lived here from 1975 until her death. The
house had been adapted by Dame Margot Fonteyn
(see page 79) for her paraplegic husband and therefore
suited Du Pré as her multiple sclerosis worsened.

Though no longer able to play herself, she continued
teaching to the end. (See also Croydon, Camden 1 and
Westminster 2.)

EISENHOWER, Dwight D. (1890–1969),
American, soldier, President
31 St James's Square, St James's, SW1.
US Department of Defense
This was another of Eisenhower's headquarters in the
run-up to the D-Day invasion, 6 June 1944. (See also
Westminster 3 and Kingston.)

ESSEX STREET
Essex Hall, Essex Street, WC2.
London County Council
Essex Street was laid out by Nicholas Barbon
(see above) in 1675. He was the leading property
developer in London in the late seventeenth century
and overcame objections from the Middle Temple to
his plans here by building New Court for them.
The plaque lists several distinguished former residents
(see pages 72 and 79).

ETTY, William (1787–1849), English, painter
14 Buckingham Street, WC2. *London County Council*
Etty occupied the top floor of this house from 1826
until his death, though in his last few years he was
rarely in London. He specialised in painting 'God's
most glorious work, woman'. Among his subjects were
Cleopatra, Venus, Judith, Sappho and *Pandora*. He was
elected to the Royal Academy in 1828. Redgrave, in
his *Dictionary of English Artists* (1873), evokes him thus:
'He was of a gentle, amiable nature, and lived a long
bachelor life, though always falling in love.'

EVANS, Dame Edith
(1888–1976), English,
actress
**109 Ebury Street,
Victoria, SW1.**
English Heritage
This was Dame Edith's
childhood home. In a stage
career of over sixty years, she
created six Shaw (q.v.) roles, was
the definitive Nurse in *Romeo and Juliet* (1932–5), but
will be above all remembered for her Lady Bracknell
in *The Importance of Being Earnest* (stage 1939, film
1952). 'A handbag!', she said, and people have been
mimicking her ever since.

EWART, William
(1798–1869), English,
politician, reformer
**16 Eaton Place,
Belgravia, SW1.**
London County Council
Ewart lived here. In
forty years in the House
of Commons
(1828–68),
he achieved the abolition of capital punishment for
many minor offences and pushed through the Public
Libraries Act of 1850 in the teeth of Conservative
opposition. It was his original suggestion that plaques
should be put up on the former homes of distinguished
citizens. (See also Richmond.)

FIELDING, Henry (1707–54), English, novelist,
lawyer
Essex Hall, Essex Street, WC2.
London County Council
19–20 Bow Street, WC2. *London County Council*
Fielding lodged in Essex Street in the 1730s, and in the
1740s was magistrate at Bow Street, where he and his
half-brother John (see below) founded the Bow Street
Runners in 1749. (See Richmond for his main entry.)

FIELDING, Sir John (1721–80), English,
magistrate, social reformer
19–20 Bow Street, WC2. *London County Council*
Like his half-brother Henry (see above), Fielding is
listed on the Bow Street plaque among the
distinguished former residents of the street. Blinded in
an accident when he was nineteen, John took over
Bow Street magistrates' court when Henry retired in
1754 and ran it till his death. Known as 'the Blind
Beak', he could allegedly recognise three thousand
criminals by their voices. Among his innovations was
the regular circulation of a 'police gazette' listing
known criminals, which is seen as the origins of police
criminal records departments.

**FISHER, Admiral of
the Fleet Lord**
(1841–1920), English,
naval officer
**16 Queen Anne's
Gate, Westminster,
SW1.**
Greater London Council

Fisher lived here from 1904 to 1910, when he was
First Sea Lord. In a naval career of over sixty years,
'Jackie' Fisher went from wooden sailing ships to
dreadnoughts and aircraft carriers. His drive for
improvements in the Navy makes him the second most
important figure in British naval history after Nelson.

FLEMING, Ian (1908–64), English, novelist
22 Ebury Street, Victoria, SW1. *English Heritage*
Fleming lived in a flat (which he bought from Oswald
Mosley) here from 1934 to 1945. Before the Second
World War he worked, not very happily, in banking
and stockbroking. When war broke out, his mother's
influence got him into naval intelligence, where he
blossomed as personal assistant to Rear Admiral
Godfrey. Although he himself never saw action, this
experience in intelligence operations gave Fleming the
background for the phenomenally successful James
Bond novels.

**FLETCHER, WPC
Yvonne** (1959–84),
English, police officer
**St James's Square,
SW1.** *Police Memorial Trust*
On the morning of
17 April 1984 WPC
Fletcher was one of
thirty police officers
monitoring a
demonstration by
Libyan dissidents
opposed to Colonel
Gaddafi outside the
Libyan legation at 5 St James's Square. At 10.18 a.m.
shots rang out, it is thought from the second floor of
the legation: several demonstrators were hit, none
being seriously injured, but WPC Fletcher was fatally
wounded in the stomach and died an hour later. In the
wake of this incident, the Police Memorial Trust was
founded, and this is the first plaque they erected. To
date, the Trust has put up thirty-six memorials
nationwide to police officers killed in the line of duty.

FONTEYN, Dame Margot (1919–91), English,
prima ballerina
2 Rutland Garden Mews, SW7. *Private*
Dame Margot owned this house from 1967, when the
Royal Academy of Dancing, of which she was
president, was nearby at South Lodge. Born Margaret

Hookham, she had a glorious autumn to her career when she partnered Rudolf Nureyev. She had this house adapted for her paraplegic husband, Roberto Arias. When they retired to a farm in Panama, the house was a suitable purchase for Jacqueline Du Pré (see page 78) as her multiple sclerosis advanced.

FOUNTAIN TAVERN
Savoy Buildings, 91 Strand, WC2. *Private*
The tavern, which stood from 1708 to 1770, was the meeting place of the Fountain Club, which was opposed to Sir Robert Walpole (q.v.). The club was celebrated in verse: 'From this fam'd Fountain freedom flow'd, For Britain and the people's good.'

FRANKLIN, Benjamin (1706–90), American, scientist, diplomat
36 Craven Street, Strand, WC2.
London County Council
Franklin lived here from 1757 to 1770, with brief returns to America. Noted for his experiments in electricity, which led to many discoveries and inventions, he was a regular correspondent with progressive English thinkers such as David Hartley (q.v.). Active in the negotiations for independence from Britain, he was the most complete American of his age.

GAINSBOROUGH, Thomas (1727–88), English, painter
82 Pall Mall, St James's, SW1. *London County Council*
Gainsborough was Reynolds's (q.v.) archrival, bringing charm, light and grace to his work, which includes *The Blue Boy* (1770), *The Morning Walk* (1780) and *Mrs Siddons* (1785). A founder member of the Royal Academy, he lived here from 1777 to his death.

GALSWORTHY, John (1867–1933), English, novelist
1–3 Robert Street, WC2. *London County Council*
Galsworthy lived here from 1912 to 1918. He was working on *The Forsyte Saga*, his most successful novels, throughout this time, apart from when he was a hospital orderly in France, having been passed over for military service. (See also Camden 1.)

GALTON, Sir Francis (1822–1911), English, scientist, explorer, eugenicist
42 Rutland Gate, SW7. *Private*
Galton lived here, says the plaque, for fifty years. A true polymath, his study of heredity led to the science

of eugenics, a word he coined, along with the phrase 'nature versus nurture'. He also invented the statistical concept of correlation, psychometrics, and produced the first weather map.

GARRICK, David (1717–79), English, actor-manager
27 Southampton Street, WC2. *Duke of Bedford*
The New Adelphi, WC2. *London County Council*
Garrick lived at the first address from 1750 to 1772, and at the second from 1772 to 1779. He came to London from Lichfield with his friend Dr Johnson (q.v.), becoming the greatest actor of the eighteenth century, and making a greater fortune than any actor since Alleyn. During his management of Drury Lane Theatre from 1747 to 1776, it rose to be one of the most famous theatres in Europe. Painted by Hogarth (q.v.), Zoffany (q.v.) and Reynolds (q.v.), he was the first of his profession to be buried in Westminster Abbey (the second being Sir Laurence Olivier in 1989). (See also Richmond.)

GAS, LIGHT & COKE COMPANY
Great Peter Street, SW1. *City of Westminster*
The plaque records this as the former site of a gasworks that from 1813 provided the first public supply of gas in the world. It closed and was demolished in 1937.

GERALD ROAD POLICE STATION
Gerald Road, Belgravia, SW1. *Private*
This was Gerald Road police station, built in 1846, rebuilt in 1894 and again in 1925. The station was purchased on closure in 1993 by the young Count Bismarck, who converted it at some expense into a private dwelling.

GIBBONS, Grinling (1648–1720), Dutch, woodcarver, sculptor
19–20 Bow Street, WC2. *London County Council*
Gibbons, who lived here from 1678 until his death, is one of the several notable former residents of Bow Street listed on the plaque. Discovered by John Evelyn in Deptford and brought to the attention of Wren (q.v.), who hired him to carve stalls and pulpits in St Paul's and other churches, he was subsequently employed at Windsor, Whitehall and Kensington, and appointed master carver to Charles II, James II, William III and George I.

GLADSTONE, William Ewart (1809–98), English, Prime Minister
11 Carlton House Terrace, SW1. *London County Council*
10 St James's Square, SW1.
London County Council
Gladstone, the 'Grand Old Man', lived at the first address from 1856 to 1875 and is one of three Prime Ministers to have lived at the second (see Derby, page 78, and Pitt, page 89), though in his case only briefly, 'for the Parliamentary season' in 1890. He was four times Prime Minister (1868–74, 1880–5, 1886 and 1892–4) and his rivalry with Disraeli (q.v.) is the overarching motif of Parliamentary life in the second half of the nineteenth century. (See also Westminster 2 and Greenwich.)

GORT, Field Marshal Viscount, VC (1886–1946), English, army officer
34 Belgrave Square, SW1. *English Heritage*
Gort, who lived here from 1920 to 1926, was awarded the Victoria Cross for gallantry in the battle of the Canal du Nord near Flesquières on 27 September 1918. He commanded the British Expeditionary Force to France in September 1939, which was outflanked by the Germans on its right and made vulnerable on its left by the collapse of Belgian resistance, but nonetheless his skilful manoeuvring enabled the retreat to Dunkirk and the rescue of a substantial part of the force to fight another day.

GRAY, Henry (1827–61), English, anatomist
8 Wilton Street, Belgravia, SW1.
London County Council
Gray lived here. His famous work *Anatomy* was published in 1853 and remains the standard introduction to the subject for medical students to this day. Fellow of the Royal Society at the age of twenty-five, he died of smallpox before the second edition of *Anatomy* was published.

GREY, Sir Edward (1862–1933), English, politician
3 Queen Anne's Gate, Westminster, SW1.
Greater London Council
Sir Edward lived here from 1906 to 1912. As Liberal Foreign Secretary (1905–16), he tried and failed to prevent the outbreak of the First World War and on the eve of the war famously said: 'The lamps are going out all over Europe; we shall not see them lit again in our lifetime.'

GWYNNE, Nell (c.1650–87), English, orange-seller, actress
79 Pall Mall, SW1. *Private*
Nell Gwynne lived in a house on this site from 1671 until her death. Humbly born, she sold oranges before

going on the stage at Drury Lane. She was Charles II's most famous mistress, bearing him two sons. His dying words supposedly were: 'Let not poor Nelly starve.'

HALDANE, Lord (1856–1928), Scottish, politician, lawyer, philosopher
28 Queen Anne's Gate, Westminster, SW1.
London County Council
Lord Haldane lived here from 1907 until his death. He was a Liberal MP from 1885 to 1911, Secretary of State for War (1905–12), during which time the Territorial Army was founded, and twice Lord Chancellor. His philosophical works include *The Pathway to Reality* (1903), *The Philosophy of Humanism* (1922) and *Human Experience* (1926).

HALIFAX, Lord (1881–1959), English, politician
86 Eaton Square, Belgravia, SW1. *English Heritage*
Lord Halifax lived here. He was viceroy of India (1926–31) and, as Foreign Secretary (1938–40), was heavily involved in the appeasement policy towards Hitler. When Chamberlain (q.v.) was ousted in 1940, Halifax declined to succeed him, opening the way for Churchill (q.v.) to be wartime Prime Minister. Halifax was appointed ambassador to the United States (1941–6).

HARDY, Thomas (1840–1928), English, novelist, poet
The New Adelphi, WC2. *London County Council*
Hardy is listed among the several distinguished names associated with the former Adelphi Terrace on this site. Not a resident, he worked at No. 8 in the offices of the architect Arthur Blomfield from 1862 to 1867. Becoming homesick, he returned to his native Dorset but remained friends with Blomfield, even after he abandoned architecture as a career. (See also Westminster 2 and Wandsworth.)

HARLEY, Robert (1661–1724), English, politician
14 Buckingham Street, WC2. *London County Council*
Harley is one of several names listed as resident in a house formerly on this site. He was Speaker of the House of Commons (1701), Secretary of State for the Northern Department (1704) and Chief Minister to Queen Anne (1711–14). He was an early practitioner of 'spin', recognising the value of media manipulation, and used both Defoe (q.v.) and Swift to write pamphlets supportive of his policies, or attacking his opponents.

HAYGARTH, Arthur (1825–1903), English, cricketer, historian
88 Warwick Way, SW1. *City of Westminster*
Haygarth lived and died here. He was a decent amateur cricketer for Sussex but achieved more lasting fame as a historian of the sport after his playing days were over. He compiled *Frederick Lillywhite's Cricket Scores and Biographies* (fifteen volumes, 1862–79), of which volume 1, covering 1744–1826, remains the main source of reference for late eighteenth-century cricket.

HEINE, Heinrich (1797–1856), German, poet
32 Craven Street, Strand, WC2.
London County Council
Heine stayed here in 1827. He was a romantic lyric poet, whose works were widely set to music as *Lieder* by many German composers, including Schumann, Schubert, Brahms and Mendelsohn. A utopian socialist and friend of Karl Marx (q.v.), he spent most of his life in exile in Paris, his works banned in Germany and, long after, burned by the Nazis. He wrote in despair of Germany: 'Where they burn books, they will ultimately also burn people.' The plaque wrongly dates his birth to 1799.

HERVEY FAMILY
6 St James's Square, SW1. *Private*
On this site from 1676 to 1955 was the house of the Hervey family, earls of Bristol from 1714 onwards. In the eighteenth century there was a fashionable quip in reference to the family's eccentric strain, 'When God created the human race, he made men, women and Herveys', which was ascribed variously to Voltaire (q.v.) or to Lady Mary Wortley Montagu.

HO CHI MINH (1890–1969), Vietnamese, President
New Zealand House, Haymarket, SW1. *Britain Vietnam Association*
Ho Chi Minh, born Nguyen Tat Thanh, worked in the kitchens of the Carlton Hotel on this site in 1913. The founder of Vietnam, known as 'Uncle Ho', he was

prime minister of North Vietnam from 1945 to 1955 and president from 1945 to 1969. He directed the successful wars against the French (1946–54) and United States-backed South Vietnam (1954–75) but did not live to see liberation. The South Vietnamese capital, Saigon, was renamed Ho Chi Minh City in his memory.

HOOD, Thomas (1799–1845), English, poet, humorist
1–3 Robert Street, WC2. *London County Council*
Hood lived at No. 2 from 1828 to 1830. During this time he started his *Comic Annual*, a humorous review of current events, initially overrun with punning, which abated as his style matured. He also started contributing to *The Athenaeum*. (See also Enfield, City and Westminster 1.)

HORE-BELISHA, Lord (1893–1957), English, politician
16 Stafford Place, Westminster, SW1.
Greater London Council
Hore-Belisha lived here from 1936 until his death. While Minister of Transport (1934–7), he made three major innovations: rewriting the Highway Code, introducing the driving test, and introducing flashing lights at pedestrian crossings, immediately dubbed 'Belisha beacons' by the public.

HUGHES, William Morris (1862–1952), Australian, Prime Minister
7 Moreton Place, Pimlico, SW1.
Commonwealth of Australia
Hughes was born here. Known as 'the Little Digger', he served a record fifty-one years in the Australian federal parliament (1901–52). As prime minister of Australia, he gave unstinting support to Britain in the First World War and established Australia as an independent nation at the Paris Peace Conference (1919).

HUSKISSON, William (1770–1830), English, politician
28 St James's Place, St James's, SW1.
London County Council
Huskisson lived here from 1804 to 1806. A supporter of Pitt (q.v.), he was Secretary of the Treasury

(1804–9), President of the Board of Trade (1823) and Colonial Secretary (1827). He was the first person to be killed by a train, at the opening ceremony of the Liverpool & Manchester Railway.

JEROME, Jerome K. (1859–1927), English, novelist, humorist
91–94 Chelsea Gardens, Chelsea Bridge Road, SW1. *English Heritage*
Jerome is remembered for his one enduring success, *Three Men in a Boat* (1889), written while living here in Flat 104. The story of George, Harris, the author and the dog Montmorency going up the Thames in a skiff, it was so successful that the number of registered boats on the river went up by 50 per cent in a year.

JOHNSON, Denis (*c.* 1760–1833), English, engineer
Acre House, 69–76 Long Acre, WC2.
City of Westminster / Covent Garden Area Trust and Veteran-Cycle Club
Johnson was a coachmaker who in 1819 produced and patented a 'hobby horse', or 'pedestrian curricle' as he called it, from his workshop on this site. The forerunner of the bicycle, it had an elegant wooden frame, a tiller for steering, and was propelled by the rider 'walking' his feet. Johnson set up a riding school, and his machine was briefly a craze among the fashionable in London.

JOHNSON, Dr Samuel (1709–84), English, lexicographer
8 Russell Street, WC2. *Greater London Council*
9 Gerrard Street, W1. *Westminster City Council / Honsway C & E Foundation*
Essex Hall, Essex Street, WC2.
London County Council
Dr Johnson first met James Boswell at the first address in 1763, founded The Club with Joshua Reynolds (q.v.) and others at the Turk's Head, formerly on the second site, in 1764, and founded an 'Evening Club' at the Essex Head alehouse at the third site in 1783. This last was dismissed by Reynolds, who declined to join, as 'a strange mixture of very learned and very ingenious odd people'. (See also City.)

KEAN, Edmund (1787–1833), English, actor
Savoy Buildings, 91 Strand, WC2. *Private*
The plaque recalls a tavern called the Coal Hole on this site, which was in the 1820s the meeting place of the Wolf Club, of which Kean was a leading member.

Kean was an alcoholic, and the club existed for heavy drinking in the company of loose women. Considered the greatest tragedian of his age, he has been the subject of plays by Dumas Père and Sartre.

KELVIN, Lord (1824–1907), Irish, physicist, inventor
15 Eaton Place, Belgravia, SW1.
English Heritage
This was Lord Kelvin's London home. He introduced the absolute temperature scale, and the SI unit of temperature is named after him. He also invented and improved ships' compasses and many electrical and telegraphic instruments, and he supervised the laying of the transatlantic cable. He was the first scientist elevated to the peerage and in 1902 was a founder member of the Order of Merit.

KENYATTA, Jomo (*c.*1894–1978), Kenyan, President
95 Cambridge Street, SW1. *English Heritage*
Kenyatta lived here from 1933 to 1937, while studying social anthropology at the London School of Economics. He had been involved in Kenyan politics since joining the Kikuyu Central Association in 1924 and went on to found the Pan-African Federation in 1946 with Kwame Nkrumah (q.v.). Known universally as 'Mzee', the Swahili for a respected old man, he is regarded as the founder of Kenya.

KIPLING, Rudyard (1865–1936), English, poet, children's writer
43 Villiers Street, Strand, WC2.
London County Council
Kipling lived here from 1889 to 1891, when he was launched on the London literary scene, and while here he published *The Light that Failed*, *Mandalay* and *Gunga Din*. His later works include *The Jungle Books* (1894–5), *Kim* (1901), *Just So Stories* (1902) and *Puck of Pook's Hill* (1906). He was awarded the Nobel Prize for Literature in 1907.

KITCHENER, Lord (1850–1916), English, soldier
2 Carlton Gardens, St James's, SW1. *London County Council*
Kitchener lived here from 1914 to 1915. Victor of the battle of Omdurman in 1898, defeating the Mahdist forces in the Sudan, he cemented his place in national iconography with the First World War recruiting poster 'Your country needs you!' While he was travelling to Russia on a diplomatic mission in 1916, his ship was torpedoed with the loss of all on board.

KNIGHT, John Peake (1828–86), English, engineer
12 Bridge Street, SW1.
City of Westminster / J. P. Knight Group Ltd
Knight was the inventor of the world's first traffic lights, which he erected here on 9 December 1868. He lived in Bridge Street and observed the traffic into and round Parliament Square regularly becoming snarled up and, as an expert on railway signalling, he saw how the system could be applied to road traffic.

LANGTRY, Lillie (1853–1929), English, actress
8 Wilton Place, Belgravia, SW1. *Private*
Langtry lived here from 1899 until her retirement to the south of France in 1919. She was now Lady de Bathe, from her second marriage in 1899 to Hugo de Bathe,

a baronet some years her junior. Their house here was lavishly decorated and featured a 7-foot-tall stuffed grizzly bear in the hall, as well as a large collection of trophies won by Lillie's successful string of racehorses. (See also Kensington & Chelsea 2.)

LAWRENCE, T. E. (1888–1935), Welsh, soldier, philosopher
14 Barton Street, SW1. *Greater London Council*
After returning from his exploits in the Middle East in the First World War, Lawrence lived in an attic room in this house, lent to him by a friend, whenever he was in London. He wrote much of *Seven Pillars of Wisdom* here during 1919–20 and completed his *Odyssey* translation here in 1931. (See also Waltham Forest.)

LEIGH, Vivien (1913–67), English, actress
54 Eaton Square, Belgravia, SW1. *English Heritage*
Vivien Leigh (the stage-name of Vivien Hartley) moved into her flat here in 1967 and died later in the year. The flat had previously been a London *pied à terre* for her and Laurence Olivier (her husband from 1940 to 1960), with whom she appeared frequently on stage, especially in Shakespearian roles. She won two Oscars, for *Gone with the Wind* (1939) and *A Streetcar Named Desire* (1951).

LEWIS, Rosa (1867–1952), English, chef, hotelier
Cavendish Hotel, Jermyn Street, SW1. *City of Westminster*
Rosa Lewis ran, or rather ruled, the Cavendish Hotel here from 1902 until her death. Trained by Escoffier, who called her 'the Queen of Cooks', her cuisine was much in demand among the aristocracy in the late nineteenth century, and her purchase of the Cavendish Hotel in 1902 was reportedly bankrolled by Edward VII. This was run as a rather louche establishment and prompted the 1976–7 BBC television drama series *The Duchess of Duke Street*, based on the racy history of Rosa and the hotel.

LILLY, William (1602–81), English, astrologer
Aldwych Underground Station, WC2.
City of Westminster
Lilly lived near this spot. He supposedly predicted the Great Fire of London fourteen years before it happened and was therefore suspected by some people of starting it. He was tried for the offence in Parliament but found innocent. His most famous book, *Christian Astrology* (1647), remains a seminal work.

LINDSEY, Reverend Theophilus (1723–1808), English, cleric
Essex Hall, Essex Street, WC2.
London County Council
Lindsey is one of several names formerly associated with Essex Street listed on the plaque. A friend of Joseph Priestley (q.v.), he resigned from the Anglican ministry and in April 1774 commenced Unitarian services in rooms here, continuing until his retirement in 1793. His principal publication was *An Historical View of the State of the Unitarian Doctrine and Worship from the Reformation to Our Own Times* (1783).

LOPEZ-PUMAREJO, Alfonso (1886–1959), Colombian, politician, diplomat
33 Wilton Crescent, Belgravia, SW1. *Private*
A progressive liberal who had studied at the London School of Economics, he was twice President of Colombia (1934–8 and 1942–5), both times promoting the *Revolución en Marcha*, and both times ousted by reactionary pressure. He died in office as Colombian ambassador to London while living here.

LOVELACE, Ada (1815–52), English, mathematician
12 St James's Square, St James's, SW1.
English Heritage
Ada, Lord Byron's only legitimate daughter, lived here from 1835, on her marriage to the future Earl of Lovelace, until her death. She had met Charles Babbage (q.v.) in 1833. He called her 'the Enchantress of Numbers', and she, in writing about his Analytical Engine, produced a method for calculating Bernoulli numbers with the engine, now recognised by historians as the world's first computer programme. The language Ada, created in 1980, is named in her honour.

LUBBOCK, John, first Baron Avebury
(1834–1913), English, banker, scientist, politician
29 Eaton Place, SW1. *London County Council*
John Lubbock was born here. (See Bromley for his
main entry.)

LUGARD, Lord (1858–1945), English, soldier,
colonial administrator
51 Rutland Gate, Knightsbridge, SW7.
Greater London Council
Lugard lived here from 1912 to 1919. As High
Commissioner for Northern Nigeria (1899–1906) and
Governor-General of Nigeria (1914–19), he
strenuously sought to advance the native population,
arguing that it was best for Britain to run affairs with
the locals, and developing the system of indirect rule
through traditional local structures.

MACKLIN, Charles (*c.*1697–1797), Irish, actor
19–20 Bow Street, WC2. *London County Council*
Macklin is one of several former residents of Bow
Street mentioned on the plaque. His fame began with
his sensational performance as Shylock, first given in
1741. He restored the play to the original Shakespeare
text, did not play Shylock as a comic character (as had
been the norm then for fifty years) and carefully
studied the mannerisms of Italian Jews in London to
enhance his portrayal. Pope (q.v.) wrote of his
performance: 'This is the Jew that Shakespeare drew.'
He went on playing the part for nearly fifty years until
incipient senility set in.

MACMILLAN, Douglas (1884–1969), English,
founder of Cancer Support
15 Ranelagh Road, SW1. *English Heritage*
Macmillan, a civil servant who lived here, founded the
Society for the Prevention and Relief of Cancer in
1911 after the death of his father from the disease.
Today known as Macmillan Cancer Support, it offers
home nursing and hospices to cancer sufferers who are
past further medical treatment.

**MANNING,
Cardinal Henry**
(1808–92), English,
prelate
**22 Carlisle Place,
Victoria, SW1.**
London County Council
Cardinal Manning

lived here. Anglican archdeacon of Chichester (1841),
he converted to Rome in 1851, becoming archbishop
of Westminster in 1865 and a cardinal in 1875.
Important events during his primacy were the building
of Westminster Cathedral and the expansion of
Catholic education in Britain.

McCALL, Charles (1907–89), Scottish, artist
1a Caroline Terrace, SW1. *Private*
McCall, who lived here, was born in Edinburgh,
where he studied at the College of Art, and had the
unusual distinction of gaining a fellowship aged only
thirty-one. He exhibited at the Royal Academy and
with the London Group.

MELVILLE, Herman (1819–91), American, novelist
25 Craven Street, Strand, WC2. *English Heritage*
Melville lodged here for five weeks in 1849 on his first
visit to London, paying one guinea a week for a room
on the fourth floor. He had already published four
novels, to some critical acclaim, but his great work,
Moby Dick, was still two years off. Almost forgotten
when he died, his reputation revived dramatically in
the twentieth century, and *Moby Dick* is now recognised
as one of the greatest novels of the nineteenth century.

METTERNICH, Prince
(1773–1859), Austrian,
politician
**44 Eaton Square,
Belgravia, SW1.**
Greater London Council
Metternich lived here
in 1848, after being
driven from Vienna in the
year of revolution. As the host
of the Congress of Vienna in 1815, he was the original
exemplar of nineteenth-century diplomatic realism,
and an early proponent of the idea of 'balance of
power'. Lauded as a pragmatist, cursed as a
reactionary, he continues to be a controversial
historical figure.

MILLBANK PRISON
Millbank, SW1. *London County Council*
The prison stood near this spot from 1816 to 1890.
Designed by Jeremy Bentham (q.v.), it was described
in the *Handbook of London* of 1850 as 'a mass of
brickwork equal to a fortress'. The *Handbook* also
noted that around four thousand convicts a year were

then being transported, embarking from the steps by the present plaque. Tate Britain now stands on the site.

MOORE, George (1852–1933), Irish, novelist
121 Ebury Street, Victoria, SW1.
London County Council
Moore lived here from 1911 until his death. He was among the first modern realists. His novels include *A Modern Lover* (1883), *A Mummer's Wife* (1885), *Esther Waters* (1894) and *The Brook Kerith* (1916), all of which shocked his contemporary readership with their depictions of extra-marital sex, prostitution and lesbianism.

MORRISON, DC James (1965–91), English, police officer
Montreal Place, WC2. *Police Memorial Trust*
Detective Constable Morrison, while off duty, chased and attempted to arrest a thief and was fatally stabbed. He was posthumously awarded the Queen's Police Gallantry Medal.

MOUNTBATTEN OF BURMA, Countess (1901–60), English, socialite
2 Wilton Crescent, SW1. *English Heritage*
Married to Earl Mountbatten (see below) in 1922, she was notorious for a life dedicated exclusively to pleasure in the 1920s and 1930s, and there were affairs on both sides of the marriage. The Second World War, however, brought a seriousness and dedication to good causes, and she remains a heroine in many Indian eyes for her work there as vicereine during the last days of the Raj.

MOUNTBATTEN OF BURMA, Earl (1900–79), English, naval officer, viceroy
2 Wilton Crescent, SW1.
English Heritage
Mountbatten, who lived here, was Chief of Combined Operations (1941–3), Supreme Allied Commander South East Asia (1943–5), and received the Japanese surrender at Singapore in 1945. In 1947–8, as the last Viceroy of India, he oversaw the partition of the Indian sub-continent into India and Pakistan. He was assassinated on 28 August 1979 by

the IRA while sailing his small boat off Mullaghmore, County Sligo, where he had his holiday home.

MOZART, Wolfgang Amadeus (1756–91), Austrian, composer
180 Ebury Street, Pimlico, SW1.
London County Council
On a grand tour of Europe, the prodigy Mozart lived here from 5 August to 24 September 1764, during which time, aged eight, he composed his first symphony. He went on to prolific composition across all genres, creating some of the most popular music in the classical canon. (See also Westminster 3.)

NAPOLEON III of France (1808–73), French, President, Emperor
1c King Street, St James's, SW1.
Royal Society of Arts
Napoleon III lived here in temporary exile during the upheavals of 1847–8.
A nephew of Bonaparte, he returned to France after the dust had settled and was elected first President of the French Republic (1848–52), and subsequently Emperor of the Second Empire (1852–70). He is unique in world history in having been head of state of both a republic and an empire. He died in England, once more in exile. This is the oldest extant plaque in London, put up in 1867.

NEWTON, Sir Isaac (1642–1727), English, scientist
87 Jermyn Street, SW1.
London County Council
35 St Martin's Street, WC2.
City of Westminster
Sir Isaac lived in a house on the site of the first address from 1700 to 1709, and in a house on the second site from 1710 until his death. He was recognised as the greatest scientist England had ever produced, a status that has not slipped in the

succeeding three hundred years. His *Philosophiae Naturalis Principia Mathematica* (1687) is still held to be the most important book in the history of science.

NICOLSON, Harold (1886–1968), English, diplomat, biographer, diarist
182 Ebury Street, Pimlico, SW1. *English Heritage*
Nicolson lived here with his wife, Vita Sackville-West (see page 90). After time in the diplomatic service, and after his marriage in 1913, he turned to writing literary biography, of Verlaine, Tennyson, Byron, Swinburne and others. His diaries are a prime source of British political history.

NOEL-BAKER, Philip (1889–1982), English, athlete, politician
16 South Eaton Place, Belgravia, SW1.
English Heritage
Noel-Baker lived here. He was captain of the British Olympic team in 1912 and managed the team, as well as competing, in the 1920 and 1924 games. As a Quaker, he ran a Friends' ambulance unit in the First World War. He was heavily involved in founding the League of Nations and was a Labour MP from 1929 to 1931 and 1936 to 1970. He was awarded the Nobel Peace Prize in 1959, for his lifelong disarmament campaigning.

NORWEGIAN GOVERNMENT IN EXILE
Kingston House North, Princes Gate, SW7.
City of Westminster
This was the headquarters of the Norwegian government in exile from 1940 to 1945. (See also Kensington & Chelsea 1.)

NOVELLO, Ivor (1893–1951), Welsh, composer, actor-manager
11 Aldwych, WC2.
Greater London Council
Novello occupied a flat in this building. He is best remembered for his songs, including 'Keep the Home Fires Burning', a great morale booster in the First World War, and 'We'll Gather Lilacs'. His musicals included *The Dancing Years* (1939), *King's Rhapsody* (1949) and *Gay's the Word* (1951).

OLD SLAUGHTER'S COFFEE HOUSE
77–78 Cranbourn Street, WC2.
City of Westminster / RSPCA
The coffee house was established in 1692 by Thomas Slaughter and run by him till his death in 1740. Thereafter it was known as Old Slaughter's. It was initially noted for chess playing, and subsequently as an artistic gathering place frequented by Hogarth (q.v.), Roubiliac, Hayman and Gainsborough (q.v.). The plaque records that on 16 June 1824 the organisation now called the Royal Society for the Prevention of Cruelty to Animals was founded here. The premises were demolished in the 1830s.

PALMERSTON, Lord (1784–1865), English, Prime Minister
20 Queen Anne's Gate, Westminster, SW1.
London County Council
4 Carlton Gardens, St James's, SW1.
London County Council
Lord Palmerston was born at the first address and lived at the second from 1846 to 1855. During this time he was Foreign Secretary for the second time, until his dismissal by Lord John Russell (see page 90) in 1851 for expressing approval of Louis Napoleon's *coup d'état* without consulting the cabinet. (See also Westminster 3.)

PEABODY, George (1795–1869), American, banker, philanthropist
80 Eaton Square, Belgravia, SW1.
Greater London Council
Peabody lived and died in this house. 'The Father of Modern Philanthropy' moved to London in 1837 as a successful banker and established the Peabody Trust in 1862 to provide quality housing for 'the artisans and labouring poor of London', opening his first blocks in Whitechapel in February 1864. The Trust continues the work to this day.

PELHAM, Henry (*c.*1695–1754), English, Prime Minister
Rear elevation, 22 Arlington Street, St James's, SW1. *English Heritage*
This house was built for Pelham by William Kent in 1741. Pelham is the most colourless man ever to hold high office, which, it has been suggested, is why he lasted so long as Prime Minister (1743–54). He was also sustained by an extensive network of corruption.

PENNY POST
39 Gerrard Street, W1. *City of Westminster*
This building was the site of the Westminster office of
the Penny Post, later the Two-Penny Post
(1794–1834).

PEPYS, Samuel (1633–1703), English, civil servant,
diarist
12 Buckingham Street, WC2. *London County Council*
14 Buckingham Street, WC2. *London County Council*
Pepys lived at No. 12 from 1679 to 1688, then moved
next door to No. 14, where he lived until 1700. His
famous diary, begun in 1660, was ended in 1669 when
he feared he was losing his sight. During his time in
Buckingham Street he was President of the Royal
Society (1684–6), Chief Secretary of the Admiralty
(1684–9) and Master of Trinity House (1676–89).
(See also City.)

**PITT, William, the
Elder** (1708–78),
English, Prime
Minister
**10 St James's
Square, SW1.**
London County Council
Pitt was the first of
three Prime
Ministers to live in
this house (see Derby and Gladstone, pages 80 and
81). He lived here from 1759 to 1762. During the first
years he was in an unhappy coalition government with
the Duke of Newcastle, which ended shortly after
George III's accession, and for a time Pitt was in
opposition. 10 St James's Square is today named
Chatham House in Pitt's honour (he was made Earl of
Chatham) and houses the Royal Institute for
International Affairs. (See also Camden 1 and Enfield.)

**PITT-RIVERS, Lieutenant General Augustus
Henry Lane Fox** (1827–1900), English, soldier,
archaeologist
4 Grosvenor Gardens, Victoria, SW1.
Greater London Council
This house was Pitt-Rivers's London home. His
interest in archaeology began in the 1850s and
gathered momentum when in 1880 he inherited the
Cranborne Chase estate in Dorset, which was
crammed with ancient sites. Retiring from the army in
1882, he had already amassed and ordered a substantial

collection of artefacts from various postings, which
formed the basis of the Pitt-Rivers Museum in
Oxford. He was appointed Britain's first Inspector of
Ancient Monuments in 1882, a post created by his
son-in-law, Sir John Lubbock (q.v.).

PUNCH'S PUPPET SHOW
St Paul's Church, Covent Garden, WC2. *Society for
Theatre Research / British Puppet and Model Theatre Guild*
This was the site of the first Punch performance in
Britain. 9 May 1662 is thought of as Punch's birthday;
on that day Pepys noted a performance by Pietro
Gimonde, operating as 'Signor Bologna': 'an Italian
puppet play, which is very pretty, the best I ever saw.'

RADCLIFFE, Dr John (1652–1714), English,
physician
19–20 Bow Street, WC2. *London County Council*
Dr Radcliffe is listed among several distinguished
former residents of Bow Street. He was Royal
Physician to William and Mary, and when he died he
left his estate to benefit the University of Oxford,
where the Radcliffe Camera, the Radcliffe
Observatory and the Radcliffe Infirmary are named in
his honour.

RATHBONE, Eleanor (1872–1946), English,
politician, reformer
Tufton Court, Tufton Street, Westminster, SW1.
Greater London Council
Eleanor Rathbone, who lived here, came from the
Rathbone family of Liverpool, noted for their
involvement in social action and reform. An
Independent MP from 1929 to her death, she had
campaigned on the issue of family allowances since
1919 and finally, in 1945, the year before her death,
she saw the Family Allowances Act passed by the Attlee
government.

REITH, Lord (1889–1971), Scottish, creator of the
BBC
6 Barton Street, Westminster, SW1.
English Heritage
Lord Reith lived here from 1924 to 1930. He ran the
BBC from 1922 to 1938 as its first director-general,
laying down a firm, principled tradition of impartial
public service, fending off government attempts to
make it their mouthpiece, and establishing a duty to
educate, inform and entertain. The rest of his career
was an anticlimax.

REYNOLDS, Sir Joshua (1723–92), English, painter

5 Great Newport Street, WC2. *Private*

9 Gerrard Street, W1. *Westminster City Council / Honsway C & E Foundation*

Fanum House, Leicester Square, WC2. *Private / London County Council*

Reynolds lived at the first address from 1753 to 1761, founded The Club with his friend Dr Johnson (see page 83) in 1764 at the former Turk's Head at the second address, and lived in a house on the site of the third address from 1761 until his death. One of the founders and first President of the Royal Academy in 1768, he is generally reckoned to be the greatest portrait painter Britain has produced.

ROWLANDSON, Thomas (1757–1827), English, painter, caricaturist

16 John Adam Street, Strand, WC2. *London County Council*

Rowlandson lived in a house on this site. He could have been a serious artist, but a gambling habit got in the way and caricature came quick and easy. He is best known for his three *Dr Syntax* books (1812, 1820 and 1821). With his friends Gillray and Cruikshank (q.v.), he developed the comic figure of John Bull.

ROYAL AIR FORCE

80 Strand, WC2. *City of Westminster*

The Royal Air Force was formed at a meeting here at the former Hotel Cecil on 1 April 1918. The hotel, once London's largest, had been requisitioned in 1917 and was the RAF's headquarters for its first year, before the senior officers moved to Kingsway, in 1919. The hotel was demolished in the 1930s to make way for Shell Mex House.

ROYAL SOCIETY FOR THE PREVENTION OF CRUELTY TO ANIMALS

77–78 Cranbourn Street, WC2. *City of Westminster / RSPCA*

The RSPCA was founded at a meeting here on

16 June 1824 in Old Slaughter's Coffee House (see above), which formerly stood on this site.

RUSSELL, Admiral Edward (1653–1727) , English, naval officer

43 King Street, Covent Garden, WC2. *Duke of Bedford*

Admiral Russell lived in this house, built for him by Thomas Archer, from 1717 until his death. In 1688 he was one of the 'Immortal Seven' who invited William of Orange to depose James II. In the subsequent War of the Grand Alliance he commanded an Anglo-Dutch fleet at the decisive victories of Barfleur and La Hougue in 1692. He was First Lord of the Admiralty three times between 1694 and 1717.

RUSSELL, Lord John (1792–1878), English, Prime Minister

37 Chesham Place, Belgravia, SW1. *London County Council*

Lord John, who lived here, was not a great success in either of his periods at 10 Downing Street (1846–52 and 1865–6), being ineffectual at healing internal party rifts and overshadowed by the belligerent Palmerston (q.v.). He must have been a decent man though, because Dickens dedicated *A Tale of Two Cities* to him 'In remembrance of many public services and private kindnesses'. He was the last Whig and the first Liberal.

SACKVILLE, Charles, Earl of Dorset (1638–1706), English, poet

19–20 Bow Street, WC2. *London County Council*

Sackville is listed among several former residents of Bow Street. He was a favourite of Charles II and noted for his dissipation. Grahame Greene described him as 'a light-hearted debauchee into whose charming verse seriousness seldom entered'. His most famous work is the engaging ballad 'To All You Ladies Now at Land', spuriously supposed to have been written at sea on the eve of a naval battle in 1665.

SACKVILLE-WEST, Vita (1892–1962), English, poet, novelist, gardener

182 Ebury Street, Pimlico, SW1. *English Heritage*

Vita Sackville-West lived here with her husband,

Harold Nicolson (see page 88). She is the only poet to have won the Hawthornden Prize twice. Living in an open marriage with Nicolson, she had many lesbian affairs, notably with Virginia Woolf (q.v.), who modelled *Orlando* on her. The garden she created at Sissinghurst Castle, Kent, is today the most visited of National Trust properties.

SARGENT, Sir Malcolm (1895–1967), English, conductor
Albert Hall Mansions, Kensington Gore, SW7.
English Heritage
Sir Malcolm lived and died in a flat here, alongside his most famous place of work, the Albert Hall. An organist by training, he conducted the Royal Choral Society from 1928, the Liverpool Philharmonic from 1942 to 1948, and the BBC Symphony Orchestra from 1950 to 1957. Known to a wide public as the chief conductor of the Proms from 1948 to 1967, and always impeccably turned out, he was nicknamed 'Flash Harry'.

SASSOON, Siegfried (1886–1967), English, poet, memoirist
54 Tufton Street, SW1. *City of Westminster*
Sassoon lived and worked in a house on this site from 1919 to 1925. During this time he was literary editor of the *Daily Herald*, commissioning work from E. M. Forster (q.v.), Arnold Bennett (q.v.) and Osbert Sitwell (q.v.). He also formed a close friendship with William Walton (q.v.), who dedicated his overture *Portsmouth Point* (1925) to Sassoon in gratitude for his patronage and support. (See also Kensington & Chelsea 1.)

SAVAGE, James (1779–1852), English, architect
Essex Hall, Essex Street, WC2.
London County Council
Savage had his offices in Essex Street. He designed several London churches, notably St Luke, Chelsea (1824), St James, Bermondsey, and Holy Trinity, Tottenham (both 1829). He published *Observations on Style in Architecture* (1836) and is regarded as a precursor of the Victorian Gothic Revival.

SAVAGE, Richard (1660–1712), English, soldier, courtier
9 Old Queen Street, SW1. *Private*
Savage lived in a house on this site. One of the most conspicuous rakes of the Restoration period, he

commanded troops with distinction in Ireland, Flanders and Lisbon. He was an intimate of Swift and of the Harley circle, and a member of the Saturday Club. His last appointment was as Constable of the Tower of London (1710–12). The poet Richard Savage claimed to be his illegitimate son.

SAVOY THEATRE
Savoy Court, Strand, WC2.
Westminster City Council / Savoy Theatre
Built by Richard D'Oyly Carte (see above) and opened in 1881 to be a permanent home for his staging of Gilbert and Sullivan operas, this was the first public building in the world to be lit by electricity. The auditorium was demolished and rebuilt in 1929, and restored to its original Victorian splendour after a fire in 1990.

SCOTLAND YARD
Ministry of Agriculture, Whitehall Place, SW1.
Greater London Council
This is the site of the original Metropolitan Police headquarters (1829–90). Great Scotland Yard, according to tradition, took its name from a house owned by the Scottish royal family, dating back to Kenneth II in the 970s. From here the Met moved to Norman Shaw's (q.v.) New Scotland Yard in 1890, and in 1966 to its present headquarters in Broadway.

SHAW, George Bernard (1856–1950), Irish, playwright, critic
The New Adelphi, WC2. *London County Council*
Shaw lived at No. 10 in the former Adelphi Terrace on this site from 1897 to 1927. Probably the most famous theatre critic before Kenneth Tynan, he championed Fabianism, vegetarianism and women's rights. A prodigious writer, he produced over fifty plays, of which *Pygmalion* (1913) (the basis of *My Fair Lady*) and *St Joan* (1923) stand out. He won the Nobel Prize in 1925. (See also Camden 2.)

SHELLEY, Mary (1797–1851), English, novelist, poet
24 Chester Square, SW1. *English Heritage*
Shelley lived here from 1846 until her death. She wrote her celebrated *Frankenstein* after a challenge by Byron; on a stormy night in June 1816, Mary Godwin and her future husband, the poet Shelley, were visiting Byron at his Villa Diodati by Lake Geneva. Byron suggested they all try to write a

supernatural tale; he gave up pretty quickly but his doctor, John Polidori (q.v.), took his fragment and wrote *The Vampyre*, so two great horror genres were born on the same occasion.

SIKORSKI, General Władysław (1881–1943), Polish, soldier, prime minister
Rubens Hotel, 43 Buckingham Palace Road, SW1.
Private
In 1939 Sikorski was made commander-in-chief of all Free Polish forces, and from 1940 prime minister of the Polish government in exile in London. After taking off from Gibraltar in 1943, he was killed in a plane crash that still provokes speculation about a conspiracy.

SMITH, F. E. (1872–1930), English, lawyer, politician
32 Grosvenor Gardens, Victoria, SW1.
London County Council
This was Smith's London home from 1915 until his death. He was a noted advocate at the bar, made 'the most brilliant maiden speech in history' in the Commons on 15 April 1906, and held various offices in Conservative governments in the 1920s, while also being Churchill's best friend and drinking companion. Margot Asquith said of him: 'F. E. Smith is very clever, but sometimes his brains go to his head.'

SMITH, William (1756–1835), English, politician, pioneer of religious liberty
16 Queen Anne's Gate, Westminster, SW1.
Greater London Council
A dissenter and independent MP, Smith, who lived here, was a member of the Clapham Sect (q.v.) and co-founder with Zachary Macaulay (q.v.) of the London Society for the Abolition of Slavery in 1823. In 1813 he persuaded Parliament to pass an Act legalising Unitarianism.

STANFIELD, Clarkson (1793–1867), English, painter
14 Buckingham Street, WC2. *London County Council*
Stanfield lived in this house from the 1820s until his

move to Hampstead in 1847. Regarded as one of the best English marine painters, he benefited from the patronage of William IV, who commissioned two major works from him, *The Opening of New London Bridge* (1832) and *The Entrance to Portsmouth Harbour*, both still in the Royal Collection. (See also Camden 1.)

STANLEY, Sir Henry Morton (1841–1904), Welsh, journalist, explorer
2 Richmond Terrace, Whitehall, SW1.
Greater London Council
Born John Rowlands, Stanley, who lived and died here, was not above embroidering his biography. His book *How I Found Livingstone* (1872) recounts their meeting and the famous phrase 'Dr Livingstone, I presume?', but this is now widely assumed to be an invention. His nickname in Africa was 'Bula Matari', meaning 'Breaker of Rocks', though it is far from clear whether this was affectionate or a reference to his harsh treatment of the Africans who worked for him.

STEAD, William T. (1849–1912), English, journalist, reformer
5 Smith Square, SW1.
City of Westminster
Stead lived here from 1904 until his death. He inaugurated the 'new journalism'; he was directly responsible for the dispatch of General Gordon to Khartoum in 1884, and 'purchased' thirteen-year-old Eliza Armstrong as part of his campaign against child prostitution. He died on the *Titanic*.

STUART, Prince Charles Edward (1720–88), Scottish, royalty
Essex Hall, Essex Street, WC2.
London County Council
'Bonnie Prince Charlie' stayed in a house in Essex Street while visiting London incognito in 1750. During his visit he took Anglican communion at St Mary-le-Strand to indicate to his British supporters that he was ready to convert to Protestantism if it would advance his chances of gaining the English throne. After being defeated at Culloden (1746), he spent the rest of his life in drunken exile on the Continent, with three short semi-secret visits to London in 1750, 1752 and 1754.

SULLIVAN, Arthur Percy, VC (1896–1937), Australian, banker, soldier
Birdcage Walk, SW1. *Australian Coronation Contingent* Gunner Sullivan was awarded his Victoria Cross for extreme gallantry, rescuing four members of his platoon who had fallen into a deep swamp under heavy fire in the retreat across the Sheika River during the North Russia Relief Expedition of 1919. In London for the Coronation of George VI, he slipped here in Birdcage Walk, striking his head fatally on the kerb.

TENNYSON, Alfred, Lord (1809–92), English, Poet Laureate
9 Upper Belgrave Street, Belgravia, SW1.
English Heritage
Tennyson lived here in 1880 and 1881. He was Poet Laureate from 1850 to his death, the first English writer to be raised to the peerage, the second most quoted writer in the *Oxford Dictionary of Quotations*, and author of many enduring poems, of which 'The Charge of the Light Brigade' (1854) has perhaps the most resonance. (See also Richmond.)

TERRISS, William (1847–97), English, actor
Adelphi Theatre stage door, Maiden Lane, WC2. *City of Westminster / Adelphi Theatre Co Ltd*
Terriss, 'Hero of the Adelphi Melodramas' as the plaque styles him, met an untimely end outside this theatre on 16 December 1897 when he was fatally stabbed by a jealous out-of-work rival. After his death a fund was set up to finance the Terriss Memorial Lifeboat House at Eastbourne, where the RNLI Lifeboat Museum now stands.

TEXAS LEGATION
Pickering Place,
St James's, SW1.
Anglo-Texan Society
The Republic of Texas existed for ten years from 1836 to 1846, having broken away from Mexico, and included parts of present-day New Mexico, Oklahoma, Kansas, Colorado and Wyoming. Although the British never officially recognised Texas, because they had friendly relations with Mexico, they were in favour of Texas remaining independent as a counterweight to the growth of the United States. When the USA annexed Texas it took over its enormous debts, and Texas, in return, in 1852 gave up all the parts of other states that it had briefly held.

THOMPSON, David (1770–1857), English, explorer
Grey Coat Hospital School, Greycoat Place, SW1. *City of Westminster / Grey Coat Hospital Foundation*
Thompson studied at this school from 1777 to 1784. His life was devoted to mapping Canada and the north-west United States. It has been calculated that he travelled 55,000 miles on horseback, by canoe, dog sled and on foot. He first crossed the Rockies in 1807 and his 'Great Map', the authority on the western territories for a century, was produced in 1813–14. He died in obscurity, but his fame was restored with the discovery and publication of his journals, *The Narrative of David Thompson*, in 1916.

TOWNLEY, Charles (1737–1805), English, antiquary, collector
14 Queen Anne's Gate, Westminster, SW1.
Greater London Council
After several grand tours, Townley built this house (then 7 Park Street) in 1778 to house his fabulous

collection of marbles and terracotta reliefs. After his death they were purchased by the British Museum and form the core of the museum's Graeco-Roman galleries to this day.

TURK'S HEAD
9 Gerrard Street, W1. *Westminster City Council*
This is the site of the Turk's Head, where Dr Johnson and Joshua Reynolds (see pages 83 and 90) formed The Club in 1764. The Club met once a week, at 7 p.m., and discussions continued 'till a pretty late hour', according to Boswell. The Turk's Head existed on this site from 1751 until some time in the 1780s, after which The Club moved to a tavern in Dover Street. Although the plaque calls the Turk's Head a tavern, Boswell and other sources call it a coffee house.

TURNER, Joseph Mallord William (1775–1851), English, painter
21 Maiden Lane, WC2.
City of Westminster / Turner Society
Turner was born in a house on this site.
(See also Kensington & Chelsea 2, Richmond and Westminster 2.)

VIVEKANANDA, Swami (1863–1902), Bengali, philosopher
63 St George's Drive, SW1. *English Heritage*
Vivekananda was on a world tour when he stayed here in 1896. He had addressed the World Parliament of Religions at Chicago in 1893 and was described in a contemporary newspaper account as 'the greatest figure at the parliament'. As the first Hindu missionary to the west, he is credited with elevating Hinduism to the status of a world religion. Every subsequent Indian leader, without exception, has acknowledged a debt to him.

VOLTAIRE (1694–1778), French, philosopher, playwright, satirist
10 Maiden Lane, Covent Garden, WC2.
Westminster City Council / Voltaire Foundation
Voltaire stayed in a house on this site in 1727–8. The towering genius of the French Enlightenment was twice imprisoned and spent most of his life banished from Paris. His works of history,

poetry, drama, philosophy and satire all supported his theme: '*Écrasez l'infâme*' ('Stamp out abuses').

WAKEFIELD, Edward Gibbon (1796–1862), English, colonial pioneer
1–5 Adam Street, Strand, WC2.
New Zealand Historic Places Trust
In prison (1826–9) for abducting a fifteen-year-old heiress, he wrote a paper on the theory of colonisation. He was subsequently involved in developing both South Australia and Canada and formed the New Zealand Association in 1837. In 1853 he emigrated to New Zealand, founded the Anglican colony at Canterbury and died there.

WALPOLE, Horace (1717–97), English, novelist, man of letters
5 Arlington Street, SW1. *Greater London Council*
The youngest son of Sir Robert (see below), Walpole became fourth Earl of Orford on the death of his brother in 1791. Over four thousand of his letters have been published, his main correspondents being Sir Horace Mann and Madame du Deffand. He coined the word 'serendipity'. (See also Richmond.)

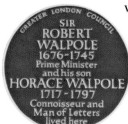

WALPOLE, Sir Robert (1676–1745), English, Prime Minister
5 Arlington Street, SW1.
Greater London Council
This was the Walpole family's London home. Britain's first Prime Minister (1715–17 and 1721–42), Walpole was notorious for embezzlement, bribery and corruption, and has been called 'the most despicable creature ever to hold high office'. However, as the first Prime Minister to study finance and commerce, he laid the foundations of free trade and colonial policy.

WEBB, Sidney (1859–1947), English, reformer, social scientist
44 Cranbourn Street, Covent Garden, WC2.
Westminster City Council / London School of Economics & Political Science
Webb was born in a house on this site on 13 July 1859. (See also Camden 1.)

94

WESLEY, Charles (1707–88), English, Methodist, hymn writer
WESLEY, John (1703–91), English, Methodist
24 West Street, WC2. *Private*
Here at the West Street Chapel, built in 1700 and first used by Huguenots, Charles and John preached frequently when it was leased by Methodists (1743–98). (See also City, Islington, Tower Hamlets and Westminster 2.)

WHEELER, Sir Mortimer (1890–1976), English, archaeologist
27 Whitcomb Street, WC2. *English Heritage*
Sir Mortimer lived here. Influenced by Pitt-Rivers (q.v.), he developed the grid system in excavations at St Albans (*Verulamium*) and Maiden Castle, Dorset. His appearances on BBC Television's quiz series *Animal, Vegetable, Mineral?* (1952–60) brought archaeology to a whole new audience. He was Television Personality of the Year in 1954, and his jolly autobiography, *Still Digging* (1955), was a bestseller.

WILDE, Oscar (1854–1900), Irish, playwright, poet, wit
Rear of Theatre Royal, Suffolk Street, SW1.
Westminster City Council / Oscar Wilde Society
The plaque records that the first performances of *A Woman of No Importance* (19 April 1893) and *An Ideal Husband* (3 January 1895) were presented at this theatre. The plaque was unveiled by Sir John Gielgud on the centenary of the second première. (See also Kensington & Chelsea 2.)

WILHELMINA, Queen of the Netherlands (1880–1962), Dutch, royalty
77 Chester Square, SW1. *Private*
Queen Wilhelmina had her secretariat here from 1940 to 1945 during her exile from Holland in the Second World War. Although she had wanted to remain in Holland, the rapidity of the German advance made that impossible and she was obliged to accept British hospitality, despite a frosty relationship since her support of the Boers. Churchill described her as the only real man among the various governments in exile in London. (See also Westminster 2.)

WINGFIELD, Major Walter Clopton (1833–1912), Welsh, inventor of lawn tennis
33 St George's Square, Pimlico, SW1.
Greater London Council
Wingfield, who lived here, took out a patent in 1874 for 'Sphairistikè' (Greek for 'ball game'), which he had invented as a game suitable for both sexes to play at a country house party. Sold as a kit, the game was instantly popular, and the first Wimbledon Lawn Tennis Championships took place in 1877.

WINSOR, Frederick (1763–1830), German, engineer
100 Pall Mall, SW1.
City of Westminster / Institute of Gas Engineers and Managers
Born Friedrich Albrecht Winzer, but changing his name to Frederick Albert Winsor, this gas engineer and pioneer of street lighting illuminated Pall Mall from a retort on this site in June 1807.

WOLF CLUB
Savoy Buildings, 91 Strand, WC2. *Private*
This club flourished in the basement of a tavern called the Coal Hole on this site in the 1820s, ostensibly as a refuge for husbands whose wives did not like them singing in the bath. In fact, it was simply a resort for heavy drinkers and prostitutes, and Edmund Kean (see page 83) was its most famous member.

WYCHERLEY, William (1641–1715), English, playwright
19–20 Bow Street, WC2. *London County Council*
Wycherley is among the several former residents of Bow Street listed on this plaque. His last two plays, *The Country Wife* (1675) and *The Plain Dealer* (1677), are still regularly revived and are enjoyed for their satire and social criticism of conventional views on marriage and sexual morality. He is credited by the *Oxford English Dictionary* with coining the word 'nincompoop' and the phrase 'happy-go-lucky'.

THE
INNER LONDON
BOROUGHS

THE INNER LONDON BOROUGHS are a fairly self-evident bunch, comprising the area formerly administered by the London County Council. This means that, rather oddly, Greenwich is an 'Inner' borough, while Newham, directly north across the Thames, is 'Outer'. Among this inner circle there are some spectacular enclaves of plaque activity, and two of these boroughs, Camden and Kensington & Chelsea, are so richly endowed that I have divided them each in two, along easily recognised main roads that bisect them both.

Of the Inner London boroughs, the most innovative with its plaque programme is Southwark. Anciently, Southwark was the place across the river, beyond the laws of the City, where Londoners went for all sorts of pleasure, not necessarily licit, and there are plenty of 'Historic Southwark' plaques memorialising the sites of theatres and bear-baiting arenas. But, since 2003, Southwark has introduced a new scheme of blue plaques, voted for by the people. Each year the council puts forward a shortlist of ten to fifteen names of local sites and citizens, and the ratepayers vote for four or five of them to be honoured. This means Southwark has more plaques to people still living than any other borough, but, they would argue, why should someone have to be dead before he or she is honoured? Indeed, why not ask Sir Michael Caine himself to unveil the plaque at his birthplace?

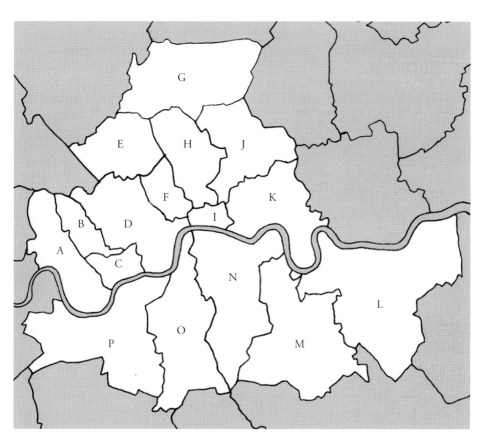

A   Hammersmith & Fulham
B   Kensington & Chelsea 1
C   Kensington & Chelsea 2
D   City of Westminster
E   Camden 1
F   Camden 2
G   Haringey
H   Islington
I   City of London
J   Hackney
K   Tower Hamlets
L   Greenwich
M   Lewisham
N   Southwark
O   Lambeth
P   Wandsworth

CAMDEN

Directly north of Westminster, Camden is an amalgamation of the three former metropolitan boroughs of Hampstead, Holborn and St Pancras. It is liberally endowed with plaques, so for convenience I have divided it along the axis of Prince Albert Road–Parkway–Camden Road.

Camden 1:
Kentish Town, Primrose Hill, South Hampstead, Gospel Oak, Hampstead and South Highgate
North of Prince Albert Road–Parkway–Camden Road

AMBEDKAR, Dr Bhimrao Ramji (1893–1956), Indian, politician
10 King Henry's Road, NW3. *Private*
Educated in New York and at the London School of Economics (he stayed in this house while completing his London education), Dr Ambedkar became a member of the Bombay Legislative Assembly and, as the leader of sixty million 'untouchables', was a lifelong campaigner against the Indian caste system. Appointed law minister at independence in 1947, he was the main author of the Indian constitution. The plaque errs in his birth year: he was born in 1893, not 1891.

ANDERSON, Lindsay (1923–94), English, film director
Stirling Mansions, 12 Canfield Road, NW6. *British Film Institute*
One of the founders of the influential Free Cinema movement in the 1950s, he worked particularly with the dramatist David Storey and filmed several of his works, notably including *This Sporting Life* (1963). He also wrote the definitive biography of John Ford. He lived here from 1977 until his death.

ASQUITH, Herbert Henry (1852–1928), English, Prime Minister
27 Maresfield Gardens, NW3. *Hampstead Plaque Fund*

Asquith lived here. During his tenure as Prime Minister (1908–16), the foundations of the modern welfare state were laid with the introduction of old-age pensions, medical inspection of children, health insurance, workmen's compensation and labour exchanges. He was created an earl in 1925. (See also Westminster 2.)

BAILLIE, Joanna (1762–1851), Scottish, poet, dramatist
Bolton House, Windmill Hill, NW3. *Royal Society of Arts*
Baillie lived here for almost fifty years. Her works were championed by Sir Walter Scott, who called her 'the Immortal Joanna'. In her time this house was a considerable salon, visited by all the notable literary figures of the day.

BARNETT, Dame Henrietta (1851–1936), English, reformer
Heath End House, Spaniards Road, NW3. *Greater London Council*
Dame Henrietta, who lived here with her husband (see page 99), was a campaigner on a

98

range of issues, raising a considerable sum to preserve Hampstead Heath from development, and founding the Hampstead Garden Suburb Trust, which launched the new development in 1907.

BARNETT, Canon Samuel (1844–1913), English, reformer, churchman
Heath End House, Spaniards Road, NW3.
Greater London Council
Barnett was the founder, in 1884, of Toynbee Hall, the original 'settlement' from which a worldwide movement sprang. His watchword, inscribed on his tomb in Westminster Abbey, is from Browning (q.v.): 'Fear not to sow because of the birds.'

BARRATT, Thomas J. (1841–1914), English, businessman, historian
East Heath Road, NW3. *Hampstead Borough Council*
Barratt was a deputy-lieutenant of the City of London and chairman of Pears, the soap manufacturers. His three-volume *Annals of Hampstead* was published in 1912.

BARRETT, Wilson (1846–1904), English, actor
Mansion Gardens, West Heath Road, Hampstead, NW3. *Hampstead Plaque Fund*
Barrett, who lived in a house called The Grange on this site, was an actor-manager with a strong suit in melodrama. His greatest success was *The Silver King* by Henry Arthur Jones, which he played for three hundred consecutive nights in 1882. By the 1890s, however, melodrama was passé, and his star waned.

BAYES, Gilbert (1872–1953), English, sculptor
4 Greville Place, NW6. *English Heritage*
Bayes lived here from 1931 until his death. He was particularly good at sculpture applied to buildings; his most familiar work is probably the *Queen of Time* (1931), the richly decorated bronze group over the entrance to Selfridges. Also worth mentioning are his frieze on the Odeon, Covent Garden (1931), and his panel *Play Up and Play the Game* (1934) at Lord's cricket ground. He was president of the Royal British Society of Sculptors from 1938 to 1945

BEATON, Sir Cecil (1904–80), English, photographer, designer
21 Langland Gardens, NW3.
Heath and Old Hampstead Society
Beaton, who was born and lived here till 1911, is primarily noted for elegant society and fashion portraiture, but his work as a stage and film designer, of both sets and costume, included his greatest success, *My Fair Lady*, on stage in London (1956), and on film in Hollywood (1963), for which he won two Oscars.

BEERBOHM TREE, Sir Herbert (1853–1917), English, actor-manager
Mansion Gardens, West Heath Road, Hampstead, NW3. *Hampstead Plaque Fund*
Beerbohm Tree, who lived in a house called The Grange on this site, was a noted Shakespearian and character actor. As actor-manager, he built and managed His Majesty's Theatre and was a founder of the Royal Academy of Dramatic Art. (See also Kensington & Chelsea 2.)

BESANT, Sir Walter (1836–1901), English, novelist, historian, reformer
106 Frognal, Hampstead, NW3. *Private*
18 Frognal Gardens, NW3.
London County Council
His novels, the early ones written in collaboration with James Rice, described conditions in London slums but are largely forgotten. His memory is sustained by his many books on London's history and topography, and by his activities as a social reformer. He lived at both addresses, barely a hundred yards apart.

BETJEMAN, Sir John (1906–84), English, poet, conservationist
31 Highgate West Hill, N6. *English Heritage*
Betjeman lived here as a child from 1908 to 1917 and evoked the memory in his poetic autobiography, *Summoned by Bells* (1960). He was a founder member of the Victorian Society in 1958. A passionate conservationist, he led the successful fight to save the St Pancras Hotel but lost the battle to save the Euston Arch. Made Poet Laureate in 1972, he reached a wide public with a number of charming and eccentric television documentaries. (See also City.)

BEVAN, Robert Polhill (1865–1925), English, artist
14 Adamson Road, NW3. *English Heritage*
Founder of the Camden Town Group with Walter Sickert (q.v.) and Philip Wilson Steer (q.v.), Bevan brought Impressionist techniques to English art. He is noted for his horse paintings and for local street scenes. This house, where he lived from 1900 until his death, was a focal point for young artists, including Wyndham Lewis (q.v.).

BLAKE, William (1757–1827), English, poet, artist
Old Wyldes, Wildwood Terrace, NW3.
Greater London Council
John Linnell (see page 108), with whom Blake shares this plaque, moved here in 1824, and Blake was a constant visitor over the last three years of his life, playing with the Linnell children. Linnell was his main support in these years and arranged his funeral in Bunhill Fields. (See also Lambeth and Westminster 3.)

BLISS, Sir Arthur (1891–1975), English, composer
East Heath Lodge, 1 East Heath Road, NW3.
English Heritage
Sir Arthur, who lived here from 1929 to 1939, wrote over 150 compositions across all genres: symphonies, ballets, operas, concertos, film scores. As the BBC's Director of Music from 1942 to 1944, he was part of the process that led to the creation of Radio 3. He was made Master of the Queen's Musick in 1953 and created a Companion of Honour in 1971.

BOMBERG, David (1890–1957), English, painter
10 Fordwych Road, Cricklewood, NW2.
English Heritage
Bomberg, who lived and worked here from 1928 to 1934, studied under Sickert (q.v.) at the Westminster School of Art (1908–10) and under Henry Tonks at the Slade (1911–13). His early belief in the aesthetics of the machine age was shaken by his First World War experiences and thereafter he turned to a more expressionist style.

BOULT, Sir Adrian (1889–1983), English, conductor
78 Marlborough Mansions, Cannon Hill, NW6.
English Heritage
Sir Adrian, who lived at Flat 78 here from 1966 to 1977, was conductor of the BBC Symphony Orchestra from 1930 to 1950, and of the London Philharmonic from 1950 to 1957. He was a champion of twentieth-century English music, and among his vast discography are the complete Vaughan Williams symphonies, recorded with the composer present. He was made a Companion of Honour in 1969.

BOWLER, Clifford Norman (1899–1993), English, watchmaker
Mill Lane, West Hampstead, NW6. *Private*
The plaque records that Bowler traded in Mill Lane for over sixty-seven years as a jeweller and watchmaker. This is an example of a plaque put up out of simple affection for the person honoured, rather than his celebrity. See, for instance, Elisabeth Hagedorn, also in NW6, Maggie Richardson in NW3 and 'Miss Rose' in SW3.

BRAILSFORD, H. N. (1873–1958), English, journalist
27 Belsize Park Gardens, NW3.
Greater London Council
Brailsford, who lived here, is described on the plaque as a 'Champion of Equal and Free Humanity'. A lifelong committed socialist, he edited *The New Leader* (1922–6) and wrote for several newspapers, including *The Guardian* and the *Daily Herald*. He was one of the few writers associated with the Left Book Club of the 1930s to attack the Soviet show trials.

BRAIN, Dennis (1921–57), English, horn player
37 Frognal Gardens, NW3. *English Heritage*
Brain, who lived here, had many works written for him by, among others, Britten (q.v.), Arnold and Berkeley (q.v.). His recording of Mozart's Horn Concertos, with von Karajan and the Philharmonia, is still thought definitive. He memorably played a hosepipe at one of the legendary Hoffnung concerts. He liked driving fast cars fast, and that led to his death at the age of thirty-six.

BROWN, Ford Madox (1821–93), English, artist
56 Fortess Road, Kentish Town, NW5.
Greater London Council
Brown, who lived here, was associated with the Pre-Raphaelites, but never a member of the Brotherhood. He was a painter of moral and historical subjects, his most important creations being *Work* (1852–63), *The Last of England* (1855) and the murals in Manchester Town Hall (1878–93).

BUSS, Frances Mary (1827–94), English, educationalist

Camden School for Girls, Sandall Road, NW5. *English Heritage*

Buss founded the Camden School for Girls, to offer education to girls whose families could not afford private education, and was its first headmistress (1879–94). She was a lifelong suffragette, co-founding the Kensington Society in 1865 with Emily Davies (q.v.), Elizabeth Garrett Anderson (q.v.) and others – from which came the London Suffrage Committee, the earliest body to campaign for votes for women.

BUTT, Dame Clara (1873–1936), English, contralto

7 Harley Road, NW3. *Greater London Council*

Dame Clara lived here from 1901 to 1929. A concert contralto, with a striking presence at 6 feet 2 inches tall, she toured widely, gave many Royal Command performances and was made a dame for her charity concerts during the First World War. Sir Thomas Beecham (q.v.) said of her: 'On a clear day, you could have heard her across the English Channel.'

CHARLES, Elizabeth Rundle (1828–96), English, novelist

Coombe Edge, Oak Hill Way, NW3. *Rundle Charles Memorial Fund*

Mrs Charles, who lived here from 1874 until her death, wrote her most famous book, *The Chronicles of the Schönberg-Cotta Family*, in 1862. It remains the object of a devoted cult. 'The design of the author is so to reproduce the times of the Reformation as to place them more vividly and impressively before the mind of the reader than has been done by ordinary historical narratives.'

CLOCK TOWER

Heath Street, Hampstead, NW3.

Hampstead Plaque Fund

This well-known local landmark, at the corner with Holly Hill, began life as the local fire station, with a lookout being posted in the tower. It was built by the Metropolitan Board of Works in 1873, designed by George Vulliamy, though Pevsner (q.v.) says 'probably by Robert Pearsall'. It was a fire station till 1915 and is now flats.

COLE, Sir Henry (1808–82), English, civil servant, reformer

3 Elm Row, Hampstead, NW3.

Hampstead Plaque Fund

Sir Henry, who lived here in 1879–80, published the first Christmas card in 1843, with artwork by John Calcott Horsley. As 'Felix Summerly' he wrote several children's books. He ran the Great Exhibition in Hyde Park in 1851 and was founder and first director of the Victoria and Albert Museum. (See also Kensington & Chelsea 2.)

COLERIDGE, Samuel Taylor (1772–1834), English, poet, critic

3 The Grove, Highgate, N6.

St Pancras Borough Council

Coleridge lived here from 1823 until his death. A friend of Wordsworth and Charles Lamb (q.v.), he is a major figure in English Romanticism, best known for 'The Rime of the Ancient Mariner' (1798) and 'Kubla Khan' (1816), the writing of which was famously cut short by the arrival of 'a man from Porlock'. He was an opium addict in later life. (See also Westminster 2 and Hammersmith & Fulham.)

CONSTABLE, John (1776–1837), English, painter

2 Lower Terrace, Hampstead, NW3.

Hampstead Plaque Fund

Mansion Gardens, West Heath Road, Hampstead, NW3.

Hampstead Plaque Fund

40 Well Walk, Hampstead, NW3.

London County Council

Constable is widely considered to be England's finest romantic landscape painter, especially of his native area around Dedham Vale in Essex, now inevitably called 'Constable Country'. Among his best-loved works are

The Haywain (1821) and *Flatford Mill* (1825). The three plaques record his various homes in Hampstead between 1819 and his death. He is buried in the parish churchyard.

COOK, Don
Kennistoun House, Leighton Road, Kentish Town, NW5. *Private*
Cook was the leader of the famous St Pancras Rent Strike of the late 1950s; residents in Kennistoun House lived for several weeks behind barricades in protest against proposed swingeing rate rises for council flats (typically from £1 15s to £2 14s 3d per week). Under the eyes of the media, the bailiffs forced entry in September 1960 and Cook's family, along with two others, were finally evicted.

CORY, William Johnson (1823–92), English, poet, educator
8 Pilgrim's Lane, Hampstead, NW3.
Hampstead Plaque Fund
Cory, who lived here, was a brilliant teacher, and composer of 'The Eton Boating Song'. Recalled with affection by at least three Prime Ministers – Rosebery, Balfour and Asquith – he was unfortunately forced to resign from Eton in 1872 under suspicion of improper relations with boys.

CROSFIELD, Sir Arthur
(1865–1938), English, soap magnate, politician
Kenwood House, Hampstead, NW3.
Private
Sir Arthur bought Witanhurst, the largest private house in London, in 1913 and refurbished it lavishly for his socialite wife. He was a Liberal MP and chairman of the National Playing Fields Association. The plaque was designed and executed by Richard Kindersley.

CRUIKSHANK, George (1792–1878), English, cartoonist, illustrator
263 Hampstead Road, NW1. *Royal Society of Arts*
Cruikshank, who lived here from 1850, made his name as a political satirist. He was once offered a bribe of £100 not to show George III in any compromising

situation. He is also known for his illustrations to Dickens's (q.v.) *Sketches by Boz* and *Oliver Twist*, and Daniel Defoe's (q.v.) *Robinson Crusoe*. In later life he was a fervent supporter of the Temperance Movement, perhaps because his father, Isaac, also a caricaturist, died of alcoholism. (See also Islington.)

DALE, Sir Henry (1875–1968), English, physician
Mount Vernon House, Mount Vernon, NW3.
Greater London Council
Sir Henry, who lived here, was the director of the National Institute for Medical Research (1928–42). He was chairman of the Wellcome Trust (1938–60). He shared the Nobel Prize for Medicine in 1936 for work on the chemical transmission of nervous effects. He was awarded the Order of Merit in 1944.

DE GAULLE, Charles (1890–1970), French, soldier, President
99 Frognal, Hampstead, NW3.
Hampstead Plaque Fund

Leader of the Free French in the Second World War, when he lived here, De Gaulle was often a thorn in Churchill's (q.v.) side. He was once advised by Clementine Churchill, who admired him: 'General, you must not hate your friends more than you hate your enemies.' (See also Westminster 4.)

DE LASZLO, Philip (1869–1937), Hungarian, painter
3 Fitzjohn's Avenue, Hampstead, NW3. *Private*
De Laszlo, who lived and worked here, painted portraits of many society figures and European and British royalty, including Edward VII, the Queen Mother and the future Queen Elizabeth II, aged seven. He was president of the Royal Society of British Artists from 1930.

DELIUS, Frederick (1862–1934), English, composer
44 Belsize Park Gardens, NW3. *English Heritage*
From 1890 Delius lived mainly in France, but at this address when in London. His output included six operas, concertos and orchestral pieces. His works were especially championed by Sir Thomas Beecham (q.v.). Blind for the last ten years of his life, he continued to compose with the help of his friend Eric Fenby (1906–97).

DEVANT, David (1868–1941), English, magician
1 Ornan Court, Ornan Road, NW3.
English Heritage
Born David Wighton, Devant formed a partnership with Nevil Maskelyne in 1904 and for the next ten years their 'House of Magic' at St George's Hall was described as 'the headquarters of the conjurer's art'. He was three times selected for Royal Command performances and noted for the humorous patter running through his tricks.

DU MAURIER, George (1834–96), French, novelist, illustrator
28 Hampstead Grove, Hampstead, NW3.
Private, adopted by the LCC
Du Maurier came to England from his native Paris in 1851 and made his name as a satirical illustrator, especially in *Punch* (1864–96). He is, however, remembered today for the best of his three novels, *Trilby* (1894), which continues to exercise the public's imagination. He lived here from 1874 to 1895. (See also Camden 2.)

DU MAURIER, Sir Gerald (1873–1934), English, actor-manager
Cannon Hall, Cannon Place, Hampstead, NW3.
Greater London Council
Son of George du Maurier (see above), he made his reputation on stage in criminal roles, becoming joint manager of Wyndham's Theatre (1910–25), and later manager of the St James's Theatre (1926–34). He was knighted in 1922.

DU PRÉ, Jacqueline (1945–87), English, cellist
5a Pilgrim's Lane, NW3.
Heath and Old Hampstead Society

Du Pré, who lived here from 1970 to 1975, started her concert career aged sixteen, having studied under Casals and Rostropovich. While married to the pianist and conductor Daniel Barenboim, she contracted multiple sclerosis and spent the last fourteen years of her life teaching from a wheelchair, universally lamented as the great lost talent of post-war British music. (See also Croydon, Westminster 2 and Westminster 4.)

EDWARDS, John Passmore (1823–1911), English, philanthropist, journalist
51 Netherhall Gardens, Hampstead, NW3.
English Heritage
As a journalist, Edwards, who lived here, worked for progressive causes from the Anti-Corn Law movement onwards. He is particularly remembered for founding some seventy free public libraries, as well as hospitals and convalescent homes, an art gallery in Newlyn and University Hall in Clare Market. He declined a knighthood.

ELGAR, Sir Edward (1857–1934), English, composer
42 Netherhall Gardens, NW3. *Elgar Plaque Fund*
Sir Edward, who lived in a house on this site from 1911 to 1921, won international acclaim with his *Enigma Variations* (1899) and *The Dream of Gerontius* (1900). His many other works include two symphonies, the much-loved Cello Concerto and the *Pomp and Circumstance* marches. He was made Master of the King's Musick in 1924. (See also Hammersmith & Fulham and Westminster 1.)

ENGELS, Friedrich (1820–95), German, political theorist
121 Regent's Park Road, Primrose Hill, NW1.
Greater London Council
Engels, who lived here from 1870 to 1894, wrote *The Communist Manifesto* (1848) together with Karl Marx (q.v.), and after Marx's death in 1883 he continued editing and translating his work, including *Das Kapital*. His own *Condition of the Working Class in England* (1845) was very influential.

FARMAN, Noel Bertram,
English, physician
60 Haverstock Hill,
NW3. *Private*
The plaque records that
Dr Farman practised
here from 1930 to 1970
and was greatly loved by all
his many patients. This appears
to be another plaque based on
personal affection, rather than renown or celebrity.

FENTON, Roger (1819–69), English, photographer
2 Albert Terrace, Primrose Hill, NW1.
English Heritage
Fenton, who lived here, is known as 'the Father of War
Photography' for his images from the Crimea in 1855,
including *The Valley of the Shadow of Death*, a post-battle
view of the location of the Charge of the Light Brigade,
strewn with cannonballs, which is included in the
famous anthology *100 Images that Changed the World.*

FERRIER, Kathleen (1912–53), English, contralto
97 Frognal, Hampstead, NW3.
Greater London Council
Ferrier lived here from 1942 until her early death.
She did not train until after winning an amateur
competition in 1937. On account of her sublime voice
and personality, she was a much-loved performer,
noted specially for her role in Gluck's *Orfeo.*

FIELDS, Dame Gracie
(1898–1979), English,
popular singer
20 Frognal Way,
Hampstead, NW3.
Heath and Old Hampstead Society
Dame Gracie had this house built for her in 1934 in a
vaguely Hollywood-Spanish style. The best-known
product of Rochdale apart from the Co-op movement,
she appeared in no less than ten Royal Variety Shows
and had huge hits on stage and film with her comic
personality and songs like 'The Biggest Aspidistra in
the World' (1928) and 'Sally' (1931). She retired to
Capri. (See also Hackney.)

FISHER, Sir Ronald Aylmer (1890–1962),
English, statistician, geneticist
Inverforth House, North End Way, NW3.
English Heritage

Sir Ronald lived here as a boy from 1896 to 1904.
He was, according to Anders Hald, 'a genius who
almost single-handedly created the foundations for
modern statistical science'. Among his ground-
breaking works are *The Correlation between Relatives on
the Supposition of Mendelian Inheritance* (1918) and
The Genetical Theory of Natural Selection (1930). In
later years he apparently became the archetype of the
absent-minded professor.

FREUD, Anna (1895–1982), Austrian, psychoanalyst
20 Maresfield Gardens, NW3. *English Heritage*
The sixth of Sigmund Freud's children, Anna came to
London with him in 1938 to escape the Nazi
persecution of the Jews. In 1923 she had opened her
own psychoanalysis practice, specialising in work with

children. Her 1936 work *The Ego and the Mechanisms of
Defence* established her as a pioneering theoretician of
analysis in her own right. She and her father (see
below) are accorded separate plaques on the same
frontage.

FREUD, Sigmund (1856–1939), Austrian,
psychoanalyst
20 Maresfield Gardens, NW3. *English Heritage*
Coming here in 1938 to escape Nazi persecution,
Freud was already seriously ill and lived only a year in
London. Recognised as 'the Father of Psychoanalysis',
he published numerous ground-breaking works,
introducing ideas such as the existence of the
unconscious mind, amongst which are *The
Interpretation of Dreams* (1899), *The Psychopathology of
Everyday Life* (1901) and *Totem and Taboo* (1913).

GAITSKELL, Hugh (1906–63), English, politician
18 Frognal Gardens, Hampstead, NW3.
Greater London Council
Gaitskell, who lived here, first entered Parliament in
1945, was Minister of Fuel and Power (1947) and
Chancellor of the Exchequer (1950–1). He took over
the leadership of the Labour Party from Clement
Attlee (q.v.) in 1955 and would most likely have won
the 1964 election and become Prime Minister but for
his sudden premature death, which has been the
subject of conspiracy theories ever since.

GALSWORTHY, John (1867–1933), English,
novelist, playwright
Grove Lodge, Admiral's Walk, NW3.
London County Council
Galsworthy lived here from 1918 until his death. He is
best remembered for *The Forsyte Saga*, a trilogy of
novels with two 'interludes', which he completed here
in 1922. It concerns an upper-middle-class 'new
money' family; while sympathetic to his characters, he
was plain about their insularity and snobbery. He was
awarded the Nobel Prize for Literature in 1932. After
his death his popularity waned, but the television
adaptation of *The Forsyte Saga* in 1967 brought a
massive revival of interest. (See also Westminster 4.)

GERTLER, Mark (1891–1939), English, painter
**Penn Studio, 13a Rudall Crescent, Hampstead,
NW3.** *Hampstead Plaque Fund*
**1 Well Mount Studios, Well Mount,
Hampstead, NW3.** *Hampstead Plaque Fund*
Gertler, who lived at the first address from 1915 to
1932 and briefly at the second, was the model for the
sinister sculptor Loerke in D. H. Lawrence's *Women in
Love*, and for Gombauld in Aldous Huxley's *Chrome
Yellow*. Patronised by Lady Ottoline Morrell (q.v.), he
had early success as a portrait painter, but his unstable
temperament alienated potential sitters and he was
always struggling with poverty. In 1930 he married
Marjorie Hodgkinson; the marriage was troubled from
the start and his melancholic temperament, coupled
with tuberculosis and worries about his work, led him
to suicide in 1939. (See also Tower Hamlets.)

GILLIES, Sir Harold (1882–1960), New Zealander,
plastic surgeon
71 Frognal, Hampstead, NW3. *English Heritage*
Gillies, 'the Father of Plastic Surgery', lived here. He
founded the Queen's Hospital at Sidcup in the First

World War specifically
to deal with facial
reconstruction.
The hospital
performed eleven
thousand operations
on five thousand
patients. His cousin
Archibald McIndoe
(q.v.) joined his
practice in 1930 and went on to do similar pioneering
work with Royal Air Force burns victims in the Second
World War.

GREEN, Anthony (b.1939), English, artist
Lissenden Mansions, Lissenden Gardens, NW5.
Lissenden Gardens Tenants Association
Green, who lived here in the early 1960s, is a realist
artist whose work invariably depicts his own domestic
family life. Elected a Royal Academician in 1977, he is
now a trustee of the Academy and lives and works in
Cambridgeshire.

GREENAWAY, Kate (1846–1901), English, artist,
illustrator
39 Frognal, Hampstead, NW3.
London County Council
Greenaway was so successful as an artist and illustrator
of children's books that she was able to commission
Richard Norman Shaw (q.v.) to design this house for
her in 1884. One of her most successful publications was
Mother Goose (1881). At the same time she exhibited
regularly at the Royal Academy and garnered praise
from no less than John Ruskin (q.v.). There is an
annual Kate Greenaway Prize for the best children's
book illustrator. (See also Islington and Hackney.)

**HAGEDORN,
Elisabeth**
(1892–1945),
English, mother
**15 Ravenshaw
Street, West
Hampstead, NW6.**
Private
This heart-shaped
plaque was erected
by Mrs Hagedorn's two daughters, who considered
her an exceptional mother, well worth a memorial on
the house where she had brought them up.

HALL, Newman (1816–1902), English, churchman
8 Hampstead Square, NW3. *Private*
Hall was a liberal Congregationalist, one of the most active and vocal British supporters of the North in the American Civil War. His tract *Come to Jesus* (1846) sold four million copies in forty languages. He lived at Vine House nearby at the time of his death. The plaque refers to homes for the aged here, given in his memory by his widow.

HAMMOND, Barbara (1873–1961), English, historian
Hollycot, Vale of Health, Hampstead, NW3.
Greater London Council
Barbara (née Bradby) married J. L. Hammond (see below) in 1901 and they collaborated on a number of works of social history, in particular revealing the harsh conditions endured by the working classes at the onset of the Industrial Revolution. They lived here from 1906 to 1913.

HAMMOND, J. L. (1872–1949), English, historian
Hollycot, Vale of Health, Hampstead, NW3.
Greater London Council
Among the works written in collaboration with his wife, Barbara (see above), were *The Village Labourer* (1911), *The Town Labourer* (1917), *The Skilled Labourer* (1919), *The Age of the Chartists* (1930) and *The Bleak Age* (1934). He also edited the liberal paper *The Speaker* from 1899 to 1906.

HANLEY, James (1897–1985), English, novelist, playwright
46–55 Lissenden Gardens, NW5.
Lissenden Gardens Tenants Association
Hanley, who lived here from 1963, never had much commercial success, perhaps because of his generally bleak subject matter, but was critically acclaimed on both sides of the Atlantic by William Faulkner, Henry Miller and John Cooper Powys. His second novel, *Boy* (1931), was suppressed after an obscenity trial and was not published in full until 1990, five years after his death.

HARMSWORTH, Alfred (1865–1922), Irish, newspaper magnate
32 Pandora Road, West Hampstead, NW6.
Greater London Council
Harmsworth lived here for a time early in his career. A pioneer of tabloid journalism, he founded the *Daily Mail* (1896) and the *Daily Mirror* (1903),

rescued *The Observer* (1905) and took over *The Times* and the *Sunday Times* (1908). He was made Viscount Northcliffe in 1918 and shortly afterwards a nervous breakdown, with a strong trace of megalomania, led to his death.

HEARTFIELD, John (1891–1968), German, montage artist
47 Downshire Hill, NW3.
English Heritage
Born Helmut Herzfeld, he anglicised his name in 1916 out of disgust for the rabid anti-English nationalism in Germany. A key figure in the Dada movement, associated with Georg Grosz and Brecht, he developed photomontage as an artistic form of political expression. One of his most famous works, *Hurrah, die Butter ist Alle!* ('Hooray, the Butter is Finished!') (1935), showed a German family, surrounded by swastikas, trying to eat pieces of metal.

HILL, Sir Rowland (1795–1879), English, reformer
Royal Free Hospital, Pond Street, NW3.
Royal Society of Arts
Sir Rowland lived in a house on this site for the last thirty years of his life. He conceived the idea of postage stamps and introduced the first in 1840, the famous Penny Black. He went on to introduce successive developments in the postal service. He was also an educational reformer, founding and designing a school with a science laboratory, a swimming pool and forced air heating. (See also Westminster 2 and Camden 2.)

HOARE, John Gurney (1810–75), English, banker
Inverforth House, North End Way, NW3.
Hampstead Plaque Fund
Hoare was born in a house near this spot. He was a leading member of the Commons Preservation Society and set up a Hampstead Heath Protection Fund to cover the legal costs of the battle with Sir Thomas Maryon Wilson, lord of the manor and owner of the Heath, who in 1829 tried to push through an Act of Parliament allowing him to build on the Heath. The struggle lasted till Sir Thomas's death in 1869, after which his heir was more amenable and sold the land to the City of London in 1871.

HOPKINS, Gerard Manley
(1844–89),
English, poet
9 Oak Hill Park, Hampstead, NW3.
Hampstead Plaque Fund
Hopkins lived at Oak Hill Park from 1852 to 1863. He was ordained a Catholic priest in 1877. Virtually none of his writings was published in his lifetime, but his friend Robert Bridges brought out a collected edition in 1918, and his reputation has continued to grow. The plaque quotes one of his famous lines: 'The world is charged with the grandeur of God.' 'Inscape', 'instress' and 'sprung rhythm' were concepts he introduced, which have proved much to be discussed ever since. (See also Wandsworth and Newham.)

HUNT, Leigh (1784–1859), English, poet, essayist
Vale of Health, NW3. *Private*
Hunt lived in a cottage on this site from 1816 to 1821. In 1813 he and his brother had been fined £500 and sentenced to two years in jail for a libel on the Prince Regent. When he emerged, he continued editing his journal, the *Examiner*, in which he published early work by Keats (q.v.). His aim as a critic was 'to reap pleasure from every object in creation'. (See also Merton, Enfield, Kensington & Chelsea 2 and Hammersmith & Fulham.)

HUXLEY, Aldous (1894–1963), English, novelist
16 Bracknell Gardens, Hampstead, NW3.
English Heritage
Huxley lived here as a boy with his father, Leonard, and brother, Julian (see below). His novels include *Antic Hay* (1923), *Point Counter Point* (1928) and *Brave New World* (1932). In later life, living in California, he became interested in psychedelic drugs and wrote an account of a 'trip', *The Doors of Perception* (1954), which was required reading in the 1960s.

HUXLEY, Julian (1887–1975), English, biologist, zoologist
16 Bracknell Gardens, Hampstead, NW3.
English Heritage
31 Pond Street, Hampstead, NW3. *Private*
Huxley lived at the first address as a boy, and at the second from 1943 until his death. He was Professor of Zoology at King's College, London (1925–7),

Secretary of the Zoological Society (1935–42) and first Director-General of UNESCO (1946–8). A great populariser, he was a regular on the radio *Brains Trust* and BBC Television's *Animal, Vegetable, Mineral?*

HUXLEY, Leonard (1860–1933), English, teacher, editor
16 Bracknell Gardens, Hampstead, NW3.
English Heritage
Leonard was the son of Thomas Huxley (q.v.) and father of Aldous and Julian (see above). After teaching at Charterhouse (1884–1901), he joined the *Cornhill Magazine* as assistant editor, later editor (1901–33).

HYNDMAN, Henry Mayers (1842–1921), English, politician
13 Well Walk, NW3. *Greater London Council*
An apostle of Karl Marx, Hyndman, who lived and died here, attempted to explain Marxism in *England for All* (1881) and founded the Social Democratic Federation in the same year. His unfortunate authoritarian style drove away early members such as William Morris (q.v.) and Eleanor Marx (q.v.), but his thinking was nevertheless an important tributary to the eventual formation of the Labour Party. (See also Islington.)

JENNINGS, Humphrey (1907–50), English, documentary film maker
8 Regent's Park Terrace, NW1. *English Heritage*
A co-founder of Mass Observation, Jennings was also involved with British surrealism in the 1930s. He worked for the Crown Film Unit (q.v.) in the Second World War, famously making *Listen to Britain* and *A Diary for Timothy*. According to Lindsay Anderson (q.v.), Jennings was 'the only real poet that British cinema has yet produced'. He lived here from 1944 until his death.

KARSAVINA, Tamara (1885–1978), Russian, ballerina
108 Frognal, Hampstead, NW3. *English Heritage*
An original member of Sergei Diaghilev's company, Karsavina came to London in 1918 with her English husband and lived here. She taught and wrote about

ballet, helping to found the Royal Academy of Dance in 1920. Among her pupils were Alicia Markova and Margot Fonteyn (q.v.).

KEATS, John (1795–1821), English, poet
Keats Grove, NW3. *Royal Society of Arts*
While living here, in 1818–20, Keats fell deeply in love with Fanny Brawne and became engaged to her. He also had what is known as his 'Great Year', starting in September 1818, in which the bulk of his most memorable works were written, including 'The Eve of St Agnes', '*La Belle Dame sans Merci*' and 'Ode to a Nightingale'. In 1819–20 his tuberculosis progressively worsened and he was invited to Italy by Shelley, where he died in February 1821. (See also Enfield and City.)

KNOX, E. V. (1881–1971), English, poet, humorist
110 Frognal, Hampstead, NW3. *Private*
Knox joined *Punch* in 1921 and was particularly noted for his ability to produce a topical poem in a pastiche of the style of any well-known contemporary poet, such as Masefield (q.v.) or de la Mare (q.v.). He published numerous collections of his *Punch* pieces. He lived here from 1945 until his death.

LAWRENCE, D. H. (1885–1930), English, novelist
1 Byron Villas, Vale of Health, Hampstead, NW3. *Greater London Council*
Noted for his unvarnished treatment of sex, Lawrence was routinely in conflict with the obscenity laws. His first success was *Sons and Lovers* (1913), followed by *Women in Love* (1921) and *Lady Chatterley's Lover* (1928), the last not published in Britain unexpurgated until 1960. He lived here briefly in 1915.

LEVER, William, first Viscount Leverhulme (1851–1925), English, soap magnate, philanthropist
Inverforth House, North End Way, NW3.
English Heritage
Lord Leverhulme, who lived and died here, entered his father's grocery business in Bolton in 1867, began trading on his own account in 1884 and started his soap-making business in 1885. Using vegetable rather than mineral oil, he developed the 'Sunlight' brand. He founded the community of Port Sunlight on the Mersey as a site for his works and a garden village for his workforce, endowing it with many facilities, including an art gallery.

LEWIS, John (*c.*1836–1928), English, department store owner
Grange Gardens, Templewood Avenue, NW3.
Hampstead Plaque Fund
John Lewis, who lived at Spedan Tower near this site from 1888 until his death, was the youngest silk buyer in London, working for Peter Robinson at Oxford Circus. He set up his own first shop in Oxford Street in 1864, and acquired Peter Jones in Sloane Square in 1905. He handed over to his son (see below) in 1914.

LEWIS, John Spedan (1885–1963), English, department store owner
Grange Gardens, Templewood Avenue, NW3.
Hampstead Plaque Fund
Running the Peter Jones store from 1914, and the whole empire on his father's death in 1928, he gradually converted the business into an employee-owned partnership, completing the process in 1950. After retiring in 1955, he was known as 'the Founder'.

LINNELL, John (1792–1882), English, painter
Old Wyldes, Wildwood Terrace, NW3.
Greater London Council
Disliked by many fellow artists because of rumours of sharp practice in his dealings, Linnell, who lived here, was constantly rejected for election to the Royal Academy and, when at last offered it in old age, turned it down. One admirable thing in his life was his support for William Blake (see page 100), who stayed here in the last years of his life.

MacDONALD, Ramsay (1866–1937), Scottish, Prime Minister
9 Howitt Road, Hampstead, NW3.
London County Council
103 Frognal, Hampstead, NW3.
Hampstead Plaque Fund
MacDonald, who lived at the first address from 1916 to 1925 and the second from 1925 to 1937, was leader of the Labour Party from 1911 to 1914 and 1922 to 1931. He was the first Labour Prime Minister (January to October 1924, and 1929–35). His second premiership was a coalition with the Conservatives from 1931 onwards, a betrayal for which he was expelled from the party,

and his name has been mud among traditional Labour supporters ever since.

MANSFIELD, Katherine (1888–1923), New Zealander, writer
17 East Heath Road, Hampstead, NW3.
Greater London Council
Mansfield lived here with her husband, John Middleton Murry (see page 110). The couple were the inspiration for the two central characters in D. H. Lawrence's (q.v.) *Women in Love*. Mansfield published three collections of stories, *In a German Pension* (1911), *Bliss and Other Stories* (1920) and *The Garden Party and Other Stories* (1922).

MARVELL, Andrew (1621–78), English, poet, politician
Outside wall of Waterlow Park, High Street, Highgate, N6. *London County Council*
Marvell lived in a cottage on this spot. In his day he was known as a wit, a liberal politician and an opponent of tyranny, but practically unknown as a poet. Charles Lamb (q.v.) began the revival of his reputation, but it was not until T. S. Eliot (q.v.) wrote an article about him in *The Times Literary Supplement* in 1921 that his poetry was rediscovered and poems such as 'To His Coy Mistress' joined the national treasury.

MARX, Karl (1818–83), German, political theorist
101–108 Maitland Park Road, Hampstead, NW3.
Camden Borough Council
Marx lived and died in a house on this site from 1875 to 1883. 'The Father of Communism' came to London in 1849, a year after publishing *The Communist Manifesto*, co-written with Engels (q.v.). He produced volume 1 of *Das Kapital* in 1867, volumes 2 and 3 being edited and published posthumously by Engels and Marx's daughter, Eleanor (q.v.). (See also Westminster 3.)

MASARYK, Tomás Garrigue (1850–1937), Czech, President
21 Platts Lane, Hampstead, NW3.
Czechoslovak Colony
Masaryk fled his native land when the First World War broke out and came to London. Living here, he was on the staff of the new School of Slavonic and Eastern European Studies and supplied useful intelligence to the Allies. Subsequently, from 1918 to 1935, he was the first president of an independent Czechoslovakia.

MATTHAY, Tobias (1858–1945), English, piano teacher
21 Arkwright Road, Hampstead, NW3.
Greater London Council
Matthay, who lived here, was Professor of Advanced Piano at the Royal Academy of Music from 1876 to 1925. He had many famous pupils, the most distinguished being Myra Hess (q.v.). He wrote several standard books, including *The Art of Touch* (1903) and *First Principles of Pianoforte* (1908).

McCORMACK, John (1884–1945), Irish, tenor
24 Ferncroft Avenue, NW3. *English Heritage*
McCormack, who lived here from 1908 to 1913, trained in Italy and made his Covent Garden debut in 1907 in *Cavalleria Rusticana*, becoming the company's youngest principal tenor. Famous for his breath control, he turned more towards the concert stage later in his career. He was a supporter of Irish nationalism, and his recording of 'The Wearing of the Green' and the songs of Thomas Moore gave impetus to the cause. His greatest honour was to be made a papal count in 1928 by Pope Pius XI.

MILLER, Lee (1907–77), American, photographer
21 Downshire Hill, NW3. *English Heritage*
Miller lived here with Roland Penrose, who shares the plaque with her, from 1937 to 1949. After being the most sought-after model in New York, she came to Europe in 1929 and became the muse and lover of the photographer Man Ray. Many of the photographs credited to him were in fact taken by her. Subsequently, during the Second World War, she worked as a war correspondent and photographer. She and Penrose married in 1947 when she found she was pregnant, and they shortly afterwards moved to Sussex. Her archive is curated by her son, Anthony.

MONDRIAN, Piet (1872–1944), Dutch, painter
60 Parkhill Road, Hampstead, NW3.
Greater London Council
Mondrian lived here from 1938 to 1940. A co-founder

of the De Stijl group, he evolved his own abstract painting style, which he called Neoplasticism, characterised by an irregular grid of vertical and horizontal black lines between blocks of white and the three primary colours.

MOORE, Henry (1898–1986), English, sculptor
11a Parkhill Road, NW3. *English Heritage*
Moore lived and worked here from 1929 to 1940. He moved in shortly after marrying Irina Radetsky and they formed part of a small avant-garde artistic community in the area, including Barbara Hepworth, Ben Nicholson and Naum Gabo. With Hepworth, in particular, Moore traded ideas as they both developed towards modernism. Moore left this house for Hertfordshire after it was damaged by shrapnel in 1940. (See also Hammersmith & Fulham.)

MURRY, John Middleton (1889–1957), English, literary critic
17 East Heath Road, Hampstead, NW3.
Greater London Council
Murry shares this plaque with his wife Katherine Mansfield (see page 109). Though he married three more times, he kept the Mansfield flame alive, editing two posthumous collections of her stories, and letters and reminiscences. He was also editor of various literary magazines and wrote books on Keats, Dostoevsky, Lawrence and Shakespeare.

NICHOLSON, Ben (1894–1982), English, painter
2b Pilgrim's Lane, NW3. *English Heritage*
Nicholson, who lived and died here, was a leading painter of abstracts. He won the first Guggenheim Award in 1957 and was given the Order of Merit the following year. The second of his three wives was the sculptor Barbara Hepworth.

NKRUMAH, Kwame
(1909–72), Ghanaian, prime minister, president
60 Burghley Road,
NW5. *English Heritage*
While living here, Nkrumah organised the fifth Pan-African Congress in Manchester and founded the West African National Secretariat, aiming for the complete decolonisation of Africa. Leader of the Gold Coast from 1952, he declared Ghana the first independent African former colony in 1957. Subsequently he was a founder of the Organisation of African Unity in 1963. At home, his exercise of power became more repressive, and he himself more remote from affairs, until he was deposed by a military coup in 1966.

ORWELL, George
(1903–50), English, novelist, essayist
77 Parliament Hill,
NW3.
Hampstead Plaque Fund
50 Lawford Road, NW5. *Greater London Council*
1 South End Road, NW3. *Private*
George Orwell (pen-name of Eric Arthur Blair) repudiated his privileged Etonian background and studied poverty by experience, notably in *Down and Out in Paris and London* (1933) and *The Road to Wigan Pier* (1937). He was a member of the International Brigade in the Spanish Civil War, in which he was wounded, and from which came his poignant *Homage to Catalonia* (1938). His essays remain an object lesson in the simple expression of ideas, ranging from how to make a proper cup of tea to the postcard art of Donald McGill (q.v.). His most famous books are *Animal Farm* (1945) and *1984* (1949), bleak novels about the inhumanity of the modern state. He lived at the first two addresses and worked in a bookshop at the third address. (See also Hillingdon, Islington and Kensington & Chelsea 1.)

ÖSTERBERG, Martina Bergman (1849–1915), Swedish, physical educationalist
1 Broadhurst Gardens, NW6. *English Heritage*
She qualified from the Royal Central Gymnastics Institute in Stockholm in 1877 and by 1882 was training physical education teachers in London. Realising there was a shortage, she opened a college

here, where she lived in Broadhurst Gardens. Among other things, she got rid of the corset and invented the gym slip. The college's growth led to a move in 1895 to Dartford, where it was described in 1897 as 'the most remarkable educational establishment in the world'.

PARISH LOCK-UP
11 Cannon Lane, Hampstead, NW3.
Hampstead Plaque Fund
This dark, single-cell lock-up was built about 1730 into the garden wall of Cannon Hall, where the local magistrates held court. When the police force was

formed in 1829, business transferred to the Watch House in Holly Walk (q.v.). Somehow this lock-up has survived, one of the handful left in London, and is now a listed building.

PARK, John James (1793–1833), English, lawyer, historian
18 Church Row, NW3.
Hampstead Antiquarian and Historical Society
His *Topography and Natural History of Hampstead* was first published in 1814, when he was only twenty. He went on to a career in the law, and his *Treatise on the Law of Dower* (1819), written while still a student, was the standard work for many years. He was briefly Professor of English Law at King's College, London, in 1831, before his health failed. He shares this plaque with his father (see below), who also lived here.

PARK, Thomas (1759–1834), English, historian, bibliographer
18 Church Row, NW3.
Hampstead Antiquarian and Historical Society
Trained as an engraver, Park gave up that occupation in 1797 and devoted himself to literature and antiquarian

research. He also published several volumes of verse, in which he was encouraged by Cowper. He was consulted constantly by Steevens in preparing his edition of Shakespeare, and Southey said of him: 'His knowledge of English bibliography has never been surpassed.'

PEARSON, Karl (1857–1936), English, statistician, mathematician
7 Well Road, Hampstead, NW3.
Greater London Council
Pearson, who lived here, was the founder of the world's first university statistics department in 1911 at University College, London, where he remained till 1933. A protégé and biographer of Galton (q.v.), he was also a controversial and aggressive proponent of eugenics.

PENROSE, Sir Roland (1900–84), English, surrealist
21 Downshire Hill, NW3. *English Heritage*
Penrose, who lived here with Lee Miller (see page 109) from 1938 to 1949, organised the London International Surrealist Exhibition of 1936, based on contacts made while living in Paris from 1922 to 1934, which launched British surrealism. He co-founded the Institute of Contemporary Arts with Herbert Read in 1947 and organised the first two hugely influential exhibitions there, *40 Years of Modern Art* and *40,000 Years of Modern Art*.

PETRIE, Sir Flinders (1853–1942), English, Egyptologist
5 Cannon Place, Hampstead, NW3.
London County Council
Petrie, who lived here from 1919 to 1935, was a grandson of Matthew Flinders (q.v.), from whose work he learnt early the importance of accurate surveying. Applying this to his work in Egypt, he is known as 'the Father of Modern Scientific Archaeology'. Professor of Egyptology at University College, London, from 1892 to 1933, his most famous find was the Merneptah stele at Thebes in 1896.

PEVSNER, Sir Nikolaus (1902–83), German, architectural historian
2 Wildwood Terrace, NW3. *English Heritage*
Sir Nikolaus, a refugee from Nazism, who lived here from 1936 until his death, was the founding author of the forty-six-volume *Buildings of England* series

Sir
NIKOLAUS
PEVSNER
1902-1983
Architectural
Historian
lived here from 1936
until his death

(1951–74), the indispensible aid to any walking architecture student, as well as numerous other books on art and architectural history. The *Buildings* series continues to be revised and updated, but will forever be called 'Pevsner' for short.

PITT, William, the Elder (1708–78), English, Prime Minister
Chatham House, North End Avenue, NW3.
Private
Pitt lived in a house on this site. One of the outstanding figures in British political history, known as 'the Great Commoner', he was the first political leader whose strength lay in his support among the public at large rather than his connections at court. This support came because of his notable integrity; while Paymaster General, for example, he creamed off nothing for himself, a startling break with tradition. Pittsburgh, Pennsylvania, and numerous other smaller communities in the United States are named in his honour. (See also Enfield and Westminster 4.)

PLATH, Sylvia (1932–63), American, poet
3 Chalcot Square, NW1. *English Heritage*
Plath met and married the future Poet Laureate Ted Hughes in 1956, and they lived here in 1960–1. She began to suffer from bouts of depression and parted from him in late 1962, taking her own life in February 1963. Her novel *The Bell Jar*, published posthumously in 1963 under the pen-name of 'Victoria Lucas', parallels the events of her life. 'Is there no way out of the mind?', she wrote.

PRIESTLEY, J. B. (1894–1984), English, novelist, playwright
3 The Grove, Highgate, N6. *English Heritage*
Priestley, who lived here, first achieved fame with his novel *The Good Companions* (1929). His first stage play was *Dangerous Corner* (1932), and his most famous play *An Inspector Calls* (1946). He was also a consummate broadcaster and his Second World War *Postscripts* (1940–1) on the BBC on Sunday nights were very popular, though abruptly cancelled because someone thought they were too left-wing. A 1957 article by him in the *New Statesman* led to the foundation of the Campaign for Nuclear Disarmament.

RACKHAM, Arthur (1867–1939), English, illustrator
16 Chalcot Gardens, Hampstead, NW3.
Greater London Council
Uncommonly prolific, Rackham, who lived here, is best remembered for his children's book illustrations, such as *Peter Pan* (1906), *Alice in Wonderland* (1907) and *Anderson's Fairy Tales* (1932), but he also produced noteworthy illustrations for adult works by Poe, Wagner, Shakespeare and others.

RAYMOND, Ernest (1888–1974), English, novelist
22 The Pryors, West Heath Drive, NW3.
Hampstead Plaque Fund
Raymond, who lived here from 1941 until his death, was ordained in 1914 but renounced holy orders in 1923, after his war experiences. His first novel, *Tell England* (1922), was one of the best to come out of the First World War. It had sold 300,000 copies by 1939 and reached its fortieth printing by 1965. He wrote nearly fifty other books, of which *We the Accused* (1935) won him the Gold Medal of the Book Guild.

REYNOLDS, Alfred (d.1993), Hungarian, poet, philosopher
Lower Lodge, Branch Hill, NW3. *Private*
An elusive figure, surprisingly impervious to research, he lived here from 1980 to 1993, according to the plaque. Born Alfred Reinhold, he was a refugee from Nazism in 1936. His position as 'Hungary's greatest modern poet' depends on a single volume, *First and Last Book of Poetry* (1932), which he allegedly resisted having translated because 'Hungarian is the only language of poetry'. Philosophically he was an atheistic liberal, regarding religion as superstition and priests as 'crows in black', as expressed in his book *Jesus versus Christianity* (1988).

RICHARDSON, Maggie (1901–74), English, flower-seller
1 Hampstead High Street, NW3. *Heath and Old Hampstead Society*
At the corner with Willoughby Road, this plaque evokes a Hampstead High Street rather different from the one we see today. Maggie was evidently a much-loved presence on the local scene, and long may her shade hover as the chain stores advance.

RIZAL, Dr José (1861–96), Filipino, novelist, politician
37 Chalcot Crescent, Primrose Hill, NW1.
Greater London Council
Unequivocally the national hero of the Philippines, Dr Rizal lived here in exile. A prolific writer and commentator, his most famous books are his two novels *Noli Me Tangere* (1887) and *El Filibusterismo* (1891), which got him in trouble with the Spanish colonial authorities, who tried and executed him in 1896, on the date now celebrated in the Philippines as Rizal Day.

ROBERTS, William (1895–1980), English, artist
14 St Mark's Crescent, NW1. *English Heritage*
Roberts lived and worked here from 1946 until his death. He passed through Roger Fry's Omega Workshop, was associated with the Vorticist movement, joined the Royal Artillery in 1916, and became an official war artist. He is often called 'the English Cubist'.

ROBESON, Paul (1898–1976), American, bass, actor
The Chestnuts, Branch Hill, NW3.
English Heritage
A college football hero in his youth, Robeson went on the stage in the 1920s, thrilling audiences with his bass voice. He appeared in many films, including *Showboat* (1928), in which he sang 'Ol' Man River'. His Othello in London in 1930, when he stayed here, was a sensation. He suffered from racism throughout his life, which was redoubled when he showed some sympathy for the Soviet Union.

ROMNEY, George (1734–1802), English, painter
Holly Bush Hill, NW3. *London County Council*
With Reynolds (q.v.) and Gainsborough (q.v.), Romney, who lived here, was one of the leading portrait painters of the eighteenth century. He met Emma, Lady Hamilton, in 1782 and she became his muse, posing for him over sixty times in a variety of guises, historical and mythological.

SALISBURY, Francis Owen (1874–1962), English, painter
23 West Heath Road, NW3. *Hampstead Plaque Fund*
Salisbury, who lived here, was known in his heyday as 'Britain's Painter Laureate'. He was deeply conservative and contemptuous of contemporary modern artists: as far as he was concerned, Picasso and company were not artists. His many portraits include twenty-five members of the Royal Family, six American Presidents, Churchill several times, and numerous panoramas of historic pageantry.

SCOTT, Sir George Gilbert (1811–78), English, architect
Admiral's House, Admiral's Walk, NW3.
London County Council

A leader of the Victorian Gothic Revival, Scott, who lived here, designed many public buildings, including the Albert Memorial, the Foreign Office and the Midland Hotel at St Pancras. Surveyor of Westminster Abbey from 1849 to 1878, he did little damage and is buried there.

SHARP, Cecil (1859–1924), English, musicologist, folklorist
4 Maresfield Gardens, NW3. *Greater London Council*
Sharp, who lived here from 1918 until his death, is the pre-eminent figure in the folk revival of the early twentieth century, his *Book of British Song* (1902) and *English Folk Song* (1907) being seminal. He founded the English Folk Dance and Song Society in 1911 and was its director until his death. The society's headquarters in Regent's Park Road is named in his honour.

SHAW, Martin (1875–1958), English, composer
42–51 Clevedon Mansions, Lissenden Gardens, NW5. *Lissenden Gardens Tenants Association*

Shaw, who lived here, is described on the plaque as the 'quiet revolutionary of English music'. With Dearmer (q.v.) and Vaughan Williams (q.v.), he edited and arranged *Songs of Praise* (1925) and *The Oxford Book of Carols* (1928). He himself composed over three hundred works of church music, the best-loved being *The Redeemer*, an oratorio for Easter, and the hymn 'All Things Bright and Beautiful'.

SHAW, Richard Norman (1831–1912), Scottish, architect
6 Ellerdale Road, NW3. *English Heritage*
Shaw, who designed this house for himself and lived in it from 1876 to his death, was the most influential British architect from the 1870s to the 1890s. He believed architecture was an art, not a profession. Among his most familiar work are New Scotland Yard (1887–1900) and the majority of the houses in Bedford Park, W4, as well as the church and inn there. Misnamed the 'Queen Anne' style, his designs are characterised by homely red-brick warmth. (See also Harrow.)

SIM, Alastair (1900–76), Scottish, comic actor
8 Frognal Gardens, Hampstead, NW3.
English Heritage
Described by Ronnie Corbett as having 'the voice of a fastidious ghoul', Sim, who lived here from 1953 to 1975, had a busy career on stage, film and television. He is best remembered for his Ebenezer Scrooge in *A Christmas Carol* (1951) and Miss Fritton, the headmistress in the 'St Trinian's' films, permanently in a tizz.

SITWELL, Dame Edith (1887–1964), English, poet
Greenhill, Hampstead High Street, NW3.
English Heritage
Dame Edith, who lived here in Flat 42, was 6 feet tall and always dressed in quasi-medieval gowns, with very large jewellery, a *grande dame* of the literary scene. Her poetry was set to music by Walton (q.v.) and Britten (q.v.) and she was acclaimed for her poems about the Blitz in the Second World War. Her book *English Eccentrics* (1933) could hardly have been written by anyone else.

SOKOLOW, Dr Nahum (1859–1936), Polish, journalist, Zionist
43 Compayne Gardens, South Hampstead, NW6.
Private
Dr Sokolow lived and worked here from 1921 until his death. After a thirty-year career on the Hebrew newspaper *Ha Tzefirah* in Poland, progressing from cub reporter to editor and co-owner, he was asked in 1906 to be secretary of the World Zionist Congress, to which he energetically devoted the rest of his life, finally serving as its president (1931–6). The kibbutz Sde Nahum is named in his honour.

STANFIELD, Clarkson (1793–1867), English, painter
Stanfield House, 86 Hampstead High Street, NW3. *Hampstead Plaque Fund*
Serving as a seaman for a number of years, Stanfield, who lived here from 1847 to 1865, developed a skill at sketching ships and seascapes. On his discharge from the Navy in 1818, he worked for the next decade as an admired painter of scenery for theatres, including Drury Lane. Abandoning that, he concentrated on marine paintings, where his knowledge of ships gave truth to his pictures. One of his best works was *The Battle of Trafalgar* (1836), commissioned by the United Services Club. (See also Westminster 4.)

STEVENS, Alfred (1817–75), English, sculptor
9 Eton Villas, Belsize Park, NW3.
London County Council
Stevens, who lived here, was responsible for the vases on the railings outside the British Museum, but most of his time from 1856 onwards was devoted to the Wellington monument in St Paul's, where he was constantly subject to harassment, unhelpful suggestions and budgetary constraints. He did not live to see the work completed.

STEVENSON, Robert Louis (1850–94), Scottish, novelist
Abernethy House, 7 Mount Vernon, NW3.
Hampstead Plaque Fund
Stevenson lived here briefly in the 1880s. In Samoa, where he lived the last five years of his sickly life, he was known as *Tusitala*, 'the Storyteller'. His works,

which besides novels include poetry and travel writing, remain constantly in print and have regularly been filmed, among them *Treasure Island* (1883), *The Strange Case of Dr Jekyll and Mr Hyde* (1886) and *Kidnapped* (1886).

STEWART, Donald Ogden (1894–1980), American, playwright
103 Frognal, NW3. *Hampstead Plaque Fund*
Stewart, who lived here, won an Oscar for his screenplay for *The Philadelphia Story* (1940). He wrote many other successful films, including *The Barretts of Wimpole Street* (1934), *The Prisoner of Zenda* (1937) and *Life with Father* (1947). Blacklisted in 1950, he retired to England.

STOPES, Marie (1880–1958), Scottish, family planning pioneer
14 Well Walk, NW3. *Hampstead Plaque Fund*
Stopes lived here during her marriage to Reginald Gates (1911–14). A palaeobotanist by training, she was a fearless advocate of women's rights, editor of *Birth Control News*, giving explicit advice on sex and contraception. Her controversial book *Married Love* (1918) was written while she was still a virgin, her marriage having been annulled on grounds of non-consummation. (See also Camden 2 and Islington.)

TAGORE, Rabindranath (1861–1941), Bengali, poet, philosopher
3 Villas on the Heath, Vale of Health, NW3.
London County Council
Tagore stayed here in 1912. He was the first Asian Nobel laureate, winning the Prize for Literature in 1913. His poems *Gitanjali* (1910) were translated into English and introduced by W. B. Yeats (q.v.). Although poetry is his first claim to posterity, he was also a playwright, short-story writer, painter and philosopher, engaging worldwide with the leading thinkers of his time. Two of his songs are the national anthems of India and Bangladesh.

TAWNEY, R. H. (1880–1962), English, economic historian
21–30 Parliament Hill Mansions, Lissenden Gardens, NW5. *Lissenden Gardens Tenants Association*

A Christian socialist, Tawney, who lived here, was involved with the Workers' Education Association throughout his career from 1905 and was its president from 1928 to 1944. He has been called 'the patron saint of adult education'. He is claimed as a forerunner by various modern strands of New Labour and Liberal Democrat thinking, but he was in truth as 'Old Labour' as they come. (See also Camden 2.)

TOPHAM, Frank (1838–1924), English, painter
4 Arkwright Road, NW3. *Hampstead Plaque Fund*
A genre painter in oil and watercolour, Topham, who lived here, exhibited regularly at the Royal Academy from 1863 and was elected an Academician in 1879. Typical of his improving historical works are *Pepys Saves a Saddler's Child from the Plague* and *Savonarola Calls on the People of Florence to Give Up Their Luxuries*.

UNWIN, Sir Raymond (1863–1940), English, architect, town planner
Old Wyldes, Wildwood Terrace, NW3. *Private*

A disciple of William Morris (q.v.), Unwin, who lived here from 1906 until his death, was involved in designing several new communities, including New Earswick near York, Letchworth Garden City, the Brentham Garden Suburb in Ealing, and, most famously, Hampstead Garden Suburb. His book *The Art of Building a Home* (1901), written with his brother-in-law, Barry Parker, was hugely influential on the house-building of the early twentieth century.

VANE, Sir Harry (1613–62), English, politician, diplomat
Vane House, Rosslyn Hill, Hampstead, NW3.
Royal Society of Arts

Sir Harry, who lived here, was a committed Parliamentarian. Briefly governor of Massachusetts (1636–7), he was civil head of Parliament (1643–53), conducting critical negotiations with the Scots. After the Restoration he was accused of high treason and executed on Tower Hill. The plaque incorrectly gives his birth year as 1612.

VENTRIS, Michael (1922–56), English, architect, linguist
19 North End, Hampstead, NW3.
English Heritage
Ventris, who designed this house and lived here for the last six years of his life, was an architect of no particular distinction, working on post-war school building. His fame rests on his decipherment of the Linear B language. Sir Arthur Evans, who had excavated tablets at Knossos, Crete, with Linear B on them, was convinced they were a 'Minoan' language, thus holding up their decipherment for decades. Ventris, an amateur with a flair for languages, proved, by a combination of inspired guesswork and rigorous analysis, that they were early Greek.

VON HÜGEL, Baron Friedrich (1852–1925), Austrian, philosopher
4 Holford Road, Hampstead, NW3.
Greater London Council
Von Hügel, who lived here from 1882 to 1903, is recognised as one of the most important lay Catholic thinkers of his time, though he had neither a degree nor a university post. He founded the London Society for the Study of Religion (1905) and his writings include *The Mystical Element of Religion* (1908), *Eternal Life* (1913) and *The Reality of God* (1931).

WALTON, Sir William (1902–83), English, composer
10 Holly Place, Holly Walk, NW3.
Hampstead Plaque Fund
Sir William, who lived here, was branded avant-garde for his musical adaptation of the poet Edith Sitwell's (q.v.) *Façade* (1923), but his Viola Concerto (1929), oratorio *Belshazzar's Feast* (1931), *Coronation Marches* (1937 and 1953) and the music for Olivier's three Shakespeare films show him to be in the best classical traditions. One of his most striking late compositions was the music for the climactic battle sequence in the film *Battle of Britain* (1969), in which the planes wheel about the sky silently behind his jaggedly phrased soundtrack.

WATCH HOUSE, Hampstead
9 Holly Place, Holly Walk, NW3.
Hampstead Plaque Fund
This is one of three old watch houses surviving in Greater London; it is now a private dwelling. For the others, see Hackney and Waltham Forest.

WEBB, Beatrice (1858–1943), English, social scientist, political reformer
10 Netherhall Gardens, Hampstead, NW3.
Greater London Council
Beatrice Potter married Sidney Webb (see below) in 1892, and they lived here. The Webbs, a couple at the core of the early Labour movement, are always mentioned in the same breath. Her two memoirs, *My Apprenticeship* (1926) and *Our Partnership* (1948), are a valuable record of early socialist politics. When Sidney became Lord Passfield, she refused to be known as Lady Passfield.

WEBB, Sidney (1859–1947), English, social scientist, political reformer
10 Netherhall Gardens, Hampstead, NW3.
Greater London Council
An early member of the Fabian Society, founder of the London School of Economics and the *New Statesman*, Sidney Webb, who lived here with his wife, Beatrice (see above), was a major extra-Parliamentary figure in early Labour politics, finally becoming an MP from 1922 to 1929. The Webbs have been widely criticised for their uncritical appraisal of life in the Soviet Union, but they were hardly alone in swallowing the Stalin line. (See also Westminster 4.)

WESTFIELD COLLEGE
6 Maresfield Road, NW3. *Hampstead Plaque Fund*
Founded by Constance Maynard (1849–1935) and Ann
Dudin Brown (1823–1917), the college opened here
on 2 October 1882, for the higher education of
women. It became co-educational in 1964, though
keeping the sexes' accommodation segregated, and
merged with Queen Mary, University of London, in
1989; the campus is now at Mile End.

WILLIS, 'Father' Henry (1821–1901), English,
organist, organ builder
9 Rochester Terrace, Camden Town, NW1.
Greater London Council
Henry Willis, who lived here, was an organist turned
organ builder. His firm, founded in 1845, became the
pre-eminent organ makers of the nineteenth century.
Willis organs are found all round the world, notably at
St Paul's Cathedral, the Royal Albert Hall, Alexandra
Palace and Windsor Castle. He is known as 'Father' to
distinguish him from three further generations of
Henrys, who ran the firm until 1997, when Henry
Willis IV retired.

WOOD, Haydn (1882–1959), English, composer
**25 Parliament Hill Mansions, Lissenden
Gardens, NW5.** *Lissenden Gardens Tenants Association*
Wood, who lived here, was a prolific composer of light
orchestral music, including fifteen suites, nine
rhapsodies, eight overtures and over 180 songs, often
for his wife, the soprano Dorothy Court, and most
memorably 'Roses of Picardy' (1916). He was a
director of the Performing Rights Society from 1939.

WOOD, Sir Henry (1869–1944), English,
conductor
4 Elsworthy Road, NW3. *Greater London Council*
Sir Henry, who lived here from 1905 to 1937, began
his career as an organist at the age of ten. At twenty he
conducted his first opera, and at twenty-six, in 1895,
he was engaged to conduct the Promenade Concerts at
the newly opened Queen's Hall, which he continued
to do for all but fifty years, conducting his last Prom
three weeks before he died. During that time he is
credited with improving musicianship in British
orchestras and introducing British audiences to a range
of new composers. (See also Westminster 2.)

ZIMMERN, Alice (1855–1939), English,
educational reformer
**41 Parliament Hill Mansions, Lissenden
Gardens, NW5.** *Lissenden Gardens Tenants Association*
An early graduate of Girton College, Cambridge,
Zimmern, who lived here from 1906 until her death,
translated many classics to make them interesting and
accessible to young people. She studied school systems
in several countries and argued that girls should have
the same educational opportunities as boys. Her book
Women's Suffrage in Many Lands (1909) was a powerful
argument for votes for women. She was also a
practical feminist, promoting early labour-saving
devices that made domestic life less arduous.

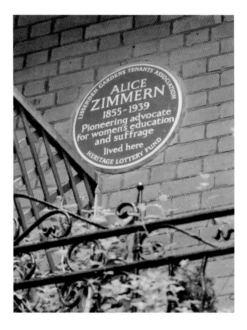

Camden 2:
Camden Town, Somers Town, St Pancras, Bloomsbury and Holborn
South of Prince Albert Road–Parkway–Camden Road

ABBAS, Ali Mohammed (1922–79), Pakistani, lawyer, politician
33 Tavistock Square, WC1. *Camden Borough Council*

Abbas, who lived here from 1945 until his death, was the son of a poor Bengali farmer. As secretary of the All India Muslim League, he believed there should be representation in London, and he called his flat here 'Pakistan House'. He was noted for his oratory and was the first Asian barrister to appear at all levels of the English legal system.

AIR RAIDS, First night (First World War)
Hotel Bedford, Southampton Row, WC1. *Private*
On 24 September 1917 thirteen people were killed and twenty-two injured near this spot on the steps of the old Bedford Hotel by a 112 pound bomb dropped by a Gotha in one of London's first night air raids. The Gotha bombers were a replacement for the Zeppelins, whose raids (see page 134) in 1915–16 had proved too costly. Between May and August 1917 the Germans flew daylight raids, but improved British defences led to a switch to night attacks in the autumn. (See also Islington and Hackney.)

ANAESTHETIC, First in the UK
52 Gower Street, WC1.
Association of Anaesthetists of Great Britain and Ireland
Here, on 19 December 1846, in the home of an American botanist, Francis Boott, James Robinson, a dental surgeon, administered ether to a Miss Lonsdale and removed a troublesome tooth. This was just two months after William Morton gave the first public demonstration of anaesthesia at Massachusetts General Hospital.

BARBIROLLI, Sir John (1899–1970), English, conductor
Bloomsbury Park Hotel, Southampton Row, WC1. *Private*
Sir John was born here. His early career as a cellist has been eclipsed by his later fame as conductor of the New York Philharmonic and of the Hallé Orchestra in Manchester, with which he was associated for twenty-seven years. Vaughan Williams (q.v.) called him 'Glorious John'.

BEAUCLERK, Lady Diana (1734–1808), English, artist
100 Great Russell Street, WC1. *Duke of Bedford*
Eldest daughter of the second Duke of Marlborough, she married Viscount Bolingbroke but was unhappy and obtained a divorce. She married Topham Beauclerk (see below) in 1768. An accomplished amateur artist, her works include illustrations for Dryden's *Fables*. (See also Westminster 4.)

BEAUCLERK, Topham (1739–1780), English, dandy, courtier
100 Great Russell Street, WC1. *Duke of Bedford*
Descended from Charles II and Nell Gwynne (q.v.), Topham Beauclerk enjoyed the friendship of Dr Johnson (q.v.). When he died, Johnson wrote to Boswell: 'His wit and his folly, his acuteness and maliciousness, his merriment and his reasoning, are now over. Such another will not often be found.' (See also Westminster 4.)

BEDFORD COLLEGE FOR WOMEN
48 Bedford Square, WC1. *Private*
Founded here in 1849 by Elizabeth Jesser Reid (see page 128) to provide a liberal, non-sectarian higher education for women, Bedford College was the first of its kind in the United Kingdom and played a prominent part in the advancement of women. It became part of the University of London in 1900.

BELL, Clive (1881–1964), English, critic
50 Gordon Square, Bloomsbury, WC1.
Camden Borough Council
Bell was an important champion of post-Impressionist art. His theory of 'significant form', outlined in *Art* (1914), held that form, rather than content, was the key element in a work of art. A member of the Bloomsbury Group (see below), which this plaque celebrates, he was married to Vanessa, Virginia Woolf's (q.v.) sister.

BELLO, Andrés (1781–1865), Chilean-Venezuelan, poet, jurist
58 Grafton Way, W1. *English Heritage*
Bello, who lived here in 1810, features on the banknotes of both Venezuela and Chile. He published the first Spanish-American grammar in 1847 and drew up the civil code of Chile in 1852. He was rector for life of the University of Santiago from 1842.

BERNAL, John Desmond (1901–71), Irish, scientist
44 Albert Street, NW1. *English Heritage*
Bernal, who lived and died here, is cited on the plaque as a crystallographer, which hardly does justice to the range of his activities. He was one of the founders of molecular biology and the social philosophy of science. He was elected a Fellow of the Royal Society in 1937, and in the same year became Professor of Physics at Birkbeck College. He was scientific adviser for the D-Day landings.

BLOOMSBURY GROUP
50 Gordon Square, Bloomsbury, WC1.
Camden Borough Council

The Bloomsbury Group were intellectual friends who began to meet here and in neighbouring houses in 1905–6 and had a great influence on the British Modernist movement, though condemned by F. R. Leavis as dilettante and élitist. Members included the Woolfs (q.v.), the Bells (q.v.), the Stracheys (q.v.), Duncan Grant, J. M. Keynes (q.v.), E. M. Forster (q.v.) and Roger Fry.

BRITTAIN, Vera (1893–1970), English, writer, reformer
58 Doughty Street, WC1. *English Heritage*
Her most famous book, the poignant *Testament of Youth* (1933), recounted her First World War experiences, when she lost both her brother and her fiancé. It brought her instant fame. She was the mother of the Labour, later Liberal Democrat, politician Shirley Williams. She shares this plaque with Winifred Holtby (see page 125). Holtby's premature death led Brittain to write *Testament of Friendship* (1940), which recounted how the two women had been drawn to their friendship and radical positions by their reactions to the First World War. (See also Westminster 1.)

BURNE-JONES, Sir Edward (1833–98), English, painter
17 Red Lion Square, WC1. *London County Council*
Burne-Jones was in the orbit of William Morris (q.v.) and D. G. Rossetti (q.v.), who share this plaque with him. His mystical romantic style was gently satirised in Gilbert and Sullivan's *Patience* as 'greenery yallery, Grosvenor Gallery'. Stanley Baldwin (q.v.) said of him: 'What he did for us common people was to open magic casements on a land of faery in which he lived throughout his life.' (See also Hammersmith & Fulham and Kensington & Chelsea 1.)

BUTTERFIELD, William (1814–1900), English, architect
42 Bedford Square, WC1. *Greater London Council*
Butterfield, who lived here, was a Gothic Revivalist. He designed Keble College, Oxford, which a wag has described as looking as though it was knitted, St Augustine's College, Canterbury, and All Saints', Margaret Street, W1.

CALDECOTT, Randolph (1846–86), English, illustrator, artist
46 Great Russell Street, Bloomsbury, WC1.
Greater London Council

Caldecott, who lived here from 1872 to 1879, worked mainly illustrating children's books, including *The House that Jack Built* (1878) and Aesop's *Fables* (1883). He was also a fine watercolourist and painter of travel scenes, and contributed regularly to *Punch* magazine.

CARLYLE, Thomas (1795–1881), Scottish, historian, essayist
33 Ampton Street, St Pancras, WC1.
London County Council
Hugely influential on many later Victorians, Carlyle, who lived here, became known in later life as 'the Sage of Chelsea'. His works included *Sartor Resartus* (1833), *The French Revolution* (1837), *Chartism* (1839) and *Frederick the Great* (1858–65). Moving from youthful leftism to ultra-conservatism, he was a firm believer in the 'great man' version of history, revering Cromwell among others. (See also Kensington & Chelsea 2.)

CAVENDISH, Henry (1731–1810), English, physicist
11 Bedford Square, Bloomsbury, WC1.
Duke of Bedford
Cavendish, who lived here, was the discoverer of hydrogen, which he called 'inflammable air'. He also invented a device for estimating the density of the earth and was responsible for early research into

electricity. The Cavendish Laboratory at Cambridge is named in his honour.

CHALLONER, Bishop Richard (1691–1781), English, prelate
44 Old Gloucester Street, Bloomsbury, WC1.
Private
Converted to Catholicism in childhood, Challoner, who lived here, spent twenty-six years at the English College in Douai (1704–30), before taking up missionary work in London, and in 1758 becoming Vicar-Apostolic of the London District. He was the author of thirty-four books, many still used by Catholics today.

CHATTERTON, Thomas (1752–70), English, poet
39 Brooke Street, EC1.
Corporation of the City of London
Chatterton, who committed suicide in a house on this site on 24 August 1770, wrote poems in a 'medieval' style purporting to be the work of a fifteenth-century monk, Thomas Rowley. In 1769 he sent an essay to Horace Walpole (q.v.), also supposedly by this monk, but Walpole was only briefly deceived. Living in poverty, Chatterton killed himself the following year. The 'Rowley' story was believed by some for another century.

CHESTERFIELD, Philip, second Earl of
(1633–1713), English, aristocrat
45 Bloomsbury Square, WC1. *Duke of Bedford*
According to Pepys, Chesterfield, who lived here, was a ladies' man in a promiscuous world. Three times married, he was also a gambler and drunkard, committed to the Tower for duelling and for his involvement with Royalist plots.

CHESTERFIELD, Philip, third Earl of
(1673–1726), English, aristocrat
45 Bloomsbury Square, WC1. *Duke of Bedford*
Born to his father's third wife, the third Earl passed almost unnoticed across the pages of history, known only for fathering the fourth Earl (see below).

CHESTERFIELD, Philip Dormer, fourth Earl of
(1694–1773), English, politician
45 Bloomsbury Square, WC1. *Duke of Bedford*
Chesterfield, who lived here, was noted in his time as a wit, orator and diplomat. He was ambassador at The Hague (1728–32) and Lord Lieutenant of Ireland

(1745–6), but his reputation now rests on his almost daily letters to his (illegitimate) son and to his godson, which set out the ways a gentleman should behave. They were not written for publication but have been steadily reprinted ever since.

COCKERELL, C. R. (1788–1863), English, architect
13 Chester Terrace, Regent's Park, NW1.
English Heritage
Cockerell, who lived and died here, was Professor of Architecture at the Royal Academy (1840–57). His best-known buildings are the Ashmolean Museum and Taylorian Institute at Oxford, the Fitzwilliam Museum, Cambridge, and St George's Hall, Liverpool.

DANCE, George, the Younger (1741–1825), English, architect
91 Gower Street, Bloomsbury, WC1.
Greater London Council
Dance, who lived and died here, was one of the great architects of the eighteenth century, but little of his work survives. He was one of the founding members of the Royal Academy (1768) and its Professor of Architecture (1798–1805). When he died, he was the last surviving founder of the Academy.

DANIELL, William (1769–1837), English, artist
135 St Pancras Way, NW1. *English Heritage*
Daniell, who lived and died here, went to India with his uncle Thomas (q.v.) at the age of fourteen, spent ten years there and produced the six-volume *Oriental Scenery*. He was elected a Royal Academician in 1822.

DARWIN, Charles (1809–82), English, scientist
Biological Science Building, Gower Street, WC1.
London County Council
Darwin's theory of evolution, outlined in his *On the Origin of Species* (1859), remains the basis of all modern natural sciences. He and his wife lived in a house on this site from 1838 to 1842, calling it 'Macaw Cottage', on account of its gaudy interiors.

DE MIRANDA, Francisco (1750–1816), Venezuelan, soldier, politician
58 Grafton Way, Fitzrovia, W1. *English Heritage*

De Miranda, who lived here from 1802 to 1810, had been active in the American War of Independence and in France during the Revolution. These experiences fired him with visions of liberating the whole of South America. He was leader of the first Venezuelan republic (1811–12) but was overthrown by conservative forces, handed over to Spain and died in prison four years later.

DENMAN, George (1819–96), English, lawyer, politician
50–51 Russell Square, Bloomsbury, WC1. *Private*
Denman was the fourth son of Thomas Denman (see below), with whom he shares the plaque. Born in this house in 1819, he was a Liberal MP from 1859 to 1872, and a judge in the High Court (1872–92). By way of relaxation, he published in 1871 a translation of Gray's *Elegy* into Greek verse.

DENMAN, Thomas (1779–1854), English, lawyer, politician
50–51 Russell Square, Bloomsbury, WC1. *Private*
Denman lived in this house from 1816 to 1834. With Brougham (q.v.), he was a member of Queen Caroline's legal team in 1820, which earned him the enmity of George IV. He sat in Parliament as a Whig

from 1816 to 1826, was Attorney-General (1830–2), drafting the great Reform Bill, and was finally Lord Chief Justice from 1834 to 1850.

DICKENS, Charles (1812–70), English, novelist
141 Bayham Street, NW1. *The Dickens Fellowship*
Prudential Buildings, 138–142 Holborn, EC1.
Private
48 Doughty Street, WC1. *London County Council*
BMA House, Tavistock Square, WC1. *Private*
14 Great Russell Street, WC1. *Private*

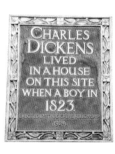

The man with the most plaques in London, Dickens lived at all the above addresses, except Great Russell Street, which was the home of the fictional Charles Kitterbell in *Sketches by Boz*. Dickens is the pre-eminent figure in Victorian literature, peopling the nation's consciousness with unforgettable characters from Mr Micawber to Fagin, from Ebenezer Scrooge to Miss Havisham, from Sam Weller to Mrs Gamp, from Mr Pickwick to Abel Magwitch. Filmed and adapted for television many times, his books are still widely available in print. (See also Haringey, Westminster 2, Westminster 4 and Southwark.)

DISRAELI, Benjamin (1804–81), English, Prime Minister, novelist
22 Theobalds Road, WC1. *London County Council*
Disraeli was born here. His twin careers, as politician and novelist, are entwined in that he wrote novels to influence public opinion; his best-known books, *Coningsby* (1844), *Sybil* (1845) and *Tancred* (1847), propounded his melancholy idea that Britain consisted of 'two nations, between whom there is no intercourse and no sympathy'. (See also City, Westminster 3 and Waltham Forest.)

D'ISRAELI, Isaac (1766–1848), English, literary historian
6 Bloomsbury Square, Bloomsbury, WC1.
Duke of Bedford
Father of Benjamin Disraeli (see above), he lived here from 1818 to 1829. Among his many works is the six-volume anthology *Curiosities of Literature* (1791–1834),

which remains a stimulating and unusual read. His *The Literary Character* (1795), admired by Byron, tried to determine the traits common to all creative writers.

DOOLITTLE, Hilda (1886–1961), American, poet, novelist
44 Mecklenburgh Square, St Pancras, WC1.
Private
Doolittle, known as 'HD', lived here in 1917–18. She was a figure in bohemian London in the early twentieth century; her works, both poetry and novels, explored the borderland between heterosexual and lesbian desire. She had relationships with Ezra Pound (q.v.) and D. H. Lawrence (q.v.), but women were her preferred companions.

DU MAURIER, George (1834–96), French, novelist, illustrator
91 Great Russell Street, Bloomsbury, WC1.
London County Council
Du Maurier lived here from 1863 to 1868. (See a full entry in Camden 1.)

DUFF, Peggy (1910–81), English, radical
11 Albert Street, Camden Town, NW1.
Camden Borough Council
Duff, who lived here, was a founder of the Campaign for Nuclear Disarmament in 1958 and, as the organisation's first General Secretary, organised the Aldermaston Marches. She resigned from the Labour Party in 1967 over Harold Wilson's diplomatic support for the Americans in Vietnam. Her memoir, *Left Left Left* (1971), had the accolade of being derided by Bernard Levin.

EARNSHAW, Thomas (1749–1829), English, clockmaker
119 High Holborn, WC1. *London County Council*
Known as 'the Father of the Chronometer', Earnshaw

had his business premises on this site. He first simplified the production of marine chronometers, improved the transit clock at Greenwich and invented the chronometer escapement and the bimetallic compensation balance.

EASTLAKE, Sir Charles (1793–1865), English, painter
7 Fitzroy Square, W1. *Greater London Council*
Painter of historical subjects, Eastlake, who lived here, was noted for two full-length portraits of Napoleon and for his views of the countryside round Rome. He was president of the Royal Academy (1850–65) and the first Director of the National Gallery (1855–65).

ELDON, Lord (1751–1838), English, lawyer, politician
6 Bedford Square, Bloomsbury, WC1.
London County Council
Lord Eldon, who lived here, was an MP (1782), Solicitor General (1788), Attorney General (1793) and Lord Chancellor (1801–27). He was notoriously reactionary, zealous against reform and against Catholics, and the only progressive bill he is said ever to have supported was the abolition of trial by combat.

ELIOT, T. S. (1888–1965), American, poet, playwright
24 Russell Square, WC1. *Camden Borough Council*
Eliot, a major figure in the British literary landscape of the twentieth century, worked here as an editorial director for Faber & Faber from 1925 to 1965. As a poet, critic and playwright, he spoke for the disillusioned post-First World War generation. In *The Hollow Men* (1925), he wrote: 'This is the way the world ends, not with a bang but a whimper.' However, he was not all gloom and doom, producing *Old Possum's Book of Practical Cats* (1939), a classic of children's verse. (See also Kensington & Chelsea 1 and Westminster 2.)

FABIAN SOCIETY
White House,
Osnaburgh Street,
NW1.
Greater London Council
The Fabian Society was formed at 17 Osnaburgh Street on this site on 4 January 1884. A left-wing group, it took its name from the Roman general Fabius Cunctator, noted for his cautious military strategy. The society's members have included H. G. Wells (q.v.), G. B. Shaw (q.v.), Sidney and Beatrice Webb (q.v.) and Edith Nesbit (q.v.). Dismissed by the more radical as merely a reformist bourgeois discussion group, it remains the leading centre-left think tank.

FAWCETT, Dame
Millicent Garrett
(1847–1929),
English, suffragist
2 Gower Street,
Bloomsbury, WC1.
London County Council
Dame Millicent, who lived and died here, co-founded Newnham College, Cambridge, in 1871 and was President of the National Union of Women's Suffrage Societies (1897–1919), but opposed to some of the more militant actions of her fellow members. She was the sister of Elizabeth Garrett Anderson (q.v.).

FIRST, Ruth (1925–82), South African, freedom fighter
13 Lyme Street, NW1. *English Heritage*
Active in the South African Communist Party, Ruth First was held in solitary confinement for 117 days and fled South Africa on her release. She lived here in exile from 1966 to 1978 with her husband, Joe Slovo (see page 131). They were key activists in the British anti-apartheid movement during their exile. Among her many books, *The Barrel of a Gun* (1970) explored the African vulnerability to the *coup d'état*. She was killed by a parcel bomb in Mozambique, where she was working for the African National Congress.

FLINDERS, Captain Matthew (1774–1814), English, explorer, sailor
56 Fitzroy Street, W1. *London County Council*
Flinders, who lived here, surveyed the coast of New South Wales (1795–1800) and circumnavigated Australia (1801–3). A range of mountains, a bay, a group of islands, two other islands and a river in Australia are named after him. His grandson was Sir Flinders Petrie (q.v.).

FONTANE, Theodor (1819–98), German, novelist
6 St Augustine's Road, NW1. *English Heritage*
Fontane, who lived here in 1857–8, came to London
as a journalist and turned to novel-writing at the age of
fifty-seven. Among his works, *Vor dem Sturm* (1878)
and *L'Adultera* (1882) are widely considered to make
him the most important nineteenth-century realist
writer in the German language.

**FORBES-
ROBERTSON,
Sir Johnston**
(1853–1937),
English, actor-
manager
**22 Bedford
Square, WC1.** *Duke
of Bedford*
Sir Johnston, who
lived here, first
appeared on the
London stage in
1874. He became manager of the Lyceum Theatre in
1895, where his *Hamlet* in 1897, at the age of forty-
four, was acclaimed as the best melancholy Dane of the
nineteenth century. Shaw (q.v.) wrote the part of
Caesar in *Caesar and Cleopatra* for him.

FURNIVAL'S INN
Prudential Buildings, 138–142 Holborn, EC1.
Corporation of the City of London
This is the site of Furnival's Inn, demolished in 1897.
Leased to law students by William de Furnival in 1383,
it was one of the Inns of Chancery until 1817, when it
was dissolved. It was demolished shortly afterwards
and replaced by a new building, retaining the name
Furnival's Inn. Dickens (see page 122) lived here while
working as a reporter for the *Morning Chronicle*
(1834–7) and wrote *Pickwick Papers* here.

GOON SHOW
Camden Palace Theatre, Camden High Street,
NW1. *Comic Heritage*
The plaque notes that the last *Goon Show* of all, starring
Peter Sellers (q.v.), Spike Milligan (q.v.) and Harry
Secombe, was recorded by the BBC in this theatre on
30 April 1972. This was a special edition of the show,
commissioned as part of the BBC's fiftieth anniversary
celebrations. It gave delirious fans one last
appointment with Hercules Grytpype-Thynne,

Count Jim Moriarty, Bluebottle, Henry Crun, Minnie
Bannister, Major Bloodnok, Eccles and Neddie
Seagoon, of whom, of course, Little Jim said, for one
last time, 'He's fallen in the water!'

GRESLEY, Sir Nigel (1876–1941), Scottish,
locomotive engineer
West Offices, King's Cross Station, NW1.
English Heritage
Sir Nigel, who had his offices here from 1923 to 1941,
was the foremost train designer of his generation,
thrilling boys of all ages with his latest innovations.
His *Flying Scotsman* was the first locomotive recorded
at over 100 mph, and his *Mallard* still holds the world
speed record for a steam locomotive at 126 mph.

HARRISON, John
(1693–1776), English,
watchmaker
**Summit House, Red
Lion Square, WC1.**
London County Council
Harrison, who lived and
died in a house on this site,
invented and developed five
versions of the marine
chronometer, designed to determine longitude, which
was a crucial requirement for accurate navigation. His
ideas were constantly rejected by the Board of
Longitude, as they were convinced the answer lay in
astronomy. But eventually they recognised his work
and he was belatedly rewarded.

HERFORD, Robert Travers (1860–1950), English,
churchman, scholar
Dr Williams's Library, 14 Gordon Square, WC1.
English Heritage
Herford, a Unitarian minister, lived and worked here.
He was noted and respected as an expert on Judaism
and a student of comparative religion. Among his
books are *Christianity in Talmud and Midrash* (1903),
Pharisaism (1912) and *The Effect of the Fall of Jerusalem
upon the Character of the Pharisees* (1917).

HILL, Sir Rowland (1795–1879), English, reformer
Cartwright Gardens, WC1.
London Borough of Camden
Hill wrote the pamphlet leading to the creation of the
modern postal service at a house on this site in 1837.
He conceived the idea of postage stamps and

introduced the first in 1840, the famous Penny Blacks, establishing the concept of a uniform postal rate, based on weight rather than distance. Despite some reactionary opposition, he went on to introduce successive developments in the postal service. (See also Camden 1 and Westminster 2.)

HODGKIN, Thomas

(1798–1866), English, physician, philanthropist
35 Bedford Square, Bloomsbury, WC1.
Greater London Council
A Quaker, Hodgkin, who lived here, wrote the classic of pathology *The Morbid Anatomy of Serous and Mucous Membranes* (1829), identified the disease which bears his name (1832) and was a pioneer of preventive medicine. He was also passionately involved in the anti-slavery campaign.

HOFMANN, A.W. (1818–92), German, chemist
9 Fitzroy Square, W1. *English Heritage*
Hofmann, who lived here, was director of the Royal College of Chemistry from 1845 and chemist to the Royal Mint (1856–65), after which he returned to Berlin. He made a special study of coal tar derivatives, discovering many organic compounds, most especially formaldehyde.

HOLTBY, Winifred (1898–1935), English, novelist, journalist
58 Doughty Street, WC1. *English Heritage*
Holtby shared this house with Vera Brittain (see page 119). Her best-known novel is *South Riding*, published posthumously in 1936. Her First World War experiences led her to lecture and campaign on international issues, and she was a prolific journalist, contributing to the *Manchester Guardian* and many periodicals. Vera Brittain wrote a moving obituary in her book *Testament of Friendship* (1940).

HOPE, Anthony (1863–1933), English, novelist
41 Bedford Square, Bloomsbury, WC1.
Greater London Council
Anthony Hope was the pen-name of Sir Anthony Hope Hawkins, who lived here from 1903 to 1917. Although he wrote thirty-four novels and a handful of plays, Hope is remembered today only for *The Prisoner of Zenda* (1894) and its sequel, *Rupert of Hentzau* (1898),

featuring the dashing Rudolf Rassendyll, and set in Ruritania, a fictional central European kingdom.

HOWARD, John

(1726–90), English, prison reformer
23 Great Ormond Street, WC1.
London County Council
John Howard, who lived here, was travelling to Lisbon in 1755 when he was captured by French privateers and imprisoned in Brest before being exchanged for a French officer held in Britain. It is thought this experience led to his interest in prison conditions. As High Sheriff of Bedfordshire in 1773, he made a tour of hundreds of British prisons and was appalled. He published *The State of Prisons* in 1777 and his campaigning led to two acts of Parliament for improvement. The Howard League for Prison Reform, founded in 1866, was named after him.

HUGHES, Hugh Price (1847–1902), Welsh, Methodist
8 Taviton Street, WC1. *English Heritage*
Hughes, who lived and died here, was the founder of the *Methodist Times* (1885), first Superintendent of the West London Methodist Mission (1887) and first President of the National Free Church Council (1896).

JACOBS, W.W. (1863–1943), English, short-story writer
15a Gloucester Gate, Regent's Park, NW1.
English Heritage
Jacobs lived here; his stories generally are lightly humorous and mostly set in the Wapping area, where he was born. The best remembered is probably *The Monkey's Paw*, a macabre tale published in his collection *The Lady of the Barge* (1902).

KEYNES, John Maynard (1883–1946), English, economist
46 Gordon Square, Bloomsbury, WC1.
Greater London Council
Keynes, who lived here from 1916 until his death, was one of the most influential economists of the twentieth century. He led the British delegation to the 1944 conference that set up the International Monetary

Fund and advised the Treasury in both world wars. He was also a member of the Bloomsbury Group (q.v.).

KHAN, Sir Syed Ahmed (1817–98), Indian, reformer, educationalist
21 Mecklenburgh Square, WC1. *English Heritage*
Khan lived here in 1869–70. During the Indian Mutiny of 1857, he remained loyal to the Raj and rescued many imperilled Britons, but nonetheless afterwards published a critical book about British rule. As mentor to the leaders of the Muslim community, he was an early advocate of the two-nation theory on the destiny of the sub-continent.

KIRK, Sir John (1847–1922), English, philanthropist
32 John Street, WC1. *Private*
Sir John, who lived here, was known as 'the Children's Friend' from his forty-year involvement with the Ragged School Union, the Shaftesbury Society and other charitable bodies. His friendship, counsel and help were always available to needy children, and particularly to the crippled.

KRISHNA MENON, V. K. (1896–1974), Indian, politician
57 Camden Square, Camden Town, NW1.
Camden Borough Council
Krishna Menon was the voice of the Indian independence movement in Britain. He was also involved with Allen Lane (q.v.) in the foundation of Penguin Books. After serving as High Commissioner to the United Kingdom, he was Indian ambassador to the United Nations (1952–62) and Defence Minister (1957–62).

LAMBERT, Constant (1905–51), English, composer
197 Albany Street, Regent's Park, NW1.
English Heritage
Lambert lived here from 1947 until his death. A prodigy, he began writing orchestral work at thirteen

and was commissioned, aged twenty, to write *Romeo and Juliet* (1925) for Diaghilev. He was one of the first 'serious' composers to recognise jazz, which influenced his *Rio Grande* (1929). His major choral work *Summer's Last Will and Testament* (1936) fell somewhat on deaf ears, with the nation mourning the death of George V, but was hailed by Alan Franks as his 'finest work'.

LAUGHTON, Charles (1899–1962), English, actor
15 Percy Street, Fitzrovia, W1. *English Heritage*
Laughton lived here from 1928 to 1931. While here, he made his first films, going on to achieve stardom, and an Oscar, in *The Private Life of Henry VIII* (1934). Later, in Hollywood, he starred in *Ruggles of Red Gap* and *Mutiny on the Bounty* (both 1935) and as Quasimodo in *The Hunchback of Notre Dame* (1939).

LETHABY, W. R. (1857–1931), English, architect, teacher
Central School, Southampton Row, WC1.
London County Council
20 Calthorpe Street, WC1. *Greater London Council*
Lethaby, who lived in Calthorpe Street from 1880 to 1891, co-founded the Central School of Arts and Crafts with George Frampton (q.v.) and was its first principal (1896–1911). Later he was appointed the first Professor of Design at the Royal College of Art (1901) and Surveyor of Westminster Abbey (1906).

MACDONALD, George (1824–1905), Scottish, poet, novelist
20 Albert Street, NW1. *English Heritage*
Macdonald, who lived here from 1860 to 1863, was a professor at Bedford College. He published two collections of poetry, *Within and Without* (1856) and *Poems* (1857), and the novels *David Elginbrod* (1863) and *Lilith* (1895). He is best known for his children's books, which include *The Princess and the Goblin* (1872) and *The Princess and the Curdie* (1883). (See also Hammersmith & Fulham.)

MARSDEN, William (1796–1867), English, physician
65 Lincoln's Inn Fields, Holborn, WC2.
Greater London Council
Marsden lived here. He founded the Royal Free Hospital in Hampstead in 1828, after discovering the great difficulty poor people had in getting treatment. Subsequently he founded the Marsden Hospital in

Chelsea in 1851, and it is today recognised as a world centre of excellence in the study and treatment of cancer.

MAXIM, Sir Hiram (1840–1916), American, inventor

57d Hatton Garden, EC1. *Greater London Council*
Hiram Maxim came to England in 1881 and perfected his famous weapon, the first machine-gun, two years later in a workshop on these premises. Its role in imperial conquest was pinpointed by Hilaire Belloc (q.v.) in *The Modern Traveller*:

'Whatever happens, we have got
The Maxim Gun, and they have not.'

MAYHEW, Henry (1812–87), English, journalist, social researcher

55 Albany Street, Regent's Park, NW1.
London County Council
Mayhew lived here. Besides co-founding *Punch*, he is remembered for the four volumes of *London Labour and the London Poor* (1851–62), which were originally articles in the *Morning Chronicle* and were influential on the thinking of Christian socialists such as F. D. Maurice (q.v.) and Charles Kingsley (q.v.).

MAZZINI, Giuseppe (1805–72), Italian, statesman

5 Hatton Garden, EC1. *Private*
187 North Gower Street, NW1.
London County Council
10 Laystall Street, EC1. *Private*
Mazzini lived at all three addresses. An apostle of modern democracy, he formed *Giovine Italia* (Young Italy), which inspired other groups such as Young Poland, Young Germany and the Young Turks, all aiming for independence and unity for their countries. His stormy career included periods of exile and imprisonment, but paved the way for Garibaldi and Cavour to establish a united Italy.

MORRELL, Lady Ottoline (1873–1938), hostess, patron of the arts

10 Gower Street, Bloomsbury, WC1.
Greater London Council

Lady Ottoline, who lived here, was the pre-eminent literary hostess of the early twentieth century, with a London salon here in Bloomsbury and a country retreat at Garsington, Oxfordshire. She had affairs with many of the leading figures in the literary world, both male and female, and was the model for fictional characters in novels by Aldous Huxley (q.v.), D. H. Lawrence (q.v.) and Graham Greene.

MORRIS, William (1834–96), English, poet, designer, socialist

17 Red Lion Square, WC1. *London County Council*
Morris, who lived here from 1856 to 1859, was the leading figure in the Arts and Crafts movement of the second half of the nineteenth century. His influence on art, architecture, design and political thought was all-pervading, and, if nothing else, his wallpaper and fabric designs continue to be popular long after his death.
(See also Bexley, Waltham Forest, Redbridge, Hackney, Hammersmith & Fulham and Westminster 3.)

NASH, Paul (1889–1946), English, painter

Queen Alexandra Mansions, Bidborough Street, WC1. *English Heritage*
Nash, who lived in Flat 176 from 1914 to 1936, was an official war artist in both world wars. His paintings from the Western Front in the First World War are among the best British evocations of the trenches. Later, with Henry Moore (q.v.) and others, he founded Unit One, a short-lived but key group in revitalising British art.

NEPALI COMMUNITY

145 Whitfield Street, W1. *London Borough of Camden*
The plaque records that the first settlement of the Nepali community in London began on this site in 1965.

NEWMAN, Cardinal John Henry (1801–90), English, prelate

17 Southampton Place, Holborn, WC1.
Duke of Bedford
John Newman lived here in early life. Ordained into the Anglican church in 1824, he converted to Catholicism in 1845. His *Apologia Pro Vita Sua* (1864) was an exploration of his spiritual evolution and is

recognised as a theological and literary classic. He became a cardinal in 1879. (See also City and Richmond upon Thames.)

PATMORE, Coventry (1823–96), English, poet, essayist
14 Percy Street, Fitzrovia, W1.
London County Council
Patmore, who lived here in 1863–64, was a librarian at the British Museum from 1846 to 1866 and a member of the Pre-Raphaelite circle. His best-known work, *The Angel in the House* (1854–63), is a eulogy to Victorian ideals of marriage. He married three times and had six children.

PERCEVAL, Spencer (1762–1812), English, Prime Minister
59–60 Lincoln's Inn Fields, WC2.
London County Council
Perceval, who lived here, was Prime Minister from 1809 to 1812, his term of office brought to an end by John Bellingham, a mentally unsound man with a grievance, who shot him in the lobby of the House of Commons. He is so far the only British Prime Minister to have been assassinated.

PITT, David, Lord (1913–94), Grenadian, physician, politician
200 North Gower Street, NW1.
London Borough of Camden
Lord Pitt worked here as a general practitioner from 1950 to 1984. His basement was used as the informal headquarters and talking shop for all the exiled leaders of African independence movements. He was the first black chair of the Greater London Council in 1974 and was made a life peer in 1975.

PRE-RAPHAELITE BROTHERHOOD
7 Gower Street, Bloomsbury, WC1.
English Heritage
Meeting in Millais's parents' house here in 1848, John Everett Millais (q.v.), Dante Gabriel Rossetti (q.v.) and William Holman Hunt (q.v.), all students at the Royal Academy, were the founders. By the autumn they were seven, including Thomas Woolner (q.v.). As a formal group they lasted barely four years, but they made a major impact, being assailed by Sir Charles Eastlake (q.v.), the President of the Royal Academy, and by Dickens (q.v.), but powerfully supported by Ruskin (q.v.), both critically and financially.

PUGIN, Augustus Charles (1762–1832), French, painter, illustrator
106 Great Russell Street, Bloomsbury, WC1.
Duke of Bedford
Pugin, who lived here, came to England in 1792 and worked as an architectural draughtsman and producer of topographical prints. He illustrated numerous books such as *The Public Buildings of London* (1825–8) and *Architectural Antiquities of Britain* (1826). He shares the plaque with his son (see below).

PUGIN, Augustus Welby Northmore (1812–52), English, architect
106 Great Russell Street, Bloomsbury, WC1. *Duke of Bedford*
Pugin, who lived here with his father (see above), was the leader of the Gothic Revival, a prolific creator of churches and houses, notable for designing every feature of his buildings down to the screws. His book *Contrasts* (1836) is his manifesto. He is most famous for his work on the Houses of Parliament, with Barry (q.v.).

PYTHON, Monty, English, Flying Circus leader
Neal's Yard, Covent Garden, WC2.
Animation Lighting and Recording Studios
The plaque is erected where the *Monty Python* team had their production offices and editing facilities from 1976 to 1987, during their post-television, film-making careers. Monty Python himself is a seminal figure in late twentieth-century British culture – the brains behind the legendary *Flying Circus*, seen on BBC television from 1969 to 1974. Spoken of with awe by those who met him, he is rumoured to have had affairs with most of the world's beautiful women. There are no known photographs of this showbiz colossus.

REID, Elizabeth Jesser (1789–1866), English, reformer, philanthropist
48 Bedford Square, WC1. *Private*
Reid founded Bedford College for Women (see page 119) here in 1849. She was active in the anti-slavery campaign, and in close touch with various movements in the European revolutions of 1848. She left her

fortune in trust to the college, and a hall of residence in the modern college is named in her honour.

RICARDO, Sir Harry (1885–1974), English, engineer
13 Bedford Square, WC1. *English Heritage*
Sir Harry, who was born here, was one of the foremost pioneers in the early development of the internal combustion engine. He helped improve the engines in the early tanks, oversaw research into octane ratings, and developed the sleeve valve and the diesel pre-combustion chamber.

RIMBAUD, Arthur (1854–91), French, poet
8 Royal College Street, NW1. *Private*
The original *enfant terrible*, Rimbaud stayed here in 1873 with Paul Verlaine (see page 133) during their tempestuous eighteen-month relationship, which was to end in Brussels with a drunken Verlaine shooting Rimbaud in the hand. While here, Rimbaud was working on *Une Saison en Enfer* (1873) and his major work *Illuminations* (1874). One of the greatest figures in French literature, he continues to inspire devotees from Jim Morrison to Bob Dylan.

ROBINSON, James (1813–62), English, physician
14 Gower Street, Bloomsbury, WC1.
English Heritage
Robinson lived and worked here. On 19 December 1846, in the home of an American botanist, Francis Boott, at 52 Gower Street, Robinson administered ether (for the first time in Britain) to a Miss Lonsdale, and removed a troublesome tooth. (See also Anaesthetic, page 118.)

ROMILLY, Sir Samuel (1757–1818), English, lawyer, reformer
6 Gray's Inn Square, Holborn, WC1. *Private*
21 Russell Square, Bloomsbury, WC1.
Duke of Bedford
Sir Samuel occupied legal chambers in Gray's Inn from 1778 to 1791 and lived in Russell Square. While at Gray's Inn he wrote his *Thoughts on Executive Justice* (1786), outlining his ideas on law reform. The death penalty was then still applicable wholesale and he fought, largely without success, to reduce the number of offences to which it applied. His one notable success was the repeal in 1812 of an Elizabethan statute which made it a capital offence for a soldier or mariner to beg without permission from a magistrate or his commanding officer.

ROSSETTI, Christina Georgina (1830–94), English, poet
30 Torrington Square, Bloomsbury, WC1.
Duke of Bedford
Rossetti, who lived and died here, was in poor health most of her life, which may explain the melancholy which characterises her work. Her poem 'In the Bleak Midwinter' (1875) was set to music by Holst (q.v.). She was hailed in her time, forgotten in the onrush of modernism, and is now being rediscovered. She was the sister of D. G. Rossetti (see below).

ROSSETTI, Dante Gabriel (1828–82), English, poet, painter
17 Red Lion Square, WC1.
London County Council
A founder of the Pre-Raphaelite Brotherhood, Rossetti, who lived here from 1851, was a major influence on William Morris (q.v.) and Edward Burne-Jones (q.v.), who share this plaque with him. His sensual, medievalist ideas were realised in a series of portraits of his wife, Elizabeth Siddal, and mistresses Fanny Cornforth and Jane Burden (Morris's wife). In his grief at Siddal's death, he buried his poems with her at Highgate, but they were subsequently exhumed and published in 1870, to great controversy since they were found rather racy by the standards of the day. (See also Kensington & Chelsea 2 and Westminster 2.)

ROY, Ram Mohun (1772–1833), Bengali, scholar, reformer
49 Bedford Square, Bloomsbury, WC1.
Greater London Council
Roy, who lived here, is best remembered for his struggle against suttee, the Indian custom of burning widows on their husbands' funeral pyres, but he also fought for women's rights more generally: to inherit, and not to be forced into child marriage, nor into a polygamous marriage. He came to England as ambassador of the Mughal Empire and died here.

RUSHTON, Willie (1937–96), English, comic actor, cartoonist
Mornington Crescent Underground Station, NW1. *Comic Heritage*
A co-founder of *Private Eye*, Rushton achieved fame as a member of the *That Was The Week That Was* team on BBC television and subsequently achieved national treasure status as a panellist on the radio programme *I'm Sorry I Haven't a Clue* (1974–96), featuring the surreal game of 'Mornington Crescent', which is why the plaque is here, rather than in Earl's Court, where he lived.

RUSSELL, Bertrand (1872–1970), English, philosopher, peace campaigner
Russell Chambers, Bury Place, WC1.
English Heritage
Russell, who lived here in Flat 34 from 1911 to 1916, published innumerable books on a wide range of topics. His most important work of philosophy was *Principia Mathematica*, written with Alfred Whitehead in 1910. He was awarded the Nobel Prize for Literature in 1950. He was one of the founders of the Campaign for Nuclear Disarmament in 1958, and even in very great age remained an active figurehead of the movement.

SALISBURY, third Marquess of (1830–1903), English, Prime Minister
21 Fitzroy Square, Fitzrovia, W1.
London County Council
Lord Salisbury lived here. He was descended from Elizabeth I's adviser William Cecil and was three times Prime Minister (1885–6, 1886–92 and 1895–1902). During his last term of office he was also effectively Foreign Secretary and saw the British Empire at its zenith. He was deeply conservative, yet, for example, a supporter of Octavia Hill (q.v.). Arguably the greatest of Victoria's Prime Ministers, he was the last holder of that office to sit in the House of Lords.

SALMOND, Sir John Maitland (1881–1968), English, air force officer
27 Chester Terrace, NW1. *English Heritage*
Sir John, who lived here from 1928 to 1936, commanded various Royal Flying Corps units in the

First World War. On the creation of the Royal Air Force, he was appointed General Officer Commanding the RAF in the field. In 1923–4 he was GOC Iraq Command, suppressing rebellion from the air by bombing villages thought to harbour rebels – a new use for aircraft. From 1930 to 1933 he was Chief of the Air Staff. In retirement he was president of the RAF Club for twenty-three years.

SAYERS, Dorothy L. (1893–1957), English, novelist
24 Great James Street, WC1. *English Heritage*
Dorothy Sayers, who lived here from 1921 to 1929, is best remembered for the Lord Peter Wimsey stories, classics of the detective genre, perhaps the most famous of them being *The Nine Tailors* (1934). In 1937 she abandoned detective fiction to work on radio plays and her translation of Dante.

SAYERS, Tom (1826–65), English, boxer
257 Camden High Street, NW1.
English Heritage
Sayers, who lived here from 1860 until his death, became English heavyweight champion in 1857, when boxing was still illegal and conducted with bare knuckles. In a career running from 1849 to 1860, he lost only once. His last fight was for the world crown against the American John Heenan; after two hours and twenty minutes, amid scenes bordering on riot, it was declared a draw. A public subscription raised £3,000 for his retirement. A year after he retired, the Anti Prize Fight Act of 1861 ended the bare-knuckle era.

SHAW, George Bernard (1856–1950), Irish, playwright, critic
29 Fitzroy Square, W1. *St Pancras Borough Council*
Shaw, who lived here from 1887 to 1898, was probably the most famous theatre critic prior to Kenneth Tynan. With an opinion on everything, he championed Fabianism, vegetarianism and women's rights. A prodigious writer, he produced over fifty plays, of which *Pygmalion* (1913) and *St Joan* (1923) stand out. He was awarded the Nobel Prize for Literature in 1925. (See also Westminster 4.)

SICKERT, Walter (1860–1942), English, painter
6 Mornington Crescent, NW1.
Greater London Council
Sickert, who lived and worked here, was encouraged early in his career by Whistler (q.v.) and Degas. He was an Impressionist, but very English; he said he preferred the kitchen to the drawing room as a scene

for a painting. He was a co-founder of the Camden Town Group in 1911. He is, ridiculously, one of the suspects in the ongoing 'Who was Jack the Ripper?' debate. (See also Islington.)

SIEBE, Augustus (1788–1872), German, inventor
5 Denmark Street, WC2. *English Heritage*
Siebe lived and worked here from 1830 until his death. He designed the first diving helmet and sealed suit in which air was pumped from above. Similar diving suits remained in use with the Royal Navy until 1989.

SLOANE, Sir Hans (1660–1753), English, physician, naturalist
4 Bloomsbury Place, Bloomsbury, WC1.
London County Council
Sir Hans, who lived here from 1695 to 1742, began his plant collection while physician to the governor of Jamaica. He later became secretary of the Royal Society (1693–1713) and physician to Queen Anne, George I and George II. In 1721 he ceded his Chelsea Physic Garden in perpetuity to the Apothecaries' Company. His wide-ranging collection of books and artefacts was sold to the nation by his executors for

£20,000 and formed the nucleus of the British Museum. He also invented the milk chocolate drink. (See also Kensington & Chelsea 2.)

SLOVO, Joe (1926–95), South African, freedom fighter
13 Lyme Street, NW1. *English Heritage*
Slovo lived here with his wife, Ruth First (see page 123), from 1966 to 1978. A leading member of the South African Communist Party (SACP), he was one of the key figures in setting up *Umkhonto we Sizwe*, the military organisation formed jointly by the African National Congress and the SACP in 1961. He went into exile in 1963 after the Rivonia state of emergency, and in England he and Ruth First became central figures in the anti-apartheid movement. He was Minister of Housing in Nelson Mandela's first cabinet.

SMIRKE, Sir Robert (1781–1867), English, architect
81 Charlotte Street, Fitzrovia, W1.
Greater London Council
Sir Robert, who lived here, was an architect in the classical mode. His works include the Royal Mint (1809), the British Museum (1823–31), the Royal College of Physicians (now Canada House) on Trafalgar Square (1824–7), and the east wing of Somerset House (1831).

SMITH, Sydney (1771–1845), English, clergyman, wit
14 Doughty Street, WC1.
London County Council
Smith, who lived here, was the least reverend clergyman in the history of the Church of England. He founded and edited the *Edinburgh Review* (1802–28). Churches were always packed for his sermons. Among his thoughts was: 'My idea of heaven is eating *pâté de foie gras* to the sound of trumpets.'

STOPES, Marie (1880–1958), Scottish, reformer, writer
108 Whitfield Street, Fitzrovia, W1. *Private*
Stopes opened her Mothers' Clinic in Upper Holloway but moved it here to be more central in 1925, and

here it remains to this day. Marie Stopes International now operates in thirty-eight countries, with 452 clinics. (See also Camden 1 and Islington.)

STRACHEY, Lytton (1880–1932), English, essayist, biographer
51 Gordon Square, Bloomsbury, WC1.
Greater London Council
50 Gordon Square, Bloomsbury, WC1.
Camden Borough Council
Strachey, who lived at No. 51, was a prominent member of the Bloomsbury Group (whose group plaque is at No. 50). A landmark in the history of biography, his *Eminent Victorians* (1918) by its wit and iconoclasm broke through to a very wide audience. His *Queen Victoria* (1921), affectionate but far from unctuous, similarly blew away the fawning of previous biographies.

SUN YAT-SEN (1866–1925), Chinese, politician
4 Warwick Court, Holborn, WC1.
Private
Sun Yat-sen, who lived in a house on this site when in exile, was provisional president in 1912 of the first post-imperial government of China. He is known as 'the Father of Modern China', and his name, uniquely, is honoured in both Beijing and Taiwan. His political philosophy was based on the 'three principles' – nationalism, democracy and socialism.

SYMONS, George James (1838–1900), English, meteorologist
62 Camden Square, Camden Town, NW1. *Private*
Symons, who lived here from 1868 until his death, joined the Meteorological Office under Fitzroy (q.v.) in 1860, and in that year he published the first *Annual Report of British Rainfall*, with data from 168 stations. By the time of his last *Report*, in 1899, the data was being collected from 3,528 stations.

TAWNEY, R. H. (1880–1962), English, economic historian, Christian socialist
21 Mecklenburgh Square, WC1.
Greater London Council

Tawney, who lived here, was involved with the Workers' Education Association from 1905 throughout his career and was its president from 1928 to 1944. He has been called 'the patron saint of adult education'. His greatest work was *Religion and the Rise of Capitalism* (1926), which remains influential, long after his brand of socialism has largely disappeared from the Houses of Parliament. (See also Camden 1.)

THOMAS, Dylan (1914–53), Welsh, poet
54 Delancey Street, Camden Town, NW1.
Greater London Council
Thomas, who lived here, was a romantic, exuberant, musical poet, and a noted public reader of his own work, which won him a following on both sides of the Atlantic. His most famous work, *Under Milk Wood*, a verse play set in the fictional village of Llareggub, was broadcast on BBC Radio in 1954 with Richard Burton as First Voice.

THURLOE, John (1616–68), English, politician, lawyer
Lincoln's Inn, Chancery Lane, WC2.
Cromwell Association
Thurloe, who lived in Old Square at various times in his life, was between 1653 and 1660 the Protectorate's head of intelligence and broke up several Royalist plots against Cromwell and Parliament. On the Restoration he was arrested for high treason, but released on condition that he assisted the new regime if asked.

TREVITHICK, Richard (1771–1833), English, engineer, inventor
The Chadwick Building, UCL, Gower Street, WC1.
Trevithick Centenary Memorial Committee
Trevithick was one of the greatest engineers in history. In 1808, near this spot, his engine *Catch Me If You Can* ran on a circular track in

'Trevithick's Steam Circus' and successfully demonstrated that locomotion by steam was faster than by horse. Admission cost one shilling, including a ride.

UNITY THEATRE
Unity Mews, Chalton Street, NW1.
St Pancras Housing Association
Unity Theatre arose out of the agitprop movement of the early 1930s. Based in a converted chapel, with support from Bernard Shaw (q.v.), H. G. Wells (q.v.) and Sybil Thorndike (q.v.), it presented a roster of left-wing drama, including the first Brecht production in England in 1938, the same year that Paul Robeson starred there, and a political pantomime, *Babes in the Wood*, caused a sensation. The theatre was destroyed by fire in 1975, but a trust continues the work.

VERLAINE, Paul (1844–96), French, poet
8 Royal College Street, NW1. *Private*
Verlaine, a major figure in *fin de siècle* French poetry, stayed here with Arthur Rimbaud (see page 129) during their tempestuous eighteen-month affair, which had begun with Rimbaud seducing Verlaine away from his wife and son. As a member of the Symbolist movement, Verlaine was noted for the musicality of his verse, exemplified in his most important work, *Romances sans Paroles* (1874), which he was working on in between the rows while staying here.

WAKLEY, Thomas (1795–1862), English, physician, journalist
35 Bedford Square, Bloomsbury, WC1.
London County Council
Wakley, who lived here, founded *The Lancet* in 1823, attacking the jobbery then common in the medical profession. He was a Radical MP for Finsbury from 1835 to 1852 and campaigned for the setting up of coronerships. As coroner for West Middlesex (1839–62), he fought against flogging in the army, which was finally abolished in 1868.

WELLCOME, Sir Henry (1853–1936), Anglo-American, pharmacist
6 Gloucester Gate, Regent's Park, NW1.
English Heritage
Sir Henry, who lived here, founded Burroughs Wellcome Pharmaceuticals in 1880, which grew to be one of the largest drugs companies in the world and is now part of GlaxoSmithKline. He set up the Wellcome

Foundation in 1924, which is now a major charity funding medical research and holding Sir Henry's vast collection of medical books, manuscripts, pictures, equipment and other artefacts.

WILLAN, Dr Robert (1757–1812), English, dermatologist
10 Bloomsbury Square, Bloomsbury, WC1.
London County Council
Dr Willan, who lived here, was from a Yorkshire family of physicians. He was the founder of dermatology as a separate medical specialism, his work *On Cutaneous Diseases* (1808) being the first to classify diseases of the skin systematically. Many of the terms he coined are still in use.

WILLIAMS, Sir George (1821–1905), English, Christian reformer
13 Russell Square, Bloomsbury, WC1.
Private
Sir George, who lived here from 1879 until his death, was the founder of the Young Men's Christian Association in 1844. It grew rapidly across the world, and on the fiftieth anniversary of its foundation Sir George was knighted by Queen Victoria and given the Freedom of the City of London. The YMCA now operates in 124 countries and claims 45 million members. (See also City.)

WOLLSTONECRAFT, Mary (1759–97), English, feminist writer
Oakshott Court, Werrington Street, NW1.
Camden Borough Council
Wollstonecraft, who lived in a house on this site, worked as assistant to the publisher Joseph Johnson and became acquainted with Thomas Paine (q.v.) and William Godwin, whom she married. Her most famous book, *A Vindication of the Rights of Women* (1792), advocated equal rights for women, and she is honoured as a feminist a century before the term was invented. (See also Southwark and Hackney.)

WOOLF, Virginia (1882–1941), English, novelist, critic
29 Fitzroy Square, W1. *Greater London Council*
50 Gordon Square, Bloomsbury, WC1.
Camden Borough Council
Virginia Woolf, who lived at 29 Fitzroy Square from 1907 to 1911, was a daughter of Sir Leslie Stephen (q.v.). It was while resident here that she, with her sister Vanessa, became the nucleus of the Bloomsbury Group (the plaque at 50 Gordon Square), the hugely influential group of friends who virtually frog-marched English art and literature into the twentieth century. She is regarded as a key innovator in modern novel-writing; her major works include *Mrs Dalloway* (1925), *To the Lighthouse* (1927) and *The Waves* (1931). She suffered from bouts of mental instability throughout her life and eventually committed suicide. (See also Richmond upon Thames.)

WYATT, Thomas Henry (1807–80), English, architect
77 Great Russell Street, Bloomsbury, WC1.
Greater London Council
Wyatt, who lived and died here, was a prolific architect, regarded as a safe pair of establishment hands, not wedded to any one style. Most of his work was in Wiltshire and Monmouthshire. His interesting Garrison Church at Woolwich (1863) is now a Second World War bomb site, preserved as the Guards' Memorial. He was President of the Royal Institute of British Architects from 1870 to 1873.

YEATS, William Butler (1865–1939), Irish, poet, playwright
5 Woburn Walk, St Pancras, WC1.
St Pancras Borough Council
23 Fitzroy Road, Fitzrovia, W1.
London County Council
Yeats, who lived at both addresses, was a giant of English language literature of the twentieth century and a key figure in the Irish literary revival as co-founder of the Abbey Theatre (1904). He was awarded the Nobel Prize in 1923, and his lines speak for the age: 'Things fall apart, the centre cannot hold.' (See also Hounslow.)

ZEPPELIN RAID
Lincoln's Inn Chapel, Old Square, Chancery Lane, WC2. *Private*
Although the Zeppelin raids had a psychological effect, after the dust had settled it was calculated that the cost of building the airships was six times the amount of damage they caused. (See Air raids, page 118; also Hackney and Islington.)

GREENWICH

Lying south of the river, the London Borough
of Greenwich is an amalgamation of the former
metropolitan boroughs of Greenwich and
Woolwich (minus North Woolwich, which
went to Newham).

ARNOLD, John (1736–99), English, watchmaker
Well Hall Pleasaunce, SE9.
London Borough of Greenwich
Arnold lived at Well Hall House on this site from
1779 until his death. He had a great rivalry with
Thomas Earnshaw (q.v.) in the production of
chronometers. He secured patents for escapement
and balance spring designs, and one of his
chronometers travelled with Cook (q.v.) on his
second voyage (1772–5). In 1788 he produced the
first pocket chronometer. He shares this plaque with
Edith Nesbit (see page 137).

BARLOW, William Henry (1812–1902), English,
engineer
Highcombe, 145 Charlton Road, SE7.
English Heritage
Barlow, who lived and died here, worked extensively
on the design of the Midland Railway, and the
'saddleback' form of rail bears his name. He worked
with Hawkshaw to complete Brunel's Clifton
Suspension Bridge. He was also a member of the
court of enquiry into the Tay Bridge disaster.

BLACKHEATH FOOTBALL CLUB
The Princess of Wales, Montpelier Row, SE3.
Private
There are two plaques. The first records that
Blackheath, the oldest rugby union club in the
world, founded in 1858, was based here and played
on the heath for many years. The second records the
picking of the first England fifteen here in 1871;
they played Scotland in Edinburgh on 25 March and
lost.

CHESTERFIELD, Philip Dormer, fourth Earl of
(1694–1773), English, writer
**Ranger's House, Chesterfield Walk, Greenwich,
SE10.** *London County Council*

PHILIP
4th EARL OF CHESTERFIELD
(1694-1773)
STATESMAN AND AUTHOR
Lived here

Chesterfield, who bought this house in 1748 and made
extensive alterations, famously incurred the wrath of
Dr Johnson (q.v.) by failing to carry out his offer to be
patron of Johnson's *Dictionary*. Noted as a wit and
orator, his reputation rests on his letters to his
(illegitimate) son (published in 1774) and to his
godson (published in 1890), which set out the ways a
gentleman should behave. He was a member of the
circle of Swift, Pope (q.v.) and Bolingbroke. (See also
Camden 2.)

DAY-LEWIS, Cecil (1904–72), English, poet,
novelist
6 Crooms Hill, Greenwich, SE10. *English Heritage*
Day-Lewis, who lived here from 1957 until his death,

was associated in left-wing causes with Auden and Spender in the 1930s. He was Professor of Poetry at Oxford (1951–6) and Poet Laureate (1968–72). He also wrote, under the pseudonym Nicholas Blake, a very successful string of detective stories, featuring the sleuth Nigel Strangeways.

DEPTFORD CREEK
Creek Road, SE10. *Greenwich and Deptford History Trail*
The plaque, situated in the middle of a defunct swing bridge carrying the main road from Deptford to Greenwich, does not mention that the creek was formerly the site of a thriving shipbuilding industry, with numerous small slipways, much of it doing sub-contracted work for the Royal Dockyard at Deptford.

DYSON, Sir Frank
(1868–1939), English, astronomer
6 Vanbrugh Hill, Blackheath, SE3.
English Heritage
Sir Frank, who lived here from 1894 to 1906, was Astronomer Royal for Scotland (1905–10), and then for England (1910–33). He was an authority on the spectrum of the corona in solar eclipses, and in 1924 he invented the Greenwich time signal 'pips'.

EDDINGTON, Sir Arthur (1882–1944), English, physicist
4 Bennett Park, Blackheath, SE3.
Greater London Council
Sir Arthur, who lived here, was a leading exponent of Einstein's theory of relativity, which he endeavoured to explain to a wider public in several publications in the 1920s and 1930s. He was involved with Sir Frank Dyson (see above) in the 1919 eclipse expeditions, which first confirmed relativity. The story is told of someone approaching him and saying: 'There are only three people in the world who understand Einstein's theory.' After a pause, Sir Arthur replied: 'Really, I was just trying to work out who the third one could be.'

GLADSTONE, William Ewart
(1809–98), English, Prime Minister
Eglinton Road School, SE18.
Private
Among the great man's thoughts in his last speech, delivered here, were 'National injustice is the surest road to national downfall' and 'The disease of an evil conscience is beyond the practice of all the physicians of all the countries in the world'. (See also Westminster 2 and Westminster 4.)

GOUNOD, Charles François (1818–93), French, composer
17 Morden Road, SE3. *London County Council*
Gounod, who stayed here in 1870, lived in England from 1870 to 1875 to avoid the Franco-Prussian War. His best-known works are his operas *Faust* (1859) and *Roméo et Juliette* (1867). His short piece *Funeral March for a Marionette* was used as the theme music for the television series *Alfred Hitchcock Presents*.

GPO FILM UNIT
47 Bennett Park, Blackheath, SE3.
English Heritage
The GPO Film Unit, which later became the Crown Film Unit, had its studios here from 1933 to 1943. Created by John Grierson, the father of British documentary film, it produced a number of ground-breaking films in the 1930s, most famously *Night Mail* (1936), with music by Britten (q.v.) and verse commentary by Auden. During the Second World War, as the Crown Film Unit, it produced morale boosters such as *London Can Take It!* (1940), made by Humphrey Jennings (q.v.) and Harry Watt.

HAWTHORNE, Nathaniel (1804–64), American, novelist
4 Pond Road, Blackheath, SE3.
London County Council

Hawthorne, who stayed here in 1856, was in England as United States consul in Liverpool. His works include *The House of Seven Gables* (1851), *Tanglewood Tales* (1853) and, most famously, *The Scarlet Letter* (1850), his fictionalised account of the Salem witch trials.

HOPE, Bob (1903–2003), American, actor, comedian
44 Craigton Road, Eltham, SE9.
British Film Institute
Bob Hope was born in this house, but his family emigrated when he was five and he became an American at the age of seventeen. He worked in vaudeville as a comedian and dancer and made his first film appearance in 1934. Best-known for the 'Road' films made with Bing Crosby from 1940 to 1961, he also hosted the Oscars ceremony on innumerable occasions, his running gag being his frustration at never receiving an award himself. As he said, 'Welcome to the Academy Awards, or, as it's known at my house, Passover'.

JEFFERIES, Richard (1848–87), English, naturalist, novelist
59 Footscray Road, Eltham, SE9.
Greater London Council
Jefferies, who lived here, was noted for his depiction of English rural life, whether in fiction such as *Bevis* (1882) and *After London* (1885), or in essays such as *Round about a Great Estate* (1880) and *Nature near London* (1883), or in his autobiography *Story of My Heart* (1883). (See also Lewisham.)

McGILL, Donald (1875–1962), English, cartoonist
5 Bennett Park, Blackheath, SE3.
Greater London Council
From 1904 to his death, McGill, who lived here, produced over twelve thousand postcard cartoons, characterised by what George Orwell (q.v.) called 'enthusiastic indecency', featuring large wives, weedy husbands, buxom wenches and *double entendres* to drive the censors wild. One of his postcards, 'Do you like Kipling?' – 'I don't know, you naughty boy, I've never kippled!', supposedly holds the world record for selling the most copies at over six million.

MORRISON, Herbert (1888–1965), English, politician
55 Archery Road, Eltham, SE9.
Greater London Council
Morrison, who lived here from 1929 to 1960, was founder and secretary in 1915 of the London Labour Party, Mayor of Hackney (1920–1), joined the London County Council in 1922, became its leader in 1934, MP for South Hackney three times between 1923 and 1945, Home Secretary in the War Cabinet, and Leader of the House from 1945 to 1951.

NESBIT, Edith (1858–1924), English, children's writer
Well Hall Pleasaunce, SE9.
London Borough of Greenwich
Nesbit, who lived here from 1899 to 1920 in a house demolished in 1931, was the author of forty children's books, among which *The Story of the Treasure Seekers* (1898), *The Wouldbegoods* (1899) and *The Railway Children* (1906) are still popular. She was also a committed socialist and one of the founders of the Fabian Society (q.v.). (See also Lewisham.)

SVEVO, Italo (1861–1928), Italian, novelist
67 Charlton Church Lane, SE7. *English Heritage*
Svevo, pen-name of Ettore Schmitz, lived here from 1903 to 1913. His early novels were unsuccessful, but with the encouragement and patronage of James Joyce (q.v.) he achieved recognition for his work. He is best remembered for *As a Man Grows Older* (1898) and *Confessions of Zeno* (1923).

VANBRUGH, Sir John (1664–1726), English, architect, playwright
Vanbrugh Castle, Maze Hill, SE10. *Private*
Sir John was imprisoned in France from 1688 to 1692, accused of being a spy, in the wake of being part of the plot to depose James II and put William III on the English throne. His radicalism was manifest also in his architecture and plays. He invented the style called English Baroque, and Castle Howard and Blenheim Palace show his uninhibited grandeur. His plays *The Relapse* (1696) and *The Provok'd Wife* (1697) were far ahead of their time both in explicit sexual content and in championing women's rights.

WAUGH, Reverend Benjamin (1839–1908), English, churchman
26 Crooms Hill, SE10. *Greater London Council*

While working as a Congregationalist minister in the Greenwich slums, Waugh, who lived here, was particularly shocked at the circumstances of the children. He wrote a polemic, *The Gaol Cradle, Who Rocks It?* (1873), arguing for the creation of juvenile courts and detention centres, as necessary, to divert children from the inevitable slide into crime. A few years later he went on to found the National Society for the Prevention of Cruelty to Children. (See also Barnet and Enfield.)

WOLFE, General James (1727–59), English, soldier
McCartney House, Greenwich Park, SE10.
London County Council
Wolfe, who lived here, served gallantly at Dettingen, Falkirk, Culloden and Louisbourg. At Culloden he famously refused a direct order from Cumberland to shoot a wounded Scots prisoner, saying his honour would not allow it. As a major-general, he was given the task of taking Quebec by Pitt (q.v.). His troops scaled the cliffs, surprised the French and defeated them on the Plains of Abraham, ending French rule in North America. Wolfe died in the hour of victory.

WOLSELEY, Field Marshal Garnet (1833–1913), English, soldier
Ranger's House, Chesterfield Walk, SE10.
London County Council
Wolseley, who lived here, entered the army in 1852 and had a career of unparalleled distinction and gallantry, from the Crimea, the Indian Mutiny, the

Second Opium War and the Red River Rebellion to his most brilliant campaign, the Ashanti War of 1873–4. He was commander-in-chief (1890–5), and the description 'All Sir Garnet' meant something was absolutely correct.

HACKNEY

Lying directly north of the City, the London Borough of Hackney is made up of the three former metropolitan boroughs of Hackney, Shoreditch and Stoke Newington.

ABNEY HOUSE
82 Stoke Newington Church Street, N16.
London Borough of Hackney
Abney House, which stood on this site from 1700 to 1843, was described by Dr Isaac Watts (see page 148) as 'Manly and plain, such was the builder's soul'. It had 25 acres of grounds, in which the longtime lady of the manor, Lady Mary Abney, planted such a variety of trees that for a time there were more kinds here than at Kew Gardens. The house was demolished and the grounds became Abney Park Cemetery.

AIR RAID PRECAUTION CENTRE
24 Rossendale Street, E5.
London Borough of Hackney
Possibly the least prepossessing location for a plaque in London, this building is Grade II listed for its significance in the Second World War. Built in 1938, the centre co-ordinated information on bombing raids in the area, the deployment of emergency rescue teams and the organisation of repair work.

BALCON, Sir Michael (1896–1977), English, film producer
Poole Street, Hoxton, N1.
London Borough of Hackney
This was the site of the Gainsborough Film Studios (see page 142), founded by Sir Michael Balcon in 1924. Balcon is a major figure in British cinema history. He remained here until 1936, when he was briefly seduced to MGM in Hollywood. In 1938 he returned and took over Ealing Studios. (See also Westminster 4 and Ealing.)

BARBAULD, Anna Laetitia (1743–1825), English, poet
113 Stoke Newington Church Street, N16.
London Borough of Hackney
Barbauld lived here from 1802 until her death. Her poetry, admired by Wordsworth, includes the prescient *Eighteen Hundred and Eleven*, which foresees the decline of Britain and the rise of the United States, from where tourists will come to visit with nostalgia 'the gray ruin and the mouldering stone' of England.

BOLAN, Marc (1947–77), English, rock star
25 Stoke Newington Common, N16.
London Borough of Hackney
Bolan, stage-name of Mark Feld, lived here until he was fifteen. He was lead singer and mainspring of the superstar glam rock boogie duo T Rex, which had four number one hits, and their every record between October 1970 and June 1973 made the top ten. He was killed in a car crash in 1977 on Queen's Ride, Barnes; the site is still a shrine.

BOMB, First of the First World War
31 Nevill Road, N16.
London Borough of Hackney
The first bomb of the First World War fell here in the garden of the Nevill Arms pub on 30 May 1915, dropped from a Zeppelin. The Zeppelins were regarded as yet another example of the perfidy of the Hun, though their effectiveness was more psychological than due to their causing any major damage. (See also Islington and Camden 2.)

BRADLAUGH, Charles (1833–91), English, politician
Regan Way, N1. *London Borough of Hackney*
The plaque records that Bradlaugh, 'Freethinker, Malthusian and Republican', was born near this site. In 1877 he and Annie Besant (q.v.) published *The Fruits of Philosophy*, Charles Knowlton's book advocating birth control, which earned them six months in prison for uttering an obscene libel. Elected to Parliament in 1880, he asked to affirm the oath of office rather than swear on the Bible and ended up in the Tower for contempt. He was finally admitted to the House in 1886.

BRAIDWOOD, Thomas (1715–1806), Scottish, teacher
Chatham Place, E9. *London Borough of Hackney*
The plaque records that the Braidwood Academy for the Deaf and Dumb, the first such school in England, stood on this site from 1783 to 1799. Thomas Braidwood had opened his original school for the deaf and dumb in Edinburgh in 1760 and developed a sign language system, still known as the Braidwoodian Method.

BRITANNIA THEATRE
103–104 Hoxton Street, N1.
London Borough of Hackney
The plaque records that on this site stood the Britannia Saloon, opened in 1841, which became the Britannia Theatre when rebuilt in 1858. As well as music hall, it was famous for presenting shocking melodramas such as *The Murder in the Red Barn* and *Sweeney Todd*, and for its annual pantomimes, which often ran until Easter. Bomb-damaged in 1940, it was demolished in 1941.

BROOKE HOUSE
Community College, Kenninghall Road, E5.
London Borough of Hackney
The plaque records that Brooke House stood on this site from the late fifteenth century until it was demolished in 1955, after bomb damage in the Second World War. The house had an eventful history, owned by Thomas Cromwell and later Henry VIII (q.v.), occupied by the Greville family (see below) in the seventeenth century, and run as a private mental asylum from 1759 to 1940.

BROOKS, James (1825–1901), English, architect
42 Clissold Crescent, N16.
London Borough of Hackney
The plaque records that Brooks designed and built this house and lived in it from c.1862 until his death. His field was church architecture, and he was a convinced high churchman, building large, simple, solid churches, usually of brick. His London designs include St Michael, Shoreditch, St Columba and St Chad, both in Hoxton, Holy Innocents, Hammersmith, and St John the Baptist, Kensington.

BROWN, PC Laurence (1963–90), English, police officer
Pownall Road, E8. *Police Memorial Trust*
On 28 August 1990 PC Brown was shot dead here with a sawn-off shotgun as he approached a suspect in an ambush, having responded to a routine 999 call.

BURBAGE, James (d.1597), English, actor
86–90 Curtain Road, EC2.
London Borough of Hackney
The plaque records that this is the site of 'The Theatre' built by James Burbage and that Shakespeare's works were performed here. The Theatre was built in 1576 for the Earl of Leicester's Company, and when the lease expired in 1597 the company dismantled the structure and rebuilt it in Southwark as the Globe (q.v.). Burbage was the father of the more famous Richard Burbage. There is also an LCC plaque on the site (see below).

BURTT, John (1855–1925), English, evangelist
13–14 Hoxton Market, N1.
London Borough of Hackney
Burtt and his brother Lewis (see page 141) were the founders, secretary and honorary superintendent respectively, of the Hoxton Market Christian Mission,

begun in 1886, and operating from these premises from 1915 'for the benefit of local people'.

BURTT, Lewis 'Daddy' (1860–1935), English, evangelist
13–14 Hoxton Market, N1.
London Borough of Hackney

Lewis and his older brother John (see page 140) had themselves been educated at a Ragged School, having been found living on the streets. Their mission offered the hundreds of children still in that situation food, clothing and a warm place to sleep. The interior was destroyed by enemy action in 1941 and the building is now a Greek restaurant.

CALMAN, Mel (1931–94), English, cartoonist
64 Linthorpe Road, Stoke Newington, N16.
London Borough of Hackney
Calman lived here from 1931 to 1957. His immortal angst-ridden 'Little Man' first appeared in the *Sunday Telegraph* in 1962 and travelled round the press, ending in *The Times* from 1979 until Calman's death. The character's anxieties reflected Calman's own lifelong depressive tendencies.

CAVELL, Edith (1865–1915), English, nurse
St Leonard's Hospital, Kingsland Road, N1.
London Borough of Hackney
Cavell was assistant matron here from 1903 to 1906. Subsequently she became matron at the Berkendael Institute in Brussels. For helping hundreds of British soldiers to escape German-occupied Belgium, she was arrested and executed by a German firing squad on 12 October 1915. The Allies gained a major propaganda weapon, and Cavell was raised to mythic status. Taking communion the night before her execution, she told the priest: 'Patriotism is not enough; I must have no hatred or bitterness towards anyone.' (See also Tower Hamlets.)

CURTAIN THEATRE
18 Hewett Street, EC2. *London Borough of Hackney*
Near this site stood the Curtain Theatre from 1577 to *c.*1627, the second English public playhouse, where Shakespeare acted and plays by him and Ben Jonson were performed.

DE VERE, Edward (1550–1604), English, poet
173 Stoke Newington Church Street, N16.
London Borough of Hackney
A medieval mansion stood on this site from the fourteenth century until *c.*1714. It was at one time the home of Edward De Vere, a prominent figure at Elizabeth I's court from 1564 until 1582, who married Cecil's daughter. For a time in 1582–3 he was banished from court owing to his violent temper but redeemed himself with service against the Armada in 1588. He is one of the many people suggested to have written Shakespeare's plays.

DEFOE, Daniel (1661–1731), English, novelist, journalist
95 Stoke Newington Church Street, N16.
London County Council
Defoe, who lived in a house on this site from 1714, was three times bankrupt and imprisoned for his satirical pamphlet *The Shortest Way with Dissenters* (1702). He is best known for *Robinson Crusoe* (1719), *Moll Flanders* (1722) and his travel book

A Tour thro' the Whole Island of Great Britain (1724–7). He was a reckless and prolific pamphleteer and editor of one of the earliest newspapers.

EAGLE TAVERN
Shepherdess Walk, N1. *London Borough of Hackney*
The Eagle Tavern was an old pub, rebuilt as a music hall in 1825 and adding the Grecian Saloon in the 1830s. The establishment offered 'Unrivalled galas, brilliant fireworks, cosmoramas, fountains, grottoes, singing, music … all rendering it a fairy scene of which a due estimate can only be formed by inspection'. It was bought by the Salvation Army in 1883, which put a stop to all that. It was demolished in 1901 and rebuilt as just a pub.

ELECTRICITY GENERATING SUB-STATION
32 Rivington Street, EC2. *London Borough of Hackney*
This was a transformer station for the London County Council tramway scheme. It was designed in 1905 by Vincent Harris (q.v.), an LCC architect, and built in 1905–7.

FIELDS, Dame Gracie (1898–1979), English, actress, singer
Poole Street, Hoxton, N1.
London Borough of Hackney
Dame Gracie is one of the stars mentioned here who worked at Gainsborough Films. Among her many popular hits made here were *Sally in Our Alley* (1931), *Sing as we Go* (1934) and *Shipyard Sally* (1939). (See also Camden 1.)

FIENNES, Celia (1662–1741), English, traveller, diarist
Unit 5, 8–20 Well Street, Homerton, E9.
London Borough of Hackney
Fiennes lived in a house near this site from 1738 until her death. Travelling round England on horseback between 1684 and 1703, 'to regain my health by variety and change of air', she is accepted as the first woman to visit every county, covering over a thousand miles in 1698 alone. Her diaries, not intended for publication, came out in 1888 and have been in print ever since.

FRY, Elizabeth (1780–1845), English, reformer
195 Mare Street, E8. *London Borough of Hackney*
This was the site of the Elizabeth Fry Refuge for women in need (1849–1913). Fry was a Quaker,

and her principal life campaign was for the reform of prisons and asylums, having discovered the appalling conditions in Newgate jail. Her face appears on the reverse side of the £5 note. (See also City.)

GAINSBOROUGH FILM STUDIOS
Poole Street, Hoxton, N1.
London Borough of Hackney
The studio building was originally a power station for the Metropolitan Railway and had briefly been run by the American film company Famous Players-Lasky, and so, when Michael Balcon (q.v.) bought it from them and founded Gainsborough Films in 1924, he took over a small efficient team, already including the young Alfred Hitchcock (see page 143). The studios eventually ceased production in 1949 and are now a mixed development of offices and flats.

GERMAN HOSPITAL
Dalston Lane, E8. *London Borough of Hackney*
These buildings were formerly the German Hospital, designed by T. L. Donaldson and E. A. Gruning and built in 1863, primarily to serve the large local German and German-speaking immigrant population, though it also treated other locals. Until after the Second World War it was staffed by German consultants and the nurses were German nuns. With the coming of the National Health Service, it was converted to a psycho-geriatric unit. It has now been redeveloped as flats.

GOSSE, Sir Edmund
(1849–1928), English, poet, critic
56 Mortimer Road, De Beauvoir Town, N1.
Greater London Council
Gosse was born here, in his father's house (see page 143). As a critic, both of literature and art, he is credited with introducing Ibsen's work to Britain and coining the phrase 'New Sculpture' to describe the late Victorian renaissance. He wrote *Father and Son* (1907) about his father, a 'Bible-soaked romantic'.

GOSSE, Philip Henry (1810–88), English, zoologist
56 Mortimer Road, De Beauvoir Town, N1.
Greater London Council
Gosse, who lived here, was a prolific populariser of
natural science, sparking the Victorian craze for
aquaria with *The Aquarium* (1854). He is remembered
above all for *Omphalos* (1857), a gallant, convoluted
attempt to reconcile God's creation with the evidence
of geology.

GREENAWAY, Kate (1846–1901), English, artist,
illustrator
Sylvia Court, Cavendish Street, N1.
London Borough of Hackney
Greenaway was born at 1 Cavendish Street, which
stood near this site. Her illustrations for children's
books, including *Mother Goose* (1881) and *The Language
of Flowers* (1884), made her pre-eminent in the field,
her only rivals being Walter Crane (q.v.) and Randolph
Caldecott (q.v.). The Kate Greenaway Medal has been
awarded annually in her memory to illustrators since
1955. (See also Camden 1 and Islington.)

GREVILLE, Fulke (1554–1628), English, poet,
politician
Community College, Kenninghall Road, E5.
London Borough of Hackney
Greville lived in Brooke House on this site from 1609
until his death. A favourite of Elizabeth I, he was
Secretary for Wales from 1583 to 1628 and Chancellor
of the Exchequer from 1614 to 1621. Author of many
sonnets and other poems, he also wrote a notable
biography of his friend Sir Philip Sidney.

GUNPOWDER PLOT
244–278 Crondall
Street, Hoxton, N1.
*London Borough of
Hackney*
The plaque records that
in a house near this site
on 12 October 1605
Lord Monteagle received a
letter unmasking the plot led
by Guy Fawkes to blow up the Houses
of Parliament. The letter, probably from Francis
Tresham, one of the plotters and Monteagle's brother-
in-law, said: 'I would advise you as you tender your life
to devise some excuse to shift your attendance at this
Parliament…'

HANCOCK, Thomas (1786–1865), English,
inventor
Banstead Court, Green Lanes, N4.
Plastics Historical Society
Hancock lived and worked on this site. In 1820 he
patented rubber fastenings for gloves, suspenders,
shoes and stockings. In 1821 he joined with Charles
Macintosh to produce waterproof clothes –
mackintoshes. He was the first to make vulcanised
india-rubber in 1843. In his seventieth year in 1857 he
published an account of his early struggles, *The Origin
and Progress of the Caoutchouc or India-Rubber Industry in
England.*

HARRIS, Vincent (1876–1971), English, architect
32 Rivington Street, EC2. *London Borough of Hackney*
Harris designed this electricity sub-station in 1906
while in the London County Council Architects
Department (1901–7). Setting up in private practice, he
went on to design, *inter alia*, Leeds Civic Hall (1933),
Sheffield City Hall (1934) and the Ministry of Defence
(1939–59). Often criticised by Modernists, he was not
abashed; accepting the RIBA Gold Medal in 1951 he
said: 'Look, I know a lot of you here tonight don't like
what I do, and I don't like what a lot of you do…'

HENRY VIII (1491–1547), English, royalty
Community College, Kenninghall Road, E5.
London Borough of Hackney
Brooke House (see above), which formerly stood on
this site, was owned by Henry VIII from 1537 until his
death. In July 1536 the house was the scene of a
reconciliation between Henry VIII and his daughter
Mary. The king and queen (Jane Seymour) met Mary,
who had not spoken to her father in five years, and she
remained in the house with her father for several days.
(See also Kensington & Chelsea 2.)

HITCHCOCK, Alfred (1899–1980), English, film
director
Poole Street, Hoxton, N1. *London Borough of Hackney*
Hitchcock is one of the big names mentioned on the
plaque celebrating Gainsborough Film Studios here.
This was the early English phase of Hitchcock's career,
which included successful films such as *Blackmail*
(1930), *Murder* (1931), *The Man Who Knew Too Much*
(1935), *The Thirty-Nine Steps* (1936) and *The Lady
Vanishes* (1939). Then he went to Hollywood and
became even more famous. (See also Waltham Forest
and Kensington & Chelsea 2.)

HOLYWELL PRIORY
98 Curtain Road, Shoreditch, EC2.
London Borough of Hackney
Holywell Priory, founded around 1152–8, dissolved in 1539, was named after a holy well, and its grounds were bounded by the present Curtain Road, Holywell Lane, Bateman Row and Shoreditch High Street. The ruins were sketched by Wyngaerd in 1540.

HOWARD, Sir Ebenezer (1850–1928), English, garden city pioneer
50 Durley Road, N16.
English Heritage
Howard, who lived here, worked for Hansard from 1876 but is remembered for his thinking on town planning. He founded the Garden Cities Association (now the Town and Country Planning Association) in 1899, and his book *Garden Cities of Tomorrow* (1902) argued the case for communities without slums enjoying the benefits of both town and country. This led to the building of Letchworth (1903) and Welwyn Garden City (1919) and has continued to influence the design of places such as Stevenage and Milton Keynes. (See also City.)

HOWARD, John (1726–90), English, prison reformer
157–159 Lower Clapton Road, Clapton, E5.
London Borough of Hackney
The plaque records that Howard was born in his father's house near this site. After an exhaustive tour of British prisons, he wrote *The State of Prisons* (1777) and conducted a campaign for reform which secured two Acts of Parliament. The Howard League for Prison Reform, founded in 1866, was named to honour his memory. (See also Camden 2.)

HOXTON HALL
128 Hoxton Street, N1. *London Borough of Hackney*
Built in 1863 as Macdonald's Music Hall, it lost its licence in 1871 after police complaints. Purchased for the Blue Ribbon Gospel Temperance Mission in 1879, it passed in 1893 to the Bedford Institute, a Quaker organisation running adult schools and relieving poverty. It is today a community centre, retaining much of the original 1863 interior, and listed Grade II*.

HOXTON MARKET CHRISTIAN MISSION
13–14 Hoxton Market, N1.
London Borough of Hackney
See entries for the Burtt brothers above.

JONSON, Ben (1572/3–1637), English, playwright
Arden House, Pitfield Street, N1.
London Borough of Hackney
18 Hewett Street, EC2. *London Borough of Hackney*
The first plaque records this as the site of the Pimlico Hostelry and Pleasure Grounds (see page 146) and also mentions that Ben Jonson, 'playwright, poet and writer of court masques' fought a duel here. The duel took place on 22 September 1598 and Jonson killed his opponent, an actor called Gabriel Spenser. For this he was briefly imprisoned in Newgate. At his trial he pleaded guilty but was released through 'benefit of clergy', having recited some of the Bible in Latin and being branded on his thumb. The second plaque celebrates the Curtain Theatre (see page 141) and mentions that Jonson's plays were performed there. Among his plays that are still performed today are *Volpone* (1605), *The Alchemist* (1610) and *Bartholomew Fair* (1614).

LEE, Nelson (1806–72), English, actor-manager, impresario
67 Shrubland Road, Hackney, E8.
London Borough of Hackney
Lee, who lived here from 1851 until his death, was the writer and star of over two hundred pantomimes, which were eagerly anticipated at the various East End theatres he managed. He also produced open-air Shakespeare shows running for fifteen minutes, precursor of today's *Complete Shakespeare in an Hour*.

LLOYD, Marie (1870–1922), English, music-hall artiste
55 Graham Road, E8.
Greater London Council
Shepherdess Walk, N1.
London Borough of Hackney
Lloyd lived at the first address and made her stage debut in 1885, aged fifteen, at the Eagle Tavern (see page 142), formerly at the second address. Marie Lloyd was the stage-name of Matilda Alice Victoria Wood, in her heyday the 'Queen of the Music Hall', noted for her saucy cockney repartee, and having a succession

of songs that still resonate today, such as 'The Boy I Love is Up in the Gallery', 'My Old Man Said Follow the Van' and 'I'm One of the Ruins that Cromwell Knocked About a Bit'.

LODDIGES NURSERY
Paragon Road, E9. *London Borough of Hackney*
This is part of the site of the nursery founded by Joachim Conrad Loddiges, a German gardener, in 1785, and greatly expanded by his son George. Seeds were solicited from all over the world and George built the world's largest hothouse to display Britain's finest collection of palms and orchids. The nursery was visited and admired by Loudon (q.v.) and Darwin (q.v.).

MANOR HOUSE
387 Mare Street, E8. *London Borough of Hackney*
The Manor House was built by John Robert Daniel Tyssen (see page 147) in 1845. Of plain yellow brick, in a late Georgian style, it survives, though shops were inserted on the ground floor in the 1890s. Tyssen demolished the New Mermaid Tavern on the site, of which it may be noted that the aeronaut Margaret Graham made a balloon ascent from the pub gardens in August 1837.

MEDIEVAL MANSION
173 Stoke Newington Church Street, N16.
London Borough of Hackney
Here stood a medieval mansion, built in the fourteenth century and demolished around 1710. It was for a time the home of Edward de Vere (see page 141). The pair of early Georgian houses now on the site, known as Sisters Place, were built *c*.1714.

MORRIS, William (1834–96), English, artist, designer, socialist
91–101 Worship Street, EC2.
London Borough of Hackney
This row of buildings was built as workshops and dwellings by Morris's friend and colleague Philip Webb (see page 148) in 1862. The plaque also notes that they were co-founders of the Society for the Protection of Ancient Buildings in 1877. (See also Bexley, Camden 2, Hammersmith & Fulham, Redbridge, Waltham Forest and Westminster 3.)

NEW MERMAID TAVERN
387 Mare Street, E8. *London Borough of Hackney*
See the entry above for the Manor House.

NEWINGTON GREEN CHURCH
39 Newington Green, N16.
London Borough of Hackney
This is the oldest nonconformist place of worship still in use in London. It was built in 1708, when Stoke Newington was a centre of nonconformist activity, by Edward Harrison, a goldsmith, to house a congregation that had been together since 1682.

NEWLEY, Anthony (1931–99), English, actor, singer
Mandeville Primary School, Oswald Street, E5.
London Borough of Hackney
Newley, the plaque notes, was a pupil at this school and spent his childhood at 14 Oswald Street, now demolished. He appeared in many films, beginning as the Artful Dodger in *Oliver Twist* (1948). He had a number one hit with the old cockney song 'Pop Goes the Weasel'. He was Joan Collins's first husband and latterly made his career as a singer and entertainer in the United States.

NOVELLO, Ivor (1893–1951), Welsh, singer-songwriter, actor
Poole Street, Hoxton, N1.
London Borough of Hackney
Novello is listed here as one of the star names associated with Gainsborough Films in these studios. He is best remembered for his songs, including 'Keep the Home Fires Burning', a great morale booster in the First World War, and 'We'll Gather Lilacs'. His musicals included *The Dancing Years* (1939), *King's Rhapsody* (1949) and *Gay's the Word* (1951). (See also Westminster 4.)

PARKES, Alexander (1813–90), English, scientist
Berkshire Road/Wallis Road, E9.
London Borough of Hackney
This was the site of Parkes's works, where he made the world's first plastic, 'Parkesine', in 1866. It was a celluloid based on nitrocellulose with an ethanol solvent, but it proved expensive to make and prone to cracking, and the works shut down in 1868. Despite this, he is recognised as the father of the plastics industry. (See also Lambeth.)

PARKINSON, James (1755–1824), English, physician, geologist
1 Hoxton Square, N1. *Private*
Parkinson, who lived here, is most famous for his 1817

treatise on *paralysis agitans*, the first description of what is now called Parkinson's disease. In 1812 he assisted his son in the first described case of appendicitis in England, showing perforation to have caused death. As an enthusiastic fossil hunter, he published three volumes on *Organic Remains of the Former World* (1804–11) and in 1807 was a co-founder of the Geological Society.

PICKWICK BICYCLE CLUB
Downs public house, Downs Road, E5.
London Borough of Hackney
The plaque records that the Pickwick Bicycle Club, the oldest cycling club in Britain, first met at this hotel on 22 June 1870. This was the week Dickens had died, and the club was named in honour of one of his most celebrated characters. The club is still in existence to this day but is now more of a gentlemen's luncheon club.

PIMLICO HOSTELRY AND PLEASURE GROUNDS
Arden House, Pitfield Street, N1.
London Borough of Hackney
This was the site of the Pimlico Hostelry and Pleasure Grounds, 'a noted place of entertainment' established by the 1590s. Ben Jonson (see page 144) fought a duel in the grounds.

PLASTIC, First in the world
Berkshire Road / Wallis Road, E9.
London Borough of Hackney
See the entry for Alexander Parkes, page 145.

POE, Edgar Allan (1809–49), American, poet, short-story writer
172 Stoke Newington Church Street, N16.
London Borough of Hackney
Poe was a pupil at the Manor House School (1817–20), which stood on this site. He was not happy here, and the experience featured in his story *William Wilson*. His work has been often filmed: *The Fall of the House of Usher* (1839), *The Murders in the Rue Morgue* (1841) and *The Pit and the Pendulum* (1843). His poem 'The Raven' (1845) echoes to this day: 'Quoth the Raven, nevermore.'

POLLOCK'S TOY THEATRE SHOP
McGregor Court, Hoxton Street, N1. *London Borough of Hackney*
The plaque records that Pollock's Toy Theatre Shop stood near this site. It was founded by John Redington in 1851 and subsequently run by Benjamin Pollock and his family. The premises were bombed in the Second World War and the business failed. It was revived in 1954 by Marguerite Fawdry and flourishes to this day, a shop and toy museum combined, at 41 Whitfield Street, W1.

PRIESTLEY, Joseph (1733–1804), English, scientist
113 Lower Clapton Road, E5.
London Borough of Hackney
Ram Place, E9. *London Borough of Hackney*
Priestley lived in a house at the first address from 1792 to 1794 and was minister to the Gravel Pit Meeting on the site of the second address in 1793–4. He was a scientist, philosopher and theologian, producing over 150 books and pamphlets on a vast range of topics, but posterity remembers him above all for one thing, the discovery of oxygen, which he called 'dephlogisticated air'.

ST JOHN THE BAPTIST, HOLYWELL
86–90 Curtain Road, EC2. *London County Council*
See the entry for Holywell Priory, page 144. This plaque also notes that nearby stood The Theatre (see page 147), London's first building devoted to the performance of plays.

ST MARY'S, HAGGERSTON
Queensbridge Road, E2.

London Borough of Hackney

On this site stood St Mary's, Haggerston, designed by John Nash and built in 1826–7. It had an unusually tall tower because, it is suggested, Nash instructed the builder to go on until told otherwise, and then went away to the country and forgot. The church was destroyed by enemy action in 1941 and the site is now a playground between Queensbridge and Thurtle Roads.

SHAKESPEARE, William
(1564–1616), English, actor, poet, playwright
86–90 Curtain Road, EC2. *London Borough of Hackney*
18 Hewett Street, EC2. *London Borough of Hackney*

The first plaque celebrates The Theatre (see page 140), built by James Burbage (see above), and notes that plays by Shakespeare were performed here. The second plaque celebrates the Curtain Theatre (see page 141), where, it says, Shakespeare acted and his plays were also performed. (See also Southwark.)

SHOREDITCH REFUSE DESTRUCTOR
Coronet Street, N1.

London Borough of Hackney
This was an early attempt to deal with refuse by burning it to produce steam and in turn produce electricity. It was inaugurated in 1897, with a Latin text across the frontage, *E pulvere lux et vis* ('Light and power

from dust'), a splendidly green notion a century before the idea became the ambition of every town hall. The building is now occupied by Circus Space.

STOKE NEWINGTON MANOR HOUSE
Town Hall, Stoke Newington Church Street, N16. *London Borough of Hackney*

On this site stood Stoke Newington Manor House from *c.*1500 to 1695, and then a terrace called Church Row from 1695 until demolition to make way for the town hall in 1936.

SYNAGOGUE, First in Hackney
25 Thistlethwaite Road, Highbury, N5.

London Borough of Hackney
The synagogue was built in 1779–80 (5539–40 in the Jewish calendar) and stood to the rear of this building in the grounds of Clapton House. Jews, mainly from Spain, had been moving into the Hackney area for over a century when Israel Levin Salomons 'spent lavishly' on building this, the first local synagogue.

TANDY, Jessica
(1909–94), English, actress
58a Geldeston Road, Clapton, E5. *London Borough of Hackney*

Tandy was born here. After a distinguished London stage career, playing opposite Olivier and Gielgud in Shakespeare, she moved to the United States and won a Tony for her Blanche Dubois on Broadway. Her career had a glowing Indian summer with an Oscar in 1989 for *Driving Miss Daisy*.

THE THEATRE
86–90 Curtain Road, EC2. *London County Council*
86–90 Curtain Road, EC2.
London Borough of Hackney

See entries for James Burbage and Holywell Priory (pages 140 and 144). There are two plaques here.

TYSSEN, John Robert Daniel (1805–82), English, steward of the manor
387 Mare Street, E8. *London Borough of Hackney*

Apart from building the Manor House (see page 155), Tyssen's claim on history is his notable collection of books, manuscripts and transcripts of records relating to Hackney history, which now form the basis of the local history archive.

WATCH HOUSE, Stoke Newington
6–8 Lordship Road, N16. *London Borough of Hackney*
The plaque records that these buildings were erected as the parish watch house, lock-up and fire-engine room. The engine room was built in 1821 and the watch house and lock-up were put up in 1824.

WATSON, Joshua (1771–1855), English, merchant, educationalist, reformer
117 Lower Clapton Road, Clapton, E5.
London Borough of Hackney
Watson lived in a house on this site from 1811 to 1823 and again from 1841 until his death. He gave up his City business in 1814 and devoted the rest of his life to the service of the church. A founder of the National Society for Promoting Religious Education in 1811, and a co-founder of King's College, London, in 1828, he was called 'the best layman in England'. William Wordsworth suggested that to the petition in the Litany there should be added, after the clause 'all Bishops, Priests and Deacons', the words 'and also Joshua Watson'.

WATTS, Isaac (1674–1748), English, poet, hymn writer
82 Stoke Newington Church Street, N16.
London Borough of Hackney
The plaque records that Watts stayed here at Abney House (see page 139) from 1734 to 1748. He composed six hundred hymns, of which the most enduring is 'O God, Our Help in Ages Past'.

WEBB, Philip (1831–1915), English, architect
91–101 Worship Street, EC2.
London Borough of Hackney
This terrace of spaces for living and working was designed by Philip Webb in 1862. It was commissioned by the philanthropist Colonel William Gillum as an example of enlightened workspaces, by contrast with the normal overcrowded sweatshops of the East End.

WOLLSTONECRAFT, Mary (1759–97), English, writer, campaigner
373 Mare Street, E8. *London Borough of Hackney*
Wollstonecraft stayed in a house on this site in 1784 and lived some of her early years in Hoxton. Subsequently, working for the publisher Joseph

Johnson, she became acquainted with William Godwin, whom she married and with whom she had Mary Shelley (q.v.). Her most famous book, *A Vindication of the Rights of Women* (1792), was partly written in response to Thomas Paine's (q.v.) *The Rights of Man* (1791), feeling he had missed out half of humanity. In it she advocated equal educational rights for women, and she is justly remembered as a feminist *avant la lettre*. (See also Southwark and Camden 2.)

WOOLLEY, Sir Leonard (1880–1960), English, archaeologist
Bridge on Southwold Road, Upper Clapton, E5. *London Borough of Hackney*
Woolley was born in a house on this site. He was one of the first 'modern' archaeologists, his most important excavations being of Sumerian sites at Ur in Mesopotamia (Iraq) from 1922 to 1934. He published several accounts of his work, including *Spadework: Adventures in Archaeology* (1953).

HAMMERSMITH & FULHAM

This amalgamation of the former metropolitan
boroughs of Hammersmith and Fulham was
initially called just 'Hammersmith' but protests
by the residents of SW6 got 'Fulham' added to
the name of the borough in 1979.

BIRD FAMILY
190 Shepherds Bush Road, W6.
Hammersmith and Fulham Historic Buildings Group
This was the site of the family home of George Bird
in the nineteenth century; as leading local builders
and brickmakers, the family was responsible for
much of the building in Hammersmith, including
Nazareth House, Sacred Heart School and the
original Hammersmith Bridge of 1829. They were
also involved in civic welfare and founded the old
West London Hospital in Hammersmith Road. The
plaque is set into the entrance to the 2003 fire
station.

BRANGWYN, Sir Frank (1867–1956), English,
painter
51 Queen Caroline Street, W6. *English Heritage*
Sir Frank lived and worked here from 1900 to 1938.
Apprenticed to William Morris (q.v.), he produced

furniture, pottery and interior designs, as well as oil
paintings, etchings, lithographs and murals. His British
Empire murals for the Houses of Parliament were
rejected as 'too exotic' and are now in Brangwyn Hall,
Cardiff.

**BURNE-JONES, Sir
Edward** (1833–98),
English, painter
**Samuel Richardson
House, North End
Crescent, W14.**
*London Borough of
Hammersmith & Fulham*
Sir Edward lived at The
Grange on this site from 1867
until his death. His mystical romantic style was gently
satirised in Gilbert and Sullivan's *Patience* as 'Greenery
yallery, Grosvenor Gallery'. Stanley Baldwin (q.v.)
said of him: 'What he did for us common people was
to open magic casements on a land of faery in which
he lived throughout his life.' (See also Camden 2 and
Kensington & Chelsea 1.)

CLARK, William Tierney (1783–1852), English,
engineer
Upper Mall, W6.
London Borough of Hammersmith & Fulham
Clark lived on this site *c*.1839. He was the designer
of the first Hammersmith Bridge in 1827 and the
suspension bridge at Marlow (1832), which was a
prototype for his grandest achievement, the Széchenyi
Chain Bridge linking Buda and Pest across the Danube
in Hungary (1849).

COBDEN-SANDERSON, Thomas James
(1840–1922), English, printer
15 Upper Mall, Hammersmith, W6.
Greater London Council
Cobden-Sanderson founded the Doves Bindery in
1893 and the Doves Press in 1900 in this house and
later lived and died here, working with William Morris
(q.v.), Burne-Jones (q.v.) and Emery Walker (q.v.).
The press closed in 1916 after some fifty publications,
and Cobden-Sanderson threw the type into the
Thames.

COLERIDGE, Samuel Taylor (1772–1834),
English, poet, critic
7 Addison Bridge Place, W14.
London County Council
Coleridge, who lived here, was a friend of Wordsworth
and Charles Lamb (q.v.) and is best known for 'The
Rime of the Ancient Mariner' (1798) and 'Kubla Khan'
(1816), the writing of which was famously cut short
by the arrival of 'a man from Porlock'. (See also
Camden 1 and Westminster 2.)

COLLINS, Michael
(1890–1922), Irish,
politician
**5 Netherwood Road,
W14.** *London Borough of
Hammersmith & Fulham*
Collins lived here in
1914–15 shortly before
returning to Ireland and becoming prominent in the
Easter Rising of 1916, in which his practical skills as a
military organiser were in marked contrast to the
romantic 'blood sacrifice' ideas of many participants.
Known as 'the Big Fella', he was later a member of the
Irish delegation to the Anglo-Irish talks on
independence, and Chairman of the Provisional
Government. He was killed in an ambush by anti-
treaty republicans during the Irish Civil War.

DE HAVILLAND, Sir Geoffrey (1882–1965),
English, aircraft designer
32 Barons Court Road, W14. *English Heritage*
While living here in 1909–10, De Havilland built his
first aircraft and, when that crashed, his second in a
hut off Bothwell Road, Fulham. His company went on
to produce the Tiger Moth (1930), the Mosquito
(1941) and the Comet (1952), the world's first
passenger jet airliner.

DEVINE, George (1910–66), English, actor, stage
director
9 Lower Mall, W6. *English Heritage*
Devine, who lived here, founded, with Tony
Richardson, the English Stage Company at the Royal
Court Theatre (1956–65), intended as a writers'
theatre, breaking away from the upper-class 'Anyone
for tennis?' genre. The result was revolutionary, with
the debuts of Osborne, Wesker, Jellicoe and Sillitoe.

**DISTRESSED GENTLEFOLK'S AID
ASSOCIATION**
75 Brook Green, W6. *Private*
The organisation, founded here on 5 May 1897, is still
active, under the name of Elizabeth Finn Care, named
in honour of the founder.

**ELECTRIC
TELEGRAPH, First
Coach House, 26
Upper Mall, W6.**
Private
The first electric
telegraph, 8 miles long,
was constructed here in
1816 by Sir Francis
Ronalds (see page 154).
The idea was turned
down by the Admiralty.

ELGAR, Sir Edward (1857–1934), English,
composer
51 Avonmore Road, W14. *London County Council*
Sir Edward lived here in 1890–1. His *Enigma Variations*
(1899) and *The Dream of Gerontius* (1900) won him
international acclaim. His many other works include
two symphonies, the much-loved Cello Concerto and
the *Pomp and Circumstance* marches. He was made
Master of the King's Musick in 1924. (See also
Westminster 1 and Camden 1.)

FINN, Elizabeth and Constance, English,
philanthropists
75 Brook Green, W6. *Private*
Elizabeth (1825–1921) and her daughter, Constance
(born 1851), founded the Distressed Gentlefolk's Aid
Association (see above) here in May 1897, 'in the
hope of alleviating some of the distress which has
overtaken ladies and gentlemen who have seen better
days'.

FOX, PC Geoffrey
(1925–66), English,
police officer
Braybrook Street,
W12. *Police Memorial Trust*
PC Fox was a local
police officer, detailed to
drive two detectives in
an unmarked car. In
Braybrook Street, at
about 3.15 p.m. on 12 August 1966, they spotted a
battered Vanguard estate van with three men in it.
Being near Wormwood Scrubs prison, and the van
having no tax disc, the detectives started questioning
the driver. Two minutes later all three policemen were
dead, shot without warning in what the trial judge
later called 'the most heinous crime to have been
committed in this country for a generation or more'.

GANDHI, Mahatma
(1869–1948), Indian,
lawyer, spiritual leader
20 Barons Court
Road, West
Kensington, W14.
Greater London Council
Aged nineteen, Gandhi
came to England in 1888 and
lived here as a law student. He was
well received but could not stand his landlady's mutton
and cabbage, which led him, through Annie Besant
(q.v.) and the Theosophical Society, to lifelong
vegetarianism thereafter. (See also Tower Hamlets.)

GARVEY, Marcus (1887–1940), Jamaican, politician
2 Beaumont Crescent, W14. *London Borough of*
Hammersmith / Marcus Garvey Memorial Trust
53 Talgarth Road, W14. *English Heritage*
Garvey lived at the first address, and lived and died at
the second. He was the founder of the Universal
Negro Improvement Association in 1914, aiming to
achieve human rights for black Americans. He lived
mainly in the United States, and a park is named after
him on Manhattan Island, New York.

GOOSSENS FAMILY, English/French, musicians
70 Edith Road, West Kensington, W14.
English Heritage
This was the home of the celebrated Goossens family
of musicians from 1912 to 1927: Eugène Goossens

(1867–1958), violinist and conductor; his sons, Sir
Eugène (1893–1962), composer and conductor;
Adolph (1896–1916), horn player; Leon
(1897–1988), oboist; and their sisters, Marie
(1894–1991) and Sidonie (1899–2004), harpists.

HAGGARD, Sir H. Rider (1856–1925), English,
novelist
69 Gunterstone Road, West Kensington, W14.
Greater London Council
Rider Haggard lived here from 1885 to 1888. While
here, he wrote the spellbinding adventure stories
King Solomon's Mines (1885), *She* (1887) and *Allan*
Quartermain (1887), which remain in print and have
been many times filmed. Jung cited *She* ('She who
must be obeyed') in discussing his *anima* concept.

HAMMERSMITH SOCIALIST SOCIETY
The Coach House, 26 Upper Mall, W6. *Private*

The Hammersmith Socialist Society was formed by
William Morris (q.v.) after he left H. M. Hyndman's
(q.v.) Socialist League. The Society had Emery Walker
(q.v.) as its secretary and offered free Sunday evening
lectures by George Bernard Shaw (q.v.), Sidney Webb
(q.v.) and others, as well as open-air soapbox rallies
near Hammersmith Bridge.

HEAD, Detective Sergeant Christopher
(1936–66), English, police officer
Braybrook Street, W12. *Police Memorial Trust*
See the entry for PC Fox, above.

HERBERT, Sir Alan (1890–1971), English,
politician, humorist
12 Hammersmith Terrace, W6. *English Heritage*
Sir Alan lived and died here. As Independent MP for
Oxford University (1935–50), he campaigned

vigorously for the reform of outdated laws on divorce, obscenity and gambling. As 'APH', he contributed a satirical column on the law called 'Misleading Cases' to *Punch* for many years. His motor launch *The Water Gypsy* was at Dunkirk.

HOLST, Gustav (1874–1934), English, composer
St Paul's Girls School, Brook Green, W6.
English Heritage
Holst was music master here. Though he wrote in all genres of music, his most famous and enduring work is *The Planets Suite* (1917). A friend of Ralph Vaughan Williams (q.v.), he shared his interest in English folk music. His great-grandfather was Swedish. (See also Richmond.)

HUNT, Leigh (1784–1859), English, poet, essayist
16 Rowan Road, W6.
London Borough of Hammersmith & Fulham
Hunt lived here from 1853 until his death. He had been on a Civil List pension since 1847 and produced his last book, *The Old Court Suburb* (1855), essays on Kensington, while here. (See also Enfield, Merton, Kensington & Chelsea 2 and Camden 1.)

IRVING, Sir Henry (1838–1905), English, actor
St Paul's Girls School, Brook Green, W6.
London Borough of Hammersmith & Fulham
Sir Henry (John Henry Brodribb) lived on this site from 1881 to 1889. He was considered the finest actor of his generation and was the first actor to be knighted. (See also Westminster 2.)

JOHNSTON, Edward (1872–1944), English, type designer, calligrapher
3 Hammersmith Terrace, W6.
Greater London Council
Johnston lived here from 1905 to 1912. He is credited with the modern revival of penmanship and is most famous for designing the sans-serif type used throughout the London Underground system, as well as the roundel station ident. In 1921 he founded the Society of Scribes and Illuminators.

LASKI, Harold (1893–1950), English, political theorist, economist
5 Addison Bridge Place, West Kensington, W14.
Greater London Council
Laski moved here in 1926, when he was appointed Professor of Political Science at the London School of Economics. Among his books are *A Grammar of Politics* (1925), *Liberty in the Modern State* (1930) and *Reflections on the Revolution of Our Time* (1943). He has legendary status in India, having taught a generation of Indian political leaders during the struggle for independence.

LE MESURIER, John (1912–83), English, actor
Barons Keep, Gliddon Road, West Kensington, W14.
Dead Comics Society
Le Mesurier, stage-name of John Elton Halliley, lived here from 1966 to 1977. His screen persona of good-natured, well-mannered vagueness, exemplified in his role as Sergeant Wilson in *Dad's Army* (BBC Television 1968–77), is said to be not unlike his real self. He composed his own death notice in *The Times*, informing his friends that he had 'conked out', and his last words were reportedly: 'It's all been rather lovely.'

LOVELY, William (*fl.*1887), English, civil servant
1 Askew Road, W12.
Private
The plaque notes that Lovely, the Fleet Paymaster of the Royal Navy, lived here at Delhi Lodge in 1887. Why he merits a plaque, and who put it up, are a mystery. Delhi Lodge has come down in the world since his time.

MACDONALD, George (1824–1905), Scottish, poet, novelist
25 Upper Mall, W6. *Private*
MacDonald lived here from 1867 to 1877. He was a professor at Bedford College, London, and wrote the poetry collections *Within and Without* (1856) and *Poems* (1857), and the novels *David Elginbrod* (1863) and

Lilith (1895). He is best remembered today for his children's stories, written while living here, such as *At the Back of the North Wind* (1871) and *The Princess and the Goblin* (1872). (See also Camden 2.)

MARK, Connie (1923–2007), Jamaican, community activist
Mary Seacole House, Invermead Close, W6.
London Borough of Hammersmith & Fulham / Nubian Jak Community Trust
Constance Winifred MacDonald, or 'Connie Mark' as she was universally known, lived the last two years of her life in the sheltered housing here. Her experience in the British Army led to her writing *West Indian Women at War: British Racism in World War Two*. Her campaigning, especially for recognition of Mary Seacole (q.v.), won her a British Empire Medal in 1991 and an MBE in 1993.

MOORE, Henry (1898–1986), English, sculptor
3 Grove Studios, Adie Road, W6.
Hammersmith and Fulham Historic Buildings Group
This was Moore's first studio after studying at the Royal College of Art and Leon Underwood's Brook Green School. He shared the studio with his college friend Raymond Coxon, for whose fiancée, Edna, he conceived an unrequited passion. But it all ended happily with Moore's marriage to Irina Radetsky and move to Hampstead. (See also Camden 1.)

MORE, Kenneth (1914–82), English, actor
27 Rumbold Road, Fulham, SW6. *Private*
More lived and died here. His most successful period was the 1950s, when he established a persona as a likeable, unflappable English hero in films such as *Genevieve* (1953), *Doctor in the House* (1954) and, above all, *Reach for the Sky* (1956), in which he played Douglas Bader, the legless Second World War fighter ace.

MORRIS, William (1834–96), English, poet, designer, socialist
26 Upper Mall, W6. *Private*
Morris lived in this house from 1878 until his death. While here he founded the Hammersmith Socialist Society (see page 151) and the Kelmscott Press in 1890. His rather dense output of prose and poetry is really only for the devotee, but his exquisite fabric and wallpaper designs continue to be bestsellers.
(See also Hackney, Bexley, Waltham Forest, Redbridge, Camden 2 and Westminster 3.)

OUIDA (1839–1908), French-English, novelist
11 Ravenscourt Square, W6. *London County Council*
Ouida was the pen-name of Marie Louise de la Ramée, who lived here until 1874. Her forty-five novels were in her time hugely successful, though mocked in some quarters for the unreality of the fashionable milieu portrayed, and the extravagant charms of her romantic heroes. She considered herself to be a serious artist and did not like comparisons with other contemporary popular authors.

PHILLIPS, Morgan (1902–63), Welsh, politician
115 Rannoch Road, W6.
London Borough of Hammersmith & Fulham
Phillips lived here from 1959 until his death. He rose in Labour ranks through steady party work: Secretary of West Fulham Labour Party (1928–30), Fulham councillor (1934–7), moving to party headquarters in 1937, and becoming Secretary in 1944. He is given much credit for Labour's two election victories of 1945 and 1950, through his modernisation of the party machine.

PRITT, Denis Nowell (1887–1972), English, politician
446 Uxbridge Road, W12.
London Borough of Hammersmith & Fulham
Pritt was a fellow-travelling socialist of the old school, representing North Hammersmith from 1935 to 1950. In 1932 he was a member of the New Fabian Research Group that visited the Soviet Union and he bought the Stalin line completely. In 1940 he was expelled from the Labour Party for supporting the Soviet invasion of Finland and in 1949, with other fellow-travellers like Konni Zilliacus and John Platts-Mills, he formed the Labour Independent Group.

RAVILIOUS, Eric (1903–42), English, painter, designer, illustrator
48 Upper Mall, Hammersmith, W6.
English Heritage
Ravilious lived here from 1931 to 1935. Versatile across a number of genres, he produced watercolour landscapes, woodcuts, engravings, ceramics for Wedgwood and book illustrations. An official war artist, he was lost on an RAF mission somewhere near Iceland. His reputation has revived lately after post-war neglect.

RONALDS, Sir Francis (1788–1873), English, scientist
Coach House, 26 Upper Mall, W6. *Private*
Ronalds's electric telegraph (see page 150) was constructed here in 1816 and turned down by the Admiralty. Ronalds also invented a system of photographic registration. He was elected a Fellow of the Royal Society in 1844 and was director of the Meteorological Office at Kew from 1843 to 1852.

ST VINCENT'S Queen Caroline Street, W6.
Hammersmith and Fulham Historic Buildings Group
The modern care home, built in 2006, is on the site of previous caring organisations, as outlined on the plaque. The Sisters of the Misericorde of Seez, an order from Normandy, made it their business to care for local sick people in their own homes.

SHORT, Sir Frank (1857–1945), English, painter, engraver
56 Brook Green, Hammersmith, W6.
London County Council
Sir Frank lived here. Encouraged by Ruskin (q.v.), he revived the mezzotint process in England and made many fine prints after Turner (q.v.), but his own compositions, with their interpretation of light in the mezzotint medium, are also much admired.

SILVER STUDIO
84 Brook Green, Hammersmith, W6.
Greater London Council

Established here in 1880, and run successively by Arthur Silver (1853–96) and his sons Rex (1879–1965) and Harry (1881–1971), this was one of the most important independent design studios, selling fashionable stylised Art Nouveau designs in Britain, the United States and on the Continent. The Museum of Domestic Design at Middlesex University houses their archive, including over forty thousand designs.

SIMMS, Frederick Richard (1863–1944), English, engineer, car salesman
Railway Arch, Ranelagh Gardens, Fulham, SW6.
Society of Motor Manufacturers and Traders
Having made the acquaintance of Gottlieb Daimler, Simms opened his first workshop here in 1893 with the British rights to Daimler engines. Here he made the first British cars and motor launches. In 1895 he sold the company and Daimler moved to Coventry.

SRI AUROBINDO (1872–1950), Indian, spiritual leader
49 St Stephen's Avenue, W12. *English Heritage*
Sri Aurobindo lived here from 1884 to 1887, while a pupil at St Paul's School, then in Hammersmith. After early involvement in the Indian nationalist movement, he turned wholly to the spiritual life and developed a new vision which he called 'integral yoga'. *The Times Literary Supplement*, reviewing a collection of his writings in 1944, said: 'To study his writings is to enlarge the boundaries of one's knowledge … He is a yogi who writes as though he were standing among the stars, with the constellations for his companions.'

TIBBLE, PC Stephen (1954–75), English, police officer
Charleville Road, W14. *Police Memorial Trust*
PC Tibble had been a serving officer for only six months. On 26 February 1975, while he was off duty, riding his motorcycle, he noticed three policemen chasing a suspect. He overtook them and the suspect and dismounted to stop the man, who shot him twice in the chest. The killer was Liam Quinn, an American of Irish descent who belonged to an IRA active service unit in London. PC Tibble was posthumously awarded the Queen's Police Medal for Gallantry.

TURNER, Alfred (1874–1940), English, sculptor
44 Munster Road, SW6. *Private*
Turner, who lived and worked here from 1914 to
1937, was the son and father of sculptors. His best-
known works are the Queen Victoria Memorial at
Tynemouth (1902), the Owain Glyndwr Memorial
outside Cardiff Town Hall (1912) and the Fulham war
memorial (1920). He was sculptor by appointment to
George V and elected a Royal Academician in 1931.

WALKER, Sir Emery (1851–1933), English,
typographer, antiquary
7 Hammersmith Terrace, Hammersmith, W6.
London County Council
Sir Emery, who lived here from 1903 until his death,
was a moving spirit, with Morris (q.v.), in the revival
of fine printing in the late nineteenth century. He
helped found the Kelmscott Press, and later the Doves
Press with T. J. Cobden-Sanderson (q.v.). He was
active in the Art Workers Guild and the Society for the
Protection of Ancient Buildings, and was secretary of
the Hammersmith Socialist Society (see page 151).

WHALL, Christopher Whitworth (1849–1924),
English, stained glass artist
19 Ravenscourt Road, Hammersmith, W6.
Greater London Council
Whall, who lived here, was a leading member of the
Arts and Crafts movement, active in the Art Workers
Guild and the Arts and Crafts Exhibition Society. His
most important work is in the Lady Chapel at
Gloucester Cathedral (1898–1913). His *Stained Glass
Work* (1905) remains the standard textbook.

WHITE, Antonia
(1899–1980), English,
novelist
**22 Perham Road,
W14.**
*London Borough of
Hammersmith & Fulham*
White, who lived her
first twenty-one years
here, struggled with mental
instability all her life, and her work was interrupted
for long intervals by breakdowns. Her novels, which
include *Frost in May* (1933), *The Lost Traveller* (1950),
The Sugar House (1952) and *Strangers* (1954) are
autobiographical and have enjoyed a critical revival
with re-publication by Virago. Elizabeth Bowen,

introducing *Frost in May*, wrote: 'White's style as a
story teller is as precise, clear and unweighty as Jane
Austen's.'

WOMBWELL, TDC David (1941–66), English,
police officer
Braybrook Street, W12. *Police Memorial Trust*
See the entry for PC Geoffrey Fox, page 151.

WOOD, Lieutenant Charles Campbell (d.1919),
South African, airman
Hammersmith Bridge, W6. *Sir William Bull*
The bronze plaque, which is situated on the handrail
mid-bridge on the upstream side, records that
Lieutenant Wood, a South African member of the RAF,
dived from this spot into the Thames at midnight on
27 December 1919 and saved a woman's life. He
unfortunately died from injuries sustained during the
rescue. Sir William Bull, a major figure in
Hammersmith at the time, had the plaque designed by
A. O. Collard, FRIBA, made by J. W. Singer & Sons
and installed by Rosser & Russell.

ISLINGTON

An inner London borough, lying directly north
of the City, Islington is formed from two
former Metropolitan Boroughs, Islington and
Finsbury.

ALLEYN, Edward (1566–1626), English, actor-
manager
Fortune Street, EC1. *Private*
Alleyn was one of the major figures of the Elizabethan
stage. Here he headed the Admiral's Men, starring
himself in major Marlowe roles. After the death of
Queen Elizabeth I he retired from the stage and turned
very successfully to business, founding Alleyn's School
and Dulwich College.

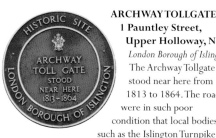

**ARCHWAY TOLLGATE
1 Pauntley Street,
Upper Holloway, N19.**
London Borough of Islington
The Archway Tollgate
stood near here from
1813 to 1864. The roads
were in such poor
condition that local bodies
such as the Islington Turnpike
Trust and the Highgate and Hampstead Trust levied
tolls to pay for repair and maintenance.

BAXTER, George (1804–67), English, printer
City University, Northampton Square, EC1.
Private
Baxter, 'a central figure in coloured picture printing'
(says the plaque), lived in a house on this site from
1844 to 1860. He invented a process (patented in
1835), incorporating the aquatint method of colour
printing, which made reproductions of paintings
available on a mass scale for the first time. Others
capitalised on his invention more than he, and he died
in poverty.

BRITTEN, Benjamin
(1913–76), English,
composer
8 Halliford Street, N1.
London Borough of Islington
Britten lived here from
1970 until his death. He
began composing at the age
of five and went on to work in
many forms, but he is best-known for his operas,
including *Peter Grimes* (1945), *Albert Herring* (1947)
and *Billy Budd* (1951). Among his later works, the *War
Requiem* (1961) and the Cello Symphony (1964) are
much admired. He founded the Aldeburgh Festival in
1948, was made a Companion of Honour in 1953 and
awarded the Order of Merit in 1965. (See also
Kensington & Chelsea 2 and Westminster 1.)

BRITTON, Thomas (1644–1714), English, musician
Jerusalem Passage, EC1. *London Borough of Islington*
Britton, who lived here and was known as 'the
Musical Coalman', founded a musical club over his
coal shop. Its weekly concerts were attended by
the composers of the day, including Handel (q.v.).
A student of chemistry and the occult, he was one of
the founders of the Harleian Collection now in the
British Museum.

BROCKWAY, Fenner (1888–1988), English,
politician
60 Myddleton Square, EC1.
London Borough of Islington
Brockway, who lived here from 1908 to 1910, was on
the left wing of the Labour Party, regularly falling out

with the centrists. He was a founder of War on Want (1951) and of the Campaign for Nuclear Disarmament (1957). Unusually, this plaque was erected in his lifetime, showing the affection which he universally inspired.

BRUCKNER, Anton (1824–96), Austrian, composer
City Gate House, 39–45 Finsbury Square, EC2. *Brunel University*
Bruckner stayed in a house on this site in 1871 and began work on his Second Symphony while in London. Initially he was the organist at Linz Cathedral (1856–68) and a professor at the Vienna Conservatoire, but in his forties, encouraged by the emperor Franz Josef, he turned to composition, producing nine symphonies in a classic-romantic mode.

BUNTING, Jabez (1779–1858), English, Methodist
30 Myddleton Square, EC1.
London Borough of Islington
Dr Bunting lived here from 1833 until his death. He became a Wesleyan minister in 1799 and from 1833 was stationed at the organisation's headquarters. He was president of the Theological Institute in 1835 and organised the final separation of Methodism from the Anglican church. He is regarded as the second founder of Methodism.

CALEDONIAN MARKET
The Clocktower, Market Road, Holloway, N7.
London Borough of Islington
Originally called the Metropolitan Cattle Market, it was built by the City of London and opened by Prince Albert in 1855 to take the live cattle trade away from Smithfield. When that trade declined, it became a vast antiques and bric-à-brac market, surviving until 1939. See also Copenhagen House, page 158.

CASLON, William (1692–1766), English, typefounder
21–23 Chiswell Street, EC1. *London County Council*
The plaque records that Caslon's type foundry stood on this site from 1737 to 1909. His typefaces were immediately popular and were used in many important documents, including the first printed

version of the American Declaration of Independence. They fell out of fashion in the late nineteenth century, but their popularity revived in the late twentieth century.

CHAMBERLAIN, Joseph (1836–1914), English, politician
25 Highbury Place, Highbury, N5.
London County Council
Chamberlain, who lived here, made his fortune from a screw-manufacturing business. He was three times mayor of Birmingham, before entering Parliament in 1876. Subsequently he became president of the Board of Trade in 1880 and Colonial Secretary in 1895. He was the father of Neville Chamberlain (q.v.). (See also Southwark.)

CHARLOTTE, Queen (1744–1818), German, royalty
Whitbread's Brewery, Chiswell Street, EC1.
Private
The plaque records a royal visit to the brewery in 1787. Despite not meeting her husband until their wedding day in 1761, Charlotte of Mecklenburg-Strelitz had a happy marriage, producing fifteen children, and George III never took a mistress, unlike his predecessors and successors. A keen amateur botanist, she helped found Kew Gardens. See pages 158 and 163 for George III and Samuel Whitbread.

CHEESMAN, Wallace Bligh (1866–1947), English, trade unionist
8 Highbury Grange, Highbury, N5.
London Borough of Islington
Cheesman lived here in 1926–7. A delegate to the Trades Union Congress and the Executive of the Labour Representation Committee, he founded the Fawcett Association (1890) and the Civil Service Federation (1906), two early trade unions. He was also a delegate to the founding conference of the Labour Party in 1900.

CHISHOLM, Caroline (1808–77), English, philanthropist
32 Charlton Place, Islington, N1.
Greater London Council

Chisholm, who lived here, was known as 'the Emigrants' Friend'. She settled in Australia in 1838, setting up a shelter for new arrivals and helping them find work. She also founded the Family Colonisation Loan Society. When she finally retired home to England in 1866, she was granted a civil pension.

CITY PESTHOUSE
Bath Street, EC1. *London Borough of Islington*
This was the site of an isolation hospital for people suffering from incurable diseases such as leprosy or infectious diseases like plague. Built in open fields in 1593, and used during the Great Plague of 1665, it was later devoted to sick French Protestant refugees (1693–1718), until a French hospital was built nearby. After years in ruins, it was demolished in 1736.

CITY ROAD TURNPIKE
112 City Road, EC1. *London Borough of Islington*
The turnpike, which stood near here from 1766 to 1864, was built as a result of petitions from the villages of Marylebone, Paddington and Islington, who wanted a route to drive sheep and cattle to Smithfield, skirting what was then the built-up north end of London. For other turnpike/tollgate sites see Archway (page 156), Coppice Row and St John Street (page 162), and Barnet.

CLERKS' WELL
14–16 Farringdon Lane, EC1.
Borough of Finsbury
The Clerks' Well, sited here, was mentioned as early as 1174 and gave its name to Clerkenwell. Here miracle plays were performed in medieval times. A pump was installed in 1800 but lost during rebuilding in the later nineteenth century. The well was rediscovered in 1924 during building work.

COLLINS MUSIC HALL
10–11 Islington Green, N1. *Greater London Council*
Collins Music Hall stood here from 1862 to 1958. Opened by Sam Collins, a performer of the day, over the years the hall saw performances by Chaplin (q.v.),

Marie Lloyd (q.v.), Harry Lauder (q.v.) and George Robey. It was destroyed by fire in 1958.

COMPTON, William (1851–1913), English, philanthropist, politician
Northampton Square, EC1. *Private*
Compton, memorialised here by friends and tenants, served as a Liberal MP from 1885 to 1897 before becoming the fifth marquis of Northampton and moving to the House of Lords. He was responsible for the development of this area in the late nineteenth century.

COPENHAGEN HOUSE
The Clocktower, Market Road, Holloway, N7. *London Borough of Islington*
Copenhagen House was a celebrated teahouse and tavern that stood here from the early seventeenth century until 1855, when it was demolished to make way for the Caledonian Market (see page 157). Its grounds, Copenhagen Fields, were at various times used for skittles, fives, dog fighting, bear-baiting, athletics and cricket. The first mile run in under 4 minutes 30 seconds was achieved here in July 1852 by Charles Westhall.

COPPICE ROW TURNPIKE
GPO Sorting Office, Farringdon Road, EC1.
London Borough of Islington
This was one of London's many tollgates, standing here from c.1750 to 1830. Oliver Twist passed through here on his long, miserable walk to London. For other turnpike sites, see Archway (page 154) and City Road (above), St John Street (page 162), and Barnet.

CRUDEN, Alexander (1701–70), Scottish, Bible scholar
45 Camden Passage, Islington, N1.
Camden Passage Association
Cruden came to London in 1719 and in 1737 produced the first edition of his famous *Bible Concordance*, which has never been out of print since. In the 1750s he adopted the title of 'Cruden the Corrector', seeing it as his divinely appointed task to monitor the nation's spelling and grammar and, through that, its moral health. He was specially roused

by misspelt signs, graffiti, swearing and the non-observation of the Sabbath. He died here in 1770. The plaque gives his year of birth as 1690, but it is more usually reckoned to have been 1701.

CRUFT, Charles Alfred
(1852–1938), English, promoter
Ashurst Lodge, Highbury Grove, Highbury, N5.
London Borough of Islington
Cruft, who lived near here from 1913 until his death, was a travelling salesman for Spratts dog-food company. His inaugural 'Great Terrier Show', which he saw as a marketing tool, was in 1886, and the first dog show to be called 'Cruft's' was in 1891; the shows continue annually to this day and have been responsible for raising standards in breeding.

CRUIKSHANK, George (1792–1878), English, cartoonist, illustrator
69–71 Amwell Street, Finsbury, EC1.
London Borough of Islington
Cruikshank, who lived here from 1824 to 1849, made his name as a political satirist but is also known for his illustrations to Dickens's (q.v.) *Sketches by Boz* and *Oliver Twist*, and Daniel Defoe's (q.v.) *Robinson Crusoe*. In later life he was a fervent supporter of the Temperance Movement. (See also Camden 1.)

FORTUNE THEATRE
Fortune Street, EC1. *Private*
In January 1600 Edward Alleyn told carpenter Peter Street that he wanted a replica of the Globe Theatre, which Street had built in 1599. Street built the Fortune Theatre near here. It was burned down in 1621, rebuilt, continued in clandestine use under the Puritans, was dismantled in 1649, and finally demolished in 1661. See also Alleyn (page 156).

GEORGE III (1738–1820), English, royalty
Whitbread's Brewery, Chiswell Street, EC1.
Private
The plaque records a royal visit to the brewery in 1787. George III reigned from 1760 to 1820, his sympathy with ordinary people and interest in mundane matters earning him the affectionate nickname 'Farmer George'. His reign was blighted by

bouts of insanity, now thought to have been the disease porphyria. See also Queen Charlotte (page 157) and Samuel Whitbread (page 163).

GREENAWAY, Kate (1846–1901), English, artist, illustrator
147 Upper Street, Islington, N1.
London Borough of Islington
Greenaway lived here from 1862 to 1873. Her illustrations for children's books, including *Mother Goose* (1881) and *The Language of Flowers* (1884), made her pre-eminent in the field, rivalled only by Walter Crane (q.v.) and Randolph Caldecott (q.v.). The Kate Greenaway Medal has been awarded in her memory since 1955. (See also Hackney and Camden 1.)

GRIMALDI, Joseph
(1778–1837), English, clown
56 Exmouth Market, Finsbury, EC1.
English Heritage
Grimaldi lived here from 1818 to 1828. The story is told of a depressed young man going to his doctor, who, after examining him, says: 'You need uplift, why don't you go and see Grimaldi?' And the young man replies: 'But Doctor, I *am* Grimaldi.' (See also Barnet.)

GROOM, John (1845–1919), English, philanthropist
8 Seckforde Street, Clerkenwell, EC1.
English Heritage
The plaque records that Groom established workshops for disabled girls near this spot in 1866. The Watercress and Flower Girls' Christian Mission, afterwards known as John Groom's Crippleage, grew to training two hundred crippled girls as independent wage-earners, making artificial flowers, with further branches in Edgware and Clacton.

HIGHBURY BARN
Highbury Barn Tavern, Highbury Grove, N5. *London Borough of Islington*
This was the site of the Highbury Barn Pleasure Resort (1861–71). In 1861 Edward Giovanelli was

given a licence to lay out a lavish pleasure garden, including an open-air theatre with high-wire acts, and the original Siamese twins on show. Unfortunately, loose behaviour, including a riot by students of St Batholomew's Hospital in 1869, and the thronging of petty criminals, offended the neighbours, and the place shut after only ten years.

HYNDMAN, Henry Mayers (1842–1921), English, politician
54 Colebrooke Row, N1.
London Borough of Islington
This was the headquarters of the Social Democratic Federation from 1926 to 1937. Hyndman founded the SDF in 1884 and it was one of the organisations that were tributaries to the formation of the Labour Party in 1900. Hyndman was a gifted public speaker and influential in developing socialist thinking, but his dictatorial manner alienated many of his early supporters, such as William Morris (q.v.) and Eleanor Marx (q.v.), and he ended up ploughing a lonely furrow. (See also Camden 1.)

IRVING, Edward (1792–1834), Scottish, Catholic clergyman
4 Claremont Square, Islington, N1.
Greater London Council
Irving, who lived here, began preaching in 1822, after training as a schoolmaster. He founded the Catholic Apostolic Church after being convicted of heresy and excommunicated by the London Presbytery for publishing his doctrines on the humanity of Jesus Christ in 1830.

KEITH, Sir Arthur (1866–1955), Scottish, anatomist, anthropologist
17 Aubert Park, Highbury, N5.
London Borough of Islington
Sir Arthur, who lived here from 1908 to 1933, added the idea of 'group selection' to evolution theory, his writings culminating in *A New Theory of Human Evolution* (1948), which had some controversial thoughts about separate Jewish identity. Sir Arthur

may have been involved in the famous 1912 Piltdown Man hoax.

LAMB, Charles (1775–1834), English, essayist
64 Duncan Terrace, N1. *London County Council*
Lamb lived here from 1823 to 1827. Writing as 'Elia', he produced some of the best literary criticism of the early nineteenth century. Much loved by his friends, who included Coleridge (q.v.), Wordsworth, Hunt (q.v.) and Hazlitt (q.v.), he is a man of many plaques (see also City and Enfield).

LEAR, Edward (1812–88), English, painter, poet, travel writer
Bowman's Mews, Seven Sisters Road, Holloway, N7.
Lear was born near this spot. A prolific travel writer and an accomplished watercolourist, he is best remembered for his nonsense verse, first published anonymously in 1846 as *A Book of Nonsense*, followed by several others. *The Yonghy-Bonghy-Bò*, *The Chankly Bore*, *The Dong with the Luminous Nose* and *The Owl and the Pussy Cat* all continue to delight new generations of children of all ages. (See also Westminster 2.)

LENIN, Vladimir Ilyich (1870–1924), Russian, politician
Percy Circus, Finsbury, WC1. *Private*
The plaque records that Lenin stayed at 16 Percy Circus, on this site, in 1905. Lenin, more than any other revolutionary leader, grasped both the theoretical and the practical requirements of revolution. He was to save the new-born Soviet state

in the civil war of 1919–20, but his health failed and, despite his warnings, he was succeeded by Stalin in 1924.

LEYBOURNE, George (1842–84), English, music-hall comedian
136 Englefield Road, Kingsland, N1.
Greater London Council
Leybourne, born Joe Sanders, lived and died here. His stage persona as 'Champagne Charlie' was launched in 1867, an impeccably dressed toff flourishing a champagne bottle. Later he did endorsements for Moët, helping to establish champagne as the drink of the high life. He died penniless.

MacNEICE, Louis (1907–63), Irish, poet
52 Canonbury Park South, Islington, N1.
English Heritage
MacNiece lived here from 1947 to 1952. As a contemporary of Auden and a collaborator with him in the 1930s, his reputation suffered in Auden's shadow but was considerably rehabilitated by the posthumous publication in 1966 of his *Collected Poems*. He was also a noted writer for radio.

MEEK, Joe (1929–67), English, record producer
304 Holloway Road, Holloway, N7.
Private
Meek lived, worked and died here. 'Telstar' by the Tornados, produced by Meek in 1962, was the first American number one hit by a British group: that was his finest hour. In total he had forty-five top fifty hits, all recorded in a pioneering home-built studio in his flat here. But success was short-lived: afflicted by drugs, debt and paranoia, he shot himself.

O'BRIEN, James Bronterre (1805–64), Irish, Chartist
Elizabeth Garrett Anderson School, Donegal Street, N1. *London Borough of Islington*
O'Brien lived at 20 Hermes Street near this site from 1863 until his death. He was a prominent figure in the

London Chartist movement from 1838, jailed in Newcastle for seditious speaking in 1840. His writings resulted in *The Rise, Progress and Phases of Human Slavery*. He was bedridden for his last few years, exhausted by campaigning.

ORTON, Joe (1933–67), English, playwright
25 Noel Road, Islington, N1.
Islington Borough Council
Orton lived here from 1960 to 1967, while writing his macabre comedies *Entertaining Mr Sloane* (1964), *Loot* (1965) and *What the Butler Saw* (published posthumously in 1968). He was murdered here by his lover, Kenneth Halliwell, who could not handle Orton's success and then committed suicide.

ORWELL, George (1903–50), English, novelist, essayist
27 Canonbury Square, N1.
London Borough of Islington
The flat here was Orwell's last London home, where he lived from 1944 to 1947. Born Eric Arthur Blair, he repudiated his privileged background and studied poverty by experience. He was a member of the International Brigade in the Spanish Civil War, where he was wounded, and wrote one of his great books, *Homage to Catalonia* (1938). His most famous books are *Animal Farm* (1945) and *1984* (1949). (See also Kensington & Chelsea 1, Hillingdon and Camden 1.)

PAINE, Tom (1737–1809), English, political thinker
Angel Square, Islington High Street, N1.
BICC plc
Paine wrote his great work *The Rights of Man* here at the Angel in 1791. A friend of Benjamin Franklin (q.v.), he was an enthusiastic supporter of American independence, and of the French Revolution, which made him highly unpopular at home. He coined the phrase 'United States of America' and is revered in both the USA and France.

PEACOCK INN
11 Islington High Street, N1.
London Borough of Islington
The Peacock Inn stood on this site from 1564 to 1962. At first a coaching inn, it later became a pub until its demolition. Tom Brown stayed the night here before setting off for Rugby in *Tom Brown's Schooldays*. The inn also appeared in Dickens's short story *Boots at the Cherry Tree Inn*.

PHELPS, Samuel
(1804–78), English, actor-manager
8 Canonbury Square, Islington, N1.
London County Council
As actor-manager at Sadler's Wells, Phelps, who lived here, restored the original texts of Shakespeare's plays, instead of the rewrites by Tate, Cibber and Garrick that had held sway for over a century. He staged all but four of the plays, some of which had not been seen since their original productions at the Globe.

ST JOHN STREET TURNPIKE
Tunbridge House, St John Street, EC1.
London Borough of Islington
The turnpike stood here from c.1746 to 1830. St John Street is the southernmost section of the old Great North Road. The turnpike collected tolls for the upkeep of the road in this immediate neighbourhood. For other turnpike and tollgate sites see Archway, City Road and Coppice Row (pages 156 and 158), and Barnet.

SHEPHERD, Thomas
Hosmer (1793–1864), English, painter
26 Batchelor Street, Islington, N1.
Greater London Council
Shepherd, who lived here, was the master recorder of nineteenth-century London. His watercolours, with their endless attention to detail, appear as steel engravings in a number of books on the city, including *Metropolitan Improvements* (1827), *London and Its Environs* (1829), *London Interiors* (1841) and *Mighty London* (1851–5).

SICKERT, Walter
(1860–1942), English, painter
1 Highbury Place, Highbury, N5.
London Borough of Islington
Sickert ran his school of painting and engraving here from 1927 to 1934. (See also Camden 2.)

SOCIAL DEMOCRATIC FEDERATION
54 Colebrooke Row, Islington, N1.
London Borough of Islington
The SDF, founded by H. M. Hyndman (see page 160) in 1884, had its headquarters here from 1926 to 1937. From the outset, the SDF had tended to lose members on the left, who thought the group merely reformist, and on the right, among people influenced by Christian socialism, but it was nonetheless an important feeder group in the formation of the Labour Party in 1900.

STOPES, Marie
(1880–1958), Scottish, reformer, writer
61 Marlborough Road, Upper Holloway, N19.
London Borough of Islington

This was the site of Stopes's first Mothers' Clinic from 1921 to 1925, the first of its kind in Britain. (See also Camden 1 and Camden 2.)

SUESS, Eduard
(1831–1914), Austrian, geologist
4 Duncan Terrace, Islington, N1.
Geological Society of London
Suess, who was born in this house, is considered one of the greatest geologists. He was the first to posit the existence of the ancient supercontinent Gondwana, and he expounded early ideas on ecology in his great four-volume work *Das Antlitz der Erde* ('The Face of the Earth', 1883–1901).

TAYLOR, James Hudson
(1832–1905), English
missionary, physician
**6 Pyrland Road,
Highbury, N5.** *Private*
Taylor used these
premises from 1872 to
1895 as the London base
for his China Inland Mission,
which he had founded in 1865. He
spent fifty-one years in China, adopting local dress,
bringing over eight hundred missionaries, founding
125 schools, and making over eighteen thousand
Christian conversions. 'No other missionary in the
nineteen centuries since the apostle Paul has had a
broader vision.'

ZEPPELIN RAID
**61 Farringdon
Road, EC1.** *Private*
This was the most
successful Zeppelin
raid of the First
World War, causing
£500,000 damage,
mostly from L13's
successful bombing of central London. This amounted
to over half the damage caused by all Zeppelin raids.
(See also Camden 2.)

WESLEY, John (1703–91), English, Methodist
47 City Road, EC1. *London County Council*
Wesley, the founder of Methodism, lived here.
(See also City and Westminster 4.)

WHITBREAD, Samuel (1720–96), English,
brewer, politician
Whitbread's Brewery, Chiswell Street, EC1.
Private
The plaque records a royal visit to the brewery in 1787
(see Queen Charlotte and George III, pages 157 and
159). Whitbread moved his brewery to Chiswell Street
in 1750 and by the end of the century it was London's
largest, producing over 200,000 barrels a year. An MP
from 1768 onwards, he is said to have been the first to
mention slavery in the House, though the claim is also
made for David Hartley (q.v.).

WILLIAMS, Charles Walter Stansby
(1886–1945), English, poet, novelist
3 Caedmon Road, Holloway, N7. *Private*
Williams, who was born here, was a prolific author of
novels, poetry, theology, drama, history, biography and
criticism. His best-known novel is *Descent into Hell*
(1945), which was admired by T. S. Eliot and
C. S. Lewis. He worked as an editor at the Oxford
University Press.

KENSINGTON & CHELSEA

Lying directly west of Westminster, the Royal Borough
of Kensington & Chelsea is an amalgamation of the former
Royal Borough of Kensington and the Metropolitan Borough of Chelsea.
It is liberally endowed with plaques, so for convenience the
entries here are split – dividing the borough along its waistline
at the Cromwell Road–Brompton Road axis.

Kensington & Chelsea 1:
Kensington, Notting Hill and North Kensington
North of Cromwell Road–Brompton Road

ALEXANDER, William Cleverly (1840–1916),
English, patron of the arts
Aubrey House, Aubrey Walk, W8. *English Heritage*
Alexander was a wealthy banker, who moved into
Aubrey House in 1873. He was a patron in particular
of Whistler (q.v.), from whom he commissioned a
number of works, and who also did some decorative
arrangements for him here.

ANSDELL, Richard (1815–85), English, painter
1 St Albans Grove, W8. *Private*
Ansdell, who lived in Lytham House on this site from
1862 to 1884, was a painter of animal and sporting
scenes. He was often compared to Landseer, the
general view being that his work, though popular,
lacked the emotional impact of Landseer's. He was
elected a Royal Academician in 1870.

AUBREY HOUSE
Aubrey Walk, W8.
English Heritage
Aubrey House is one of
the grand mansions of
Kensington. Its heart is
thought to be a building
erected *c.*1698 beside
medicinal springs, but
it was altered and
extended several times
in the course of the
eighteenth century. For the various former inhabitants
listed on the plaque see above and below.

BADEN-POWELL, Robert (1857–1941), English,
soldier
9 Hyde Park Gate, SW7. *Greater London Council*
Baden-Powell, 'Chief Scout of the World' (says the
plaque), lived here from 1861 to 1876. He is
remembered as a soldier as the hero of the defence
of Mafeking in the Second Boer War, and universally as
the founder of the Boy Scout movement. A camp on
Brownsea Island in 1907 was a pilot for his ideas, from
which the movement grew globally.
(See also Merton.)

BAGNOLD, Enid (1889–1981), English, novelist,
playwright
29 Hyde Park Gate, SW7. *English Heritage*
Bagnold, who lived here, was an associate of Katherine
Mansfield (q.v.) and Henri Gaudier-Brzeska, who
sculpted her head. Among her novels are *National
Velvet* (1935), later a film starring Elizabeth Taylor, and
The Loved and the Envied (1950). Her best-known play is
The Chalk Garden (1955).

BAIRNSFATHER, Bruce (1888–1959), English,
cartoonist
1 Sterling Street, SW7. *Greater London Council*
Bairnsfather, who lived here, is remembered for his
First World War cartoons featuring 'Old Bill',

a curmudgeonly old soldier with a walrus moustache and balaclava (hobby, filling sandbags on rainy nights), whose best-known saying, to a whingeing mate, was 'If you know a better 'ole, go to it!'

BARBOSA, Ruy (1849–1923), Brazilian, statesman
17 Holland Park Gardens, W14.
Anglo-Brazilian Society
Treasury minister in the new Republic of Brazil (1889–94), he fled after the establishment of a military dictatorship and spent a year in exile here in 1895. Taking part in the Hague Conventions of 1899 and 1907, he was known as 'the Eagle of The Hague'.

BARTON, Sir Derek (1918–98), English, chemist
Chemistry Building, Imperial College Road, SW7. *Royal Society of Chemistry*
Having been a student at Imperial College (1938–42), Sir Derek was Professor of Organic Chemistry here (1957–78) and in 1969 was awarded the Nobel Prize for his new concept in organic conformational analysis.

BEERBOHM, Sir Max (1872–1956), English, caricaturist, essayist
57 Palace Gardens Terrace, W8.
Greater London Council
Sir Max, who was born here, succeeded G. B. Shaw (q.v.) as drama critic of the *Saturday Review* and was a prolific writer of elegant witty essays and a famous full-length novel, *Zuleika Dobson* (1911). His caricatures of his contemporaries were equally witty and he was the source of innumerable quips, such as 'Most women are not as young as they are painted'.

BENN, Caroline DeCamp (1926–2000), American, educationalist
12 Holland Park Avenue, W11. *Tony Benn*
Married to Tony Benn for fifty years, Caroline DeCamp was a leader in the campaign for comprehensive education, sending all their children to the local Holland Park Comprehensive, and a school governor for thirty-five years. She was also a constant support in her husband's various battles, and widely respected in the Labour movement.

BENSON, E. F. (1867–1940), English, novelist
25 Brompton Square, SW3. *English Heritage*
Benson, who lived here, was a prolific popular novelist. His works include *Dodo* (1893), *Queen Lucia* (1920) and *Miss Mapp* (1922), each of which spawned several sequels. *Mapp and Lucia* was a television series of the 1980s. Benson also wrote several books of reminiscence, full of amusing anecdotes.

BOOTH, Charles (1840–1916), English, social researcher
6 Grenville Place, South Kensington, SW7.
London County Council
Booth, who lived here, was the inheritor of a Liverpool shipping fortune. He settled in London in 1875 and sponsored several ground-breaking social research projects, most notably including the 'Poverty' maps of London, which were based on detailed enquiry and showed street by street the gradations of wealth and poverty.

BRIDGE, Frank (1879–1941), English, composer, conductor
4 Bedford Gardens, W8. *English Heritage*
Bridge, who lived here, was the tutor of Benjamin Britten (q.v.) and a frequent conductor at the Promenade concerts. Among his compositions are *Sea* (1912) and *Ovation* (1930), the latter recorded by Julian Lloyd Webber in 1976. He is best remembered for his chamber music.

BROWNE, Hablot Knight (1815–82), English, illustrator
239 Ladbroke Grove, W10. *English Heritage*
Browne, who lived here from 1874 to 1880, chose to sign his work 'Phiz', to chime, he said, with Dickens's 'Boz'. He illustrated ten Dickens novels, his most successful realisations being Sam Weller, Wackford Squeers, Mr Micawber, Mrs Gamp and David Copperfield.

BROWNING, Robert (1812–89), English, poet
29 De Vere Gardens, Kensington, W8. *Private*
Browning lived the last two years of his life here. His last volume of poems, *Asolando*, was published on 12 April 1889, the day of his death. It contains the

famous self-portrait, 'One who never turned his back but marched breast forward...'
(See also Westminster 1 and Southwark.)

BURNE-JONES, Sir Edward (1837–98), English, painter
41 Kensington Square, W8. *English Heritage*
Burne-Jones lived here from 1865 to 1867. His mystical romantic style was gently satirised in Gilbert and Sullivan's *Patience* as 'greenery yallery, Grosvenor Gallery'. (See also Hammersmith & Fulham and Camden 2.)

CAMPBELL, Mrs Patrick (1865–1940), English, actress
33 Kensington Square, Kensington, W8. *Private*
Mrs Campbell lived here. Married at nineteen, she went on the stage in 1888. She starred in *The Second Mrs Tanqueray* (1893) by Pinero (q.v.), played Ophelia, Juliet and Lady Macbeth for Forbes-Robertson (q.v.), and was the first ever Eliza Doolittle in *Pygmalion* (1914), written for her by Shaw (q.v.), even though she was by then forty-nine.

CAYLEY ROBINSON, Frederick (1862–1927), English, painter
Lansdowne House, 80 Lansdowne Road, W11.
Greater London Council
Cayley Robinson, who lived and worked here, was heavily influenced by the work of Burne-Jones (q.v.) and Puvis de Chavannes. His murals for Middlesex Hospital, *The Four Acts of Mercy* (1915–20), were much admired. Forgotten for fifty years, his name was revived by an article in *The Connoisseur* in 1977.

CETSHWAYO (c.1832–84), Zulu, royalty
18 Melbury Road, W14. *English Heritage*
Cetshwayo, the last king of an independent Zulu nation, stayed here for a month in August 1882. Becoming king in 1872, he had shown belligerence at Boer incursions into Zulu territory, which led to the Zulu War of 1879, in which, after inflicting the calamitous defeat of Isandlwana on the British, he was eventually defeated and dethroned. His visit to Britain was to negotiate his reinstatement as king, which Gladstone (q.v.) agreed to. He was restored to the throne in 1883 but was fatally weakened by divisions among the Zulus and died, possibly poisoned, in 1884.

CHESTERTON, G. K. (1874–1936), English, novelist, biographer, poet
32 Sheffield Terrace, Kensington, W8. *Private*
11 Warwick Gardens, West Kensington, W14.
London County Council
Chesterton was born at the first address and lived at the second. 'Bowing down in blind incredulity, as is my custom, before mere authority and the tradition of the elders, superstitiously swallowing a story I could not test at the time... I am firmly of the opinion that I was born on the 29th May 1874 on Campden Hill.' He most famously produced the 'Father Brown' stories and wrote biographies of Browning (q.v.), Dickens (q.v.), R. L. Stevenson (q.v.) and St Francis of Assisi. 'The Prince of Paradox' was best friends with Shaw (q.v.) and Belloc (q.v.).

CHEVALIER, Albert (1861–1923), English, music-hall comedian
17 St Ann's Villas, W11. *London County Council*
Chevalier was born here. After a fourteen-year career on the legitimate stage from the age of sixteen, he developed his own music-hall show built round costermonger songs of his own invention. Hugely popular in his heyday, among his most memorable songs were 'Knocked 'em in the Old Kent Road' and 'My Old Dutch'. His own 'Old Dutch' was Florrie, daughter of George Leybourne (q.v.).

CHRISTIE, Dame Agatha (1890–1976), English, detective-story writer
58 Sheffield Terrace, W8. *English Heritage*
Christie lived here from 1934 to 1941. She wrote more than seventy detective stories, mostly featuring

the characters Hercule Poirot or Miss Marple. Innumerable films and television adaptations have been made from her work. She also wrote the whodunnit *The Mousetrap*, which has been running in London since 1952. (See also Kensington & Chelsea 2.)

CHURCHILL, Sir Winston (1874–1965), English, Prime Minister
28 Hyde Park Gate, SW7. *Greater London Council*
Churchill lived here from 1945 until his death, apart from his second stint as Prime Minister (1951–5). His funeral was the grandest for a non-royal person since that of the Duke of Wellington in 1854. (See also Westminster 2 and Westminster 4.)

CLEMENTI, Muzio (1752–1832), Italian, composer, musician
128 Kensington Church Street, Kensington, W8. *London County Council*
Clementi, who lived in this house from 1820 to 1823, had settled in London in 1782 after earlier visits and opened a piano and music business. His collection of piano studies, *Gradus ad Parnassum* (1817), continues in use today as exercises.

COGAN, Alma (1932–66), English, popular singer
43–52 Stafford Court, Kensington High Street, W8. *Musical Heritage*
Cogan lived here and threw fabulous showbiz parties. Her era was the 1950s and early 1960s, singing traditional pop music such as was largely obliterated by the arrival of rock 'n' roll. Dubbed 'the Girl with a Giggle in Her Voice', she had four top ten hits, including 'Dreamboat', which was number one in May 1955.

COKE, Lady Mary (1727–1811), English, diarist
Aubrey House, Aubrey Walk, W8. *English Heritage*
Lady Mary led a life flitting around the courts and stately homes of Europe, engaging and then usually alienating her hosts with her blithe overestimation of her own importance. Her friend Horace Walpole (q.v.), who dedicated *The Castle of Otranto* to her but then wearied of her gossip and snobbery, wrote: 'She has a frenzy for royalty, and will fall in love with and at

the feet of a Great Duke and Duchess, especially the former.' Her diaries, not intended for publication, are a bizarre combination of the mundane, the preposterous and the perceptive.

COMPTON-BURNETT, Dame Ivy (1884–1969), English, novelist
Braemar Mansions, Cornwall Gardens, SW7. *English Heritage*
Dame Ivy, who lived here from 1934 until her death, was noted for her skilful way with dialogue and many of her books have been adapted for broadcasting. *Pastors and Masters* (1925), *Brothers and Sisters* (1929), *Men and Wives* (1931) and *Daughters and Sons* (1937) are among her best-known works.

CORBOULD, Edward Henry (1815–1905), English, painter
52 Eldon Road, Kensington, W8. *Private*
Corbould, who lived here, was primarily a watercolourist of literary and historical scenes, particularly a series on the Canterbury Pilgrims. He was appointed instructor of historical painting to the Royal Family, which meant tutoring the royal children, in 1851. The contract was terminated in 1871, for reasons unknown.

CRANE, Walter (1845–1915), English, painter, illustrator
13 Holland Street, Kensington, W8. *London County Council*
Crane, who lived here, was an associate of William Morris (q.v.) and a keen member of the Art Workers Guild. He was particularly noted for his book illustrations, his *Faerie Queen* (1894–6) being seen as one of his greatest achievements.

CROMPTON, Colonel R. E. B. (1845–1940), English, electrical engineer
48 Kensington Court, W8. *English Heritage*
Colonel Crompton lived and worked here from 1891

to 1939. His company was England's leading manufacturer of electricity generating and lighting equipment in the 1880s and 1890s. Among his many contracts was the Vienna Opera, the first large theatre to be lit by electricity. He also drew the first blueprints for battle tanks.

CROOKES, Sir William (1832–1919), English, scientist
7 Kensington Park Gardens, Notting Hill, W11.
Greater London Council
Sir William, who lived here from 1880 until his death, discovered the metal thallium (1861), invented the radiometer (1873–6), identified the first known sample of helium (1895) and improved vacuum tubes and electric lighting. He was elected a Fellow of the Royal Society in 1863 and awarded the Order of Merit in 1910.

DANIELL, Thomas (1749–1840), English, topographical artist
14 Earls Terrace, W8. *English Heritage*
Daniell lived and died here. He spent ten years in India with his nephew William (q.v.) and together they published *Oriental Scenery* in six volumes in 1808. According to Redgrave's *Dictionary of Artists* (1873), 'His works are characterised by great Oriental truth and beauty; the customs and manners of India are well rendered. His painting was firm, but sometimes thin, his colouring agreeable. He seldom painted any but Oriental subjects.'

DOBSON, Cowan (1893–1980), Scottish, painter
62 South Edwardes Square, W8. *Private*
Dobson lived and painted here from 1940 until his death. After the First World War he was commissioned to paint all the Victoria Cross winners of the war. These portraits are now at the Imperial War Museum. He was a noted portraitist of kings, queens and dignitaries of many countries.

DUKES, Ashley (1885–1959), English, playwright, critic
Kensington Temple, Ladbroke Road, Notting Hill, W11. *Private*

This was the site of the Mercury Theatre, which Dukes founded in 1931 as a new stage for plays by poets, and which ran until 1987. He is best remembered for his play *The Man with a Load of Mischief* (1924). From 1937 onwards he was Professor of Drama at the Royal Society of Literature. He was married to Marie Rambert (q.v.).

ELIOT, T. S. (1888–1965), English, poet, playwright, critic
3 Kensington Court Gardens, W8. *English Heritage*
Eliot, who lived and died here, was a major figure in the British literary landscape of the twentieth century. As a poet, critic and playwright, he spoke for the disillusioned post-First World War generation. In *The Hollow Men* (1925) he wrote: 'This is the way the world ends, not with a bang but a whimper.' However, he was not all gloom and doom, producing *Old Possum's Book of Practical Cats* (1939), a classic of children's verse. (See also Camden 2 and Westminster 2.)

EPSTEIN, Sir Jacob (1880–1959), American, sculptor
18 Hyde Park Gate, SW7. *Private*
25 Queen's Gate Mews, SW7. *Private*
Sir Jacob lived at the first address from 1929 until his death and worked at the second.
His muscular nude figures, such as the eighteen statues he made for the British Medical Association headquarters in the Strand (now Zimbabwe House), led to accusations of indecency, and the works were vandalised. One of his most celebrated works is *St Michael and the Devil* (1958), at Coventry Cathedral.

FILDES, Sir Luke (1844–1927), English, painter, illustrator
31 Melbury Road, West Kensington, W14.
London County Council
Sir Luke lived in this house, designed for him by Richard Norman Shaw (q.v.), from 1878 until his death. Commissioned by Dickens (q.v.) to illustrate *Edwin Drood* (1870), he was noted for his grasp of 'the tragic aspect of humanity'. He went on to huge success, including painting the coronation portraits of Edward VII and Queen Alexandra. He was elected a Royal Academician in 1887.

FLINT, Sir William Russell (1880–1969), Scottish, painter
80 Peel Street, Kensington, W8. *Private*
Sir William lived here from 1925 until his death. He will be remembered as a prolific and popular painter of ladies of the harem lounging about at their leisure, sweetly sexy and very decorative. He was elected a Royal Academician in 1933 and was president of the Royal Society of Painters in Watercolours (1936–56).

FORBES, Vivian (1891–1937), English, painter
Lansdowne House, 80 Lansdowne Road, W11.
Greater London Council
Vivian Forbes met Glyn Philpot (see page 174) in the trenches in the First World War and 'clung to him' for the rest of his life. When Philpot suddenly died of a heart attack, Forbes committed suicide with an overdose of sleeping pills the day after the funeral.

FORD, Ford Madox (1873–1939), English, novelist, critic
80 Campden Hill Road, Kensington, W8.
Greater London Council
Ford Madox Ford, who lived here, was the pen-name of Ford Hermann Hueffer, grandson of Ford Madox Brown (q.v.). Author of eighty books and editor of two literary magazines, he collaborated for a time with Conrad (q.v.). His best-known work is *The Good Soldier* (1915).

FOSCOLO, Ugo (1778–1827), Italian, poet
19 Edwardes Square, Kensington, W8.
English Heritage
Foscolo, who lived here in 1817–18, was the first modern Italian poet to deal with the crisis of his age. An admirer of Napoleon as liberator of Italy, he went into exile when the Austrians returned in 1814. In England he wrote articles for various literary reviews but died in poverty.

GABOR, Dennis (1900–79), Hungarian, electrical engineer, inventor
79 Queen's Gate, SW7. *English Heritage*
Gabor, who lived here, came to England as a refugee from Nazism in 1933. Working with the British Thompson-Houston company, he conducted research into electron optics and published a series of papers on optical imaging (1946–51), which, among many honours, led to the Nobel Prize for Physics in 1971. He said: 'The best way to predict the future is to invent it.'

GARTH, Susan, English, antique dealer
167 Portobello Road, W11. *Private*
Some local traders objected when the plaque was erected in 1975, feeling it wrong to give all the credit to Susan Garth, as there had been various antique stalls in the area since the 1940s, when she started up.

GRAHAME, Kenneth (1859–1932), Scottish, children's writer
16 Phillimore Place, Kensington, W8.
London County Council
Grahame lived here from 1901 to 1908, while secretary to the Bank of England. He wrote *The Wind in the Willows* (1908), the adventures of Ratty, Mole, Mr Badger and Mr Toad, as an amusement for his son, not at first thinking of publication. It is now recognised as one of the greatest works of children's fiction, and enjoyed by adults too. It was first dramatised for the stage by A. A. Milne (q.v.) as *Toad of Toad Hall* (1929) and has been perennially adapted for television.

GROSVENOR, Sir Edward Lloyd Richard, first Earl (1731–1802), English, politician, horse-breeder
Aubrey House, Aubrey Walk, W8. *English Heritage*
Sir Edward, among the several former inhabitants of Aubrey House listed on the plaque, was a horse-breeder and was MP for Chester (1754–61). When he became the first Earl Grosvenor in 1784, he chose the subsidiary title of Viscount Belgrave, taking the name from an estate the family owned in Cheshire. Today Belgrave Square is at the heart of the Grosvenor Estate.

HAAKON VII of Norway (1872–1957), Norwegian, royalty
10 Palace Green, W8. *English Heritage*
King Haakon led the Norwegian government in exile here from 1940 to 1945. He was the first king of Norway after the dissolution of the union with Sweden in 1905, being, unusually for a king, *elected* to the throne. He reigned fifty-two years and is regarded as one of the greatest figures in Norwegian history. (See also Westminster 4.)

HALL, Radclyffe
(1880–1943), English, novelist, poet

37 Holland Street, Kensington, W8.

English Heritage

Hall, who lived here from 1924 to 1929, is today remembered mainly for *The Well of Loneliness* (1928), the only one of her novels to deal openly with lesbianism. There was an obscenity trial and, despite support from E. M. Forster (q.v.) and others, the book was banned. It was finally published in 1949.

HENRY, Sir Edward (1850–1931), English, police commissioner
19 Sheffield Terrace, W8. *English Heritage*
Sir Edward, who lived here from 1903 to 1920, was commissioner of the Metropolitan Police (1903–18) and is particularly associated with pioneering work in the use of fingerprinting. But he also oversaw the introduction of dogs, typewriters, telephones and police boxes; during his watch the police finally moved out of the Victorian era.

HOWERD, Frankie (1917–92), English, comedian
27 Edwardes Square, Kensington, W8.
Dead Comics Society
Howerd lived here from 1966 until his death. His humour depended on a direct relationship with the audience, littered with apparently ad-lib verbal tics such as 'Titter ye not'. He would innocently deliver a risqué double-entendre and then upbraid the audience for having got the joke. When his career was in temporary eclipse, he was rescued by Peter Cook (q.v.), who gave him a season at the Establishment Club, which led to cult status, especially among students, later in life.

HUDSON, W. H. (1841–1922), English, novelist, naturalist
40 St Luke's Road, Notting Hill, W11.
Hudson's Friends Society of Quilmes
Hudson lived his last years here. Born in Argentina, he is honoured there as Guillermo Enrique Hudson. He settled in England in 1869 and was naturalised in 1900. His writings initially were on ornithology and he was a founding member of the Royal Society for the Protection of Birds. Fame came with his novel *Green*

Mansions (1904) and his countryside books, especially *A Shepherd's Life* (1910).

HUNT, William Holman (1827–1910), English, painter
18 Melbury Road, West Kensington, W14.
London County Council
Hunt, who lived and died here, was one of the founders of the Pre-Raphaelite Brotherhood, with Millais (q.v.), Rossetti (q.v.) and others. He pursued realism and truth to nature in his often deeply symbolic paintings, such as *The Scapegoat* (1854), *The Light of the World* (1853–4), *The Finding of the Saviour in the Temple* (1854–60) and *The Shadow of Death* (1870–3). Of all the Brotherhood's members, he is said to be the one who remained most faithful to their original ideas.

JAMES, Henry
(1843–1916), American, novelist
34 De Vere Gardens, Kensington, W8.
London County Council
James lived here from 1886 to 1902. His theme in his major works is the encounter between America and Europe. His innovative use of point of view and interior monologue make him a founder of the modern novel. Among a large output of novels, mention should be made of *The Portrait of a Lady* (1881), *The Bostonians* (1886) and *The Ambassadors* (1903), and among his novellas *Daisy Miller* (1879) and *The Turn of the Screw* (1898). His stories have been adapted for the cinema many times.

JINNAH, Mohammed Ali
(1876–1948), Pakistani, politician
35 Russell Road, West Kensington, W14.
London County Council
Jinnah stayed here in

1895. The next year he joined the Indian National Congress and believed in united independence for the whole sub-continent, but, after becoming President of the All-India Muslim League in 1916, he gradually shifted to the idea of a separate Muslim state and became the acknowledged founder of Pakistan.

JOYCE, James (1882–1941), Irish, novelist
28b Campden Grove, Kensington, W8.
English Heritage
Joyce, who lived here in 1931, is famous for his development of the 'stream of consciousness' style of writing – 'The flushpots of Euston and the hanging garments of Marylebone'. His works include *Dubliners* (1914), *Portrait of the Artist as a Young Man* (1916), *Ulysses* (1922) and *Finnegan's Wake* (1939).

KENNEDY, John Fitzgerald (1917–63), American, President **14 Princes Gate, South Kensington, SW7.** *Private* Kennedy lived here as a young man. The thirty-fifth president of the USA (1960–3), he was the youngest man and the first Catholic to be elected to the office. He sanctioned the disastrous Bay of Pigs invasion of Cuba (a plan he inherited) in 1961 but obtained the removal of Soviet missiles from the island in 1962. His assassination in Dallas on 22 November 1963 remains the subject of endless speculation. Like many who died young, he is protected from the compromise of age.

KOSSUTH, Louis (1802–94), Hungarian, politician
39 Chepstow Villas, Notting Hill, W11.
London County Council
Kossuth stayed here during a triumphant tour after being forced into exile. In 1848, the 'Year of Revolutions', he was the voice of Hungary and, when briefly in 1849, independence was declared from Austria, he was regent-president. But with the intervention of Russia, Hungary was again subjugated and he went into exile. During his visit to England he addressed a crowd estimated at up to 100,000 at Copenhagen Fields (q.v.) and it caused great anguish to Queen Victoria that such a virulent republican

should be so rapturously received by her subjects.

LANG, Andrew (1844–1912), Scottish, historian, writer
1 Marloes Road, Kensington, W8.
London County Council
Lang lived here from 1876 until his death. His works include *Custom and Myth* (1884), *Myth, Ritual and Religion* (1887) and *The Making of Religion* (1898). He also wrote *A History of Scotland* (1899–1904) and several books of verse and fairy tales for children.

LAO SHE (1899–1966), Chinese, novelist, playwright
31 St James's Gardens, W11.
English Heritage
Lao She, who lived here from 1925 to 1928, is considered one of the most important Chinese writers of the twentieth century. His best-known novel is *Rickshaw Boy* (1936), and his most-performed play is *Teahouse* (1957). While in London he was a lecturer at the School of Oriental Studies (now the School of Oriental and African Studies).

LEIGHTON, Lord (1830–96), English, painter, sculptor
12 Holland Park Road, West Kensington, W14.
London County Council
Lord Leighton, who lived and died here, travelled extensively in Europe and specialised in classical Greek subjects. Many of his paintings were reproduced and became popular sellers in Victorian homes. He was president of the Royal Academy (1876–96) and in 1896 was the first artist to be ennobled, but he died the next day.

LEWIS, Percy Wyndham (1882–1957), English, painter, novelist
61 Palace Gardens Terrace, Kensington, W8.
Greater London Council
Wyndham Lewis, who lived here, was a founder of Vorticism, a fusion of Cubism and Futurism, and editor of its magazine *Blast*. A reveller in controversy, he dubbed himself 'the enemy', and in later life was called by W. H. Auden 'that lonely old volcano of the Right'.

LOW, Sir David (1891–1963), New Zealander, cartoonist
Melbury Court, Kensington High Street, W8.
English Heritage
Sir David, who lived in Flat 33 here, came to London in 1919 and worked for the *Star* (1919–27), the *Evening Standard* (1927–50), the *Daily Herald* (1950–3) and the *Guardian* (1953–63). His ruthless portrayal of fascist Italy and Germany meant his work was banned in both countries, and Goebbels complained to Halifax (q.v.) about his depictions of Hitler. His most famous character was Colonel Blimp, an affectionate satire on reactionary British politics.

LOWES-DICKINSON, G. (1862–1932), English, historian, humanist
11 Edwardes Square, Kensington, W8. *Private*
This was Lowes Dickinson's London home. A Cambridge lecturer (1886–1920), his works include *The Meaning of Good* (1901), *Religion and Immortality* (1911) and *War, Its Nature, Cause and Cure* (1923). From 1914 on he threw himself into the campaign for a 'League of Nations', a phrase he may have invented.

MALLARMÉ, Stéphane (1842–98), French, poet
6 Brompton Square, SW3. *London County Council*
Mallarmé stayed here in 1863. A member of the Symbolist Group, he was a regular visitor to England and taught English in Paris. He translated Poe's (q.v.) *The Raven* into French (1875), with illustrations by Manet, and his own works inspired composers such as Debussy, Ravel, Milhaud and Boulez.

MAXWELL, James Clerk (1831–79), Scottish, physicist
16 Palace Gardens Terrace, Kensington, W8.
London County Council
Maxwell, who lived here from 1858 to 1866, developed the classical electromagnetic theory, bringing together all previous observations and speculations. This has been called the 'second great unification in physics' and Einstein described his work as 'the most profound and fruitful since Newton'.

MAY, Phil (1864–1903), English, cartoonist
20 Holland Park Road,
West Kensington, W14. *Greater London Council*
May lived and worked here. He was the cartoonist of the 'Arrys and 'Arriets on London streets, observed with tenderness and compassion. He had the unusual distinction of being elected to the Royal Institute of Painters in Watercolour in 1896. Unfortunately, early poverty and heavy drinking led to cirrhosis of the liver.

McBEY, James (1883–1959), Scottish, painter
1 Holland Park Avenue, Notting Hill, W11.
Private
Mcbey, who lived here, was an official war artist in the First World War. Subsequently, he is particularly associated with North Africa, living mostly in Tangier and Marrakesh, and producing notable watercolours and etchings with sensitive draughtsmanship and a very personal impressionistic style.

MERCURY THEATRE
Kensington Temple, Ladbroke Road, Notting Hill, W11. *Private*
A mid-nineteenth-century church hall, bought by Ashley Dukes (q.v.) and Marie Rambert (q.v.) in 1927, opened as the Mercury Theatre in 1931 with a performance by her Ballet Club (later the Ballet Rambert). The company's most celebrated production was the première of T. S. Eliot's (q.v.) *Murder in the Cathedral* (1935). The theatre was demolished in 1987.

MILL, John Stuart (1806–73), English, philosopher, economist
18 Kensington Square, Kensington, W8.
London County Council
Mill, who lived here, was a major liberal progressive thinker, ahead of his time on women's rights, proportional representation, trade unions and universal education. Among his most important writings are *On Liberty* (1859) and *Utilitarianism* (1863). He was Bertrand Russell's (q.v.) godfather.

MILLAIS, Sir John Everett (1829–96), English, painter
2 Palace Gate, W8. *London County Council*
Millais, who lived and worked here, was a child prodigy, accepted into the Royal Academy School at the age of eleven. He was a founder, in 1848, with Holman Hunt (q.v.) and D. G. Rossetti (q.v.), of the Pre-Raphaelite Brotherhood and went on to paint

some of the best-known pictures in British art, among them *Ophelia* (1852), *The Boyhood of Raleigh* (1871) and *Bubbles* (1886). (See also Kensington & Chelsea 2.)

MORGAN, Charles (1894–1958), English, novelist, critic
16 Campden Hill Square, Kensington, W8.
English Heritage
Morgan lived and died here. His novels include *The Gunroom* (1919), *Portrait in a Mirror* (1929), *The Fountain* (1932) and *The Voyage* (1940). He was also drama critic of *The Times* (1926–39). His reputation, high in his lifetime, is currently in eclipse, but he is greatly admired in France.

MORGAN, John Pierpont (1837–1913), American, financier
14 Princes Gate, SW7. *English Heritage*
This was the London home of J. P. Morgan and his father, Junius (see below). Morgan dominated the American economy in his time, arranging the merger of Edison and Thompson-Houston in 1892 to form General Electric, and the merger of Carnegie Steel and others in 1901 to form US Steel. He is credited with saving the American economy in the crises of 1895 and 1907, and also with saying: 'If you have to ask the price, you can't afford it.'

MORGAN, Junius S. (1813–90), American, financier
14 Princes Gate, SW7. *English Heritage*
Overshadowed in history by his son (see above), Junius was nonetheless smart enough to leave an estate valued at $10 million. From 1854 he was partner, with George Peabody (q.v.), in the English banking house of George Peabody & Co. In 1864 he succeeded Peabody as head of the firm and changed its name to J. S. Morgan & Co.

NABUCO, Joaquim (1849–1910), Brazilian, politician
52 Cornwall Gardens, South Kensington, SW7. *Brazilian Government*
Nabuco lived here from 1900 to 1905 while ambassador to the Court of St James. His earlier political life had largely been devoted to the fight against slavery, abolished in Brazil in 1888, principally

thanks to him. He was one of the first proponents of the idea of 'Pan-Americanism'.

NEHRU, Jawaharlal (1889–1964), Indian, politician
60 Elgin Crescent, Notting Hill, W11.
English Heritage
Nehru was studying at the Inner Temple while living here in 1910 and 1912. He became a central figure in the Indian National Congress, campaigning for independence and spending years in prison for it. He was India's first prime minister (1947–64), and a leader of the Third World non-aligned movement.

NEWBOLT, Sir Henry (1862–1938), English, poet
29 Campden Hill Road, Kensington, W8. *English Heritage*
Sir Henry, who lived here from 1918, is best known for works about seafaring, including *Admirals All* (1907), in which 'Drake's Drum' appears, *Songs of the Sea* (1904) and *Songs of the Fleet* (1910). His most famous poem is 'Vitaï Lampada', with the ultimate British line of poetry: 'Play up! Play up! And play the game!'

ORWELL, George (1903–50), English, novelist, essayist
26 Portobello Road, W11. *Private*
Orwell lived here in 1927–8, after his return from being a policeman in Burma and before his two-year stay in Paris, which was to produce his first book, *Down and Out in Paris and London* (1933). (See also Camden 1, Hillingdon and Islington.)

PALMER, Samuel (1805–81), English, painter
6 Douro Place, Kensington, W8.
Greater London Council
Palmer, who lived here from 1851 to 1861, was a friend of Blake (q.v.) and son-in-law of Linnell (q.v.). He formed a group of artists called 'The Ancients' at Shoreham, Kent (1826–35). His paintings from that time include *A Hilly Scene* (1826) and *The Magic Apple Tree* (1830), set in a mystic landscape, and are better regarded than his later, more conventional work. (See also Southwark.)

PANKHURST, Dame Christabel (1880–1958), English, suffragette
50 Clarendon Road, W11.
English Heritage
Christabel Pankhurst, who lived here with her mother (see below), earned the nickname 'Queen of the Mob' for her fervent espousal of the cause of women's rights. She and her mother and others founded the Women's Social and Political Union in 1903, and she was several times arrested for her activities. During the First World War she was ultra-patriotic; her supporters handed out white feathers to young men not in uniform. After the war, with typical enthusiasm, she moved to the United States and took up evangelism.

PANKHURST, Emmeline (1858–1928), English, suffragette
50 Clarendon Road, W11. *English Heritage*
Mrs Pankhurst lived here with her daughter (see left). She founded the Women's Franchise League in 1889, but the movement gained a new impetus when, with her daughters, she founded the Women's Social and Political Union in 1903. Altogether she was arrested

thirteen times for various demonstrations before the First World War. During the war she became an ultra-patriot, and her daughter Sylvia (q.v.) described the WSPU at that time: 'Giving its energies wholly to the prosecution of the War, it rushed to a furious extreme, its Chauvinism unexampled amongst all the other women's societies.'

PARRY, Hubert (1848–1918), English, composer
17 Kensington Square, Kensington, W8.
London County Council
Parry, who lived here from 1886 until his death, was director of the Royal College of Music (1894–1918) and Professor of Music at Oxford (1900–8), but he is best remembered for his choral settings: the hymn 'Dear Lord and Father of Mankind', the anthem 'I Was Glad', written for Edward VII's coronation in 1902, and, above all, 'Jerusalem' with the words of William Blake (q.v.).

PATER, Walter (1839–94), English, aesthete
12 Earls Terrace, W8. *English Heritage*
Pater, the archetype of aestheticism, lived and worked here from 1885 to 1893. His career at Oxford was thwarted more than once by his barely disguised homosexuality. In his philosophical novel *Marius the Epicurean* (1885) he expounded his views on the ideal aesthetic life, and it had a great effect on Oscar Wilde (q.v.). His literary judgement was acute, his style fastidious, and his views were influential across a range of subjects.

PHILPOT, Glyn (1884–1937), English, painter
Lansdowne House, 80 Lansdowne Road, W11.
Greater London Council
Philpot, who lived and worked here, was best known as a portrait painter of distinguished contemporaries such as Siegfried Sassoon (q.v.). His later work caused some controversy with its explicit sexual imagery of black men. He was elected a Royal Academician in 1923. He was the partner, professionally and privately, of Vivian Forbes (see page 169).

PLACE, Francis (1771–1854), English, political reformer
21 Brompton Square, SW3. *London County Council*
Place, who lived here from 1833 to 1851, was largely self-taught, but he had huge extra-Parliamentary influence, supplying research to the fight against the Combination Acts (repealed 1824) and agitating for

the Great Reform Bill (1832). He was an early advocate of contraception to control population.

POUND, Ezra (1885–1972), American, poet
10 Kensington Church Walk, W8. *English Heritage*
Pound lived here from 1909 to 1914. One of the central figures in the birth of modernist English literature, he was responsible for the poetic movement called Imagism – relying on precise images and clear language, in reaction against the discursive sentiment of Victorian poetry. He coined the term Vorticism for his friend Wyndham Lewis's (q.v.) art movement, and he edited his friend Eliot's (q.v.) *The Waste Land* (1920), the first modernist work to reach a wide public.

POWELL, Michael (1905–90), English, film director
8 Melbury Road, W14. *Directors Guild of Great Britain*
Powell lived here from 1951 to 1971. In partnership with the writer Emeric Pressburger, he created some of the best of English cinema: *The Life and Death of Colonel Blimp* (1944), *Black Narcissus* (1948), *The Red Shoes* (1950) and *Peeping Tom* (1961). His work is much admired by Scorsese and Coppola.

PRYDE, James (1866–1941), Scottish, artist
Lansdowne House, 80 Lansdowne Road, W11.
Greater London Council
Pryde, who lived and worked here, was mainly a graphic artist, but he experimented in various genres and, among other things, designed the sets for Paul Robeson's (q.v.) *Othello* in 1930.

PURKOVIC, Miodrag A. (1907–76), Serbian, historian
Serbian Community Centre, 89 Lancaster Road, W11. *Serbian Council of Great Britain*
Dr Purkovic lived here from 1972 until his death. He spent the whole of the Second World War as a prisoner of war and did not want to return to Serbia when the war finished. He spent time in Austria before moving permanently to England. His primary field of work was Serbian medieval history. He was chairman of the Society of Serbian Writers and Artists Abroad.

RAMBERT, Dame Marie (1888–1982), Polish, dancer, choreographer
Kensington Temple, Ladbroke Road, Notting Hill, W11.
Private
19 Campden Hill Gardens, Kensington, W8. *English Heritage*
Dame Marie, born Cyvia Rambam, taught and produced ballet at the first address and lived at the second. After dancing with Diaghilev, she settled in London in 1918 and married Ashley Dukes (see page 158). She began teaching, formed the Ballet Club in 1926, which became today's Ballet Rambert, and is recognised as the foremost champion of modern ballet technique.

Most of the early performances by her company took place at the Mercury Theatre (see page 168). She fostered the careers of Frederick Ashton and Antony Tudor.

RATTIGAN, Sir Terence (1911–77), English, playwright
100 Cornwall Gardens, SW7. *English Heritage*
Sir Terence, who was born here, had many West End successes, including *The Winslow Boy* (1946), *The Browning Version* (1948) and *The Deep Blue Sea* (1952). The 'kitchen sink' dramas of the later 1950s were a reaction against his genre, which was perceived as being aimed at a notional 'Aunt Edna' matinée audience.

RICKETTS, Charles (1866–1931), English, artist, typographer
Lansdowne House, 80 Lansdowne Road, W11.
Greater London Council
Ricketts, who lived and worked here, is best remembered for his connections with the Vale Press, for which he designed type and illustrated works by Oscar Wilde (q.v.). He also worked as a stage designer. He was elected a Royal Academician in 1928. He was partner, professionally and privately, of Charles Shannon (see below).

ROTHENSTEIN, Sir William (1872–1945),
English, artist
1 Pembroke Cottages, Edwardes Square, W8.
English Heritage
Sir William lived here from 1899 to 1902. He was
principal of the Royal College of Art (1920–35),
where he fostered the talents of Jacob Epstein (q.v.),
Henry Moore (q.v.) and Paul Nash (q.v.). An official
war artist in both world wars, he was noted for his
portraits of prominent figures. He wrote several
books, including *English Portraits* (1898) and the
autobiographical *Men and Memories* (1931).

SAMBOURNE, Edward Linley (1844–1910),
English, cartoonist
18 Stafford Terrace, Kensington, W8. *Private*
Sambourne lived here and the house has been kept as a
time capsule of a cultured Edwardian home, a museum

in his honour. He
published his first
cartoon in *Punch* in
1867 and stayed with
the magazine through
to his death, becoming
chief cartoonist on the
retirement of John
Tenniel in 1901.

SANDOW, Eugen
(1867–1925),
German-English,
bodybuilder
161 Holland Park Avenue, W11. *English Heritage*
'The Father of Body-Building' was born Friedrich
Wilhelm Müller in East Prussia. He first appeared in
London in 1889 and was an immediate sensation with
his developed musculature and feats of strength. He
published a bestseller, *Strength and How to Obtain It*
(1897), and organised the first body-building contest,
at the Royal Albert Hall in 1891. World tours brought
him international fame as 'the Great Sandow'. Having
been
naturalised
British in
1905, he
lived here
from 1906
until his
death.

SASSOON, Siegfried (1886–1967), English, poet,
memoirist
23 Campden Hill Square, W8. *English Heritage*
Sassoon lived here from 1925 to 1932. He is
remembered for his *Sherston* trilogy – *Memoirs of a
Fox-Hunting Man* (1928), *Memoirs of an Infantry Officer*
(1930) and *Sherston's Progress* (1936) – which semi-
autobiographically recounted his passage from
innocence to dreadful awakening in the horrors of the
First World War. Known to his men as 'Mad Jack' for
his exceptional bravery in the trenches, he nonetheless
loathed the war and patriotism and threw away his
Military Cross in disgust. (See also Westminster 4.)

SHANNON, Charles (1863–1937), English, painter
Lansdowne House, 80 Lansdowne Road, W11.
Greater London Council
Shannon, who lived and worked here, was Charles
Ricketts's (see above) partner, both professionally and
privately. They met at the Lambeth School of Art,
where Shannon studied wood engraving. He was
elected a Royal Academician in 1921. Their substantial
art collection was left to the British Museum.

SIBELIUS, Jean (1865–1957), Finnish, composer
15 Gloucester Walk, Kensington, W8.
English Heritage
Sibelius lived here in 1909. His music played a role in
developing the Finnish national identity, his seven
symphonies and such pieces as *Finlandia* and *Karelia*
evoking a land of long dark winters and short brilliant
summers. He wrote virtually nothing in the last thirty
years of his life.

SIMON, Sir John
(1816–1904), English,
physician
**40 Kensington
Square, Kensington,
W8.** *London County
Council*
Sir John, who lived here
from 1871 until his death, was
appointed Medical Officer of
Health to the City of London in 1846, and afterwards
to the national government. He guided the
development of sanitary science, taking public health to
a level that, according to his obituary, was 'an example to
the civilised world'.

SIMS, Joan (1930–2001), English, comic actress
Esmond Court, Thackeray Street, W8.
Comic Heritage
Joan Sims lived here. She will be best remembered as a stalwart of the 'Carry On' series of films, appearing in twenty-four of them between 1959 and 1978, usually playing slightly fluffy, faintly repressed nurses, capable of being shocked but actually quite enjoying it.

SINGH, Maharajah Duleep (1838–93), Indian, royalty
53 Holland Park, W11. *English Heritage*
The maharajah lived here from 1881 to 1886. He came to the throne of the Punjab at the age of five, but at the end of the Second Anglo-Sikh War in 1849, when he was eleven, he was deposed and spent the rest of his life in gilded exile. The Koh-i-Noor diamond was among the many royal treasures that were appropriated.

SPRINGFIELD, Dusty (1939–99), English, pop singer
38 Aubrey Walk, W8. *Musical Heritage*
Dusty Springfield, stage-name of Mary O'Brien, lived here from 1968 to 1972. She originally appeared as a member of a trio called the Springfields (1961–3). Going solo in 1963, her first hit, 'I Only Want to Be With You', was the first song played on BBC Television's *Top of the Pops*. In all she had eleven top ten hits, including the number one 'You Don't Have to Say You Love Me'. She later developed into a fine jazz singer.

STANFORD, Sir Charles (1852–1924), Irish, composer
56 Hornton Street, W8. *London County Council*
Sir Charles lived here from 1894 to 1916. He was Professor of Composition at the Royal College of Music (1882), Professor of Music at Cambridge (1887) and a key figure in the nineteenth-century revival of the English choral tradition. He wrote canticles, anthems, symphonies, oratorios and operas, which are being rediscovered after decades of neglect.

STAUNTON, Howard (1810–74), English, chess champion
117 Lansdowne Road, W11. *English Heritage*
Staunton lived here from 1871 until his death. He was acclaimed, in England at least, as world chess champion (1843–51), having beaten the Frenchman Saint-Amant. He wrote a chess column in the *Illustrated London News* from 1845 until his death and published *The Chess Player's Handbook* (1847) and *The Chess Player's Companion* (1849). He was also a Shakespeare scholar, publishing an annotated edition (1857–60).

STEPHEN, Sir Leslie (1832–1904), English, journalist, alpinist
22 Hyde Park Gate, South Kensington, SW7.
London County Council
Sir Leslie, who lived here, was editor of the *Cornhill Review* (1871–82), first editor of the *Dictionary of National Biography* (1885–91), and published numerous scholarly works and biographies. He was president of the Alpine Club (1865–8) and his book *The Playground*

of Europe (1871) is regarded as a classic of mountaineering literature. He was the father of Virginia Woolf (q.v.)

STONE, Marcus (1840–1921), English, painter
8 Melbury Road, W14. *English Heritage*
Stone lived here from 1877 until his death. Illustrator of novels by Dickens (q.v.) and Trollope (q.v.), both friends of his father, he went on to paint many pictures of Shakespearian scenes, which were reproduced and very popular in his day, the sentiment always balanced by precise execution. He was elected a Royal Academician in 1887.

STUART, John McDouall (1815–66), Scottish, explorer
9 Campden Hill Square, Kensington, W8.
London County Council
Stuart lived and died here. After accompanying Captain Sturt into the interior of Australia in 1844, when both men nearly died of scurvy, Stuart led six expeditions between 1858 and 1862, on the last of which, after a nine-month trek from Adelaide, he reached Chambers Bay, Northern Territory, the first person to cross the continent.

TAYLOR, Clementia (1810–1908), English, suffragette, philanthropist
Aubrey House, Aubrey Walk, W8. *English Heritage*
Clementia Doughty married Peter Taylor (see below) in 1842 and in their time at Aubrey House in the 1860s it became a centre for nonconformist radicalism in London. She acknowledged that she was regarded by some of her middle-class friends as 'a dangerous, go-ahead, revolutionary person' in her organising role with the London National Society for Women's Suffrage.

TAYLOR, Peter (1819–91), English, politician, philanthropist
Aubrey House, Aubrey Walk, W8. *English Heritage*
Taylor was a member of the Courtauld family, a Unitarian, a radical politician attacked by his defeated opponent in the election of 1862 as 'anti-everything'. As a young man, he had lectured on behalf of the Anti-Corn Law League (q.v.) and in 1847, with his friend Mazzini (q.v.), co-founded the People's International League, arguing for universal suffrage. Aubrey House was a considerable radical salon when he and his wife (see above) lived there in the 1860s.

TERRY-THOMAS (1911–90), English, comic actor
11 Queen's Gate Mews, SW7. *Comic Heritage*
Born Thomas Terry Hoar-Stevens, Terry-Thomas, who lived here from 1949 to 1981, came to embody a certain upper-class caddish character, often a bit of a rotter. With a distinctive gap in his upper teeth, he had endless success in a string of films on both sides of the Atlantic, regularly deploying certain catchphrases such as 'You're an absolute shower!' or simply 'Good show!'.

THACKERAY, William Makepeace (1811–63), English, novelist
16 Young Street, Kensington, W8.
London County Council
2 Palace Green, Kensington, W8.
Royal Society of Arts
Thackeray lived at the first address from 1846 to 1853, and the second from 1861 until his death. Seen as second only to Dickens (q.v.) among Victorian novelists, he is remembered above all for *Vanity Fair* (1848), many times filmed and on television. Its heroine, Becky Sharp, is one of the great female characters in fiction. (See also Kensington & Chelsea 2 and Westminster 2.)

THORNYCROFT, Sir Hamo (1850–1925), English, sculptor
2a Melbury Road, West Kensington, W14.

London County Council
Thornycroft, who lived here, was the leading figure in the 'New Sculpture' – a term coined by his friend Edmund Gosse (q.v.) in 1894. He sculpted many public monuments in London, including Gordon of Khartoum on the Embankment (1885–8), Cromwell outside Parliament (1895–9), Gladstone in the Strand (1905) and Boadicea in her chariot on Westminster Bridge (1902), daring the citizens of South London to come across.

UNDERHILL, Evelyn (1875–1941), English, philosopher
50 Campden Hill Square, Kensington, W8.
English Heritage
Underhill lived here from 1907 to 1939. In childhood she had 'abrupt experiences of the peaceful, undifferentiated plane of reality', which led her to a lifelong immersion in Christian mysticism. Her greatest book, *Mysticism* (1911), was the most widely read book of Christian philosophy of the early twentieth century.

WEIZMANN, Chaim (1874–1952), Belarusian/English/Israeli, chemist, politician
67 Addison Road, West Kensington, W14.
Greater London Council
Weizmann, who became a British citizen in 1910, lived here while directing the Admiralty laboratories during the First World War. As a chemist, he is considered the father of industrial fermentation. He took over the leadership of World Zionism in 1920, was twice president of the World Zionist Organisation (1920–31 and 1935–46), and first president of the state of Israel (1949–52).

WILKINSON, Sir Geoffrey (1921–96), English, chemist
Chemistry Building, Imperial College Road, SW7. *Royal Society of Chemistry*
Having been a student at Imperial College (1939–43), Sir Geoffrey was Professor of Inorganic Chemistry here from 1956 to 1996, winning the Nobel Prize in 1973 for pioneering studies on organo-metallic compounds.

YOVANOVITCH, Slobodan (1869–1958), Serbian, historian, prime minister
39b Queen's Gate Gardens, South Kensington, SW7.

Serbian Council of Great Britain
Professor Yovanovitch lived here in exile from 1945 until his death. One of the leaders of the Serbian intelligentsia for over fifty years, his writing style was notably crisp and dubbed the 'Belgrade style'. He was prime minister of the Yugoslav government in exile (1942–3) and not rehabilitated at home until after the break-up of Yugoslavia.

Kensington & Chelsea 2:
South Kensington, Brompton, Chelsea and Earls Court
South of Cromwell Road–Brompton Road

ALEXANDER, Sir George (1858–1918), English, actor-manager
57 Pont Street, SW1. *London County Council*
Alexander (stage-name of George Samson), who lived here, first appeared on stage in Nottingham in 1879 and later worked with Irving (q.v.) He was the leading man of the Lyceum Company (1885–9) and managed the St James's Theatre from 1891 to 1918. He was knighted in 1911.

ALLENBY, Field Marshal Viscount (1861–1936), English, soldier
24 Wetherby Gardens, SW5. *London County Council*
Allenby lived here from 1928 until his death. He served in South Africa in 1884–5 and in the Second Boer War. He commanded the Egypt Expeditionary Force (1917–18), in which his brilliant victory over the Turks at the battle of Megiddo is regarded as a precursor of the German *blitzkrieg* tactics of the Second World War.

ARBUTHNOT, WPC Jane (1961–83), English, police officer
Hans Crescent, SW1. *Police Memorial Trust*
On Saturday afternoon, 18 December 1983, Knightsbridge was busy with Christmas shoppers. WPC Arbuthnot and two colleagues were reconnoitring a suspected IRA car bomb outside Harrods when it exploded, killing all three of them.

ARNOLD, Sir Edwin (1832–1904), English, poet, journalist
31 Bolton Gardens, SW5. *London County Council*
Sir Edwin lived and died here. His time in India (1856–61) gave him a lifelong ambition to interpret in English the life and philosophy of the East, which he did in *The Light of Asia* (1879) and *The Light of the World* (1891). He was also associated with the *Daily Telegraph* for over forty years.

ASTAFIEVA, Princess Seraphine (1876–1934), Russian, ballerina
152 King's Road, SW3. *Greater London Council*
Astafieva lived and taught ballet here from 1916 until her death, after originally coming to England with Diaghilev in 1910. Pupils at her school included Dame Margot Fonteyn (q.v.), Anton Dolin (q.v.) and Dame Alicia Markova.

AUSTEN, Jane (1775–1817), English, novelist
23 Hans Place, SW1. *Private*
Austen stayed with her brother, Henry, in a house on this site in 1814–15. In these two years she completed *Emma* (1814) and *Persuasion* (1815). Her works were immediately well received and she was a particular favourite of the Prince Regent. Sir Walter Scott praised her for having 'that exquisite touch which renders ordinary commonplace things and characters interesting'. (See also Westminster 4.)

BACON, Francis (1909–92), Irish, artist
7 Cromwell Place, SW7. *National Art Collections Fund*
Bacon lived and worked on the ground floor of this house, known as the Millais (q.v.) House and now home to the National Art Collections Fund, from 1943 to 1951. Regarded as one of the foremost figures in post-war British art, Bacon is known for his semi-abstract tortured figures, many with religious associations, notably his series of reworkings of Velasquez's portrait *Pope Innocent X*. His 1976 *Triptych* was bought in May 2008 for $86 million by Roman Abramovitch.

BARTÓK, Béla (1881–1945), Hungarian, composer
7 Sydney Place, SW7. *English Heritage*
Bartók always stayed here when performing in London. As a child prodigy on the piano, he toured extensively. His composing style featured the evocative re-creation of folk music and his work includes the opera *Duke Bluebeard's Castle*, ballets, two violin and three piano concertos and six string quartets.

BEERBOHM TREE, Sir Herbert (1852–1917), English, actor-manager
76 Sloane Street, SW1. *Private*
31 Rosary Gardens, South Kensington, SW7.
London County Council
Tree lived in a house on the site of the first address and at the second address. He made his stage debut in 1879, appearing in over fifty plays in the next eight years, then running the Haymarket Theatre as actor-manager from 1887 to 1897, finally building and managing His Majesty's Theatre from 1897 onwards. He founded a drama school at His Majesty's in 1904, which later became the Royal Academy of Dramatic Art. Carol Reed (q.v.), the film director, was his illegitimate son. (See also Camden 1.)

BELLOC, Hilaire (1870–1953), English, poet, essayist, historian
104 Cheyne Walk, SW10.
Greater London Council
Belloc lived here from 1900 to 1905. Prolific across a number of genres, he wrote biographies of Cromwell, Charles II and Marie Antoinette, contemporary political critiques, novels and works of religious thought, but he is best remembered for his books of children's verses. He had a way with a couplet, for example: 'When I am dead, I hope it may be said: "His sins were scarlet, but his books were read".'

BENNETT, Arnold (1867–1931), English, novelist
75 Cadogan Square, SW1. *London County Council*
Bennett lived here from 1921 to 1930. Originally a journalist, he published his first novel in 1898. His works, the early ones mostly set in the Potteries,

where he was born, include *Anna of the Five Towns* (1902), *The Old Wives' Tale* (1908) and the *Clayhanger* series (1910–16). He also wrote a strand of lighter entertainments, including *The Card* (1911) and *Mr Prohack* (1922). (See also Westminster 1.)

BLACKIE, Dr Margery (1898–1981), English, physician
18 Thurloe Street, SW7. *English Heritage*
Dr Blackie lived and worked here from 1929 until her death. Regarded as a major pioneer, she was Dean of the Faculty of Homœopathy, London (1965–79), and physician to Her Majesty the Queen from 1968 onwards. Her teachings were collected and published posthumously as *Classical Homeopathy* (1986).

BONAR LAW, Andrew (1858–1923), Scottish, Prime Minister
24 Onslow Gardens, SW7. *London County Council*
Canadian-born Bonar Law, who lived here, was a successful businessman before entering Parliament in 1900. Leader of the Unionists from 1911 on, he served in various cabinet posts in the First World War coalition government. His tenure as Prime Minister, October 1922 to May 1923, tragically cut short by fatal illness, was the shortest of the twentieth century.

BORROW, George (1803–81), English, traveller, writer
22 Hereford Square, South Kensington, SW7.
London County Council
Borrow lived here. His journeys round Europe and Russia were mainly on foot, exploiting his linguistic abilities. He published *The Zincali* (1840), *The Bible in Spain* (1843), *Lavengro* (1851), *Wild Roses* (1862) and several other books, many about gypsy life, with which he claimed an affinity.

BRITTEN, Benjamin (1913–76), English, composer
173 Cromwell Road, SW5. *English Heritage*
Britten lived here from 1931 to 1933. He had just come to public attention for the first time with the Sinfonietta Opus 1, *A Hymn to the Virgin* (1930). He went on to compose in many forms but is best known for his operas and choral music. (See also Islington and Westminster 1.)

BRUNEL, Isambard Kingdom (1806–59), English, engineer
98 Cheyne Walk, SW10. *London County Council*
Greatest of Victorian engineers, Brunel, who lived here from 1808 to 1825 with his father (see below), was Chief Engineer of the Great Western Railway (1833). He designed the Clifton Suspension bridge (1864), as well as several great ships, including the *Great Western* (1838), the *Great Britain* (1845) and the *Great Eastern* (1858) (q.v.), which laid the first transatlantic telegraph cable. (See also Southwark and Tower Hamlets.)

BRUNEL, Sir Marc Isambard (1769–1849), French, engineer
98 Cheyne Walk, SW10. *London County Council*
Brunel came to England to escape the French Revolution and rapidly became known as an innovative engineer. His greatest achievement was the first Thames Tunnel (1825–43), between Rotherhithe and Wapping, which remains in use by trains today.

CARLYLE, Thomas (1795–1881), Scottish, historian, essayist
24 Cheyne Row, Chelsea, SW3.
The Carlyle Society
Carlyle lived here from 1834 until his death, becoming known as 'the Sage of Chelsea', even though his views travelled from liberal to reactionary. Works written while living here include *The French Revolution* (1837), *Chartism* (1839), *Cromwell's Letters and Speeches* (1845) and *Frederick the Great* (1858–65). He was the founder in 1841 of the London Library. (See also Camden 2.)

CARTER, Howard (1874–1939), English, Egyptologist
19 Collingham Gardens, Earls Court, SW5.
English Heritage
Carter, who lived here, joined Flinders Petrie's (q.v.) 1891 expedition to Egypt and from 1907 worked under the patronage of Lord Carnarvon. Among his many discoveries were the tombs of Hatshepsut, Tuthmosis IV and, most notably, in November 1922,

Tutankhamun – the most intact and lavish pharaonic tomb ever discovered.

CHELSEA CHINA
16 Lawrence Street, Chelsea, SW3.
London County Council
Chelsea china, which was manufactured in a house in Lawrence Street between 1745 and 1784, was known as 'the English Dresden'. It was much sought after, especially for the colours later developed, such as their claret, pea-green, mazarine blue and turquoise. It was china for aristocrats, and Horace Walpole (q.v.) had a large collection.

CHRISTIE, Dame Agatha (1890–1976), English, novelist, playwright
Christie Cottage, Cresswell Place, SW10.
Private
Dame Agatha lived here. See her entry in Kensington & Chelsea 1.

COLE, Sir Henry (1808–82), English, civil servant, reformer
33 Thurloe Square, South Kensington, SW7.
English Heritage
Sir Henry lived here, across the road from the Victoria and Albert Museum, of which he was the founder and first director. He published the first Christmas card in 1843, with artwork by John Calcott Horsley, and as 'Felix Summerly' wrote several children's books. He also managed the Great Exhibition in Hyde Park in 1851. (See also Camden 1.)

COPEMAN, Sydney Monckton (1862–1947), English, physician
57 Redcliffe Gardens, West Brompton, SW10.
English Heritage
Dr Copeman, who lived here, was senior medical Officer at the Ministry of Health and Emeritus Professor of Public Health, Westminster Hospital. His discovery of the first safe smallpox vaccine in the 1890s was important because Jenner's vaccine was too often contaminated with syphilis.

CRIPPS, Sir Stafford (1889–1952), English, politician
32 Elm Park Gardens, Chelsea, SW10.
English Heritage

Sir Stafford was ambassador to Moscow (1940–2), Minister of Aircraft Production (1942–5) and Chancellor of the Exchequer (1947–50). A man with a rather austere presence, he was once introduced on the BBC as 'Sir Stifford Crapps'.

CROSBY HALL
Cheyne Walk, Chelsea, SW3.
Royal Borough of Kensington & Chelsea

The hall has been owned since 1988 by Christopher Moran, a property tycoon, who has spent millions creating a 'Tudor mansion' alongside. While the work has been carried out to the very highest standards, it is argued in some quarters that it is nonetheless a fake, and a fake is a fake.

DAWSON, Margaret Damer (1875–1920), English, policewoman
10 Cheyne Row, Chelsea, SW3. *Private*
Dawson, who lived here, was Secretary of the International League of Animal Protection Societies (1906), for which she was awarded medals in Finland and Denmark, but she made her mark on history by founding and being the Commandant of the first Women's Police Service during the First World War.

DE MORGAN, Evelyn (1855–1919), English, painter
127 Old Church Street, Chelsea, SW3.
London County Council
Evelyn De Morgan, who lived and died here with her husband, William (see below), was a considerable Pre-Raphaelite artist, handling classical and mythical themes. A substantial collection of her work is in the De Morgan Centre for the Study of Nineteenth Century Art, housed at the former West Hill Library, Wandsworth.

DE MORGAN, William (1839–1917), English, ceramic artist, novelist
127 Old Church Street, Chelsea, SW3.
London County Council

De Morgan, who lived and died here, was associated with Burne-Jones (q.v.) and Morris (q.v.). His ceramic work rediscovered lustre techniques and explored a 'Persian' palette. Sadly, it was never profitable and he turned to novel-writing in his last ten years and achieved more immediate fame for that, though posterity at last values his ceramics.

DILKE, Sir Charles (1843–1911), English, politician
76 Sloane Street, SW1. *London County Council*
Sir Charles, who lived here, was a radical Liberal. He sat in Parliament from 1868 to 1886 and 1892 to 1911 and was largely responsible for the legalisation of trade unions. Touted as a future prime minister, his political rise was effectively ended by a sensational divorce case in 1886.

DOBSON, Austin (1840–1921), English, poet, essayist
10 Redcliffe Street, West Brompton, SW10.
London County Council
Dobson, who lived here, worked at the Board of Trade (1856–1901), where he was close friends with Edmund Gosse (q.v.). He published several volumes of verse, as well as biographies of a number of eighteenth-century figures. 'Time goes, you say? Ah no! Alas, Time stays, we go.'

DOBSON, Frank (1886–1963), English, sculptor
14 Harley Gardens, West Brompton, SW10.
English Heritage

Dobson, who lived here, was an official war artist in both world wars. He was Professor of Sculpture at the Royal College of Art (1946–53) and elected a Royal Academician in 1953. His reputation was eclipsed by modernism but is now reviving, and he is recognised as one of the key figures in twentieth–century British sculpture.

DODD, Inspector Stephen (1949–83), English, policeman
Hans Crescent, SW1. *Police Memorial Trust*
See entry above (page 180) for WPC Jane Arbuthnot.

DOLIN, Sir Anton (1904–83), English, dancer, choreographer
66 Glebe Place, SW3. *Private*
Sir Anton, stage-name of Patrick Healey-Kay, lived here from 1926 to 1939. He was a principal dancer with Diaghilev's Ballet Russe. He partnered Dame Alicia Markova (1935–8), including a notable *Giselle*. He was the first artistic director of the London Festival Ballet (1950–61) and he wrote several books on ballet.

DU BOULAY, William Thomas (1832–1921), English, cleric
43 Gilston Road, West Brompton, SW10. *Private*
Du Boulay, who lived here, was vicar of St Mary's, The Boltons (1868–1909). Favouring high-church ritualism, he founded a Guild of St Michael for local female servants who agreed to give up fairs, races, dances and music halls.

ELIOT, George (1819–80), English, novelist
4 Cheyne Walk, Chelsea, SW3.
London County Council
George Eliot, pen-name of Mary Ann Evans, lived here for only the last few weeks of her life; it had been hoped that the Chelsea air would be good for her health. Considered one of the greatest nineteenth-century novelists, her works include *Adam Bede* (1859), *The Mill on the Floss* (1860), *Silas Marner* (1861) and *Middlemarch* (1871–2). (See also Wandsworth.)

FITZROY, Admiral Robert (1805–65), English, sailor, meteorologist
38 Onslow Square, SW7. *Greater London Council*

Fitzroy, who lived here from 1854 to 1865, commanded the *Beagle* on a survey of South America (1828–30) and on a circumnavigation of the globe (1831–6) with Charles Darwin (q.v.). He became the first head of the Meteorological Office in 1854 and pioneered numerous developments in weather forecasting. (See also Croydon.)

FLEMING, Sir Alexander (1881–1955), Scottish, physician, biologist
20a Danvers Street, Chelsea, SW3. *Greater London Council*
Sir Alexander, who lived here, discovered penicillin in 1928, which is recognised as the beginning of modern antibiotic medicine. He shared the Nobel Prize for Medicine in 1945 with Florey and Chain, who usefully worked out how to mass-produce Fleming's laboratory curiosity. (See also Westminster 2.)

FORTUNE, Robert (1812–80), Scottish, botanist
9 Gilston Road, West Brompton, SW10.
English Heritage
Fortune, who lived here from 1857 until his death, travelled extensively in the East for the London Botanical Society and brought many previously unknown plants into Britain, but he is principally remembered for introducing tea from China into India, and thus founding the Indian tea industry.

FRANKLIN, Rosalind (1920–58), English, scientist
Donovan Court, Drayton Gardens, West Brompton, SW10. *English Heritage*
Franklin lived here from 1951 until her death. Her work on X-ray diffraction images of DNA was greatly influential on the discovery of its structure by Crick (q.v.) and Watson. Her findings were shown to Crick and Watson without her knowledge, and her contribution to the breakthrough has been recognised more by posterity than it was at the time.

FREAKE, Sir Charles (1814–84), English, builder, philanthropist
21 Cromwell Road, South Kensington, SW7.
Greater London Council
Sir Charles, who lived here, was 'the most eminent of the Kensington builder-developers' according to Pevsner (q.v.). Freake was responsible for swathes of West London, including Eaton Square, Onslow Square and Cromwell Road. He also built the Royal College of Organists at his own expense.

FROUDE, J. A. (1818–94), English, historian
5 Onslow Gardens, South Kensington, SW7.
London County Council
Froude lived here from 1873 to 1892. His major work, completed in 1869, was the twelve-volume *History of England from the Fall of Wolsey to the Defeat of the Spanish Armada*. He was literary executor of Carlyle (q.v.), and author of his *Life*, occasioning some controversy in its frank discussion of the difficulties of Carlyle's married life.

GASKELL, Mrs Elizabeth (1810–65), English, novelist
93 Cheyne Walk, West Brompton, SW10.
London County Council
Mrs Gaskell, author of seven novels and many novellas, short stories and ghost stories, as well as a much-praised biography of Charlotte Bronte, was born here. Her best remembered book is *Cranford* (1853), a charming fictional picture of Knutsford, Cheshire, in the early nineteenth century.

GILBERT, W. S. (1836–1911), English, humorist, librettist
39 Harrington Gardens, SW7.
London County Council
This house was built for Gilbert and he lived here from 1883 to 1898. His collaboration with the composer Sir Arthur Sullivan from 1875 to 1896 produced thirteen comic operas that are still regularly performed throughout the English-speaking world to this day, and whose influence has been discerned from Betjeman's poetry to *The Two Ronnies*. They include *Trial by Jury* (1875), *HMS Pinafore* (1878), *The Pirates of Penzance* (1879), *Iolanthe* (1882), *The Mikado* (1885), *Ruddigore* (1887) and *The Yeomen of the Guard* (1888). (See also Harrow.)

GISSING, George (1857–1903), English, novelist
33 Oakley Gardens, Chelsea, SW3.
Greater London Council
Gissing lived here from 1882 to 1884. His novels treat of poverty and failure, the best-known being *New Grub Street* (1891) and *The Private Papers of Henry Ryecroft* (1902). His reputation went into eclipse after his death but has subsequently revived.

GODWIN, George (1813–88), English, architect, reformer
24 Alexander Square, Chelsea, SW3.
Greater London Council
Godwin, who lived here, was the architect responsible for The Boltons in South Kensington, a pioneer in the use of concrete, and editor of *The Builder* (1844–83), in which he campaigned for better housing for working people. His hobby was collecting chairs that had once belonged to famous people.

GRAINGER, Percy (1882–1961), Australian, composer, musician
31 King's Road, Chelsea, SW3.
Greater London Council
Grainger lived here from 1901 to 1914, became interested in British folk music and in 1906 toured Britain recording on Edison wax discs, the first person to do so. His most famous piece, *Country Gardens*, was collected by Cecil Sharp (q.v.) and arranged by Grainger in 1918.

GREAVES, Walter (1846–1930), English, painter
104 Cheyne Walk, West Brompton, SW10.
Greater London Council
Greaves lived here from 1855 to 1897. He was from a family of Chelsea boatmen and took up painting under the influence of Whistler (q.v.), whom he rowed on the river and assisted for twenty years. His best work is his earliest, including *Hammersmith Bridge on Boat Race Day* (1862), painted when he was sixteen.

GRENFELL, Joyce (1910–79), English, comedienne, comic actress
34 Elm Park Gardens, SW10. *English Heritage*
Grenfell, who lived here in Flat 8 from 1957 to 1979, is best remembered for her one-woman shows and monologues, including the harassed nursery teacher ('George, *don't* do that'). She also appeared in many comic films, including *The Happiest Days of Your Life* (1950) and the St Trinian's series.

GUIZOT, François (1787–1874), French, politician, historian
21 Pelham Crescent, SW7. *English Heritage*
Guizot was Professor of Modern History at the Sorbonne (1812), subsequently Minister of the Interior (1830) and briefly prime minister (1847–8). He lived here in exile in the Year of Revolutions (1848–9) and when he returned to France he left politics and confined himself to historical scholarship. He is credited as the originator of the much-reworked dictum: 'Not to be a Republican at twenty is proof of want of heart; to be one at thirty is proof of want of head.'

HADEN-GUEST, Lord (1877–1960), English, physician, politician
38 Tite Street, Chelsea, SW3. *Private*
Lord Haden-Guest, who lived here, served in the Royal Army Medical Corps in the Boer War, First World War and Second World War, winning a Military Cross. He was a Socialist MP from 1923 to 1927 and 1937 to 1950. A founder of the Anglo-French Companions of the Red Cross Society, he was ennobled in 1950 and made a lord-in-waiting to the king in 1951.

HANSOM, Joseph Aloysius (1803–82), English, architect, inventor
27 Sumner Place, South Kensington, SW7.
Greater London Council
Hansom, who lived here, was the architect of over two hundred buildings, including Birmingham Town Hall (1831) and many Catholic churches. He was founder-editor of *The Builder* (1843) and inventor of the hansom cab in 1834, designed to combine speed and safety. Over three thousand were in use by the late nineteenth century; one remains in use today, at the Sherlock Holmes Museum.

HENRY VIII (1491–1547), English, royalty
23 Cheyne Walk, Chelsea, SW3.
Royal Borough of Kensington and Chelsea
Cheyne Studios, Cheyne Gardens, Chelsea, SW3. *Private*
Both plaques refer to King Henry's manor house, which stood at the first address and adjoined the second. Chelsea, in Henry VIII's time, was a rural retreat from London. Thomas More had his estate next door, and the preferred way of getting to and from town would have been in the royal barge.

HILL, Benny (1924–1992), English, comedian
1–2 Queen's Gate, South Kensington, SW7.
Dead Comics Society
Benny Hill lived here from 1960 to 1986. His fame rests on the worldwide success of *The Benny Hill Show* (1969–89), denounced by the new wave of comedians as 'dirty old man' humour, built round Hill's lecherous relationship with 'Hill's Angels'. *The Independent* said the attacks were 'like watching an elderly uncle being kicked to death by young thugs'. His song 'Ernie (The Fastest Milkman in the West)', was the Christmas number one in 1971. (See also Richmond.)

HITCHCOCK, Sir Alfred (1899–1980), English, film director
153 Cromwell Road, SW5. *English Heritage*
Hitchcock lived here from 1926 to 1939. This was the English phase of his career, which included successes such as *Blackmail* (1930), *Murder* (1931), *The Man Who Knew Too Much* (1935), *The Thirty-Nine Steps* (1936) and *The Lady Vanishes* (1939). (See also Hackney and Waltham Forest.)

HOPPÉ, Emil Otto (1878–1972), German, photographer
7 Cromwell Place, SW7. *National Art Collections Fund*
Hoppé is one of the names on this plaque at the Millais House, now the offices of the National Art Collections Fund. He was one of the most influential early Modernist photographers, noted for his portraits and his documenting of London before the war. Cecil Beaton (q.v.) called him 'the Master'.

HUNT, Leigh (1784–1859), English, poet, essayist
22 Upper Cheyne Row, SW3. *London County Council*
Hunt lived here. As founding editor of *The Examiner* (1808–21), he was friends with Byron, Moore (q.v.), Shelley (q.v.) and Lamb (q.v.), championing the Romantics and publishing early works by Keats (q.v.). He was imprisoned with his brother from 1813 to 1815 for libelling the Prince Regent and lived abroad from 1822 to 1825 with Shelley and Byron. (See also Enfield, Merton, Hammersmith & Fulham and Camden 1.)

IRELAND, John (1879–1962), English, composer
14 Gunter Grove, West Brompton, SW10.
English Heritage
Ireland, who lived here, developed his own brand of 'English Impressionism', his work including song settings of poems by Hardy (q.v.), Housman (q.v.) and Masefield (q.v.), piano and violin sonatas and orchestral preludes.

JACQUES, Hattie (1924–80), English, comic actress
67 Eardley Crescent, Earls Court, SW5.
Comic Heritage
Jacques lived here from 1945 until her death. She first appeared on stage at the Players' Theatre in 1944 and went quickly on to radio success with Tommy Handley (q.v.) and later Tony Hancock (q.v.). She is best remembered for fourteen 'Carry On' films, as often as not playing the Matron, and a long partnership on television with Eric Sykes (1960–79).

JELLICOE, Admiral of the Fleet Lord (1859–1935), English, sailor
25 Draycott Place, Chelsea, SW3.
Greater London Council
Jellicoe lived here from 1905 to 1907, while serving as director of naval ordnance. He was promoted in 1914 to command the Grand Fleet, which he led in the battle of Jutland (1916), his tactics being ever since a subject of debate. He was subsequently First Sea Lord (1916–17) and governor-general of New Zealand (1920–4).

JOHN, Augustus (1878–1961), Welsh, painter
28 Mallord Street, Chelsea, SW3.
Greater London Council
This house was built for John in 1913–14 by the Dutch architect Robert van t'Hoff. John is known chiefly for his portraits, including T. E. Lawrence (q.v.), G. B. Shaw (q.v.), Tallulah Bankhead, Thomas Hardy (q.v.), and many of his two wives and his children. He was noted for his fine draughtsmanship and characterisation, free handling, acute responsiveness to beauty, and a roving eye.

JORDAN, Mrs Dorothy (1762–1816), Irish, actress
30 Cadogan Place, SW1.
Greater London Council
Mrs Jordan lived here. There never was a Mr Jordan – Dorothy Bland assumed the name for respectability. She was pretty, witty and intelligent. Leigh Hunt (q.v.) thought her the epitome of the 'natural' actress, and Hazlitt (q.v.) wrote: 'It was not as an actress, but as herself, that she charmed everyone.' For twenty years (1791–1811) she was the mistress of the Duke of Clarence, the future William IV. They had ten illegitimate children, who took the surname FitzClarence. (See also Lewisham.)

KINGSLEY, Charles (1819–75), English, novelist, cleric
56 Old Church Street, Chelsea, SW3.
Greater London Council
Kingsley lived here. His best-known novels are *Westward Ho!* (1855), *The Water Babies* (1855) and *Hereward the Wake* (1866). One of the first to call himself a 'Christian socialist', he was Regius Professor of Modern History at Cambridge from 1860, and chaplain to Queen Victoria from 1873.

LANE, Sir Hugh (1876–1915), Anglo-Irish, art collector
8 South Bolton Gardens, SW5.
Private
Sir Hugh lived here. When he established Dublin's Municipal Gallery in 1908 it was the first public gallery in the world devoted to modern art. Appointed director of the Irish National Gallery in 1914, he was in office for only a year, going down with the *Lusitania* in 1915.

LANE, Sergeant Noel (1955–83), English, police officer
Hans Crescent, SW1. *Police Memorial Trust*
See the entry for WPC Jane Arbuthnot above (page 180).

LANGTRY, Lillie (1853–1929), English, actress
21 Pont Street, Chelsea, SW1.
Greater London Council
Langtry, born Emilie Charlotte Le Breton, lived here from 1892 to 1897. When she arrived in London in the 1870s, her beauty caused a sensation and she was painted by Millais (q.v.) (*A Jersey Lily*, 1878), Poynter and Burne-Jones (q.v.). Mistress of the future Edward VII for two years (1877–8), she later turned to acting and was decorative, if apparently never more than competent, on stage. (See also Westminster 4.)

LAVERY, Sir John (1856–1941), Irish, painter
5 Cromwell Place, South Kensington, SW7.
Greater London Council
Sir John lived here from 1899 until his death. After painting the official portrait for Queen Victoria's state visit to Glasgow in 1888, he had the entrée to London society and painted everyone from Churchill (q.v.) to

John McCormack (q.v.). His second wife, Hazel, appears in over four hundred of his works.

LECKY, William (1838–1903), Irish, historian, essayist
38 Onslow Gardens, South Kensington, SW7.
London County Council
Lecky lived and died here. His book *The Spirit of Rationalism in Europe* (1865), arguing that rationalism is essential to civilised society, made his name. Later works included *England in the Eighteenth Century* (1878–90), *Democracy and Liberty* (1896) and *The Map of Life* (1899).

LIND, Jenny (1820–87), Swedish, soprano
189 Old Brompton Road, SW7.
London County Council
Jenny Lind lived here from 1876 to 1886. She was an internationally celebrated soprano, known as 'the Swedish Nightingale'. She had her greatest success touring the United States (1850–2), promoted by P. T. Barnum, who paid her $1,000 a night. In her retirement, mostly spent in England, she founded and endowed many musical scholarships in England and Sweden.

LOCKYER, Sir Norman (1836–1920), English, scientist
16 Penywern Road, SW5. *English Heritage*
Sir Norman lived here from 1876 until his death. He discovered helium in 1868. He founded *Nature* in 1869, to facilitate the exchange of ideas between different scientific disciplines, and was its first editor. He was also instrumental in founding Imperial College and the Science Museum.

LOSEY, Joseph (1909–84), American, film director
29 Royal Avenue, SW3. *Private*
Losey, who lived here from 1966 until his death, moved to England in 1952 because of the McCarthy witch-hunt in Hollywood. His most successful films were *The Criminal* (1962), *The Damned* (1963), *The Servant* (1964) and *The Go-Between* (1971).

McINDOE, Sir Archibald (1900–60), New Zealander, surgeon
Avenue Court, Draycott Avenue, SW3.
English Heritage
Sir Archibald lived here in Flat 14. Appointed consultant on plastic surgery to the Royal Air Force in

1938, he developed the Queen Victoria Hospital, East Grinstead, into the outstanding centre for the treatment of burns during the Second World War. By 1945 he had operated on 3,600 patients, rebuilding the lives as well as the faces and hands of the men in his 'Guinea Pig Club'.

McMILLAN, William (1887–1977), Scottish, sculptor
64 Glebe Place, SW3. *Private*
McMillan lived here from 1921 to 1966. Among his many public works are the Beatty Memorial Fountain in Trafalgar Square and the statue of George VI in Carlton Gardens. He was elected a Royal Academician in 1933 and was master of the Royal Academy's Sculpture School (1929–40).

MEREDITH, George (1828–1909), English, novelist, poet
7 Hobury Street, West Brompton, SW10.
Greater London Council
Meredith lived here in 1858–9 after his first wife ran away with the writer Henry Wallis. He saw himself as a poet first and a novelist second, but posterity has preferred it the other way round. Among his best-known novels is *The Ordeal of Richard Feverel* (1859), which he completed while living here. He was awarded the Order of Merit in 1905. (See also Kingston.)

MILLAIS, John Everett (1829–96), English, painter
7 Cromwell Place, SW7. *National Art Collections Fund*
This is the Millais House, now home of the National Art Collections Fund. Millais was the founder in 1848, with Holman Hunt (q.v.) and D. G. Rossetti (q.v.), of the Pre-Raphaelite Brotherhood. He painted some of the best-known pictures in British art, among them *Ophelia* (1852), *The Boyhood of Raleigh* (1871) and *Bubbles* (1886). (See also Kensington & Chelsea 1.)

MILNE, A. A. (1882–1956), English, children's writer
13 Mallord Street, Chelsea, SW3.
Greater London Council
Milne lived here. Somewhat to his annoyance, the success of *Winnie-the-Pooh* (1926) and *The House at Pooh Corner* (1928) came to overshadow all the rest of his output. The characters were famously based round his son, Christopher Robin, and his toys. He also adapted *The Wind in the Willows* by Kenneth Grahame (q.v.) for the stage under the title of *Toad of Toad Hall* (1929).

MORE, St Thomas (*c*.1478–1535), English, cleric, statesman
Allen House, Beaufort Street, SW3. *Private*
More's Chelsea home stood on this site. On the fall of Wolsey in 1529 he became Henry VIII's chancellor, but, refusing to accept the king as head of the church and his marriage to Anne Boleyn, he was sent to the Tower and beheaded. He was canonised in 1935, and his story is told in *A Man for All Seasons*, the 1960 play by Robert Bolt, starring Paul Scofield as More, a role the actor repeated in the 1966 film.

MUNNINGS, Sir Alfred (1878–1959), English, painter
64 Glebe Place, SW3. *Private*
96 Chelsea Park Gardens, SW3.
Private
Sir Alfred lived at both addresses, the first from 1920 to 1922, the second from 1920 until his death. (Note that the plaque omits the final 's' of his name). He is accounted the finest British painter of equine subjects and his works continue to command high prices. An opponent of modernism, in his farewell speech to the Royal Academy in 1949, obviously drunk, he claimed that Cézanne, Matisse and Picasso had corrupted art. The speech was heard by millions on BBC radio.

ORPEN, Sir William (1878–1931), Irish, painter
8 South Bolton Gardens, SW5.
Greater London Council
Sir William, who lived here, was an official war artist in the First World War, deeply affected by what he saw.

Although he continued to paint successfully as a portrait artist, his post-war work is said to be merely efficient, showing an emotional exhaustion after his experiences in the trenches.

PANKHURST, Sylvia (1882–1960), English, suffragette
120 Cheyne Walk, SW10.
Greater London Council
Sylvia Pankhurst, who lived here, was the only Pankhurst to remain on the left. She broke from her mother, Emmeline (q.v.), and sister, Christabel (q.v.), of the Women's Political and Social Union in 1914 over their support for the First World War. She continued her suffrage campaign in the East End and was for a time a communist, reverting eventually to a socialist anti-fascist stance. As a supporter of Haile Selassie at the time of the Italian invasion of Ethiopia, she became more engaged in that country's struggle and lived the last four years of her life in Addis Ababa. (See also Tower Hamlets and Redbridge.)

PEAKE, Mervyn (1911–68), English, novelist, illustrator, poet
1 Drayton Gardens, West Brompton, SW10.
English Heritage
Peake lived here from 1960 until his death. He was a prolific illustrator, not only of his own books, but of Coleridge, Carroll, the Brothers Grimm and Stevenson. His nonsense verse was praised by Betjeman (q.v.) as 'outstanding'. He is remembered above all for the *Gormenghast* trio of novels, which were intended as the beginning of a longer series, which was thwarted by Peake's declining health. (See also Sutton.)

PLAYFAIR, Sir Nigel (1874–1934), English, actor-manager
26 Pelham Crescent, South Kensington, SW7.
London County Council
Sir Nigel, who lived here, was actor-manager of the Lyric Theatre, Hammersmith, in the 1920s, credited with the first modern pared-down productions of Shakespeare, in reaction against the over-elaboration then in vogue. 'Sir Nigel's Vintage Marmalade' is still sold at Fortnum & Mason.

POTTER, Beatrix (1866–1943), English, children's writer, artist
Corner of Old Brompton Road and The Boltons, SW3. *The Boltons Association / The Beatrix Potter Society / Frederick Warne & Co*
This is the site of the Potter family home, where she lived until 1913. She was the author and illustrator of the most successful series of children's stories ever published, beginning with *The Tale of Peter Rabbit* in 1900. She moved from here to Hill Top Farm in the Lake District and devoted her royalties to preserving the local landscape and way of life. In her will she left 4,000 acres of land, cottages and fifteen farms to the National Trust.

RACZYNSKI, Count Edward (1891–1993), Polish, politician
8 Lennox Gardens, SW1. *English Heritage*
Count Raczynski lived here from 1967 until his death. Polish ambassador in London from 1934, he was subsequently the pivotal political figure of the Polish government in exile and its president from 1979 to 1986. He was awarded the Polish Order of Merit by Lech Walesa in 1991.

REED, Sir Carol (1906–76), English, film director
213 King's Road, Chelsea, SW3. *Private*
According to the plaque Sir Carol lived here from 1948 to 1978, but in fact he died in 1976. An illegitimate son of Sir Herbert Beerbohm Tree (q.v.), he was prolific before and after the Second World War; his best films were the successive *Odd Man Out* (1947), *The Fallen Idol* (1948) and *The Third Man* (1949). He belatedly won an Oscar for *Oliver!* (1968).

ROBINSON, George Frederick Samuel (1827–1909), English, politician, colonial governor
9 Chelsea Embankment, SW3.
London County Council
Robinson, who lived here, served in every Liberal cabinet from 1861 to his death. As viceroy of India (1880–4), he tried to introduce legislation to advance

the Indians but was frustrated by the House of
Commons. His name is honoured in India, particularly
in Chennai.

ROSE, Miss (d.1966)
133 Old Church Street,
Chelsea, SW3. *Private*
The Latin inscription translates
as 'Miss Rose who held sway in
this house and holds sway, now
and forever, in our hearts'.
Miss Rose, it has been suggested, was a cat.

ROSSETTI, Dante Gabriel (1828–82), English,
artist, poet
16 Cheyne Walk, SW3. *London County Council*
A founder of the Pre-Raphaelite Brotherhood,
Rossetti, who lived here, was a major influence on
William Morris (q.v.) and Edward Burne-Jones (q.v.).
His sensual, medievalist ideas were realised in a series
of portraits of his wife, Elizabeth Siddal, and mistresses
Fanny Cornforth and Jane Burden (Morris's wife). In
his grief at Siddal's death, he buried his poems with
her at Highgate, but they were subsequently exhumed
and published in 1870, to great controversy since they
were found rather racy by the standards of the day.
(See also Camden 2 and Westminster 2.)

RUMFORD, Count (1753–1814), Anglo-American,
inventor, traveller
168 Brompton Road, SW3. *English Heritage*
Rumford, who lived here from 1799 to 1802, was
born Bernard Thompson in Massachusetts. As a
loyalist, he left for Britain in 1776. In a wandering life,
he is credited with a variety of social reforms in
Bavaria, Dublin and London and was made a count of
the Holy Roman Empire in 1784. The first scientist to
determine that 'heat is a mode of motion', he is also
credited with inventing the coffee percolator, a kitchen
range and improved fireplaces. He co-founded the
Royal Institution with Sir Joseph Banks (q.v.) in 1799.

SARGENT, John Singer (1856–1925), American,
painter
31 Tite Street, Chelsea, SW3. *Private*
Sargent lived and worked in this house from 1901 until
his death. He had settled in London in 1885, becoming
a fashionable portrait painter, his subjects including
Ellen Terry (q.v.) and R. L. Stevenson (q.v.). During
many visits to the United States, he painted two

Presidents, Roosevelt and Wilson, and was an official
war artist in the First World War.

SARTORIUS, John F. (*c*.1775–*c*.1830), English,
painter
155 Old Church Street, Chelsea, SW3.
London County Council
Sartorius lived here from 1807 to 1812. Most of his
work was portraits of horses, for which he was highly
esteemed, though overshadowed by George Stubbs. He
painted two pictures of the celebrated Hambletonian
versus Diamond challenge race at Newmarket in 1799
but, unfortunately for him, so did Stubbs.

SCOTT, Robert Falcon (1868–1912), English, naval
officer, explorer
56 Oakley Street, Chelsea, SW3.
London County Council
Scott lived here. He led two expeditions to the
Antarctic (1900–4 and 1910–12). On the second,
he reached the South Pole one month after the
Norwegian Amundsen, and he and his companions
perished in a blizzard on the way back, a very short
distance from safety.

SEBASTOPOL
FORTIFICATIONS
The Courtyard, 65–69
Old Church Street,
Chelsea, SW3. *Private*
Who brought this stone
back from the Crimea,
and why, is lost to us. The
siege of Sebastopol lasted
eleven months in
1854–5, and at the end
the victorious allied forces entered a ruined city, so
there would have been plenty of loose debris to be
taken as souvenirs. The small light-industrial courtyard
in which this charming curio was placed is now The
Courtyard, a smart development of flats (1998).

SEFERIS, George (1900–71), Greek, poet, diplomat
7 Sloane Avenue, SW3. *Private*
Seferis was Greek ambassador to the United Kingdom
(1957–62), when he lived at this address. In 1963
Seferis was awarded the Nobel Prize for Literature,
'for his eminent lyrical writing, inspired by a deep
feeling for the Hellenic world of culture'. He was the
first Greek to receive the prize. His *Complete Poems*
were published in an English translation in 1995. (See
also Westminster 3.)

SITWELL, Sir Osbert
(1892–1969), English,
poet, writer
**2 Carlyle Square,
Chelsea, SW3.**
Park Lane Group
Sir Osbert lived here
from 1919 to 1963.
Collectively known as
'the Sitwells', he and his
sister, Edith (q.v.), and his
brother, Sacheverell, knew everybody. His writings
ranged across all genres, from First World War poetry
to criticism, to the libretto for Walton's (q.v.)
Belshazzar's Feast (1931). His best work was his five-
volume autobiography (1945–50), which
affectionately and acidly evoked Sitwell family life.

SLOANE, Sir Hans (1660–1753), Irish, physician,
naturalist
23 Cheyne Walk, Chelsea, SW3.
Royal Borough of Kensington & Chelsea
Sir Hans purchased Henry VIII's manor house, which
stood on this site, from Lord Cheyne in 1712 and
eventually moved here in 1742, bringing his vast book,
manuscript and curio collection, which on his death
was bequeathed to the nation and became the nucleus
of the British Museum. (See also Camden 2.)

SMOLLETT, Tobias (1721–71), Scottish, novelist
16 Lawrence Street, Chelsea, SW3.
London County Council
Smollett lived from 1750 to 1762 in part of the house
on this site, where Chelsea china (see page 182) was
manufactured. He had been a seafarer and a surgeon
before devoting himself to writing. His best-loved
works are *Roderick Random* (1748), *Peregrine Pickle*
(1751) and *Humphrey Clinker* (1771). His readiness to
sue for libel made him a difficult contemporary.

STEER, Philip Wilson (1860–1942), English,
painter
109 Cheyne Walk, West Brompton, SW10.
Greater London Council
Steer, who lived and died here, is known for his
landscapes, such as *The Beach at Walberswick* (1890, Tate
Britain). He was a leader of English Impressionism
with Sickert (q.v.) and was one of the founders of the
New English Art Club in 1886.

STOKER, Bram
(1847–1912), Irish,
novelist
**18 St Leonard's
Terrace, Chelsea,
SW3.**
Greater London Council
Stoker, who lived
here, was personal
assistant to Henry
Irving (q.v.), for
whom he managed the Lyceum Theatre for twenty-
seven years. He wrote a number of romantic novels,
all forgotten, and one unforgettable horror novel.
Dracula (1897) was based on eight years' research into
European folklore and inspired by a visit to Slains
Castle in Aberdeenshire, which Stoker saw as 'the
castle of the dead', and a visit to the crypts under the
church of St John the Baptist in Dublin, where he had
been baptised.

SWINBURNE, Algernon Charles (1837–1909),
English, poet
16 Cheyne Walk, SW3. *London County Council*
Swinburne lived here with D. G. Rossetti (see above)
after coming down from Oxford. He had the promise
of being a great poet, and his early work remains his
best, but, as Max Beerbohm wrote, 'Youth goes, and
there was not in Swinburne that basis on which a man
may in his maturity so build as to make good, in some
degree, the loss of what is gone.' (See also Merton and
Wandsworth.)

TERRY, Ellen (1847–1928), English, actress
22 Barkston Gardens, Earls Court, SW5.
London County Council
215 King's Road, Chelsea, SW3. *Private*
Terry, who lived at the first address from 1889 to 1900
and the second from 1904 to 1920, was the leading
Shakespearian actress of her era. She played all the

He is remembered above all for *Vanity Fair* (1848), many times filmed and on television. Its heroine, Becky Sharp, is one of the great female characters in fiction. (See also Westminster 2 and Kensington & Chelsea 1.)

THORNDIKE, Dame Sybil (1882–1976), English, actress

6 Carlyle Square, Chelsea, SW3. *English Heritage*
Dame Sybil lived here from 1921 to 1932. Her debut was on an American tour with Ben Greet's (q.v.) company in 1904. Her most famous role was the title part in *Saint Joan*, which Shaw (q.v.) wrote with her in mind. From its premiere in 1924 the play was regularly revived and she last played the part in 1941, at the age of fifty-nine. She was made a Companion of Honour in 1970.

great female roles, many opposite Henry Irving (q.v.). Her three marriages and a tempestuous series of other flings made her a fascinating 'celebrity', before the term was invented. She had a famous correspondence with George Bernard Shaw (q.v.).

THE GROVE
The area surrounding The Grove Tavern once included a cricket ground, which was the setting for the first Test Match between England & Australia in 1880.

The street in which the pub stands was laid out during that era, and was originally named Grove Place to commemorate a nearby grove of trees. The Taverns name is derived from the same source

TEST MATCH, First
The Grove Tavern, Beauchamp Place, SW3. *Private*
The plaque claims that the area surrounding this pub used to have a cricket ground, and that the first test match between England and Australia took place there in 1880. Unfortunately, this claim is not supported by the official record, which states that the only test match of 1880 was played at the Kennington Oval. There had also been three test matches in Australia prior to 1880.

THACKERAY, William Makepeace (1811–63), English, novelist

36 Onslow Square, South Kensington, SW7.
London County Council
Thackeray, who lived here from 1854 to 1862, is seen as second only to Dickens among Victorian novelists.

TURNER, Joseph Mallord William (1775–1851), English, painter

119 Cheyne Walk, SW3.
Turner House Committee
Turner, who lived and worked in this house, 'looked beyond the mere details to a larger treatment of nature, seizing all the poetry of sunshine, and the mists of morn and eve, with the grandeur of storm and the glow of sunset' (Redgrave, *Dictionary of Artists of the English School*, 1873). Turner's painting *The Fighting Temeraire* (1838) was voted 'the greatest painting in a British art gallery' in 2005. (See also Richmond, Westminster 2 and Westminster 4.)

TWAIN, Mark (1835–1910), American, novelist, humorist

23 Tedworth Square, Chelsea, SW3.
London County Council
Twain, pen-name of Samuel Clemens, lived here in 1896–7. He had taken up writing books after being a journalist, printer, riverboat pilot and gold miner. His great masterpieces are *The Adventures of Tom Sawyer* (1876) and *The Adventures of Huckleberry Finn* (1884), perennially filmed. He famously said on reading a premature obituary: 'The report of my death was an exaggeration.'

TWEED, John (1869–1933), Scottish, sculptor
108 Cheyne Walk, West Brompton, SW10.
Greater London Council
Tweed lived here from 1895 to his death. He was a
close friend of Auguste Rodin, who always stayed with
the Tweeds when in London, and he has been called
'the English Rodin' – although he was a Scot. His work
is primarily monumental sculpture, including Lord
Kitchener at Horse Guards (1921–6), Sir George
White in Portland Place (1922), the Rifle Brigade
Memorial in Grosvenor Place (1924–5) and Captain
Cook at Whitby (1912).

WARLOCK, Peter (1894–1930), Anglo-Welsh,
composer, critic
30 Tite Street, Chelsea, SW3. *Greater London Council*
Warlock lived here. He wrote under his own name of
Philip Arnold Heseltine as a critic and biographer of
Delius (1923) but assumed the name Warlock for his
compositions, which were mainly songs, including
The Curlew (1920–2), a setting of four Yeats (q.v.)
poems, and his best-known work, *Capriol* (1926).

WHEELER, Sir Charles (1892–1975), English,
sculptor
49 Old Church Street, Chelsea, SW3. *Private*
Sir Charles, who lived here, specialised in architectural
sculpture, such as all the figures on the façade of the
Bank of England. His *Earth* and *Water*, at the entrance
to the Ministry of Defence, were each carved from
40 tons of Portland stone. The Treasury vetoed his
doing *Fire* and *Air* as well. He was president of the
Royal Academy (1956–66).

**WHISTLER, James
Abbott McNeil**
(1834–1903),
American, painter
**96 Cheyne Walk, West
Brompton, SW10.**
London County Council
Whistler, who lived
here, settled in London
in 1859. In 1877 he
famously sued Ruskin (q.v.) for describing his work as
'flinging a pot of paint in the public's face' and won a
farthing's damages. His most famous painting,
Arrangement in Gray and Black, is more commonly called
Whistler's Mother (1871). He and his friend Oscar Wilde
(q.v.) vied in exchanging *bon mots*. On one occasion

Wilde remarked: 'How I wish I had said that.' And
Whistler replied: 'You will, Oscar, you will.'

WILBERFORCE, William (1759–1833), English,
anti-slavery campaigner
44 Cadogan Place, SW1. *London County Council*
Having lived just long enough to see the Act abolishing
slavery pass through Parliament, Wilberforce died here
at his brother's house, where he spent his last two
years in great ill health. (See also Barnet, Hillingdon,
Lambeth, Merton and Wandsworth.)

WILDE, Lady Jane Francesca (1821–96), Irish,
poet
87 Oakley Street, SW3. *English Heritage*
Lady Jane, who lived here from 1887 until her death,
was a fervent supporter of Irish nationalism. The
mother of Oscar Wilde (see below), she contributed
poetry and essays to *The Nation* under the pseudonym
of 'Speranza'. When she was dying, she asked
permission to see Oscar, who was in prison, but was
refused.

WILDE, Oscar
(1854–1900), Irish,
playwright, poet, wit
**34 Tite Street,
Chelsea, SW3.**
London County Council
His plays include *Lady
Windermere's Fan* (1892),
A Woman of No Importance
(1893), *An Ideal Husband* (1895)
and *The Importance of Being Earnest* (1895). Hounded
for his homosexuality, he spent two years in Reading
Gaol, went into exile and died destitute in a cheap
Paris hotel. He was quipping to the end: 'My
wallpaper and I are fighting a duel to the death. One
or the other of us has to go.' He remains an icon for
the gay community. (See also Westminster 4.)

WODEHOUSE, P. G. (1881–1975), English, comic
novelist
16 Walton Street, SW3. *Private*
Wodehouse rented this house from 1918 to 1920, and
it was during this time that the legendary Jeeves and
Wooster first appeared in print in Britain, in *My Man
Jeeves* (1919). (See also Westminster 3.)

LAMBETH

Lying across the river Thames from
Westminster, the London Borough of Lambeth
is an amalgamation of the former Metropolitan
Borough of Lambeth with part of the former
Metropolitan Borough of Wandsworth,
principally Streatham and Clapham.

BARRY, Sir Charles (1795–1860), English, architect
30 Clapham Common North Side, SW4.
London County Council
Sir Charles, who lived and died here, studied in Italy
and his work shows the influence of the Italian
Renaissance. Among his designs are the Manchester
Athenaeum (1836), the Reform Club (1837) and, his
most famous work, the Houses of Parliament
(1840–60). His house here is now a Trinity Hospice.

BAX, Sir Arnold (1883–1953), English, composer
13 Pendennis Road, SW16. *English Heritage*
Sir Arnold was born here. His works, often based on
Celtic legends, include seven symphonies, tone
poems, chamber music, piano solos and concertos. He
was appointed Master of the King's Musick in 1942.

BAYLIS, Lilian (1874–1937), English, theatre
manager

27 Stockwell Park Road, SW9.
Greater London Council
Baylis, who lived and died here, started by helping
Emma Cons (q.v.) in the running of the Royal Victoria
Hall (afterwards the Old Vic), which she took over in
1912, developing it into a home for Shakespearian
productions. She also acquired Sadler's Wells in 1931
for opera and ballet. Her work laid the basis for the
Royal Ballet, the National Theatre and the English
National Opera. She was made a Companion of
Honour in 1929.

BENTLEY, John Francis (1839–1902), English,
architect
43 Old Town, Clapham, SW4. *London County Council*
Bentley lived here. His work was almost exclusively on
Catholic churches, the summit of his achievements
being Westminster Cathedral (1895–1903). He was
awarded the Gold Medal of the Institute of Architects,
but he never received it, dying before the cathedral
was opened.

BLAKE, William
(1757–1827), English,
poet, painter
**23 Hercules Road,
Lambeth, SE1.** *Private*
The plaque says Blake
lived in a house formerly
on this site in 1793, but in
fact he lived at 13 Hercules
Buildings from 1790 to 1800.
Lambeth, then still largely rural, was the inspiration
for some of his greatest writings and is the area he

picks out more than any other: 'From Lambeth we began our foundations; lovely Lambeth!' (See also Westminster 3 and Camden1.)

BLIGH, Captain William (1754–1817), English, naval officer
100 Lambeth Road, SE1. *London County Council*
Bligh lived here from 1794 to 1813. History (and Hollywood) has wronged him: he was not the cruel martinet portrayed in many accounts of the famous 1789 mutiny on the *Bounty*; he cared for his crew's health and was commended by Nelson (q.v.) for his conduct at the battle of Copenhagen. He is justly fêted for his navigation of 3,618 nautical miles in a 23-foot open boat after being cast adrift by the mutineers, reaching Timor after forty-seven days, with only one loyal crew member being lost along the way. (See also Tower Hamlets.)

CHAPLIN, Charlie (1889–1977), English, music-hall and film star
39 Methley Street, SE11. *Dead Comics Society*
287 Kennington Road, SE11. *Vauxhall Society*
Chaplin lived at both addresses as a child: at the first with his mother, and at the second with his father and his mistress (while his mother

was in an asylum). He first went to the United States with Fred Karno in 1910 and made his first film appearance in 1914. In that same year 'The Tramp' was born, almost accidentally. Chaplin wrote in his autobiography: 'I had no idea of the character. But the moment I was dressed, the clothes and the makeup made me feel the person he was. I began to know him, and by the time I walked on stage he was fully born.' (See also Westminster 1 and Southwark.)

CLAPHAM SECT
Holy Trinity Church, Clapham Common, SW4.
Greater London Council
The Clapham Sect were evangelical Christians active between 1790 and 1830 and especially associated with the fight against the slave trade. Prominent members were William Wilberforce (q.v.), his cousin Henry Thornton, and Granville Sharp, 'Father of the Anti-Slavery Movement'. Satirised in their day as 'the

Saints', they published a journal, the *Christian Observer*, edited by Zachary Macaulay (q.v.), and were also instrumental in the foundation of several missionary bodies, including the British and Foreign Bible Society and the Church Missionary Society.

COX, David (1783–1859), English, painter
34 Foxley Road, Stockwell, SW9.
London County Council
Cox, who lived here, is especially remembered for his watercolour landscapes of the Thames and of mountainous Wales and Scotland. Redgrave's *Dictionary of Artists of the English School* said of him: 'His sparkle of our English summer in shower and sunshine has never been surpassed.' There is a large collection of his work in his native Birmingham.

DUNNE, PC Patrick (1948–93), English, police officer
Cato Road, SW4. *Police Memorial Trust*
On Wednesday 20 October 1993 thirty-one-year-old William Danso was watching a football match on television with a friend. Shortly after 9 p.m. Danso answered his front door and was shot six times. Local Clapham community officer PC Patrick Dunne, forty-five, was attending an incident across the street when he heard the sound of gunfire, and as he went outside to investigate he was shot once in the chest. The killer was finally convicted thirteen years later.

ELLIS, Henry Havelock (1859–1939), English, physician
14 Dover Mansions, Canterbury Crescent, SW9. *Greater London Council*
Ellis, who lived here, is remembered as a pioneer in the scientific study of sex. His own sex life was uncommonly complicated; still a virgin, he married at the age of thirty-two in a 'new marriage' to the feminist lesbian Edith Lees, but it was not a great success and they lived apart after the honeymoon. His friends were amused that he wrote as an expert on a subject where he had little or no personal experience. Among his prolific output, the *Studies in the Psychology of Sex* (seven volumes, 1897–1928) was banned for some time in the United Kingdom.

GREET, Sir Philip Ben (1857–1936), English, actor-manager
160 Lambeth Road, Lambeth, SE1.
London County Council
Sir Ben lived here from 1920 until his death. He led a return to Shakespeare's original texts in simplified productions, often in the open air, in contrast to the elaborate style then in vogue. His company toured Britain and the United States with great success. He was director of the Old Vic (1914–18) under Lilian Baylis (q.v.).

GRIEG, Edvard (1843–1907), Norwegian, composer
47 Clapham Common North Side, SW4.
English Heritage
Grieg stayed here when performing in London. His music is the embodiment of Norwegian national consciousness, much of it based on old folk tunes. His most popular and enduring work is the *Peer Gynt* suite. An arrangement of part of his Piano Concerto made an unforgettable television appearance in 1971 in the *Morecambe and Wise Show*, conducted by André Previn.

HENDERSON, Arthur (1863–1935), Scottish, politician
13 Rodenhurst Road, Clapham, SW4.
Greater London Council
Henderson, who lived here, was stopgap leader of the Labour Party three times between 1908 and 1932. He also served as Home Secretary (1924) and Foreign Secretary (1929–31). He was awarded the Nobel Peace Prize in 1934 after chairing the Geneva Disarmament Conference.

HOBBS, Sir Jack (1882–1963), English, cricketer
17 Englewood Road, Balham, SW12.
Greater London Council
Sir Jack, who lived here, was the prince of Surrey batsmen from 1905 to 1935; he scored 61,237 runs in first-class cricket, and 197 centuries (both records unlikely to be broken), and played sixty-one tests for England. He was the second cricketer to be knighted, after Don Bradman, in 1953. He was selected as one of Wisden's 'Five Cricketers of the Twentieth Century'.

Each year on his birthday, 16 December, the Master's Club meets at The Oval for a lunch in his honour. The menu always consists of roast lamb followed by apple pie, Hobbs's favourite meal.

INNER LONDON EDUCATION AUTHORITY
County Hall, Belvedere Road, Lambeth, SE1.
Greater London Council
County Hall was the home of the Inner London Education Service. This plaque was erected just as Mrs Thatcher was putting a temporary end to London home rule by abolishing the Greater London Council, whose leader Ken Livingstone (1981–6) especially got under her skin. He returned as mayor when London regained self-government in 2000.

JAMES, C. L. R. (1901–89), Trinidadian, writer, political activist
165 Railton Road, Brixton, SE24.
English Heritage
James lived and died here. In his politics he was always of the radical left, by turns Trotskyist and Marxist; his books *World Revolution* (1937) and *The Black Jacobins* (1938), the latter about Toussaint L'Ouverture and the Haitian revolt, were both widely praised. His semi-autobiographical book *Beyond a Boundary* (1963) is regarded by many as the best single book ever written about cricket, if not about any sport.

LENO, Dan (1860–1904), English, music-hall comedian
56 Akerman Road, Stockwell, SW9.
London County Council
Leno, stage-name of George Wild Galvin, lived here from 1898 to 1901. He was on stage from the age of four, later developing a clog-dancing act with his brother, and was crowned world clog-dancing champion in 1880. His fame came with the development of his comic monologue to the audience, either in his cockney persona or as a pantomime dame, often opposite Marie Lloyd (q.v.). His funeral was said to be the biggest for a stage personality since Garrick (q.v.).

MACAULAY, Thomas Babington (1800–59), English, historian, poet, politician
5 The Pavement, Clapham, SW4.
London County Council
Macaulay lived here with his father (see below). He was a proponent of the 'Whig interpretation of history', seeing history as drama, having heroes and villains. His great work is *The History of England from the Accession of James II* (1848–55), which was completed by his sister after his early death. His *Lays of Ancient Rome* (1842) was a very successful book of ballads about great episodes in Roman history. He was also responsible for the Indian Code of Law (1860), much of which is still in force in various former British colonies.

MACAULAY, Zachary (1768–1838), Scottish, philanthropist
5 The Pavement, Clapham, SW4.
London County Council
Macaulay lived here. He was governor of Sierra Leone (1793–9) and secretary of the Sierra Leone Company (1799–1808), a utopian attempt to build a home in Africa for freed slaves. He edited the *Christian Observer* (1802–16), a paper devoted to the abolition of the slave trade, and then of slavery itself. He was a co-founder of the Anti-Slavery Society in 1823.

MEE, Arthur (1875–1943), English, journalist, writer, topographer
27 Lanercost Road, Tulse Hill, SW2.
English Heritage
Mee lived here. Described as 'torrentially productive', he calculated he wrote a million words a year for fifty years, including a complete topographic series on British counties, but his output was mostly children's books and magazines, including *The Children's Encyclopaedia* and the *Wonder Book* series, which opened the eyes of several generations.

MONTGOMERY OF ALAMEIN, Viscount (1887–1976), English, soldier
Oval House, 52–54 Kennington Oval, SE11.
English Heritage
Montgomery was born here. In the Second World War he commanded the Eighth Army in North Africa, where his victory at El Alamein (1942) was the first good news for the British since the war started. He went on to command the ground forces in the Normandy landings of 1944 and received the German surrender at Lüneberg Heath.

PARKES, Alexander (1813–90), English, scientist
32 Park Hall Road, West Dulwich, SE21.
Plastics Historical Society
Parkes, who lived here, took out sixty-five patents over forty-six years, mostly to do with the deposition of metal by electricity. He was called 'the Nestor of Electrometallurgy'. He plasticised cellulose nitrate with camphor and is recognised as the father of the plastics industry. (See also Hackney and Waltham Forest.)

RUSKIN, John (1819–1900), English, art critic
26 Herne Hill, SE24. *London County Council*
Ruskin, who lived in a house on this site, was the pre-eminent cultural thinker of the Victorian age, his writings ranging across art, architecture, education and social justice. When he received his inheritance, he said that there could not be a rich socialist and dispersed most of it to good causes, such as Octavia Hill's (q.v.) housing projects and his own charity, the Guild of St George. He was the first Slade Professor of Fine Art at Oxford (1869–79), his lectures so popular he had to give them twice. His admirers ranged from Tolstoy to Proust to Gandhi, and Ruskin College, Oxford, is named in his honour.

SOSEKI, Natsume (1867–1916), Japanese, novelist
81 The Chase, Clapham Common, SW4.
English Heritage
Soseki, the pen-name of Natsume Kinnosuke, lived here in 1901–2. His early works included the humorous *I Am a Cat* (1905) and *Botchan* (1906), which were followed by work in a more serious vein. He is regarded as one of Japan's greatest writers.

SZABO, Violette (1921–45), Anglo-French, secret agent
18 Burnley Road, Stockwell, SW9.
Greater London Council

Szabo lived here. Captured in June 1944 during her second mission for the Special Operations Executive into occupied France, she was tortured, raped, sent to Ravensbrück concentration camp, and finally executed in February 1945, having told her captors nothing. She was awarded a posthumous George Cross in 1946. Her story was told in the film *Carve Her Name with Pride* (1958), starring Virginia McKenna.

TRINDER, Tommy (1909–89), English, comedian
54 Wellfield Road, Streatham, SW16.
Streatham Society
Trinder was born in this house. He made his stage debut at the age of twelve and came to national fame after appearing in *Band Wagon* at the Palladium in 1939. He is remembered for his catchphrase 'You lucky people!'. A favourite with the Royal Family, he appeared in six Royal Variety Shows. He was chairman of Fulham Football Club (1955–76).

VAN GOGH, Vincent (1853–90), Dutch, painter
87 Hackford Road, South Lambeth, SW9.
Greater London Council
Van Gogh lived here in 1873–4. He was in London working for the Dutch art dealers Goupil & Cie. While living here, he fell in love with his landlady's daughter, Eugénie, but she rejected him. This sent him into a depression, from which he emerged with an evangelical fervour, which preoccupied him for the next several years. He did not take up painting until 1880. (See also Hounslow.)

WILBERFORCE, William (1759–1833), English, anti-slavery campaigner
Holy Trinity Church, Clapham Common, SW4.
Greater London Council
Wilberforce was a leading member of the Clapham Sect (see page 196), whose members worshipped at this church and were the intellectual force behind the campaigns to abolish first the slave trade and then slavery itself. (See also Merton, Hillingdon, Barnet, Wandsworth and Kensington & Chelsea 2.)

LEWISHAM

In south-east London, the London Borough of
Lewisham is an amalgamation of two former
metropolitan boroughs, Lewisham and
Deptford.

BAIRD, John Logie (1888–1946), Scottish,
television pioneer
3 Crescent Wood Road, Sydenham, SE26.
Greater London Council
Baird lived here from 1933 to 1944. He had been
removed from control of his pioneering company in
1933 but continued his researches in a laboratory here.
He developed systems for colour, three-dimensional
imagery, screen projection and stereophonic sound.
Unfortunately for him, there was a war on and no one
paid attention to his ideas at the time. (See also
Westminster 3 and 4.)

BARING, Sir Francis
(1740–1810), English,
banker
**Manor House Library,
Old Road, SE13.**
*London Borough of
Lewisham / Baring Brothers & Co*
Sir Francis lived here from
1797 until his death. He was the
founder of Baring's Bank in 1762 and financial adviser to
successive governments, including particularly that of
his close friend Lord Shelburne (q.v.). By the time he
retired in 1804, Baring's was the most powerful
merchant bank in London and he was able to buy this
house from his old friend Sir Joseph Plaice for £20,000.

BONHOEFFER, Dietrich (1906–45), German,
theologian, cleric
2 Manor Mount, Forest Hill, SE23.
*Borough of Lewisham / International Bonhoeffer
Society / German Evangelical Church, Sydenham*

Bonhoeffer lived here from 1933 to 1935, when he
was pastor at the German church nearby. He bravely
returned to Germany when many who shared his anti-
Nazi views were leaving. He was arrested in 1943 and
executed one month before VE Day. His best-known
theological work is *Ethics*, published posthumously in
1949.

CLARENCE, Duke of (1765–1837), English, royalty
**Ashberry Cottage, Honor Oak Road, Forest
Hill, SE23.** *Private*

This cottage was for twenty years (1791–1811) the
rural retreat of William, Duke of Clarence, the future
William IV, and his mistress, the actress Mrs Jordan
(see page 202). They had ten children and led a blissful
family life. Mrs Jordan was given a pension when they
parted, provided she did not go back on stage. The
children were given the surname FitzClarence. (See
also Westminster 3.)

CONNELL, Jim (1852–1929), Irish, socialist
22a Stondon Park, Forest Hill, SE23.
London Borough of Lewisham/Labour Party
Connell lived here from 1915 until his death. He composed 'The Red Flag', anthem of the Labour Party, while on a train home from Charing Cross. He had been inspired to write it after attending a meeting during the London dock strike of 1889, and it is thought the title comes from his seeing the train guard raise and lower the red signal flag on the platform. In 1920 he recalled: 'In writing the song I gave expression to not only my own best thoughts and feelings, but the best thoughts and feelings of every genuine socialist I knew.'

DEPTFORD FRIENDS' MEETING HOUSE
146 Deptford High Street, SE8. *Private*
The meeting house was demolished as late as 1907, and the site is now a charity shop. It is remembered because Peter the Great of Russia (see page 203) worshipped here (1697–8).

DOWSON, Ernest (1867–1900), English, poet
Dowson Court, Belmont Grove, SE13.
London Borough of Lewisham
Dowson, who lived in a house on this site, was of the 'decadent' *fin de siècle* school. He contributed to the literary quarterly *Yellow Book* (1894–7), and his poetry has given us such memorable phrases as 'days of wine and roses' and 'gone with the wind'. He died of alcoholism at the age of thirty-two.

DUNCAN, Leland Lewis (1862–1923), English, local historian
8 Lingards Road, Lewisham, SE13.
London Borough of Lewisham
Duncan lived here from 1873 until his death. His work was at the War Office, but his off-duty life was devoted to antiquarian research in Lewisham and surrounding areas. He published the standard *History of Lewisham* (1908) as well as histories of the parish church and Colfe's Grammar School.

FLECKER, James Elroy (1884–1915), English, poet, playwright
9 Gilmore Road, Lewisham, SE13.
Greater London Council
Flecker was born here. His two plays, *Hassan* and *Don Juan*, were published posthumously in 1922 and 1925. His best-known poem, 'To a Poet a Thousand Years Hence', includes the haunting lines:
O friend, unseen, unborn, unknown,
Student of our sweet English tongue,
Read out my words at night, alone:
I was a poet, I was young.
He died of tuberculosis at thirty-one.

GLAISHER, James (1809–1903), English, astronomer, meteorologist
20 Dartmouth Hill, Blackheath, SE10.
Greater London Council
Glaisher, who lived here, was Superintendent of Meteorology at Greenwich for thirty-four years. He is remembered for pioneering balloon flights to measure temperature and humidity at altitude. On an occasion in 1862 he broke the altitude record but passed out before a reading could be taken.

GRACE, W. G. (1848–1915), English, cricketer
7 Lawrie Park Road, Sydenham, SE26.
London Borough of Lewisham
Grace, who lived in a house on this site, was one of the towering figures of Victorian society. He made cricket into a major spectator sport and was its first nationwide star. In a forty-four-year career, he scored a total of 54,896 runs and took 2,876 wickets, playing in twenty-two tests for England. (See also Bromley.)

GREENING, Edward Owen (1836–1923), English, social reformer
Dowson Court, Belmont Grove, Lewisham, SE13. *London Borough of Lewisham/Co-operative Wholesale Society*

Greening lived in a house on this site from 1893 until his death. He gave his first public speech at the age of sixteen at an anti-slavery meeting. Deeply involved in the co-operative movement from the 1850s, he believed that the co-ops should do more than trade: they should encourage sport, art, hobbies and education.

GROVE, Sir George (1820–1900), English, engineer, musicologist
208 Sydenham Road, Sydenham, SE26.
London Borough of Lewisham
Sir George lived in a house on this site from 1860 until his death. As an engineer he specialised in lighthouses, but his name is preserved in *Grove's Dictionary of Music and Musicians*, originally published in 1878–99, and still, regularly revised, the standard reference work. He was knighted in 1883, when he was the first director of the Royal College of Music.

HEPWORTH, Cecil M. (1874–1953), English, film pioneer
17 Somerset Gardens, Lewisham, SE13.
British Film Institute
Hepworth was born here. His father was a popular magic-lantern entertainer and by the early 1890s Hepworth was himself touring with a photographic show. He became an assistant to Birt Acres (q.v.) and later, with his own company, filmed Queen Victoria's funeral (1901), the first screen version of *Alice in Wonderland* (1903) and, his greatest success, *Rescued by Rover* (1905), featuring a faithful dog saving a baby.

HORNIMAN, Frederick John (1835–1906), English, merchant
Horniman Museum, London Road, SE23.
Greater London Council
Horniman gave this museum and its gardens to the people of London in 1901. He and his father, whose fortune was based on tea, had been inveterate travellers and collectors. Their collection was first displayed to the public in their house, but then Frederick commissioned C. Harrison Townsend to design this striking building, erected between 1897 and 1901. (See also Croydon.)

JEFFERIES, Richard (1848–87), English, naturalist, novelist
20 Sydenham Park Road, Sydenham, SE26.
Lewisham Council
Jefferies, who lived here, was noted for his depiction of English rural life, whether in fiction such as *Bevis* (1882) and *After London* (1885), or in essays such as *Round About a Great Estate* (1880) and *Nature near London* (1883), or in his autobiography, *Story of My Heart* (1883). (See also Greenwich.)

JORDAN, Mrs Dorothy (1761–1816), Irish, actress
Ashberry Cottage, Honor Oak Road, Forest Hill, SE23. *Private*
Mrs Jordan lived here for twenty years (1791–1811) as the mistress of the Duke of Clarence (see page 200), the future William IV. They had ten children and were blissfully domesticated. Mrs Jordan was given a pension when they parted, provided she did not go back on stage. The children were given the name FitzClarence. There never was a Mr Jordan: it seemed more respectable for an apparently married woman to be on stage. (See also Kensington & Chelsea 2.)

LADYWELL MINERAL SPRING
148 Ladywell Road, SE13.
Lewisham Council / Ladywell Village Society
This was the site of the celebrated mineral spring. Among its supposed medicinal properties, the water was said to be particularly good for people with poor eyesight. Unfortunately the well dried up when a sewer was constructed nearby.

LONDON & GREENWICH RAILWAY
Deptford Station, Deptford High Street, SE8.
Private
The plaque commemorates the first passenger railway line in London, built in 1836. Deptford is the oldest station still in use.

MARX, Eleanor (1855–98) English, socialist
7 Jews Walk, Sydenham, SE26. *English Heritage*
Marx lived here from 1895 until her death. The youngest daughter of Karl Marx (q.v.), known as 'Tussy', she was her father's secretary from the age of sixteen, and when he died she oversaw the posthumous publication of *Das Kapital* (1867) in English. In 1884 she joined Hyndman's (q.v.) Social Democratic Federation but left almost immediately, along with William Morris (q.v.), to form the Socialist

League. An accomplished linguist, she produced the first English translation of Flaubert's *Madame Bovary* and of two of Ibsen's plays.

McMILLAN, Margaret (1860–1931), and **Rachel** (1859–1917), American-Scottish, educationalists, reformers
127 George Lane, SE13. *London Borough of Lewisham*
The sisters lived here from 1910 to 1913. They were Christian socialists, involved in many campaigns, especially those to do with the welfare of children. In particular their agitation led to the 1906 Provision of School Meals Act. They were memorialised by their friend Walter Cresswell: 'Such persons, single-minded, pure in heart, blazing with selfless love, are the jewels of our species. There is more essential Christianity in them than in a multitude of bishops.'

NESBIT, Edith (1858–1924), English, children's writer
28 Elswick Road, SE13. *London Borough of Lewisham*
Nesbit lived here from 1882 to 1885. She was a committed socialist and one of the founders of the Fabian Society (q.v.) in 1884. At this stage she still had hopes of being a poet and a serious writer, but her husband's bankruptcy led her in a different direction and she went on to mine a rich vein as the author of forty children's books, among which *The Story of the Treasure Seekers* (1898), *The Wouldbegoods* (1899) and *The Railway Children* (1906) are still popular. (See also Greenwich.)

PETER THE GREAT of Russia (1672–1725), Russian, emperor
146 Deptford High Street, SE8. *Private*
Peter I, who had been tsar since 1682, was on a learning tour of western Europe. In Deptford he stayed at the house of the diarist John Evelyn while studying the local shipbuilding industry. His policy of westernisation transformed Russia into a major European power. In Deptford he worshipped at the Friends' Meeting House on this site, where he, the head of

the Russian Orthodox Church, discussed religion with William Penn, the leading Quaker. Neither man was persuaded to convert.

ROSS, Sir James Clark (1800–62), English, naval officer, explorer
2 Eliot Place, Blackheath, SE3.
Sir James lived here. Between 1819 and 1831 he served on several Arctic expeditions, discovering the north magnetic pole in 1831. He led an Antarctic expedition (1839–43), during which he discovered the south magnetic pole. The Ross Shelf, Ross Island and Ross Sea are named in his honour.

SHACKLETON, Sir Ernest (1874–1922), Irish, explorer
12 Westwood Hill, Upper Sydenham, SE26.
London County Council
Sir Ernest lived here in his childhood. He accompanied Scott (q.v.) on his first expedition (1900–4) and in all made four Antarctic expeditions. His 1914–18 expedition included an extraordinary 800-mile journey in a small boat to get help after his ship, *Endurance*, was crushed by ice. On his last expedition he died of a heart attack in South Georgia and is buried there.

SMILES, Samuel (1812–1904), Scottish, reformer, writer
11 Granville Park, Lewisham, SE13.
London County Council
Smiles, who lived here, had a varied career as surgeon, journalist, secretary of railway companies and spare-time Chartist. He wrote prolifically, including multiple biographies of his engineering heroes, but is best known for 'improving' works such as *Self Help* (1859), *Character* (1871), *Thrift* (1875), *Duty* (1880) and *Life and Labour* (1887).

SMITH, Sir Francis Pettit (1808–74), English, engineer
17 Sydenham Hill, SE26. *English Heritage*
Smith, pioneer of the screw propeller for ships, built this house for himself in 1864 and lived here until

1870. His childhood enthusiasm for boats led him in 1834 to construct a model propelled by a screw driven by a spring, being convinced this was superior to the paddle system, and after further experiments he took out a patent in 1836. He loaned his boat *Archimedes* to Brunel (q.v.), who was persuaded to change the design of the SS *Great Britain* from paddle to screw propulsion.

STURDEE, Thankfull (1852–1934), photographer, local historian
16 Bolden Street, Deptford, SE8.
London Borough of Lewisham
Sturdee lived here from 1900 to 1903. On the *Daily Mirror* from 1911, he was known as 'the Father of Fleet Street Photographers'. In his spare time he took pictures around Deptford and collected historical materials, published as *Reminiscences of Old Deptford* (1895). His archive is now in Deptford Library.

TALLIS, John (1817–76), English, publisher
233 New Cross Road, SE14. *Greater London Council*
Tallis lived here from 1870 until his death. He is best known for his publication *London Street Views* (1838–40), a unique series of engravings, street by street, house by house. He also published a celebrated *Illustrated Atlas* (1851) and *Town Plan* series (1850–60). He overreached himself and went bankrupt in 1861. The plaque incorrectly gives his birth year as 1816. *London Street Views* was re-published in facsimile by the London Topographical Society in 1969.

UNWIN, Sir Stanley (1884–1968), English, publisher
13 Handen Road, Lee, SE12. *Greater London Council*
Sir Stanley was born here. He purchased a controlling interest in George Allen & Unwin in 1914, publishing serious and sometimes controversial works by Bertrand Russell (q.v.), Gandhi (q.v.) and others. In 1936 J. R. R. Tolkien submitted *The Hobbit* for publication, and Unwin paid his ten-year-old son, Rayner, a few pence to write a report on the manuscript. The boy's favourable reaction secured the book's publication and led to sequels – *The Lord of The Rings* trilogy.

WALLACE, Edgar (1875–1932), English, novelist, journalist
6 Tressillian Crescent, Brockley, SE4.
London County Council

Wallace, who lived here, was incredibly prolific: he wrote 175 novels, including *Four Just Men* (1905), *Sanders of the River* (1911) and *The Mind of Mr J. G. Reeder* (1925). 160 films have been made from his works, including *King Kong*, for which he wrote the original screenplay, though he died before the film's realisation. (See also City.)

WALLIS, Sir Barnes (1887–1979), English, scientist, designer, inventor
241 New Cross Road, New Cross, SE14.
London Borough of Lewisham
Sir Barnes, who lived here as a boy from 1892 to 1909, was a pioneer of geodesic airframes, as in his Wellesley and Wellington bombers. He is most famous for designing the bouncing bombs employed on the Dam Busters raid in 1943. He was subsequently involved in early work on swing-wing aircraft and Concorde.

WILLIAMSON, Henry (1895–1977), English, novelist
21 Eastern Road, SE4.
Borough of Lewisham / Henry Williamson Society
When Williamson was living here, as a boy and young man (1902–20), this was still a semi-rural area, and this period inspired his lifelong love of nature, represented by his best-known works, *Tarka the Otter* (1927) and *Salar the Salmon* (1935). The Henry Williamson Society was formed in 1980.

WOOLWORTH'S V2 ATTACK
277–281 New Cross Road, New Cross, SE14.
Deptford History Group
168 people were killed here in the worst single V2 incident of the war. It was 12.26 p.m. on a Saturday, and the shop was packed because word had got round that the store had just received a consignment of saucepans, which were in short supply in the war. There was only one survivor on the premises. (For other Second World War sites, see City, Tower Hamlets, Newham and Kingston.)

SOUTHWARK

Directly south across the River Thames from
the City and the East End, the London Borough
of Southwark is an amalgamation of three
former metropolitan boroughs, Southwark,
Bermondsey and Camberwell.

BOBBY ABEL IN W. G.—'LOOK HERE, WE PLAYERS INTEND TO BE SUFFICIENTLY
PAID, AS WELL AS THE SO-CALLED GENTLEMEN!'

ABEL, Bobby
(1857–1936), English,
cricketer
**Café Gallery,
Southwark Park,
SE16.** *London Borough
of Southwark*
Abel, the plaque
notes, learned his
cricket here in
Southwark Park.
Although he was only
5 feet 4 inches tall, he
was nicknamed 'the Guv'nor'. A prolific opening
batsman, he was the first England player to carry his
bat through an innings, and the first player to score
over two thousand runs in consecutive seasons, which
he did for eight seasons (1895–1902). His 357 not out
remains the Surrey County record score. Failing
eyesight ended his career, and he was blind for the last
several years of his life.

**ANCHOR
BREWERY
Park Street, SE1.**
Private
The brewery
operated on this site
from 1616 to 1986.
The plaque lists the
many successive
owners, among whom
the best-known was Henry Thrale, whose wife, Hester, is
famous for her long friendship with Dr Johnson (q.v.).

BABBAGE, Charles (1791–1871), English,
computing pioneer
Larcom Street/Walworth Road, SE17.
Southwark Council
Babbage was born near here. He devised a calculating
machine, the difference engine, and another, the
analytical engine, neither built in his lifetime, which
were forerunners of the modern computer. In 1991
the Science Museum built a Difference Engine and
showed that it worked. (See also Westminster 2.)

**BEAR-BAITING
Bear Gardens,
SE1.**
Historic Southwark
Bear-baiting, the
'sport' of setting
dogs on to a
chained bear, was popular in England from at least the
early sixteenth century until the early nineteenth
century. The Puritans were the first to try to ban it,
but it was not until the growth of wider sensitivity that
it was finally outlawed by the Cruelty to Animals Act
of 1835.

**BERMONDSEY ABBEY
Charte House, Abbey Street, SE1.** *Private*
Endowed by Aylwin Child, a wealthy local citizen, the
abbey grew in power and wealth with gifts from
successive monarchs, until the buildings were
surrendered to Henry VIII at the dissolution of the
monasteries. The stones were reused by Sir Thomas
Pope to build himself Bermondsey House nearby.

BESANT, Annie (1847–1933), English, social reformer
39 Colby Road, Norwood, SE19.
London County Council
Besant, who lived here in 1874, was a Theosophist, a social reformer and promoter of birth control, an associate of Charles Bradlaugh (q.v.) and the Fabian Society (q.v.), and sister-in-law of Sir Walter Besant (q.v.). A friend of Mahatma Gandhi (q.v.), she threw herself into the cause of Indian independence, living for many years in India and becoming President of the Indian National Congress (1917).

BIBLE, First printed English
Post Office, Borough High Street, SE1.
Borough of Southwark
The first English Bible was produced in Zürich in 1535 by Miles Coverdale. The 1537 version, produced here by John Rogers, was, however, the first to be translated from the original Hebrew and Greek, and the first to be printed in England. Rogers was later the first martyr under 'Bloody Mary' (see City).

BLYTON, Enid (1897–1968), English, children's writer
354 Lordship Lane, East Dulwich, SE22.
London Borough of Southwark
Enid Blyton was born here. See her fuller entries in Kingston and Bromley.

BRAIDWOOD, James (1800–61), Scottish, fire chief
33 Tooley Street, Southwark, SE1.
Private
Braidwood was killed by a falling wall during the great Tooley Street fire on 22 June 1861 near this spot. He was the first director of the London Fire Brigade from 1833, founding the modern service. Among his innovations was a breathing apparatus for firemen, and his manual on firefighting is quoted to this day.

BRANDON, Charles, Duke of Suffolk (?–1543), English, soldier, diplomat
Brandon House, Borough High Street, SE1.
Borough of Southwark

160 Borough High Street, SE1.
Borough of Southwark
Both plaques claim to be on or near the site of the Duke of Suffolk's palace. A close friend of Henry VIII, he was secretly married to Henry's sister, Mary, while still married to his second wife, but a papal bull straightened things out. He led a couple of invasions of France and was with Henry VIII at the Field of Cloth of Gold (1520).

BRANDON, Sir Thomas (?–1509), English, diplomat
Brandon House, Borough High Street, SE1.
Borough of Southwark
Sir Thomas was an uncle of Charles Brandon (see above). Like his nephew, he was engaged in diplomacy, concluding peace with France in 1492 and a treaty with the Emperor Maximilian in 1503. The plaque, which misspells his surname 'Branden', may confuse him with his nephew.

BROWNING, Robert (1812–89), English, poet
179 Southampton Way, Camberwell, SE5. *Private*
This is where Browning grew up, educated largely by his parents. His first poem was published in 1833. During his lifetime his wife, Elizabeth (q.v.), was a considerably more popular poet, but his reputation has continued to grow. (See also Kensington & Chelsea 1 and Westminster 1.)

BRUNEL, Sir Marc Isambard (1769–1849), French, engineer
Railway Avenue, SE16.
London Docklands Development Corporation
This building was the engine house for the world's first underwater tunnel, designed by Sir Marc, assisted by his son, Isambard Kingdom Brunel (q.v.). The engine house is now a museum about the Brunels. (See also Kensington & Chelsea 2.)

CAINE, Sir Michael (b.1933), English, film star
Lower Road, SE16.
London Borough of Southwark
The plaque records that Sir Michael (Maurice Micklewhite) was born here in 1933 in St Olave's Hospital. His breakthrough role was as Gonville Bromhead in

Zulu (1964), followed by Harry Palmer in *The Ipcress File* (1965), and *Alfie* (1966). He has won two Oscars as best supporting actor, in *Hannah and Her Sisters* (1986) and *The Cider House Rules* (1999). The plaque is affixed to the former hospital gatehouse, all the other buildings having been demolished in the 1970s.

CARR-GOMM, Richard (1922–2008), English, social activist
36 Gomm Road, SE16. *London Borough of Southwark*
Carr-Gomm lived and worked in this house. Inspired by Christian ideals, and the example of a community for older people that he came across in Cairo, he resigned his commission in the Coldstream Guards in 1955, becoming known as 'the Scrubbing Major' for his unpaid cleaning work among the elderly. He formed the Abbeyfield Society in 1957, which now provides accommodation for ten thousand senior citizens nationwide.

CATHERINE OF ARAGON (1485–1536), Spanish, royalty
49 Bankside, Southwark, SE1.
Private
This charming old plaque is purest fantasy: it claims that Catherine of Aragon (future first wife of Henry VIII) stayed here when she came to London. In fact, she was lodged at Lambeth Palace on arrival in the capital. Furthermore, this house was not built till 1710, 208 years later. Nor did Sir Christopher Wren (see page 215) watch St Paul's being built from here. The plaque and the dubious circumstances of its creation are explained in Gillian Tindall's *The House by the Thames* (Chatto & Windus, 2006).

CHAMBERLAIN, Joseph (1836–1914), English, politician
188 Camberwell Grove, Camberwell, SE5.
London County Council
Chamberlain, who was born and lived here until he was eighteen, made his fortune from a screw-manufacturing business (now part of GKN). He was three times mayor of Birmingham before entering Parliament as a Radical Liberal in 1876. Later he was president of the Board of Trade (1880) and Colonial Secretary (1895). He was father of the prime minister Neville Chamberlain (q.v.). (See also Islington.)

CHAPLIN, Charlie (1889–1977), English, music-hall and film star
277 Walworth Road, SE17. *Southwark Council*
Chaplin was born in East Lane (now East Road) here. As a child he lived at various addresses around Walworth and Kennington. His early life was tough because of his father's alcoholism and his mother's mental fragility. (See also Westminster 1 and Lambeth.)

CHAUCER, Geoffrey (1342–1400), English, poet
Talbot Yard, Borough High Street, SE1.
London Borough of Southwark
The plaque commemorates the Tabard Inn (see page 214), from which the pilgrims set off in Chaucer's *Canterbury Tales*. Chaucer was a man of many parts: diplomat, spy, Clerk of the King's Works. His greatest work was written in 1387 and, as Terry Jones, the *Monty Python* star and medieval scholar, said when unveiling this plaque, 'The pilgrims are living characters speaking the language they spoke on the street.'

CLINK PRISON
Clink Street, Southwark, SE1.
London Borough of Southwark
The Clink originally housed religious and political prisoners in the fourteenth century, when it was owned by the Bishops of Winchester. It was later 'a very dismal hole where debtors were confined' and gave its name as a term for any grim lock-up. It was burned down during the Gordon Riots (1780). Now there is a small museum.

COBHAM, Sir Alan (1894–1973), English, aviator
78 Denman Road, SE15. *English Heritage*
Sir Alan, who was born here, served in the Royal Flying Corps in the First World War, afterwards becoming a test pilot for De Havilland (q.v.). In the late 1920s he pioneered long-distance flights, to Australia, Cape Town and Rangoon. In the 1930s 'Cobham's Flying Circus' gave shows round the country.

COLE, Harry (1926–2008), English, police officer, writer
Charles Dickens School, Lant Street, SE1.
London Borough of Southwark
Cole attended this school from 1934 to 1940. Subsequently he was a police constable at Carter Street station in Walworth for thirty years, from which experience he wrote a stream of anecdotal memoirs – *Policeman's Lot*, *Policeman's Patch*, etc. He was awarded the British Empire Medal in 1958 for community work.

COOPER, Sir Henry (b.1934), English, boxing champion
322 Old Kent Road, SE1.
London Borough of Southwark

The plaque is on a former pub, the Thomas à Becket, in whose first-floor gymnasium Sir Henry trained throughout his boxing career. Phenomenally popular even beyond the world of boxing, Cooper was British, European and Commonwealth heavyweight champion in 1970. He is the only British boxer ever to win three Lonsdale belts outright. In 1963, "Enry's 'ammer' famously floored Muhammad Ali, who said later that he had been hit so hard that his ancestors in Africa felt it.

COUNTY HALL
Belvedere Road, SE1. *Greater London Council*
The plaque notes that this was the home of London government from 1922 to 1986. It was erected in the dying days of the old Greater London Council, famously killed off by Mrs Thatcher because of her dislike of the council leader Ken Livingstone's way of doing things. Subsequently London self-government was revived under Tony Blair, with Livingstone once more at the helm, now as mayor.

CROSS BONES GRAVEYARD
Redcross Way, SE1. *Friends of Cross Bones*
The plaque records that in medieval times this was an unconsecrated burial ground for prostitutes, known locally as 'Winchester geese' because this area was the

possession of the bishops of Winchester, who licensed the women. By the eighteenth century it had become simply a paupers' graveyard and it was eventually closed in 1853, filled with an estimated fifteen thousand bodies. Various subsequent attempts to develop the site have been defeated by local sentiment. It is currently a building yard for London Underground, and the Friends hope to be able to make it into a permanent garden.

DICKENS, Charles (1812–70), English, novelist
Charles Dickens School, Lant Street, SE1.
London Borough of Southwark
In 1824, at the age of twelve, Dickens lodged in an attic room in a house on the site of today's school in order to be near his father, who was imprisoned for debt in the nearby Marshalsea Prison (q.v.). Dickens would have breakfast with his parents in the prison and then go on to his work at Warren's blacking factory. He

wrote later, in *Pickwick Papers*: 'There is a repose about Lant Street which sheds a gentle melancholy on the soul.' (See also Westminster 2, Westminster 4, Haringey and Camden 2.)

DRUID STREET ARCH BOMBING
Druid Street, SE1. *London Borough of Southwark*
The plaque records that on the night of 25 October 1940 a bomb fell through this railway arch and killed seventy-seven people who were sheltering from the raid. This and other disasters, such as Stainer Street (see page 214), led to the development of deeper shelters.

DRYSDALE, Dr Charles Vickery (1874–1961), English, engineer, family planning pioneer
153a East Street, Walworth, SE17. *English Heritage*
Dr Drysdale opened his first family planning clinic here in 1921 and from the same year, as president of the Malthusian League, he argued a conservative individualistic philosophy. In his other field of activity, electrical engineering, he invented the alternating-current potentiometer, the polyphase wattmeter and the phase-shifting transformer.

FARADAY, Michael (1791–1867), English, scientist
Walworth Road, SE17. *Borough of Southwark*
Faraday was born near this spot. His experiments led to the invention of the dynamo, the transformer and the electric motor. Known as 'the Father of Modern Electrical Science', he was Professor of Chemistry at the Royal Institute from 1833 and is regarded as one of the greatest experimenters of all time. (See also Richmond and Westminster 2.)

FERDINAND, Rio (b. 1978), English, footballer
Millbrook House, Peckham Park Road, SE15. *London Borough of Southwark*
Ferdinand, born here, has played for West Ham United, Leeds United and Manchester United. A gifted central defender, he has amassed, at the time of writing, seventy-three England caps. Whether he can yet be called 'a legend', as the plaque says, is debatable: Dixie Dean, Frank Swift and Johnnie Haynes are legends: Ferdinand is not yet ready for the label.

FERRYMAN'S SEAT
Bear Gardens, SE1. *Historic Southwark*
A battered flat stone in a niche, installed in a new building at the corner with Bankside, this was the

place where ferrymen would take the weight off their feet while waiting for the next customers wishing to cross the Thames to the City.

FORESTER, C. S.
(1899–1966), English, novelist
48 Underhill Road, East Dulwich, SE22.
English Heritage
Forester, pen-name of Cecil Troughton Smith, lived here. He is famous for his series of adventurous novels in the course of which their eighteenth-century naval hero, Horatio Hornblower, rises eventually to be an admiral. Forester was also the author of *The African Queen* (1935), memorably filmed by John Huston in 1951 with Humphrey Bogart and Katherine Hepburn.

GEORGE, Sir Ernest (1839–1922), English, architect
17 Bartholomew Street, Southwark, SE1.
Southwark Council
Sir Ernest, who lived here, built a strong practice in domestic architecture, initially in Tudor and Jacobean mode, later adapting Flemish and Dutch styling for large areas of South Kensington. His office was a fashionable training ground for young architects, and he was president of the Royal Institute of British Architects (1908–9).

GEORGE INN
73 Borough High Street, Southwark, SE1.
Southwark Council
The George, in the courtyard at the rear, built in 1677 on the site of an earlier hostelry, is London's only remaining galleried inn. It was very important, and busy, in the eighteenth century as the London terminus of all coach traffic from south-east England. The plaque exaggerates in claiming that Dickens (q.v.) 'immortalized' the George in *Little Dorrit*; he merely mentions it in passing. He did visit several times, as too did Shakespeare in an earlier age.

GLOBE THEATRE
Park Street, SE1.
The Shakespeare Reading Society of London
The plaque is on the site of the original Globe Theatre, not to be confused with the modern facsimile theatre

round the corner on Bankside. The theatre stood here from 1599 until 1644, being rebuilt after a fire in 1613. Shakespeare in his time owned one tenth of it.

GOLDSMITH, Oliver (?1730–74), Anglo-Irish, poet, playwright, novelist
Oliver Goldsmith School, Peckham Road, SE15.
London Borough of Southwark
As author of *The Vicar of Wakefield* (1762), *The Deserted Village* (1770) and *She Stoops to Conquer* (1773), and supposed author of the nursery story *Goody Two-Shoes*, Goldsmith fully justifies his friend Dr Johnson's epitaph for him: 'he left scarcely any style of writing untouched, and touched nothing that he did not adorn.'

HARDY, Bert (1913–95), English, photographer
The Priory, Webber Street, SE1.
London Borough of Southwark
Hardy took innumerable documentary photographs of Britons enjoying themselves in the late 1940s and 1950s but is best remembered for his association with the magazine *Picture Post* (1941–57), especially his work with the reporter James Cameron in the Korean War, when they exposed some unpalatable truths about the allied side.

HARVARD, John (1607–38), English, cleric
103 Borough High Street, Southwark, SE1.
Borough of Southwark
This is the site of the former Queen's Head inn, owned by the Harvard family. John, a nonconformist priest educated at Emmanuel College, Cambridge, emigrated to America in 1637 but died of

consumption only a year later. He left his library of around three hundred books and £779 to the college in Cambridge, Massachesetts, which later took his name.

HILL, Octavia (1838–1912), English, social reformer
Red Cross Garden, Redcross Way, SE1.
London Borough of Southwark
These gardens, cottages and communal hall were established by Octavia Hill in 1887, as her first venture in social housing in Southwark. They were designed by her regular architect of choice, Elijah Hoole. Here too, the plaque notes, she pioneered Army cadets (1887–90). (See also Westminster 2.)

HILL, Rowland (1744–1833), English, cleric
Orbit House, 197 Blackfriars Road, SE1.
London Borough of Southwark
This is the site of Rowland Hill's Surrey Chapel, where, on 13 July 1803, the inaugural meeting of the National Sunday School Union was held, rapidly blossoming into a worldwide movement. The building later had another round of fame when it was called 'The Ring' and used for boxing. Rowland Hill, not to be confused with his namesake the postal pioneer (q.v.), was an itinerant preacher who commanded vast congregations and whose base the Surrey Chapel was.

JOHNSON, Janet (1858–1955), English, social worker
39 Redcross Way, SE1. *Historic Southwark*
Janet Johnson, who lived in a house on this site, was the first woman to sit on the Southwark Board of

Guardians (1888) and devoted her life to the welfare of the workhouse inhabitants. Later, as manager of the Central London School for Orphans and Destitute Children at Hanwell, she initiated a number of humanitarian reforms in the areas of education, clothing and diet.

KAIL, Edgar (1900–76), English, amateur footballer
Edgar Kail Way, SE22. *London Borough of Southwark*
Kail played here for the great non-league amateur club Dulwich Hamlet from 1919 to 1933 as a striker, scoring 427 goals. He resisted numerous offers to turn professional and stuck to his job as a wine and spirits salesman to preserve his amateur status. He was awarded three England caps in 1929, making him the last non-league player to be capped, but *not* the last amateur as the plaque claims (that was Bernard Joy of Casuals and Arsenal in 1936).

KARLOFF, Boris (1887–1969), English, film star
36 Forest Hill Road, East Dulwich, SE22.
English Heritage
Karloff, stage-name of William Henry Pratt, was born here. He went to North America in 1909 and, after twelve years in repertory and silent films, he achieved fame as the monster in *Frankenstein* (1931) and went on to appear in many further horror films right up to his death. His particular contribution to the genre was to give his characters vulnerability and dignity alongside their awful capacity for violence.

LIVESEY, Sir George (1834–1908), English, industrialist, philanthropist
682 Old Kent Road, SE15.
London Borough of Southwark
Sir George was chairman of the South Metropolitan Gas Company and a major figure in Southwark industry. He presented this building to the local people

in 1890 as a public library, which continued until 1966. It was then converted into a children's museum, which was very popular, until it was abruptly shut by Southwark Council in 2008, in the face of widespread local protests. Its future is currently uncertain.

MARSHALL, John (d.1631), English, baker, philanthropist
9 Newcomen Street, Southwark, SE1. *Private*
Marshall was a baker living in Axe Yard (the former name of Newcomen Street), married but with no children. He left money to trustees to fund repair and restoration of churches, cathedrals and parsonages, which Marshall's Charity still does to this day.

MARSHALSEA PRISON
Tabard Street Gardens, SE1. *Historic Southwark*
The original Marshalsea Prison dated from the fourteenth century. It was rebuilt in 1811, closed in 1842, and most of its buildings were demolished in 1849. All that is left of it now is a brick wall and two gate arches. 'The crowding ghosts of many miserable years' are remembered only by the council plaque. 'It is gone now,' Dickens wrote, 'and the world is none the worse without it.'

MARSON, Una (1905–65), English, feminist
17 Brunswick Park, SE5.
London Borough of Southwark
Una Marson was the first black female broadcaster on the BBC (1939–46), producing for the Empire Service a programme in which soldiers could send messages home, and a series, *Caribbean Voices*, that exposed West Indian culture for the first time in Britain. A lifelong active feminist, she was prominent in several campaigning organisations, including being secretary of the League of Coloured People and the Women's International League for Peace.

MAYFLOWER
The Mayflower, 117 Rotherhithe Street, SE16.
London Docklands Development Corporation
St Mary's Church, St Marychurch Street, SE16.
London Borough of Southwark
The *Mayflower*, carrying the Pilgrim Fathers, left a jetty by the present-day pub in spring 1620. Both plaques

recall the event. The ship's captain, Christopher Jones of Rotherhithe, died only a year after returning from America and is buried in St Mary's churchyard, though the location of his grave is lost.

MOODY, Dr Harold (1882–1947), Jamaican, physician, campaigner
164 Queens Road, Peckham, SE15.
English Heritage
Dr Moody, who lived and practised here, came to London to study in 1904, setting up his general practice in Peckham in 1913. A devout Christian, he fought for his coloured patients to get jobs and homes, eventually, with others, founding the League of Coloured People and being its first president (1931–47).

MYERS, George (1803–75), English, master builder
131 St George's Road, SE1. *English Heritage*
Myers, who lived here from 1842 to 1853, was particularly associated with Augustus Pugin (q.v.), responsible for the construction of over ninety churches. He also worked at Windsor Castle, the Tower of London and the Aldershot army camp, and built the Medieval Court for the Great Exhibition of 1851.

NEWLANDS, J. A. R. (1837–98), English, chemist
19 West Square, Kennington, SE11.
Royal Society of Chemistry
Newlands was born and raised here. In 1863 he prepared the first periodic table of elements arranged in order of their relative atomic mass, and in 1865 he pointed out the 'law of octaves', whereby every eighth element has similar properties. He was ridiculed at the time.

OLIVER, Percy Lane (1878–1944), English, pioneer of blood donation
5 Colyton Road, East Dulwich, SE22.
Greater London Council
In 1921 Oliver, who lived and worked here, was secretary of the local Red Cross when he had the idea of panels of voluntary blood donors. The scheme was operated by him and his wife from this house, eventually growing into the National Blood Transfusion Service, subsequently copied worldwide.

PALMER, Samuel (1805–81), English, painter
42 Surrey Square, Walworth, SE17. *Private*
Palmer, who was born here, was a friend of Blake (q.v.) and son-in-law of Linnell (q.v.). He formed a group of artists called 'The Ancients' in Shoreham, Kent (1826–35). His works from that time, which are thought to be his best, include *A Hilly Scene* (1826) and *The Magic Apple Tree* (1830), set in mystic landscapes. (See also Kensington & Chelsea 1.)

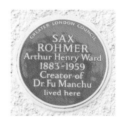

PEARSALL, Phyllis (1906–96), English, mapmaker
3 Court Lane Gardens, Dulwich, SE21. *London Borough of Southwark*
Pearsall was born here. Her great idea arose after she became thoroughly lost on a stormy night in 1935 while travelling to a dinner party and she conceived the notion of an 'A–Z'. She trudged the streets of London, and in 1936 her first edition was published. Well over 60 million copies have been published since, and the idea has been copied for every major city in the world.

PIONEER HEALTH CENTRE
St Mary's Road, Peckham, SE15.
London Borough of Southwark
Opened in 1935 by a husband and wife team of doctors, Scott Williamson and Innes Pearse, who were appalled at the level of health among the low-paid local citizenry, the health centre adopted a preventative rather than curative approach to health problems. The experiment continued until 1950, by which time the National Health Service had taken up many of their ideas.

ROHMER, Sax (1883–1959), English, novelist
51 Herne Hill, SE24.
Greater London Council
Rohmer, pen-name of Arthur Henry Ward, is remembered as the creator of Dr Fu Manchu. The first story, published in 1912, introduced the 'Yellow Peril', which sought world domination

through a secret organisation, the *Si-Fan*. Rohmer went on pumping them out till the year of his death, apparently bemused at the accusation of racist stereotyping.

ROSE THEATRE
Park Street, SE1. *London Borough of Southwark*
The Rose, the first theatre on Bankside, was built by Philip Henslowe and John Cholmley on the site of an old house called The Rose. Edward Alleyn (q.v.) first appeared here. The lease expired in 1605 and the building was shortly after demolished.

ST MARGARET'S CHURCH AND THE BOROUGH COMPTER
34 Borough High Street, Southwark, SE1.
London Borough of Southwark
This is the site of the thirteenth-century St Margaret's. In 1540 the parishes of St Margaret and St Mary Magdalen Overy were united into St Saviour, with the present cathedral as the parish church. The original church building here continued in use for some time as a courthouse with a compter (prison) attached.

ST THOMAS'S HOSPITAL
Post Office, Borough High Street, Southwark, SE1. *London Borough of Southwark*
The original St Thomas's Hospital stood on this site from 1225 to 1865. It was rebuilt in 1552 and in 1865 moved permanently west to Lambeth Palace Road. The plaque also says the first English Bible was printed here in 1537. (See Bible, page 206.)

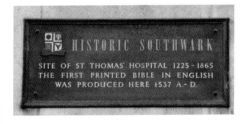

SHAKESPEARE, William (1564–1616), English,
playwright, poet, actor
Park Street, SE1.
The Shakespeare Reading Society of London
The plaque commemorates the Globe Theatre, on this site from 1598 to 1613, where many of Shakespeare's plays were first performed. (See also Hackney.)

SHAW, Sir Eyre Massey (1830–1908), English, fire chief
Winchester House, 94 Southwark Bridge Road, SE1. *English Heritage*
Shaw succeeded James Braidwood (see page 206) as London's fire chief, and under him between 1865 and 1889 the brigade built numerous new fire stations, increased the use of steam fire engines, introduced telegraph alarm systems and augmented its manpower. The brigade was taken over by the London County Council in 1889 and Shaw resigned, unable to accept a new style of management.

SHELLEY, Percy Bysshe (1792–1822), English, poet
Applegarth House, Nelson Square, SE1.
Historic Southwark
The plaque records that Shelley lived at 26 Nelson Square on a site to the north of this building. He lived here only briefly, in hiding from his creditors, from November 1814 to January 1815, in a *ménage a trois* with Mary Godwin and her stepsister, Jane 'Claire' Clairmont. The address is usually given as 2 Nelson Square. (See also Westminster 3.)

SHELTON, Anne (1928–94), English, popular singer
142 Court Lane, Dulwich, SE21.
London Borough of Southwark

Anne Shelton, stage-name of Patricia Sibley, lived in this house from 1944 until her death. Her career began with a six-year stint singing with the Bert Ambrose (q.v.) band at the May Fair Hotel. She was a 'forces' favourite' in the Second World War and was involved with veterans' charities, particularly the Not Forgotten Association. Her 1956 number one hit 'Lay Down Your Arms' was produced by Joe Meek (q.v.).

STAINER STREET ARCH BOMBING
Stainer Street, SE1. *London Borough of Southwark*
The plaque records that on the night of 17 February 1940 a bomb fell through the railway arch here, killing sixty-eight people and injuring 175. The year on the plaque is incorrect: the tragedy actually occurred in 1941.

STEAM BUS GARAGE
Nunhead Lane, SE15. *Private*
The National Steam Car Company was founded by Thomas Clarkson (1864–1933) and ran its first London buses on 2 November 1909, with four vehicles in service. This had risen to 184 by 1914. The service struggled on through the First World War, facing

> On this site stood a Garage for the Steam Buses which The National Steam Car Company Limited opened in 1911. The Clock Tower is a replica of the one which existed until 1999.

insuperable competition from petrol-driven buses. The last steam bus ran on 18 November 1919, and the garage was bought by the London General Omnibus Company.

STEELE, Tommy (b. 1936), English, entertainer
Nickleby House, George Row, SE16.
London Borough of Southwark
Steele, who lived here on the Dickens Estate from 1937 to 1944, was born Thomas William Hicks. He was discovered at the 2i's Coffee Bar (q.v.) in 1956, and is often called England's first pop idol. He had several top ten hits in the 1950s with his group, the Steelmen, including 'Singing the Blues', number one in December 1956. He went on to a showbiz career in film and stage musicals, leaving pop behind, and has developed a successful autumnal career as a sculptor.

STONES END
Police Station, Borough High Street, Southwark, SE1. *Borough of Southwark*
This was the site of 'Stones End', where 'Town Street' met the old turnpike road, and where one of the ring of forts ordered by Parliament to protect London during the Civil War was erected in 1642. It was still standing, though not in prime condition, when Daniel Defoe (q.v.) undertook his *Tour of Britain* in the 1720s.

SURREY DOCKS FIRE
1 Surrey Quays Road, SE16. *London Borough of Southwark*
Surrey Docks Fire
On September 7th 1940 the docks were set on fire in the first raid of the Blitz
Voted by the People

Although London had been bombed before, 7 September 1940 was the beginning of the Blitz proper. 348 Luftwaffe bombers, escorted by 617 fighters, hit the docks, killing 448 people in an afternoon on what became known as 'Black Saturday'. Fires among stores of pepper, paint, rum and rubber each caused particular problems. The fire in Quebec Yard in the Surrey Docks is recorded as the most intense single fire ever in Britain.

TABARD INN
Talbot Yard, Borough High Street, SE1.
London Borough of Southwark
The Tabard was established in 1307 as a gathering point for pilgrims setting off on the annual pilgrimage to the shrine of St Thomas à Becket (q.v.) in Canterbury. Destroyed by fire in 1676, it was rebuilt and renamed the Talbot. It was famous as a coaching inn up to the mid-nineteenth century, when the coming of the railway put it into decline, and it was eventually demolished in 1873.

TIME AND TALENTS
The Old Mortuary, St Mary's Churchyard, SE16. *London Borough of Southwark*
The Time and Talents Association was started by Mina Gollock and friends from the Young Women's Christian Association to do something for the over five thousand women and children employed in often appalling conditions in the various local industries associated with the docks. Originally opened in Bermondsey Street, the Association moved here in 1980 and remains a thriving neighbourhood centre,

offering a range of activities from local history workshops to tai chi.

WANAMAKER, Sam (1919–93), American, actor, director

Bankside, SE1. *London Borough of Southwark* Blacklisted in Hollywood in 1952, at the height of the 'Red Scare', Wanamaker thereafter made his career in England. In 1970 he founded the Shakespeare Globe Trust with the ambition of erecting a re-creation of the original Globe Theatre. He eventually raised over $10 million for the project, which was opened by Queen Elizabeth II in 1997, sadly four years after Wanamaker had died. The plaque memorialises him as a 'visionary' beside his creation.

WHITE HART INN
White Hart Yard, Borough High Street, Southwark, SE1. *Borough of Southwark*

This is the site of the White Hart Inn. Dating from *c*.1400, the inn was used as a base by Jack Cade's Kentish rebels in 1450, had soldiers quartered in 1640, was damaged by fire in 1669, again in 1676, and was where we first meet Sam Weller, working as 'Boots', in *Pickwick Papers*. It was demolished in 1889.

WOLLSTONECRAFT, Mary (1759–97), English, campaigner

45 Dolben Street, SE1. *London Borough of Southwark* Wollstonecraft lived at 49 George Street on this site from 1788 to 1791. It was probably her most fruitful period; she produced *The Female Reader* and *Miscellaneous Pieces for the Improvement of Young Women* (both 1789) and *A Vindication of the Rights of Man* (1790), a response to Burke's (q.v.) *French Revolution*, and she began her most important book, *A Vindication of the Rights of Women* (1792). Of the two *Vindications*, Virginia Woolf (q.v.) wrote: 'those two eloquent and daring books ... which are so true that they seem now

to contain nothing new in them – their originality has become our commonplace.' (See also Camden 2 and Hackney.)

WREN, Sir Christopher (1632–1723), English, architect
49 Bankside, Southwark, SE1. *Private*

Unfortunately this charming old plaque was created in the 1940s and is bogus. Wren did not watch St Paul's being built from here (this house was not built until 1710). He is thought to have watched from a house some way to the west, which was pulled down in 1906. The story of the plaque and its dubious origins is detailed in Gillian Tindall's *The House by the Thames* (Chatto & Windus, 2006). (See also Richmond.)

TOWER HAMLETS

Lying directly east of the City, the London
Borough of Tower Hamlets is the inner London
core of the East End, an amalgamation of three
former Metropolitan Boroughs, Bethnal Green,
Stepney and Poplar.

ANNESLEY, Susanna (1669–1742), English, mother
7 Spital Yard, E1. *Corporation of the City of London*
Annesley was born in this house. She was the twenty-
fifth child in her family and gave birth to eighteen
herself, from her marriage to Samuel Wesley in 1690.
Her fifteenth child was John Wesley (q.v.) and her
eighteenth was Charles Wesley (q.v.).

ASHBEE, C. R.
(1863–1942), English,
architect, designer
**Onyx House, 401
Mile End Road, E3.**
*London Borough of Tower
Hamlets*
In 1891 Ashbee founded
the Guild of Handicraft
in Essex House, which
formerly stood on this site, and was its director for
twenty years. Heavily influenced by Morris (q.v.) and
Ruskin (q.v.), Ashbee was a remarkable all-rounder,
specialising in church restoration, but also an
accomplished silversmith and furniture designer. He
founded the Guild as a co-operative while a resident at
Toynbee Hall. He also founded the *Survey of London*.

BARNARDO, Dr Thomas (1845–1905), Irish,
social worker
30 Coborn Street, Bow, E3. *Historic Buildings of Bow*
Solent House, Ben Jonson Road, Stepney, E1.
London County Council
Barnardo lodged in Coborn Street on first coming to
London and began his work with children in 1866 in a
building formerly at the second address. Though
always styled 'Doctor', he was not medically qualified.
Converted in 1862, Barnardo evangelised in Dublin
slums before coming to London. His first home for
boys was opened in Stepney in 1870, with the large
motto on the frontage: 'NO DESTITUTE CHILD
EVER REFUSED ADMISSION'. It multiplied into a
string of refuges and by his death he had helped
250,000 children.

BERG, Jack 'Kid'
(1909–91), English,
boxer
**Noble Court, Cable
Street, Stepney, E1.**
Stepney Historical Trust
Berg was born Judah
Bergman in a house near
this spot. Known as the
'Whitechapel Windmill', he was
World Junior Welterweight Champion in 1930 and
British Lightweight Champion in 1934. In a career
lasting twenty-one years, he had 192 fights, 157 wins,
twenty-six defeats and nine draws. He was almost
equally famous for his colourful life outside the ring,
said to have included an affair with Mae West.

BETHNAL GREEN TUBE DISASTER
**Corner of Cambridge Heath Road and Roman
Road, E2.** *London Borough of Tower Hamlets*
This is the site of the worst civilian disaster of the
Second World War. On the evening of Wednesday
3 March 1943, 173 men, women and children lost
their lives descending into the Bethnal Green tube
station air-raid shelter. It is thought that the firing of a

nearby anti-aircraft battery, using a new type of rocket making an unfamiliar sound, caused the panic, and the tragedy happened in less than a minute on steps made slippery by rain.

BILLIG, Dr Hannah (1901–87), English, physician
198 Cable Street, Stepney, E1.
Borough of Tower Hamlets
Dr Billig, known locally as 'the Angel of Cable Street', lived and worked here from 1935 to 1964. The daughter of Russian refugee Jews, she achieved a notable local reputation for never turning patients away. She was awarded the George Medal in 1941 after a heroic night's work during the Blitz, despite having a broken ankle. After the war she did famine relief work in India and finally retired to Israel.

BLIGH, Captain William (1754–1817), English, naval officer
Reardon Street, Wapping, E1.
History of Wapping Trust
Bligh lived in a house on this site from 1785 to 1790. It was while resident here that he was the victim of the famous mutiny on HMS *Bounty*. The plaque records that he transported breadfruit from Tahiti to the West Indies, intended to be the staple diet of slaves on the plantations there. (See also Lambeth.)

BOROUGH, Stephen (1525–84), English, navigator
King Edward Memorial Park, Shadwell, E1.
London County Council
The plaque commemorates several navigators who set sail from this reach of the Thames in the second half of the sixteenth century to explore northern waters. In

1553 Borough commanded the *Edward Bonadventure*, the only ship of three to make it to Russia by the north-east passage and the only ship to return from the expedition. In 1556 he discovered the entrance to the Kara Sea, and he was chief pilot and one of the masters of the queen's ships in the Medway (1563–84).

BOROUGH, William (1536–99), English, navigator
King Edward Memorial Park, Shadwell, E1.
London County Council
Younger brother of Stephen Borough (see above), he sailed to Russia as an ordinary seaman on three expeditions in 1553, 1556 and 1557. Subsequently he rose to be Comptroller of the Queen's Navy, was vice-admiral with Drake on the 'Singeing of the King of Spain's Beard' raid at Cadiz (1587) and commanded a ship against the Armada (1588).

BRUNEL, Isambard Kingdom (1806–59), English, engineer
262 West Ferry Road, E14. *London County Council*
The plaque commemorates the launch here in 1858 of the *Great Eastern* (see page 219), the largest ship ever built at the time, and Brunel's last major design. (See also Southwark and Kensington & Chelsea 2.)

BUXTON, Sir Thomas Fowell (1786–1845), English, anti-slavery campaigner
Old Truman Brewery, Brick Lane, E1.
English Heritage
As a partner in the brewery from 1811, and later as sole owner, Buxton lived and worked here. He was involved in numerous campaigns: in support of the destitute weavers of Spitalfields, with Elizabeth Fry (q.v.) on prison reform, and against the death penalty, where he succeeded in reducing the number of capital offences from over two hundred to eight. But his major effort was the anti-slavery battle; he was a co-founder with Zachary Macaulay (q.v.) and others of the Anti-Slavery Society in 1823, and, when Wilberforce (q.v.) retired in 1825, he took over the campaign in Parliament, eventually succeeding in abolishing slavery in the British Empire in 1833.

CAVELL, Edith (1865–1915), English, nurse
London Hospital, Whitechapel Road, E1.
English Heritage
Cavell trained and worked here from 1896 to 1901. For helping hundreds of British soldiers to escape

German-occupied Belgium, she was arrested and executed by the Germans on 12 October 1915. The Allies gained a major propaganda weapon, and Cavell was raised to mythic status. Her monument, by Sir George Frampton (q.v.), is in St Martin's Place. (See also Hackney.)

COBORN, Charles (1852–1945), English, music-hall singer
Coborn Street, Bow, E3. *Bow Heritage*
Charles Whitton McCallum lived in this street as a boy and took its name when he trod the boards. His biggest hits were 'Two Lovely Black Eyes' (1886) and 'The Man Who Broke the Bank at Monte Carlo' (1890). He claimed to have sung the latter 250,000 times.

COLE, King (d. 1868), Australian Aboriginal, cricketer
Meath Gardens, Mile End, E2. *Private*
Cole was given this name because the English could not get their tongues round his Aboriginal name of Bripumyarrimin. He was a member of the first Australian cricket party to tour England in 1868. They were all Aboriginals, exciting curiosity for their wiry hair, and admiration for their athletic skills. Cole died of tuberculosis during the tour, eleven days after playing at Lord's, and was buried in a pauper's grave here. A eucalyptus tree shades the plaque.

COOK, Captain James (1728–79), English, explorer
88 Mile End Road, E1. *Greater London Council*
326 The Highway, Stepney, E1.
Stepney Historical Trust
Cook lived in houses at both sites. He surveyed the St Lawrence river (1759) and, in three voyages from 1768 on, charted the coasts of New Zealand and eastern Australia, as well as wide areas of the Pacific, hitherto unexplored. He was killed by natives on the island of Hawaii.

EDWARDS, John Passmore (1823–1911), English, philanthropist, journalist
Vernon Hall, Roman Road, Bow, E3.
Borough of Tower Hamlets
The plaque records that Edwards contributed two-thirds of the cost of erecting this building, formerly Bow Library. As a journalist, he worked for progressive causes from the Anti-Corn Law movement onwards. He founded some seventy free libraries, hospitals and convalescent homes in Britain, an art gallery in Newlyn and University Hall in Clare Market. He declined a knighthood.
(See also Camden 1.)

FLANAGAN, Bud (1896–1968), English, comedian
12 Hanbury Street, Shoreditch, E1.
English Heritage
Flanagan, stage-name of Chaim Reuben Weintrop, was born here. Partnered through most of his career by Chesney Allen, he led the 'Crazy Gang' for over thirty years. He is known to today's audiences for singing 'Who Do You Think You Are Kidding, Mister Hitler', the theme song to the television series *Dad's Army*.

FLYING BOMB, First
Railway Bridge, Grove Road, Bow, E3.
English Heritage
The first flying bomb to fall on London landed here at 4.25 a.m. on 13 June 1944. This was the beginning of the second Blitz, with the Vergeltungswaffen, the 'Vengeance Weapons'. The V1 'Doodlebugs', which announced themselves by chugging along at low

altitude until the fuel expired, and the V2 rockets, which arrived straight down and unannounced, killed 8,938 civilians in London and the south-east. (See also City, Kingston, Newham and Lewisham.)

FROBISHER, Sir Martin (?1535–94), English, navigator
King Edward Memorial Park, Shadwell, E1.
London County Council
The plaque honours several navigators who set off from this reach of the Thames in the second half of the sixteenth century to explore the northern seas. Frobisher made three voyages in search of a North-West Passage and was vice-admiral in Drake's expedition to the West Indies of 1586. He commanded the *Triumph* at the head of one of the four English squadrons in the battle against the Spanish Armada in 1588 and was knighted for his services.

GANDHI, Mahatma (1869–1948), Indian, lawyer, spiritual leader
Kingsley Hall, Powis Road, Bow, E3.
London County Council
Gandhi stayed here in 1931. His policy of *satyagraha* (non-violent civil disobedience) so got under the skin of the British Raj that he was invited to London for a round table conference in 1931, which was fruitless from his point of view. Shortly after Indian independence he was assassinated by a Hindu fanatic. (See also Hammersmith & Fulham.)

GARRETT ANDERSON, Elizabeth (1836–1917), English, physician
London Guildhall University, Commercial Road, E1. *London Borough of Tower Hamlets*
Dr Garrett Anderson was born in a house formerly on this site. After being refused entry by various medical schools, the Society of Apothecaries finally allowed her to obtain their licence in 1865 and she became the first woman doctor. She was senior physician at the New London Hospital for Women (renamed in her honour after her death) from 1866 to 1892. The plaque wrongly has her dying in 1919. (See also Westminster 3.)

GARTHWAITE, Anna Maria (1690–1763), English, designer
2 Princelet Street, Spitalfields, E1. *English Heritage*
Garthwaite lived and worked here. She was 'the pre-eminent silk designer of her period'. Moving here in 1728, she created over a thousand designs, mostly vivid floral patterns. 874 original drawings by her, with detailed instructions to the weavers, are preserved in the Victoria and Albert Museum.

GERTLER, Mark (1891–1939), English, painter
32 Elder Street, Shoreditch, E1.
Greater London Council
Son of Polish-Jewish immigrants, Gertler, who lived here as a child, had considerable personal magnetism and fell in with the Bloomsbury Group (q.v.), where he conceived a doomed passion for Dora Carrington. His masterpiece, *The Merry-go-round* (1914), reflected his pacifism and melancholia. (See also Camden 1.)

GREAT EASTERN, SS
262 West Ferry Road, E14. *London County Council*
Launched here in 1858, the *Great Eastern* was the largest ship yet built, designed by I. K. Brunel (see page 217) and J. Scott Russell (see page 221) to carry four thousand passengers round the world without needing to refuel. The ship's only worthwhile period of work was from 1865 to 1878, when she was converted for cable-laying. She was broken up for scrap on Merseyside in 1889–90 and her topmast is now a flagpole at Anfield, the home of Liverpool Football Club.

GREEN, John Richard (1837–83), English, cleric, historian
St Philip's Vicarage, Newark Street, E1.
London County Council
Green lived here as the incumbent of St Philip's (1866–9). In the cholera epidemic that swept the East End in 1866 he worked heroically, himself carrying corpses away for burial. But his service in the East End broke his health and he was translated to the quiet of Lambeth Palace Library, where he was able to work on his hugely popular *Short History of the English People* (1874), which marked a new epoch in the writing of history because of its attention to the social and economic story of ordinary people. (See also Westminster 2.)

GROSER, Reverend St John (1890–1966), English, cleric
2 Butcher Row, Limehouse, E14. *English Heritage*
Groser lived here. The Royal Foundation of St Katharine dates from 1147 and moved here in 1948 under Groser's leadership. He was a leading member of various radical Christian socialist movements and saw the church's role as active and interventionist.

HUGHES, Mary (1860–1941), English, social worker
71 Vallance Road, Bethnal Green, E2.
London County Council
Hughes lived and worked here from 1926 until her death. The plaque calls her 'a friend to all in need'; she called herself a Christian communist pacifist. Moving into this former pub, she renamed it the 'Dew Drop Inn', and it became a social centre and refuge for local homeless people. As a justice of the peace, she regularly wept at the evidence and paid fines for the poor.

JEWISH BOARD OF GUARDIANS
Astral House, 129 Middlesex Street, E1. *Private*
The Jewish Board of Guardians was set up in 1859 to care for a growing Jewish population, many of whom were desperately poor. The Guardians occupied these premises from 1896 to 1956.

LANSBURY, George (1859–1940), English, politician
39 Bow Road, Bow, E3. *Bow Heritage*
Lansbury lived for twenty-three years in a house formerly on this site. Rooted in local politics, he was Mayor of Bow and a local councillor from 1903 until his death. At the same time he rose to be leader of the national Labour Party (1932–5), but was obliged to resign as his Christian pacifism was increasingly at odds with cross-party calls for rearmament in the face of Nazism.

MALLON, Dr Jimmy (1874–1961), English, reformer, social worker
Toynbee Hall, Commercial Street, Whitechapel, E1. *Greater London Council*
Dr Mallon lived here. As Warden of Toynbee Hall (1919–54), he saw the place develop from its high-minded Christian Victorian origins into a modern focal point of social work in the local multi-ethnic community. A legend in the East End, he was made a Companion of Honour in 1939.

MATCH GIRLS' STRIKE
Fairfield Road, Bow, E3. *Historic Buildings of Bow*
On this site, now redeveloped as flats, Bryant & May manufactured matches from 1861 to 1979. In 1888, organised and galvanised by Annie Besant (q.v.), the seven hundred women and girls who worked here went on strike against the harsh and dangerous conditions of match-making, in particular 'phossy jaw', a ghastly illness caused by working with yellow phosphorus. The owners caved in after three weeks.

MATCH TAX ABANDONMENT
149–151 Bow Road, Bow, E3. *Bow Council*
In 1871 the Chancellor of the Exchequer, Sir Robert Lowe, proposed to introduce a tax on matches, and his department even prepared the tax stamps with the Latin motto *Ex luce lucellum* ('From light a small gain'). As happens with politicians, he was surprised to find his proposal was universally unpopular, and the idea was rapidly withdrawn. This plaque commemorates the celebratory fountain that was erected here by Bryant & May, which was removed in 1954.

McLAGLEN, Victor
(1886–1959), English,
actor
**505 Commercial
Road, E1.** *Private*
McLaglen was born here.
After being heavyweight
boxing champion of the
British Army in 1918, he moved
to Hollywood, where he became a regular in John
Ford movies, and won the best actor Oscar in 1935 for
his role in *The Informer*.

MENDOZA, Daniel (1764–1836), English, boxer
3 Paradise Row, Bethnal Green, E2.
Tower Hamlets Environment Trust
Mendoza, who proudly billed himself as 'Mendoza the
Jew', is often called 'the Father of Scientific Boxing'.
He published *The Art of Boxing* in 1789, while living
here, and was English champion (1792–5). His career
after the ring was erratic; intelligent, charming but
disorganised, he died leaving his family in poverty.

(Plaque: HISTORIC BUILDINGS OF BOW — 45 NORMAN GROVE — E. SYLVIA PANKHURST (1882–1960) — SET UP THE EAST LONDON TOY FACTORY AND BABIES' NURSERY IN THIS HOUSE AND THE BUILDING IN THE REAR GARDEN 1914–1934 — THE FACTORY WAS FINANCED BY NORAH LYLE-SMYTH (1874–1963))

MOSES, Miriam
(1886–1965), English,
social reformer
**17 Princelet Street,
Spitalfields, E1.**
Private
Moses was born here.
A lifelong campaigner
against poverty, slums and
racial prejudice, she was a
founder member of the League of Jewish Women, and
a member of the Board of Deputies. She also founded
the Brady Girls' Club in 1927. She was not only
Stepney's first woman mayor in 1931–2, but also the
borough's first Jewish mayor.

MURDER ON A TRAIN, First
**Top o' the Morning pub, 129 Cadogan Terrace,
E9.** *London Borough of Tower Hamlets*
The plaque memorialises Thomas Briggs of Clapton,
who, on Saturday 9 July 1864, was assaulted on a
North London train near here. He was carried, near to
death, to this public house and died later that day at
home. Franz Muller, a German tailor, was arrested in
New York for the crime and his subsequent public
hanging was attended by scenes of drunkenness and
disorderly conduct.

PANKHURST,
Sylvia (1882–1960),
English, suffragette
**45 Norman Grove,
E3.**
Historic Buildings of Bow
**91–94 Tait Court,
Old Ford Road, E2.**
Bow Heritage Trail
At the first address
Pankhurst set up the East London Toy Factory and
Babies' Nursery (1914–34). On the second site
formerly stood the Gunmakers' Arms, a public house
taken over by Sylvia Pankhurst and her suffragette
associates in 1915, renamed 'the Mothers' Arms', and
used as a day nursery. (See also Kensington & Chelsea
2 and Redbridge.)

PERKIN, Sir William Henry (1838–1907),
English, chemist
Gosling House, Cable Street, Stepney, E1.
Stepney Historical Trust
Sir William had a home laboratory in the back garden
of the family home on this site. He was only eighteen
when he discovered and patented mauveine.
Previously dyes had been expensive extracts from
plants, especially Tyrian purple, traditionally the
colour of wealth and status. He went on to discover
Britannia Violet and Perkin's Green. (See also Ealing.)

ROSENBERG, Isaac (1890–1918), English, poet,
painter
Whitechapel Library, 77 High Street, E1.
English Heritage
Rosenberg lived nearby and studied here. He trained at
the Slade School of Art but is remembered for his
poetry. He enlisted in 1915 and was killed on 1 April
1918 on the Somme. His poem 'Break of Day in the
Trenches', addressed to a passing rat, has been called
the 'greatest poem of the war'.

RUSSELL, John Scott (1808–82), Scottish, naval
architect
262 West Ferry Road, E14. *London County Council*
Russell was the leading naval architect of the day,
co-designing with I. K. Brunel (see page 217) the
Great Eastern, which was launched at this site in 1858.
He was a royal commissioner for the Great Exhibition
of 1851 and is remembered for his development of the
wave-line system of ship construction.

SALVATION ARMY
23 New Road, Stepney, E1.
Tower Hamlets Environment Trust
The first indoor meeting of the Salvation Army was held here on 3 September 1865. Begun as the Christian Mission, the name was changed in 1878. William Booth (q.v.), the founder, described their work as 'the three S's; first, soup; second, soap; and finally, salvation'. The Army is now operating in 111 countries, tambourines at the ready.

SHEFFIELD, Edmond, Lord (1564–1646), English, soldier, sailor
215–217 Bow Road, Bow, E3.
Historic Buildings of Bow
Sheffield lived in a house formerly on this site. He commanded the *White Bear*, one of the two biggest vessels in the British fleet, in the battle against the Spanish Armada in 1588 and was awarded the Garter by a grateful Elizabeth I. Later, as President of the North under James I, he was 'open handed to feed the poore and cloath the naked'.

SHINWELL, Manny (1884–1986), English, politician
Brune House, Toynbee Street, E1.
Tower Hamlets Environment Trust
Shinwell was born in a house formerly on this site. After a trade union career on 'red Clydeside', he was in and out of Parliament in the 1920s and 1930s, held various posts in Attlee's (q.v.) post-war government, and finally chaired the Parliamentary Labour Party (1964–7). He was the oldest ever member of Parliament.

WAINWRIGHT, Lincoln Stanhope (1847–1929), English, cleric
Clergy House, Wapping Lane, Wapping, E1.
London County Council
Wainwright, as vicar of St Peter's, London Docks, lived here from 1884 until his death. He arrived in the parish as curate in 1873 and stayed fifty-five years, giving his all to the parishioners. On the fiftieth anniversary of his arrival, the bishop of London noted he had not had a holiday in forty-seven years and

hoped he would spend at least some of the £1,000 that had been collected on himself.

WILLOUGHBY, Sir Hugh (d.1554), English, navigator
King Edward Memorial Park, Shadwell, E1.
London County Council

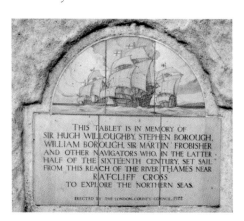

THIS TABLET IS IN MEMORY OF SIR HUGH WILLOUGHBY, STEPHEN BOROUGH, WILLIAM BOROUGH, SIR MARTIN FROBISHER AND OTHER NAVIGATORS WHO IN THE LATTER HALF OF THE SIXTEENTH CENTURY, SET SAIL FROM THIS REACH OF THE RIVER THAMES NEAR RATCLIFF CROSS TO EXPLORE THE NORTHERN SEAS.
ERECTED BY THE LONDON COUNTY COUNCIL 1922

Willoughby is one of the mariners who set off from this reach of the Thames in the second half of the sixteenth century to explore northern waters. In 1553 he was dispatched by Sebastian Cabot to search for a north-eastern passage to Cathay and India. A year later he and his crew were found frozen to death on the coast of Norwegian Lapland.

ZANGWILL, Israel (1864–1926), English, novelist, playwright, philanthropist
288 Old Ford Road, Bethnal Green, E2.
London County Council
His novel *Children of the Ghetto* (1892) brought him fame, his play *The Melting Pot* (1908) was praised by Theodore Roosevelt, and his *The Big Bow Mystery* (1891) was the first 'locked room' murder mystery. He campaigned for Zionism, for women's suffrage and for pacifism.

WANDSWORTH

An inner borough of south-west London,
the London Borough of Wandsworth is an
amalgamation of the former Metropolitan
Borough of Battersea with most of the former
Metropolitan Borough of Wandsworth,
excluding Streatham and Clapham.

BATEMAN, H. M. (1887–1970), Australian,
cartoonist
40 Nightingale Lane, SW12. *English Heritage*
Bateman, who lived here from 1910 to 1914, is most
famous for his 'The Man Who…' series of cartoons,
which made him, in the 1920s and 1930s, the highest-
paid and most-copied cartoonist of the day. G. K.
Chesterton (q.v.) called him 'the Master of Wild
Exactitude'.

BENES, Dr Edvard
(1884–1948), Czech,
statesman
**26 Gwendolen
Avenue, Putney,
SW15.**
Greater London Council
Dr Benes lived here
from 1938 to the end of
the Second World War.
In the First World War
he was a leader of the
Czech independence
movement, and between the wars he was successively
Czech foreign minister, prime minister and president.
Leader of the government in exile during the Second
World War, he returned home to be president again,
resigning at the communist coup in 1948.

BURNS, John (1858–1943), English, politician
110 North Side, Clapham Common, SW4.
London County Council
Burns, who lived here, rose to prominence as one of
the leaders of the London dock strike of 1889, entered

Parliament in 1892, and in 1906 became only the
second working-class cabinet minister. 'I am not
ashamed to say that I am the son of a washerwoman,'
he said.

DOUGLAS, Norman (1868–1952), Scottish,
novelist, essayist
**63 Albany Mansions, Albert Bridge Road,
SW11.** *Greater London Council*
Douglas, who lived here, spent most of his life from
1896 onwards in Capri, which he thinly disguised as
'Nepenthe' in his most famous novel, *South Wind*
(1917). He is also remembered for excellent travel
books, including *Fountains in the Sand* (1912) and
Old Calabria (1915).

ELEN, Gus (1862–1940), English, music-hall
comedian
3 Thurleigh Avenue, Balham, SW12.
Greater London Council
Elen lived here the last six years of his life. His stage
persona was a cockney costermonger, and his biggest

hit had the refrain: 'Wiv a ladder and some glasses you could see to 'Ackney Marshes if it wasn't for the 'ouses in between.' A friendly rival of Albert Chevalier (q.v.), he retired in 1914 and went fishing.

ELIOT, George
(1819–80), English, novelist
Holly Lodge, 31 Wimbledon Park Road, SW18.
London County Council
George Eliot moved here in February 1859 with her lover, the writer George Henry Lewes. While here, her real identity was discovered and her relationship with the married Lewes caused a scandal. She managed to write *The Mill on the Floss*, but they soon tired of the area and the gossip and moved to Regent's Park in September 1859. (See also Kensington & Chelsea 2.)

HARDY, Thomas
(1840–1928), English, novelist, poet
172 Trinity Road, SW17.
London County Council
Hardy lived here from 1878 to 1881. His Dorset upbringing provided the background to his novels, of which he wrote *The Return of the Native* (1878) while living here. After his last novel, *Jude the Obscure* (1895), he gave himself over wholly to poetry. (See also Westminster 2 and Westminster 4.)

HARTLEY, David (1732–1813), English, inventor, politician
Tibbet's Corner, Putney Heath, SW15.
City of London
In 1776 Hartley built a house on this spot and conducted experiments with 'fire plates' to prevent fire spreading upwards. On one occasion the king and queen took breakfast on the first floor, undisturbed by a fire raging on the ground floor. The experiment impressed the king, the mayor, aldermen and MPs,

and Hartley was granted £2,500 for his costs and given the Freedom of the City. He was a regular correspondent with Benjamin Franklin (q.v.) and together they drew up the treaty of 1783 between the United States and the United Kingdom.

HENTY, G. A. (1832–1902), English, novelist, journalist
33 Lavender Gardens, Battersea, SW11.
London County Council
Henty lived here. His letters home from the Crimea were published and led to a career as a war correspondent in Abyssinia, India and Paris during the Commune. At the same time his prolific stream of historical adventure stories for boys, with titles such as *Under Drake's Flag, A Tale of the Spanish Main* and *At Agincourt, A Tale of the White Hoods of Paris*, was hugely successful.

HOPKINS, Gerard Manley (1844–89), English, poet
Manresa House, Holybourne Avenue, SW15.
Greater London Council
Hopkins lived and studied at Manresa House. He was ordained a Catholic priest in 1877. Virtually none of

his writings was published in his lifetime, but his friend Robert Bridges brought out a collected edition in 1918, and his reputation has continued to grow. 'Inscape', 'instress' and 'sprung rhythm' are poetic concepts he introduced, which provoke academic debate to this day. (See also Camden 1 and Newham.)

JAGGER, Charles Sargeant (1885–1934), English, sculptor
67 Albert Bridge Road, SW11. *English Heritage*
Jagger, who lived and died here, served at Gallipoli and in Flanders in the First World War, was wounded twice and awarded the Military Cross in 1918. His personal experience of the war informs his famous memorials, notably the Artillery Memorial at Hyde Park Corner and the Great Western Railway Memorial at Paddington.

KNEE, Fred (1868–1914), English, politician, reformer
24 Sugden Road, Battersea, SW11.
Greater London Council
Knee, who lived here from 1898 to 1901, was the founder in 1898 of the Workmen's Housing Council, a pressure group for better housing. Later, as chair of the housing committee of the borough of Battersea, he instituted major construction, employing direct labour. The Latchmere Estate of 1903, described as 'exemplary' by Pevsner (q.v.), was the first to be built by a London borough.

LAUDER, Sir Harry
(1870–1950), Scottish, music-hall singer
46 Longley Road, Tooting, SW17.
Greater London Council
Sir Harry lived here from 1903 to 1911.
He was the first singer to sell over a million records. His songs, mostly written by himself, include 'Roamin'

in the Gloamin", 'I Love a Lassie', 'I Belong to Glasgow' and 'Keep Right on to the End of the Road', this last a memorial to his only son, killed in France in 1916.

LEWIS, Ted 'Kid' (1893–1970), English, boxing champion
Nightingale House, 105 Nightingale Lane, SW12. *English Heritage*
Lewis, who lived and died here, was born Gershon Mendeloff in Aldgate. He boxed professionally at various weights from 1909 to 1929, and between 1915 and 1921 the world welterweight title switched back and forth between him and the American Jack Britton. He was called the 'smashing, bashing, crashing, dashing kid'.

LLOYD GEORGE, David (1863–1945), Welsh, Prime Minister
Lloyd George Mansions, 191 Trinity Road, SW18. *Private*
3 Routh Road, SW18. *English Heritage*
Lloyd George lived at the first address from 1900 to 1904 and then moved round the corner to the second until he became Chancellor of the Exchequer in 1908. He was Chancellor (1908–15) and Prime Minister (1916–22). During this time the Liberal government introduced old-age pensions, health and unemployment benefits, and medical examinations for schoolchildren. Lloyd George played a major role in the Versailles Peace Conference after the First World War. He famously liked women.

O'CASEY, Sean (1880–1964), Irish, playwright
49 Overstrand Mansions, Prince of Wales Drive, SW11. *English Heritage*
O'Casey lived here at Flat 49. His great plays were his first three, for the Abbey Theatre in Dublin: *Shadow of a Gunman* (1923), *Juno and the Paycock* (1924) and *The Plough and the Stars* (1926). After a mixed reception for the last, he moved to London and was not the same again.

SAUNDERS, Sir Edwin (1814–1901), dentist
89 Wimbledon Parkside, SW19.
English Heritage
Sir Edwin lived and died here. Appointed Royal

Surgeon-Dentist in 1846, he treated Queen Victoria, Prince Albert and the Prince and Princess of Wales. He lectured at St Thomas's Hospital (1837–54) and was the first dentist to be knighted, in 1883.

SPURGEON, C. H. (1834–92), English, preacher **99 Nightingale Lane, Balham, SW12.** *London County Council* Spurgeon, who lived here, was a Reformed Baptist minister whose powerful oratory earned him the title 'the Prince of Preachers'. He appealed across denominations and by the mid-1850s, in his mid-twenties, he was the most popular preacher in London, routinely speaking to audiences of ten thousand people.

SURREY IRON RAILWAY
Wall of Ram Brewery, Ram Street, SW18.
Wandsworth Society
The plaque records that the Surrey Iron Railway, which ran from Croydon to the mouth of the Wandle, was the first public railway in Britain, and probably the world. Goods wagons were drawn by horses on rails with a gauge of 4 feet 2 inches. It opened in 1803 and closed in 1846 with the arrival of steam. (See also Croydon.)

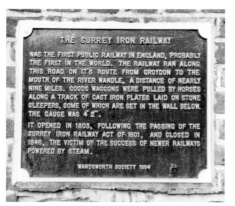

SWINBURNE, Algernon Charles (1834–92), English, poet
11 Putney Hill, SW15. *London County Council*
Swinburne was an alcoholic and enjoyed masochistic pleasures. In 1879 he had a mental and physical breakdown, brought on by these excesses, and was taken under the wing of his friend Theodore Watts-Dunton (see page 227), who looked after him here for the rest of his life. Having been a beacon of flamboyance and recklessness, he became almost respectable, a shadow of the man once touted as Tennyson's successor. (See also Merton and Kensington & Chelsea 2.)

THOMAS, Edward (1878–1917), English, poet, essayist
61 Shelgate Road, Battersea, SW11.
London County Council
Thomas lived here. After a career in journalism, he turned to poetry only when encouraged by his friend Robert Frost. He enlisted in 1915 and is thought of as one of the war poets, though his poetry is mainly about the English countryside. He was killed at Arras in 1917.

WALTER, John (1739–1812), English, merchant, newspaper owner
113 Clapham Common North Side, SW4.
Greater London Council
Walter, who lived here, was a coal merchant who played a leading part in founding the Coal Exchange but failed as a Lloyd's underwriter. In 1785 he founded *The Daily Universal Register*, a scandal sheet, which on 1 January 1788 changed its name to *The Times*.

WANDSWORTH, Lord (1845–1912), English, banker, philanthropist
Nightingale House, Nightingale Lane, Balham, SW12. *Private*
Lord Wandsworth lived here and bequeathed the house and grounds to be a home for the aged poor of the Jewish faith in memory of his father, David, Viscount de Stern, and his mother, Sophia. He took over the banking firm of Stern Brothers from his father and was involved in multiple charity work. He was unmarried, and his estate of £1.5 million was given to charity, including the foundation of Lord Wandsworth College in Hampshire.

WATTS-DUNTON, Theodore (1832–1914), poet, novelist, critic
11 Putney Hill, SW15. *London County Council*
Watts-Dunton was a figure on the London literary scene, writing prolifically in *The Athenaeum*. His poetry and novels are now quite forgotten and he is remembered as the man who looked after his alcoholic friend Algernon Charles Swinburne (see page 227) in this house for the last thirty years of his life.

WILBERFORCE, William (1759–1833), English, anti-slavery campaigner
111 Broomwood Road, SW11.
London County Council
Wilberforce lived in Broomwood House on this site from 1797 to 1807 during the campaign which climaxed in his first victory, the abolition of the slave trade in 1807. The abolition of slavery itself would take another twenty-six years of struggle. (See also Hillingdon, Kensington & Chelsea 2, Barnet, Lambeth and Merton.)

WILSON, Edward Adrian (1872–1912), English, physician, explorer, naturalist
St Mary's House, 42 Vicarage Crescent, SW11.
London County Council
Wilson, who lived here, went to the Antarctic twice with Scott (q.v.). On the second expedition (1910–12), he was one of the five-man party who reached the South Pole but perished on the return journey to base camp. Scott said he was 'the finest character I ever met'.

THE OUTER
LONDON
BOROUGHS

ONE OF THE most ancient counties of England, Middlesex formerly girdled the City of London north of the Thames from Poplar in the east, through Tottenham to the north and round to Hounslow in the west. London's grab of its territory began in 1888, when whole swathes of what is now called Inner London, including Westminster, were seized, and the process was completed in 1965 with the wholesale extinction of the rest of Middlesex, and the creation of huge new boroughs such as Hillingdon and Brent. While Greater London has also taken bites out of Essex, Kent and Surrey, and even nibbled at Hertfordshire, it has (for the moment at least) still left those counties with their flags flying, whereas poor Middlesex is a ghost. It survives, confusingly, as a postal address, as a university and as a cricket team.

Not surprisingly, plaques are comparatively thin on the ground in outer London; the great and the good have not tended to move to Romford or Hayes. In total the outer boroughs contribute some 350 plaques to the ensemble, rather less than Westminster alone. Some of them muster only a literal handful of entries here, Brent and Barking & Dagenham sharing the wooden spoon with only three entries each. In both boroughs there are pressures to get a plaque programme going but, municipal budgets being tight, this is one of those optional extras that tends to get cut. Barnet, Croydon, Enfield and Waltham Forest have had vigorous bouts of plaque erection in the past, but at the time of writing these schemes are all in abeyance.

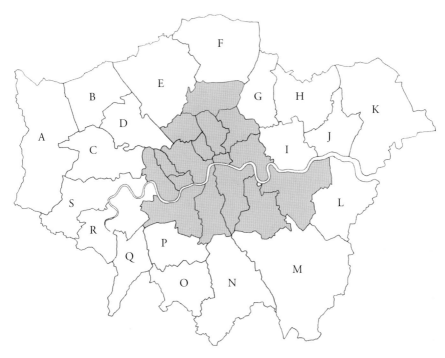

A   Hillingdon
B   Harrow
C   Ealing
D   Brent
E   Barnet
F   Enfield
G   Walham Forest
H   Redbridge
I   Newham
J   Barking & Dagenham
K   Havering
L   Bexley
M   Bromley
N   Croydon
O   Sutton
P   Merton
Q   Kingston upon Thames
R   Richmond upon Thames
S   Hounslow

BARKING & DAGENHAM

Lying in the north-east of Greater London,
once wholly in Essex, the London Borough of
Barking & Dagenham is an amalgamation of
almost all of the former Municipal Borough of
Barking (losing a bit to Newham) and almost all
of the former Municipal Borough of Dagenham
(losing a bit to Redbridge).

BECONTREE ESTATE
22–28 Chitty's Lane, Dagenham.
London County Council
The Becontree Estate was part of the post-First World
War building programme called 'Homes for Heroes'.
This was a national plan to reward returning veterans,
and this estate was the largest municipal housing
undertaking in Europe. The target was to build 29,000
dwellings to accommodate 145,000 people. The plan
also sought to encourage good citizenship and
neighbourliness, with, for example, an emphasis
placed on gardening, with the London County Council
awarding annual prizes for the best-kept gardens.

GEORGE V (1865–1936), English, royalty
20 Bushgrove Road, Dagenham. *Private*
George V and Queen Mary took tea here in June 1923
during a visit to see the Becontree Estate (see above).
He reigned from 1910 to 1936 and had the affection of
the general public for what was seen as his
conscientiousness and adherence to duty. As a family
man, he seems to have treated his children as if they
were junior ranks in the Navy, propriety and
correctness preventing any lapses into normal human
larking about.

MARY, Queen (1867–1953), English, royalty
20 Bushgrove Road, Dagenham. *Private*
Born in England as Princess Mary of Teck (a German
principality), she was clearly destined to marry into
the British royal family. She was first engaged to the
heir to the throne, Prince Albert, and when he died
young she became engaged, after a suitable interval, to
his younger brother George. Known to the public for
exemplifying rectitude on all occasions, she was
appalled at the behaviour of her son Edward VIII (later
the Duke of Windsor) and supported his brother when
he had to step in and take the throne as George VI.

THEIR MAJESTIES
KING GEORGE V & QUEEN MARY
WHEN VISITING BECONTREE
ON TUESDAY 12TH JUNE 1923
TOOK TEA IN THIS COTTAGE & PLANTED
TWO TREES ON THE ADJACENT GREEN.

BARNET

Lying at the north-west border of Greater London, incorporating substantial slices of Hertfordshire and Middlesex, the London Borough of Barnet is formed from two former municipal boroughs, Finchley and Hendon, plus three urban districts, Barnet, Friern Barnet and East Barnet.

ABRAHAMS, Harold (1899–1978), English, athlete
Hodford Lodge, 2 Hodford Road, NW11.
English Heritage
Abrahams lived here from 1923 to 1930, during which time he was the winner of the 100 metres race at the Paris Olympic Games of 1924, having done the rather un-British thing of hiring a professional coach, Sam Mussabini. His career was ended by a broken leg in 1925, and he went on to be a sports journalist and chairman of the Amateur Athletics Association. He was famously portrayed by Ben Cross in the 1981 Oscar-winning film *Chariots of Fire*, in which his memorial service was the framing device at the beginning and end of the film.

ACRES, Birt (1854–1918), American, film pioneer
19 Park Road, Barnet. *British Film Institute*
An American inventor and pioneer cameraman, he filmed the first British moving picture here in February 1895. He had come to Barnet in 1892 and worked as a manager for a local firm producing photographic plates, before setting up his own business. His film, *Incident at Clovelly Cottage*, unfortunately no longer exists.

ARUP, Sir Ove (1895–1988), Anglo-Danish, engineer
28 Willifield Way, NW11. *London Borough of Barnet*
Arup lived here from 1932 to 1939. He was the foremost architectural consulting engineer of the twentieth century, involved with the Penguin Pool at London Zoo, Highpoint in Highgate, Coventry Cathedral, Sydney Opera House and the Kingsgate Bridge in Durham, from which his ashes were scattered after his death.

BECK, Harry (1903–74), English, graphic designer
60 Court House Gardens, N3.
Finchley Society
Finchley Central Station, N3.
London Transport
Beck was an engineering draughtsman who created the original iconic London Underground map in his spare time. His key innovation was ignoring the actual distance between stations in favour of a clear schematic diagram that showed connections. He lived in Court House Gardens (1936–70) and commuted by tube from Finchley Central to work at London Transport headquarters. The station plaque is situated on the southbound platform alongside copies of his original 1933 design and its current updated version. Beck's tube map has been voted the second greatest British design of the twentieth century, after Concorde.

CASTLE TOLLGATE
The Castle, 452 Finchley Road, NW11.
Hendon Corporation
The tollgate was erected under an Act of Parliament of 1826 for 'making a turnpike road from St John's

Chapel to the north-east end of Ballard's Lane, abutting upon the North Road in the Parish of Finchley, with a branch therefrom in the County of Middlesex'. The tolls were abolished in 1851, and the gate was finally removed in 1871.

CATTLE POUND OF HENDON
The Quadrant, Hendon, NW4. *Hendon Corporation*
The purpose of the pound, which survived from medieval times until the mid-nineteenth century, was to prevent cattle straying on to the land of the lord of the manor.

CATTLEY, William (1788–1835), English, botanist
Cattley Close, Wood Street, Barnet.
London Borough of Barnet
Cattley, who lived in this house, was famous as one of the first successful growers of epiphytic orchids in England, especially the 'corsage orchid', *Cattleya labiata*. He was also a patron of John Lindley (q.v.), another pioneer orchidologist, to whom he paid a salary for drawing and describing new plants.

CHAPMAN, Herbert (1878–1934), English, football manager
6 Haslemere Avenue, Hendon, NW4.
English Heritage
Chapman lived and died in this house. Though his career as a player was undistinguished, he managed Huddersfield Town (1921–5) to an FA Cup win and two First Division titles, and then Arsenal (1925–34), also to an FA Cup and two First Division titles. He set Arsenal up to dominate the 1930s but died suddenly in 1934 and did not share their further triumphs. He was one of the game's first modernisers, introducing new tactics and training methods, and backing innovations such as floodlighting and numbered shirts for players.

CHURCH HOUSE
The Greyhound, Church End, Hendon, NW4.
Hendon Corporation
The plaque says this is the site of Church House (1321), former location of parish meetings. The Greyhound Inn is the latest in a series of buildings on the site. The vestry meetings continued here, the name 'Greyhound' being first recorded in 1655.

COATES, Eric (1886–1957), English, composer
7 Willifield Way, Golders Green, NW11. *London Borough of Barnet*
Coates lived here from 1925 to 1931. He was a prolific composer, best remembered for his theme march to the 1954 film *The Dambusters*. He also composed *By the Sleepy Lagoon* (1930), which is the theme music of *Desert Island Discs*, and *The London Suite* (1933), which includes the popular 'Knightsbridge March'.

COLLINSON, Peter (1694–1768), English, naturalist
Wall of Mill Hill School, The Ridgeway, NW7.
Hendon Corporation
Collinson lived from 1749 in Ridgeway House on this site. He was a friend and regular correspondent of Benjamin Franklin (q.v.), and they exchanged news about experiments with electricity. It was on Collinson's advice that American settlers began cultivating flax, hemp, sisal and vines. He was elected a Fellow of the Royal Society in 1728 and made notable contributions to the Hans Sloane (q.v.) collection, later the nucleus of the British Museum.

COURT LEET AND COURT BARON
The White Bear, The Burroughs, NW4.
Hendon Corporation
This was the site of two ancient courts: the Court Leet was a criminal jurisdiction under the lord of the manor in medieval times, and the Court Baron met twice a year, dealing mainly with matters to do with the manor estate, and was running until 1916. The present White Bear was built in 1932.

DONAT, Robert (1905–58), English, actor
8 Meadway, Hampstead Garden Suburb, NW11.
English Heritage
Donat, who lived in this house, made his stage debut in 1921 but is best remembered for his films, which notably include

The Count of Monte Cristo (1934), *The Thirty-Nine Steps* (1935) and *Goodbye Mr Chips* (1939), for which he won an Oscar. His final film was *The Inn of the Sixth Happiness* (1958).

EDGWARE TURNPIKE
Corner of Deansbrook and Edgware Roads,
Edgware. *Hendon Corporation*
This was the site of the Edgware Turnpike from around 1711 until 1872. Tolls were collected here by the local authorities to maintain the road in their patch. The plaque is now something for drivers to read when they are stuck here in the morning jam.

FRY, C. B. (1872–1956), English, sportsman
8 Moreland Court, Finchley Road, NW2.
Hendon Corporation
Fry lived the last six years of his life here. Known mainly as a cricketer, he also played football for England and at one time was co-holder of the world long-jump record. His feat of six consecutive centuries in first-class cricket has yet to be equalled or surpassed. He claimed he was once offered (and refused) the throne of Albania. (See also Croydon.)

GRIMALDI, Joseph (1778–1837), English, clown
Finchley Memorial Hospital, Granville Road,
N12. *London Borough of Barnet*

Mr GRIMALDI, as Clown.

The 'Garrick of Clowns' lived in a house on this site. Grimaldi's 'Joey' was the first modern clown, and the name has been used for the profession ever since. He was the forerunner of the pantomime dame and began the tradition of audience involvement in pantomimes. His health was ruined by years of acrobatic tumbling and he retired in 1823. He was broke within five years but rescued by benefits held in his honour at Sadler's Wells and Covent Garden. On the first Sunday in February every year there is a memorial service to him at All Saints, Haggerston, attended by hundreds of clowns in full regalia. (See also Islington.)

HALL, Henry (1898–1989), English, dance-band leader
38 Harman Drive, NW2. *English Heritage*
Hall lived here from 1932 to 1959. His popular radio series *Henry Hall's Guest Night* started in 1932, with the signature tune *Here's to the Next Time*, which he had composed. In the 1950s he hosted the television series *Face the Music*, always in suave white tie, and is remembered for his catchphrase 'This *is* Henry Hall speaking'. (See also Westminster 1.)

HANCOCK, Tony
(1924–68), English, actor, comedian
10 Grey Close,
Golders Green, NW11.
Dead Comics Society
Hancock lived here in 1947–8. He is remembered for his lugubrious, pretentious misfit character, a resident of 'Railway Cuttings, East Cheam', in *Hancock's Half Hour*, on radio (1954–6) and on television (1956–61), with scripts by Ray Galton and Alan Simpson. An alcoholic, at odds with his frustrated ambitions, he killed himself in 1968. (See also Richmond.)

TONY
HANCOCK
1924 ~ 1968
Comedian
LIVED HERE
1947~1948
DEAD COMICS SOCIETY

HESS, Dame Myra (1890–1965), English, pianist
48 Wildwood Road, Golders Green, NW11.
English Heritage
Famous on both sides of the Atlantic, Dame Myra, who lived in this house, achieved further renown in the Second World War, when, with the concert halls all shut, she organised lunchtime recitals at the National Gallery, which are credited as a significant contribution to popular morale.

HILL, Graham (1929–75), English, motor-racing champion
32 Parkside, NW7.
English Heritage
Hill lived here from 1960 to 1972. He was Formula 1 World Champion twice, with BRM in 1962 and with Lotus in 1968. He won the Monaco Grand Prix five times and is the only ever winner of the motor-racing 'triple crown': the Indianapolis 500, Le Mans, and the Formula 1 world title. He was killed flying his own plane.

JESSOP, Gilbert (1874–1955), English, cricketer
3 Sunnydale Gardens, Mill Hill, NW7.
Hendon Corporation
Jessop lived here from 1924 to 1936. Reckoned to be the fastest run-scorer in the history of cricket, though also noted as a fast bowler and lightning fielder, 'the Croucher' was Cricketer of the Year for 1898. The Fifth Test at The Oval against the Australians in 1902 is recalled as 'Jessop's Match'.

JOHNSON, Amy (1903–41), English, aviatrix
Vernon Court, Hendon Way, NW2.
English Heritage
Johnson lived in a flat in this block. A series of solo flights – to Australia (1930), to Japan and back (1931), and to Cape Town and back (1932) – established her as a national heroine. A ferry pilot in the Second World War, she is thought to have been shot down by 'friendly fire' over the Thames estuary.

LEMON, Mark (1809–70), English, journalist
Church Farmhouse Museum, Greyhound Hill, NW4.
London Borough of Barnet
Lemon, the co-founder and first editor of *Punch* (1841–70), lived here from 1817 to 1823. He also wrote farces, melodramas, operas and novels. He was known to his friends as 'Uncle Mark'.

LIPTON, Sir Thomas (1850–1931), Scottish, grocer, philanthropist, yachtsman
Oakdale, Southgate, N14. *London Borough of Barnet*
Sir Thomas lived in this house. He opened his first grocery in Glasgow in 1870 and was a millionaire by the age of thirty. He purchased extensive tea plantations and was benevolent in his management of them. He is affectionately remembered for his five unsuccessful challenges for the America's Cup.

LIVINGSTONE, David (1813–73), Scottish, missionary, explorer
Livingstone Cottage, Hadley Green. *Private*

In Bechuanaland from 1840, he travelled north and discovered the Victoria Falls (1852–6). He stayed here in this cottage before his second expedition (1858–64), exploring the Zambesi. He did not return from his third expedition (1866–73), during which he was 'found' at Ujiji in 1871 by H. M. Stanley (q.v.), who allegedly and famously greeted him: 'Dr Livingstone, I presume?'

MEDTNER, Nicholas (1880–1951), Russian, composer, pianist
69 Wentworth Road, Golders Green, NW11.
London Borough of Barnet
A German composer who happened to be born in Russia, he trained at the Moscow Conservatory and had a successful career as a touring recitalist before settling in London, in this house, from 1935 to his death. Facing hardship with the cut-off of revenues from Germany in the Second World War, he was rescued by the Maharaja of Mysore, who in 1946 founded a Medtner Society to record all his works.

MILLIGAN, Spike (1918–2002), Irish, writer, comedian
Holden Road, North Finchley, N12. *Finchley Society*
'Spike Milligna, the well-known typing error', lived in a house on this site from 1955 to 1974. He was the principal writer of the BBC radio series *The Goon Show* and one of its performers (1951–60). The programme was a seminal experience for a generation, including the Prince of Wales and the *Monty Python* team. He was also a prolific writer of children's books and other nonsense. His seven-part war memoirs, beginning with *Adolf Hitler – My Part in His Downfall* (1971), brought a whole new perspective to the North African campaign and beyond. (See also Westminster 2.)

MORECAMBE, Eric (1926–84), English, comedian
85 Torrington Park, North Finchley, N12.
Comic Heritage
Stage-name of Eric Bartholomew, who lived here from 1956 to 1961, Morecambe first teamed up with his comedy partner, Ernie Wise, in 1943, and at the time of their phenomenal run on BBC Television (1968–78) they were easily the most popular comedy duo in Britain, involving distinguished guest stars in appalling plays 'wot Ernie had wrote'. (See also Richmond.)

MURRAY, Sir James (1837–1915), Scottish, lexicographer
Sunnyside, Hammers Lane, Mill Hill, NW7.
Hendon Corporation
When Murray, who lived in this house from 1870 to 1885 and was a teacher at the nearby Mill Hill School, began work on the *New English Dictionary* (which became the *Oxford English Dictionary*) in 1879, the job was expected to last ten years and occupy four volumes. By the time the dictionary finally came out in 1928, it had taken forty-nine years and filled twelve volumes.

NICOLL FAMILY
Randall Court, Page Street, Mill Hill, NW7.
Hendon Corporation
This was the site of the family residence for almost six hundred years. The Nicolls crop up continuously in

records around north-west London from 1321, when a Stephen Nicoll is mentioned in a survey. The house, which was demolished in 1920, had been erected by Randall Nicoll in 1637. They also built almshouses.

NORDEN, John (1548–1625), English, cartographer
Hendon School, Golders Rise, NW4.
Hendon Corporation
The man's name was Norden but the plaque says 'Morden'; furthermore, it has been strongly asserted that his house was on the other side of Golders Rise, not where the school stands. Norden was the first Englishman to design a complete series of county histories and geographies, and his maps of London and Westminster are the best representations we have of the capital in Tudor times.

PARISH LOCK-UP
Corner of Brent Street and Bell Lane, Hendon, NW4. *Hendon Corporation*
A place for a constable to hold, typically, a recalcitrant drunk overnight, this lock-up was in use as early as the thirteenth century. It was recorded on a map of 1796, was in use until 1882 and was sold for redevelopment the next year, as modern police stations began to be built. (See also Camden 1.)

PAUL, Robert W. (1869–1943), English, film-maker
49 Sydney Road, Muswell Hill, N10.
British Film Institute
A medal-winning maker of scientific instruments, Paul developed a film camera with Birt Acres (q.v.). He became cameraman, director and exhibitor, showing the first 'news film', of the 1896 Derby, only a day after the race was run. He also built the first British film studio, with laboratory attached, in 1898. He lived here from 1914 to 1920.

PAVLOVA, Anna (1881–1931), Russian, ballerina
Ivy House, North End Road, Golders Green, NW11. *Hendon Corporation*
The greatest dancer of her age, and perhaps of all time, Pavlova's most famous role was the 'Dying Swan', choreographed for her by Fokine in 1907. Her legions of fans called themselves the *Pavlovatzi*. From 1907 she

Reckoned to be one of the most influential philosophers of the twentieth century, he defined his thinking as 'critical rationalism'. He was elected a Fellow of the Royal Society in 1976 and made a Companion of Honour in 1982.

RAFFLES, Sir Stamford
(1781–1826), English, colonial pioneer
Highwood House, Highwood Hill, Mill Hill, NW7.
Hendon Corporation
Raffles lived here for the last year of his life (1825–6). His exploits had begun during his service with the East India Company, participating in a victorious campaign against the Dutch in Java in 1811. He founded Singapore (1819) while governing Sumatra (1818–23). Returning to England, he founded the Zoological Society of London at Regent's Park Zoo in 1825 and became its first president in 1826. Sadly, he lived only three months longer.

toured the world continuously with her own company, from 1912 being based at this house, where she lived till her death.

PICK, Frank (1878–1941), English, transport executive
15 Wildwood Road, Golders Green, NW11.
Greater London Council
Pick lived here and the plaque describes him as a 'pioneer of good design for London Transport'. It was while he was commercial manager that he commissioned Edward Johnston (q.v.) to design the distinctive 'Johnston Sans' typeface and the blue and red roundel of London Transport. He later became chief executive of London Transport (1933–40) and nurtured Harry Beck (q.v.) and his famous Underground map.

POPPER, Sir Karl (1902–94), Austrian, philosopher
16 Burlington Rise, East Barnet. *English Heritage*
Popper left Austria in 1937 when the Anschluss was imminent, going first to New Zealand, and coming to London in 1946 to be Reader in Logic and Scientific Method at the London School of Economics.

RELPH, Harry ('Little Tich')
(1867–1928), English, music-hall comedian
93 Shirehall Park, Hendon, NW4.
Greater London Council
This was Little Tich's last home. Only 4 feet 6 inches tall, he made his first appearance on stage at the age of twelve and went on to international stardom, being especially popular in France. His famous Big Boot Dance, with boots 28 inches long, was filmed in 1900, and Jacques Tati said it was 'a foundation for everything that has been realised in comedy on the screen'. In 1909 Little Tich was made an officer of the French Academy for his triumphs at the Folies Bergères. (See also Bromley.)

ROSEBANK
The Ridgeway, Mill Hill, NW7. *Hendon Corporation*
This was a Quaker meeting house (1678–1719), built by Richard Haley in the weatherboarded style typical of Middlesex at that time. It is now part of the Mill Hill Conservation Area.

STEPHENS, Henry C.
(1841–1918), English, businessman, philanthropist
Avenue House, East End Road, Finchley, N3. *Finchley Society*
Son of Henry Stephens, the inventor of blue-black ink, he greatly expanded the family business. Buying Avenue House in 1874, he added a laboratory and planted an extensive garden. The house, which he bequeathed to the people of Finchley, is now a shrine to ink. He was known as 'Inky' Stephens.

TAIT, Thomas Smith (1882–1954), Scottish, architect
Gates House, Wyldes Close, NW11.
English Heritage
A partner in the firm of Sir John Burnet, Tait & Lorne, the leading British architectural practice of the 1930s, he lived here from 1928 until his death. His most famous design was the Royal Masonic Hospital, Ravenscourt Park, W6, which won the RIBA Gold Medal as the best building of 1933.

TROBRIDGE, Ernest George (1884–1942), Irish, architect
19 Heather Walk, Edgware. *Private*
The plaque refers to Trobridge as 'architect *extraordinaire*', as indeed he was. In the 1920s he built

an estate around Roe Green in Kingsbury, NW9, the houses being in one of two extraordinary styles – either sixteenth-century-style cottages, or castellated, turreted miniature fantasy castles. This house, his own, which he also designed, is conventional by comparison.

TROLLOPE, Anthony (1815–82), English, novelist
Grandon, Hadley Green. *London Borough of Barnet*
One of the most successful of Victorian novelists, Trollope lived in this house from 1836 to 1838. He wrote forty-seven novels and sixteen books in other genres. His best-known works include the Barsetshire series (1855–67) and the Palliser series (1864–79) of novels, both of which have been adapted and filmed for television. He was also responsible for introducing the pillar box while working for the Post Office. He shares this plaque with his mother (see below). (See also Westminster 2.)

TROLLOPE, Fanny (1780–1863), English, novelist
Grandon, Hadley Green. *London Borough of Barnet*
Widowed in 1835, and gifted with inexhaustible energy, Fanny Trollope travelled extensively and produced over forty books, which supported her large family and brought her wealth and fame, albeit transitory. She was apparently surprised when her son Anthony (see above) took up writing.

TUDOR HALL
Wood Street, Barnet. *London Borough of Barnet*
This Tudor hall housed the Free Grammar School of Queen Elizabeth I, who granted its charter in 1573. It was set up by Elizabeth's favourite, Robert Dudley, 'for the education, bringing up and instruction of boys in Grammar and other learning and the same to continue forever'. In 1930 the school moved from here to its present site on Queen's Road.

VARDON, Harry (1870–1937), English, golfer
35 Totteridge Lane, Whetstone, N20.
London Borough of Barnet
Vardon lived here from 1903 until his death. He was six
times winner of the Open Championship between 1896
and 1914 (a record that survives), one of the 'great
triumvirate' (with Braid and Taylor) who dominated golf
in the twenty years before 1914. The Vardon grip
continues to be used by 90 per cent of golfers.

VICTORIA MATERNITY HOSPITAL
Cattley Close, Wood Street, Barnet.
London Borough of Barnet
This building, Cedar Lawn, is the site of the former
Victoria Maternity Hospital (1924–87). Originally
opened in 1888 by public subscription, it converted to
maternity after the First World War and closed when
the service was transferred to Edgware Hospital in
1987.

WAUGH, Reverend Benjamin (1839–1908),
English, cleric
Christ Church, Friern Barnet Road, N11.
London Borough of Barnet
Waugh, a Congregationalist from 1865, served as
founder-minister of this church (1883–7). While
incumbent here, in 1884, he founded the National
Society for the Prevention of Cruelty to Children and
went on to be its Director (1889–1905). (See also
Enfield and Greenwich.)

WAUGH, Evelyn
(1903–66), English,
novelist
145 North End Road,
Golders Green,
NW11. *English Heritage*
This was Waugh's
parents' home during his
time at Oxford. An
incurable snob, he would
walk east to Hampstead to post letters in order to get
a classier postmark. Regarded as the prose stylist of his
generation, his works range from brittle comic satire
on the fast set of the inter-war years to the darker
comedy of the *Sword of Honour* trilogy (1952–61)
about the Second World War. His *Brideshead Revisited*
(1945) was made into a television classic by Granada in
1981, and his *Scoop* (1938) remains the best and
funniest book about journalism.

WILBERFORCE,
William
(1759–1833), English,
anti-slavery
campaigner
Barnet Road,
Arkley.
Hendon Corporation
St Paul's Church,
The Ridgeway, Mill
Hill, NW7. *London*
Borough of Barnet
The plaque in Arkley records the site of Hendon Park,
where Wilberforce lived in retirement (1826–31),
before spending the remaining two years of his life
being looked after at his brother's house in Chelsea.
He financed the building of St Paul's Church but died a
week before it was consecrated in August 1833. (See
also Merton, Wandsworth, Lambeth and Kensington &
Chelsea 2.)

BEXLEY

Lying at the south-east edge of Greater London, once wholly in Kent, the London Borough of Bexley is an amalgamation of the former municipal boroughs of Bexley and Erith, plus the old Crayford Urban District.

CASTLEREAGH, Viscount
(1769–1822), Irish, politician
Loring Hall, Water Lane, North Cray.
English Heritage
Castlereagh lived here. He was Chief Secretary for Ireland (1797–1801) and Foreign Secretary (1812–22). He famously fought a pistol duel with another cabinet minister, Canning (q.v.), in 1809. Perceived as reactionary, he was extremely unpopular with the general public and was skewered in Shelley's poem *The Masque of Anarchy*: 'I met Murder on the way – He had a face like Castlereagh.' He committed suicide, his mental disturbance possibly brought on by syphilis. This was covered up, and he is buried in Westminster Abbey.

MORRIS, William
(1834–96), English, poet, designer, socialist
Red House, Red House Lane, Bexleyheath.
Greater London Council
Morris commissioned this house from his friend Philip Webb (see page 240) in 1859, the year he married Jane Burden. Although their early years here were happy and produced two children, Jane then began a long affair with D. G. Rossetti (q.v.), and Morris gave up Red House after only five years. (See also Camden 2, Westminster 3, Redbridge, Waltham Forest and Hammersmith & Fulham.)

RED HOUSE
Red House Lane, Bexleyheath.
Greater London Council
Described by D. G. Rossetti (q.v.) as 'More a poem than a house', Red House is held to be a major pioneering piece of architecture, both reviving medieval styles and foreshadowing the work of Lutyens (q.v.) and Richard Norman Shaw (q.v.). It is now in the hands of the National Trust.

THORPE, John (1715–92), English, antiquary, historian
123 Bexley High Street, Bexley.
London Borough of Bexley
On his father's death in 1750, Thorpe moved in here and edited his father's researches into the history of Rochester. He was also himself a diligent student of the history of west Kent and published several accounts of the area. His passing mention in 1750 of a Roman mosaic at Lullingstone led archaeologists in 1949 to uncover a pavement and villa.

TRAD JAZZ
The Red Barn, Barnehurst Road, Barnehurst.
Private
This is the place where traditional jazz was reborn in England, with George Webb's Dixielanders, a group that at one time or another included most of the leading British jazz musicians, including Humphrey

Lyttleton and Wally Fawkes. The plaque was unveiled
by George Melly.

WEBB, Philip (1831–1915), English, architect
Red House, Red House Lane, Bexleyheath.
Greater London Council
Webb was assisting G. E. Street (q.v.) when he met
William Morris (q.v.), who encouraged him to set up
on his own and commissioned Red House from him.
They remained closely associated: Webb was a partner
in Morris & Co, and together they founded the Society
for the Protection of Ancient Buildings in 1877, a
reaction against the prevailing Victorian urge to
'improve' old buildings. Among his other extant
designs are 1 Palace Green, W8 (1868), and Standen in
West Sussex (1892–4). (See also Hackney.)

BRENT

In the north-west of Greater London, once
wholly in Middlesex, the London Borough of
Brent is an amalgamation of the two former
municipal boroughs of Wembley and Willesden.

KAUFMAN, Morris
(1919–88), English,
educationalist, historian
**5 Blackstone Road,
NW2.**
Plastics Historical Society
Kaufman lived here while
principal lecturer at the
Polytechnic of North London,
now London Metropolitan University. His expertise
was in the history of the plastics industry and his 1963
book *The First Century of Plastics* rediscovered the work
of pioneers such as Alexander Parkes (q.v.). He also
wrote *The History of PVC* (1969) and *Giant Molecules:
The Technology of Plastics, Fibres and Rubber* (1968).

LUCAN, Arthur (1885–1954), English, comedian
11 Forty Lane, Wembley. *Greater London Council*
Arthur Lucan (stage-name of Arthur Towle) moved
here for the rest of his life after starring at the Royal
Variety Performance in 1934. His 'Old Mother Riley'
was a character on stage, in pantomime, on radio and
in the cinema, usually in a double act with 'her'
daughter, Lucan's wife, Kitty McShane. He died in his
dressing room when due on stage in Hull. The plaque
incorrectly gives his birth year as 1887.

McCLOSKEY, PC Ronan (1962–87), Irish, police
officer
Dudden Hill Lane, NW10. *Police Memorial Trust*
PC McCloskey, on only his fourth day of duty at
Willesden police station, was killed on 9 May 1987, by
a drunk driver who drove off with him clinging to the
car.

BROMLEY

Lying at the south-east edge of Greater
London, once wholly in Kent, Bromley, the
largest London Borough, is an amalgamation of
the former municipal boroughs of Bromley and
Beckenham, plus the old Penge and Orpington
urban districts, and the Chislehurst part of
another old urban district.

ALDRIDGE, Ira
(1807–67), American,
actor
**5 Hamlet Road,
SE19.** *English Heritage*
Known as 'the African
Roscius', Aldridge lived
here after arriving in
England from his native
New York in the 1820s.
He had faced racism in
New York and would face it here, though more from
snobbish critics than from the general public, who
were thrilled by his deep voice and his playing of all
the major Shakespearian roles, most obviously
Othello. He also toured Europe to great acclaim,
acquiring wealth, which he used to fund progressive
black causes.

BIGGIN HILL AIRFIELD
Main Road, Biggin Hill. *London Borough of Bromley*
Two plaques on the gateposts flanking the entrance
memorialise the RAF station (1917–92), most famous
as the home of several Spitfire squadrons in the Battle
of Britain. It was heavily bombed twelve times by the
Luftwaffe between August 1940 and January 1941 but
remained operational throughout the battle (see also
Towerfields, page 245). Biggin Hill pilots shot down
1,400 enemy aircraft in the course of the war.

BLYTON, Enid (1897–1968), English, children's
writer
83 Shortlands Road, Shortlands.
London Borough of Bromley

ENID
BLYTON
1897 - 1968
AUTHORESS
lived here

With a steady output of ten
thousand words a day,
Blyton, who lived here,
produced about eight
hundred stories for
children of all ages over a
period of forty years, the
best-remembered being the
twenty-one 'Famous Five' books
(1942–63) and the fifteen 'Secret Seven' books
(1949–63), and of course the 'Toyland' adventures of
Noddy, Big Ears and friends.

FRANK
BOURNE
1855 -1945
Colour-Sergeant at the
battle for Rorke's Drift
22-23 January 1879
lived here

BOURNE, Frank
(1855–1945), English,
soldier
**16 King's Hall Road,
Beckenham.**
London Borough of Bromley
Bourne, who lived here, was
the colour sergeant at the battle
of Rorke's Drift, 22–23 January
1879. Afterwards he was awarded the Distinguished
Conduct Medal and offered an immediate
commission, which he refused. Retired in 1907, he
re-enlisted for the First World War, at the end of which
he was given the honorary rank of lieutenant-colonel.
He was the last survivor of the battle. In the 1964 film
Zulu, he was portrayed by Nigel Green.

BRIDE, Harold (1890–1956), English, radio
operator
58 Ravensbourne Avenue, Bromley Park.
London Borough of Bromley

Bride, who lived here from 1903 to 1922, had been a qualified radio operator for only nine months when the *Titanic* sailed on 10 April 1912. When the ship hit an iceberg on 14 April he conveyed messages to the bridge, while his colleague Jack Phillips sent out distress signals. Later they both clung to an overturned lifeboat but Phillips froze to death before help arrived. Bride survived with badly crushed and frozen feet. He found himself a local hero upon returning home, but he disliked recalling the experience and moved to Scotland in 1922.

CAMPBELL, Sir Malcolm (1885–1948), English, speed record holder
Bonchester Close, Camden Park Road, Chislehurst.
London Borough of Bromley
Sir Malcolm, who lived here from 1909 to 1922, broke his first world land speed record in 1924 at Pendine Sands, Carmarthenshire, with a speed of 146.16 mph. He raised the record eight further times, in an epic rivalry with Sir Henry Segrave, eventually becoming the first man to go over 300 mph at Bonneville, Utah, in 1935. He then turned to the water and raised that record three times on Coniston Water between 1937 and 1939, leaving it at 141.7 mph in August 1939. All his cars and boats were called *Bluebird*, after he had seen the Maeterlinck play of that name on the London stage.

CHISLEHURST CAVES
Caveside Close, Chislehurst.
London Borough of Bromley
The plaque recalls that people came from all across London and north-west Kent to shelter here during the Blitz. At the height of the bombardment between October 1940 and July 1941 thousands used the cave system every night. Although called 'caves', the tunnels are in fact man-made mines for chalk and flint, first recorded in the thirteenth century.

CRAPPER, Thomas (1837–1910), English, engineer, inventor
12 Thornsett Road, Anerley, SE20.
London Borough of Bromley

Crapper, who lived here, is credited with the invention of the syphonic toilet flush, though he never lodged a patent for it. One of the leading contractors in the field in the 1870s and 1880s, he installed thirty toilets at Sandringham for Queen Victoria.

CROMPTON, Richmal (1890–1969), English, children's writer
The Glebe, Oakley Road, Bromley Common.
London Borough of Bromley
Her thirty-nine books about William, a mischievous eleven-year-old, and his friends the Outlaws, were a phenomenal success. Crompton took up writing aged thirty-three, when polio obliged her to stop teaching. She was frustrated that her many novels aimed at adult readers were comparatively ignored. She had this house built for herself and her mother and lived here from 1928 to 1954.

CROSBY, Brass (1725–93), English, politician
Court Lodge, Church Road, Bromley.
London Borough of Bromley
Crosby, who lived here, was lord of the manor of Chelsfield, lord mayor of London (1770–1) and a champion of the liberty of the press. In 1771 he was imprisoned in the Tower of London after demanding that the minutes of Parliament be published. Public support led to his release and the foundation of Hansard, hence the saying 'as bold as Brass'. (See also Westminster 4.)

DE LA MARE, Walter (1873–1956), English, poet
195 Mackenzie Road, Beckenham.
London Borough of Bromley
De la Mare is best-known for his verses and short stories for children, including the celebrated *Memoirs of a Midget* (1921), which explored the world of the minute Miss M. His field was childhood, fantasy and mystery, often with a strain of melancholy. He was made a Companion of Honour in 1948 and awarded the Order of Merit in 1953. (See also Richmond.)

EVANS, Sir Geraint (1922–92), Welsh, baritone
34 Birchwood Road, Petts Wood.
London Borough of Bromley
Sir Geraint lived here. He made his Covent Garden debut in 1948 as the nightwatchman in *Die Meistersinger*. He was particularly associated with the role of Papageno in *Die Zauberflöte*, and with the title roles in *Falstaff* and *Wozzeck*, which he sang in all the world's major opera houses. After retiring from singing in 1983, he worked extensively as an opera director.

FRY, Dr John (1922–94), English, physician
138 Croydon Road, Elmers End.
GP Research Club
Dr Fry worked here as a general practitioner from 1946 to 1991, resisting all offers of prestigious research posts. Notable for the research he conducted among his own patients, producing *Profiles of Disease* (1966), he was a co-founder of the College of General Practitioners, and for forty-five years a member of the General Medical Council.

GRACE, W. G. (1848–1915), English, cricketer
Fairmount, Mottingham Lane, Mottingham, SE9. *Greater London Council*
Dr Grace lived here. He was one of the towering figures of Victorian society; he made cricket into a major spectator sport and was its first nationwide star. In a forty-four-year career he scored a total of 54,896 runs and took 2,876 wickets, playing in twenty-two tests for England. Stories of him are legion, including that of the bouncer that supposedly went through his beard: when he remonstrated with the bowler, the man said: 'Sorry, Doctor, it slipped.' (See also Lewisham.)

HARMAN, John Pennington, VC (1914–44), English, soldier
9 Shrewsbury Road, Elmers End.
London Borough of Bromley
A Lance Corporal in the 4th Battalion, the Queen's Own Royal West Kent Regiment, Harman was awarded the Victoria Cross posthumously for conspicuous bravery at Kohima, Assam, India, on 9 April 1944. He was born in this house.

HAWKINS, Benjamin Waterhouse (1807–89), English, artist, sculptor
22 Belvedere Road, SE19.
London Borough of Bromley
Hawkins lived here. Specialising in animal art, he contributed forty-nine plates to Darwin's (q.v.) *Zoology of the Voyage of HMS Beagle* (1838–43). The creation of the prehistoric 'monsters' at Crystal Palace occupied him from 1852 to 1855, and he held a famous dinner party in the iguanodon mould on 31 December 1855 to celebrate their completion.

KEEPING, Charles (1924–88), English, illustrator
16 Church Road, Shortlands.
London Borough of Bromley
Keeping live here. He illustrated Rosemary Sutcliff, Rider Haggard (q.v.), Charles Kingsley (q.v.), Horace Walpole (q.v.), Victor Hugo and the whole of Dickens (q.v.) for the Folio Society. He was twice winner of the Kate Greenaway Medal, in 1967 and 1981.

KROPOTKIN, Prince Peter (1842–1921), Russian, anarchist
6 Crescent Road, Bromley.
English Heritage
His work as a geographer exposed him to the appalling conditions of most Russians, and the indifference of the authorities. He joined the extreme wing of a working men's organisation and was imprisoned. He escaped to England, and later to France, where he was again imprisoned. He settled again in England, for a time at this house, until 1917, when he returned to Russia and retired from politics. The core of his philosophy was to establish communism without central government; when he saw the Bolsheviks in power he said: 'This buries the revolution.'

LUBBOCK, John, first Baron Avebury (1834–1913), English, scientist, banker, politician
High Elms Estate, Shire Lane, Farnborough.
London Borough of Bromley

Sir John, who lived at High Elms, was firstly a banker, but also a diligent scientific researcher, friend of Darwin (q.v.), and writer of *Pre-historic Times, as Illustrated by Ancient Remains* (1865). He also published an account of an experiment in which he tried to teach his poodle to read. He was a Liberal MP (1865–1900), steering through the Bank Holidays Act of 1871. (See also Westminster 4.)

MacCOLL, Ewan
(1915–89), Scottish, political singer, songwriter
35 Stanley Avenue, Beckenham.
London Borough of Bromley
Born Jimmie Miller, he was married to Joan Littlewood and with her established the Theatre Workshop. Later influential in the British folk-music revival, he wrote and recorded many songs and, although he abhorred the world of pop music, had a huge hit with Roberta Flack's version of 'The First Time Ever I Saw Your Face' in 1972. He lived his last thirty years here, with his third wife, Peggy Seeger.

MUIRHEAD, Alexander (1848–1920), Scottish, engineer, inventor
20 Church Road, Shortlands.
Greater London Council
Muirhead is credited with recording the world's first electrocardiogram, at St Bartholomew's Hospital, while studying for his DSc. He later specialised in wireless telegraphy, inventing duplex cabling, capable of handling messages in opposite directions at the same time. Elected a Fellow of the Royal Society in 1904, he lived here.

NASH, Heddle (1895–1961), English, tenor
49 Towncourt Crescent, Petts Wood.
London Borough of Bromley
Nash, who lived here, was the leading British lyric tenor from the 1920s to the 1950s. He made his debut in Milan in 1924 and had an Italianate style, which led one critic to suggest that he sang everything as though it was written by Verdi. Elgar (q.v.) chose him to sing The Ode of Gerontius in 1931, and his 1945 recording of it, conducted by Sir Malcolm Sargent (q.v.), is still regarded as definitive.

RELPH, Harry ('Little Tich') (1867–1928), English, music-hall comedian
Blacksmiths' Arms, Cudham Lane, Cudham.
London Borough of Bromley
One of fifteen children born to the landlord of this pub, Relph grew to only 4 feet 6 inches tall – hence his stage-name. He was hugely popular for over forty years, abroad as well as at home. His best-known routine was his Big Boot Dance, performed with a pair of 28-inch boots. (See also Barnet.)

SHEPHEARD, Sir Victor (1893–1989), English, naval architect
Manor Place, Manor Park, Chislehurst.
London Borough of Bromley
Sir Victor, who lived here from 1957 to 1989, began as an apprentice at the Devonport naval dockyard in 1907, served at the battle of Jutland and rose to be Professor of Naval Architecture at Greenwich from 1934 to 1939. Serving in the Naval Construction Department in the Second World War, he became its director in 1951. He designed the Royal Yacht *Britannia*.

THORNTON'S CORNER
102–104 High Street, Beckenham.
Bromley & Beckenham Philatelic Society

This ordinary high street premises housed the *Beckenham Journal* from 1881 to 1965 and was the site of the first British airmail post office, opened on 9 August 1902.

TOWERFIELDS
Westerham Road, Leaves Green.
London Borough of Bromley
The plaque records that following heavy bombing of Biggin Hill Airfield (see page 242) in 1940, during the

Battle of Britain, control of operations for this
defensive sector was moved to Towerfields until 1941.
Biggin Hill remained operational throughout.

WELLS, H. G. (1866–1946), English, novelist
Allders Store, High Street, Bromley. *Private*
Wells was born on this site on 21 September 1866. He
was a writer in several genres: his science fiction
earned him a reputation as a prophet; his social realist
novels remain vivid slices of lower middle-class life;
and his didactic works, such as *The Outline of History*,
show him to be a great teacher. (See also Sutton,
Westminster 1.)

WILLETT, William
(1856–1915),
English, builder
**82 Camden Park
Road, Chislehurst.**
*London Borough of
Bromley*
Willett lived in this
house, designed for
him by Ernest
Newton, from 1894
until his death. His firm, Willett Building Services, was
noted for quality work in choice areas such as Chelsea.
He first proposed Daylight Saving in 1907 in a
pamphlet called *The Waste of Daylight*, apparently
inspired by a brainwave while riding his horse early
one morning on Chislehurst Common. By the time
Daylight Saving was finally introduced, in May 1916,
Germany had already done it, and Willett was dead.

**WILLIS, Lord
(Ted)** (1918–92),
English, playwright,
screenwriter
**5 Shepherd's
Green, Chislehurst.**
*London Borough of
Bromley*
Writer of a number of
British films, including
The Blue Lamp (1950) and *Woman in a Dressing Gown*
(1957), Willis is best remembered for BBC Television's
Dixon of Dock Green (1955–76), the homely stories of an
old-fashioned London bobby, PC George Dixon, played
by Jack Warner, who always started the show with
'Evenin' all'. Willis lived here from 1959 until his death.

CROYDON

Lying at the southern edge of Greater London,
and once wholly in Surrey, the London
Borough of Croydon is an amalgamation of the
County Borough of Croydon with Coulsdon
and Purley Urban District.

ADDINGTON OLD FORGE
Addington Village Road, Addington.
London Borough of Croydon
Built around 1740, this is the last working forge in the area. The building houses a business run by the Collins family for over sixty years, making ornamental ironwork of all kinds. Though horses are no longer shod, all other aspects of the original activities are still in operation.

AMIS, Sir Kingsley
(1922–95), English,
novelist
16 Buckingham
Gardens, Norbury.
London Borough of
Croydon
Author of over
twenty novels and six
volumes of verse,
Amis was born in this
house and, says the
plaque, 'used
Norbury as
inspiration for his
books'. He is best
remembered for *Lucky Jim* (1954), which established him as a key figure in post-war British literature. In later life he cultivated a curmudgeonly personality.

ASHLEIGH AND INDIA HOUSES
137–139 Addiscombe Road, Addiscombe.
London Borough of Croydon
These two houses are all that remains of Addiscombe College. They were built in 1848 for the professors of the East India Company's seminary. The college was founded in 1809 to train officers for the East India Company's regiments. After the Indian Mutiny of 1857 the government took over the company, and the cadets were transferred to Sandhurst.

ASHMORE, Albert (1906–85), English, Salvationist
Fairfield Halls, Barclay Road, Croydon.
London Borough of Croydon
The model of an engaged local citizen, Ashmore was a lifelong member of the Salvation Army and co-founder of the Fairfield Christmas carol services here. Involved throughout his life in community projects, he was presented to the Queen on the occasion of the borough celebrating its centenary in 1983.

BARKER, Cicely
Mary
(1895–1973),
English, artist,
children's writer
23 The Waldrons,
Croydon.
London Borough of Croydon
Barker lived and worked here from 1924 to 1961. Her series of 'Flower Fairy' stories ran from 1923 to 1948. Barker was careful to point out: 'I have never seen a fairy; the fairies and all about them are just pretend.' And she was sure that 'children will be able to tell the true parts from the pretend parts'.

THE BOURNE
The Jolly Farmers, 7 Purley Road, Purley.
Bourne Society

The plaque says that the Bourne or Woe Water, which runs underground near here, traditionally floods parts of the Purley, Caterham and Coulsdon valleys every seven years and foretells national disaster!

COLERIDGE-TAYLOR, Samuel

(1875–1912), English, composer
30 Dagnall Park, South Norwood, SE25.
Greater London Council
Coleridge-Taylor was brought up here by his mother and her adopted parents, his father having returned to Africa before his birth. Championed by Elgar (q.v.), he was known as 'the African Mahler' and was interested in adapting African music to European forms.

CONAN DOYLE, Sir Arthur (1859–1930),
Scottish, novelist
12 Tennison Road, South Norwood, SE25.
Greater London Council
Conan Doyle lived here from 1891 to 1894. His immortal detective creation, Sherlock Holmes, had first appeared in *A Study in Scarlet* (1887). While living here, Conan Doyle published *The Adventures of Sherlock Holmes* (1892) and *The Memoirs of Sherlock Holmes* (1894). The house is now a residential care home for youngsters. (See also Westminster 1 and Westminster 2.)

COULSDON COURT
Coulsdon Court Road, Coulsdon. *Bourne Society*
Now the Coulsdon Manor Hotel, and clubhouse of Coulsdon Golf Club, this was the family seat of the squires Byron from 1851 to 1921.

COULSDON SOUTH STATION
Coulsdon South Railway Station, Coulsdon.
Bourne Society
The plaque was erected to commemorate the station's centenary in 1989 and records its various name changes along the way. It was originally called

'Coulsdon', renamed 'Coulsdon & Cane Hill' in 1896, then 'Coulsdon East' in July 1923, and finally 'Coulsdon South' in August 1923.

CREED, Frederick George (1871–1957),
Canadian, engineer, inventor
20 Outram Road, Addiscombe.
Greater London Council
Creed lived and died here. His teleprinter design was accepted by the British Post Office in 1902, and in 1909 he moved to Croydon, setting up Creed & Co to make teleprinters and Typex cipher machines, which were the British equivalent of the German Enigmas.

CROYDON AIRPORT TERMINAL
Purley Way, South Croydon.
London Borough of Croydon
This was one of the first purpose-built airport terminals in the world and was operational from 1928 to 1959. It was the base of Imperial Airways (forerunner of British Airways), which operated services from here to Europe and the Empire, until it merged with the British Overseas Airways

Corporation in 1939. Croydon was the first airport in the world to have air traffic control.

CROYDON CATTLE MARKET
Drovers Road and Selsdon Road, South Croydon. *London Borough of Croydon*
Croydon was an important agricultural centre, and the market here was opened in 1848. It could accommodate two hundred calves, 1,400 sheep and pigs and two hundred head of cattle. It was demolished in 1935 to make way for flats. The only surviving remnant is the cattle trough, relocated to Norbury Park.

DAVIS THEATRE
South End by Robert Street, Croydon.
Cinema Theatre Association
This building is all that remains of the Davis Theatre, opened in 1928 as a dual-purpose cinema and theatre designed in contemporary French Decorative style by Robert Cromie. It held an audience of more than 3,700 and was the largest cinema in England at the time. Among the many spectacular presentations was the Bolshoi Ballet, which performed in 1957. It closed and was demolished in 1959.

DU PRÉ, Jacqueline (1945–87), English, cellist
14 The Bridle Road, Purley.
London Borough of Croydon
It was while du Pré was living at this address, from 1948 to 1958, that the world got its first sight of her, as a guest on Huw Weldon's BBC Television children's magazine, *All Your Own*. Her prodigious talent was apparent to all. (See also Camden 1, Westminster 2 and Westminster 4.)

FITZROY, Admiral Robert (1805–65), English, sailor, meteorologist
140 Church Road, SE19. *London Borough of Croydon*
Fitzroy, who lived and died here, was the captain of the *Beagle* on the epoch-making voyage that took Charles Darwin (q.v.) to the Galapagos Islands. Subsequently he became the first head of the Meteorological Office. Sadly, he had always been prone to long bouts of depression and, stung by ill-informed criticism of his pioneering work in weather forecasting – which is now recognised as excellent, he committed suicide here on 20 April 1865. (See also Kensington & Chelsea 2.)

FRY, C. B. (1872–1956),
English, sportsman
144 St James's Road, Croydon.
English Heritage
Fry, who was born here, was known mainly as a cricketer, but he also represented Britain at athletics and football. He still holds the record of six consecutive centuries in first-class cricket. He claimed he was once offered (and refused) the throne of Albania. (See also Barnet.)

GARDNER'S PLEASURE RESORT
Godstone Road, Kenley. *Bourne Society*
This house, now converted to flats, was the headquarters of Gardner's Pleasure Resort from *c.*1893 until it closed in 1931. The pleasures on offer included a miniature railway (with tunnel), donkey rides, swings, hoopla and a monkey house. There was also an animal cemetery in which the donkeys and monkeys were affectionately remembered: 'Faithful Bess, gave rides to hundreds of visitors, died aged 17.'

GILLETT & JOHNSON FOUNDRY
Union Road, Croydon. *London Borough of Croydon*
Operational on this site from 1844 to 1957, Gillett & Johnson were internationally renowned clockmakers and bellfounders. They produced over fourteen thousand tower clocks, with or without bells, between 1844 and 1950, including the seventy-two-bell carillon for the Rockefeller Center in New York and the 10½-ton 'Freedom Bell' for Berlin Town Hall.

GRAND THEATRE AND OPERA HOUSE
Grosvenor House, 125 High Street, Croydon.
London Borough of Croydon
The theatre was opened in 1896 by Herbert Beerbohm Tree (q.v.) with a production of *Trilby*. Among performers here over the years were Sarah Bernhardt, Ellen Terry (q.v.) and Sir Henry Irving (q.v.). It was demolished, despite a 100,000-signature petition, in 1959.

HAY, Will (1888–1949), English, comic actor, astronomer
45 The Chase, Norbury, SW16. *English Heritage*
Hay, who lived here from 1927 to 1934, began his

career with a schoolmaster sketch in music hall in 1909. He later joined Fred Karno's troupe. He became a stage star in his own right in the 1920s and appeared in films in the 1930s. A keen amateur astronomer, he discovered a white spot on Saturn from his observatory in the garden here in 1933.

HORNIMAN, Frederick John (1835–1906), English, merchant, philanthropist
Coombe Cliff Centre, Coombe Road, Croydon.
English Heritage
The Hornimans, father and son, who share this plaque, lived here. They were inveterate travellers and collectors, and their collection was first displayed to the public in this house. Then Frederick commissioned C. Harrison Townsend to design the museum that bears their name (erected 1897–1901). (See also Lewisham.)

HORNIMAN, John (1803–93), English, merchant, philanthropist
Coombe Cliff Centre, Coombe Road, Croydon.
English Heritage
John Horniman, who lived here with his son (see above), was the first tea merchant to introduce mechanised packaging and by 1891 Horniman's was the largest tea company in the world. Father and son spent their money on travelling and collecting.

THE JOLLY FARMERS
7 Purley Road, Purley. *Bourne Society*
Erected in 2007 to celebrate the pub's centenary, the plaque notes that formerly on the site stood a mid-nineteenth-century wooden beerhouse called the 'Hammer and Clink', because of the blacksmith's forge at the rear.

KENLEY STATIONMASTER'S HOUSE
Kenley Station, Kenley Lane, Kenley.
Bourne Society
The plaque notes that this bijou Victorian cottage, now boarded up, was the stationmaster's house, erected in 1856.

LEAN, David (1908–91), English, film director
38 Blenheim Crescent, South Croydon. *Directors' Guild of Great Britain*
Lean, who was born here, had a glittering career but became trapped in his own grandeur. His early films such as *Brief Encounter* (1946), *Great Expectations* (1948) and *Oliver Twist* (1949) are lively and engaging, while *Lawrence of Arabia* (1965) is just big.

LOCKYER, Tom (1826–69), English, cricketer
The Queen Victoria, 98 Mitcham Road, Croydon. *London Borough of Croydon*
Lockyer, who was formerly landlord of this pub, took part in the earliest England cricket tours, to Canada, Australia and New Zealand. Playing for Surrey and England, he was regarded as the leading wicket-keeper of his era. The pub was called the Prince Albert when he ran it.

THE LORD ROBERTS
Upper Woodcote Village. *Bourne Society*
The plaque records that the Lord Roberts, the centrepiece of the model village of Upper Woodcote, was opened in 1907 as a temperance inn. It is now the village's general store. Built round a large green, Upper Woodcote was conceived and laid out by William Webb, a surveyor from Purley.

PISSARRO, Camille (1830–1903), French, painter
77a Westow Hill, SE19. *National Westminster Bank / Crystal Palace Foundation*
Pissarro, who stayed in a house on this site in 1870–1, was a prolific artist who experimented with several different styles, notably pointillism. One of the most important yet underrated of the Impressionists, he made several visits to England and painted several landscapes of this area. (See also Richmond upon Thames.)

PURLEY RAILWAY STATION
Purley Railway Station, Purley. *Bourne Society*
This plaque was erected to commemorate the
renaming of this station 'Purley' on 1 October 1888.
Originally named 'Godstone Road', it had been known
as 'Caterham Junction' since 1856.

SANDERSTEAD OLD FORGE
**Holy Family Church Hall, Limpsfield Road,
Sanderstead.** *Bourne Society*
The plaque records that Sanderstead Old Forge was
built here in the early eightenth century and was a
smithy for two centuries. Subsequently, until the early
1940s, it was 'The Skep', a private school.

STANLEY, W. F. R. (1829–1909), English, inventor,
philanthropist
12 South Norwood Hill, SE25. *English Heritage*
Stanley, who built and endowed these halls and the
technical school behind, began as an instrument
maker, inventing and improving theodolites,
anemometers, spirometers and meteorometers, and a
coin-in-the-slot machine to measure one's height. He
became 'Mr Norwood', contributing to local schools,
hospitals and charities so generously that the citizenry
erected a 'Little Ben' outside the railway station to
celebrate his golden wedding. He is known worldwide
for the Stanley knife.

SURREY IRON RAILWAY
Purley Library, Banstead Road, Purley.
Bourne Society
The plaque records that southern England's first public
railway, the Croydon, Merstham and Godstone line,
opened in July 1805. A horse-drawn service carrying
stone to Wandsworth, it ran across this site. It
eventually closed in 1846, blown away by the
development of steam locomotion. (See also
Wandsworth.)

TIVOLI LODGE
39 Beulah Hill, Upper Norwood, SE19.
London Borough of Croydon
This was the entrance lodge, designed by Decimus
Burton, to the Royal Beulah Spa and Pleasure Gardens,
which opened in 1830. The spa was built round a pure
saline well, whose water was analysed by Michael
Faraday (q.v.). It closed in 1855, because Londoners
'grew tired of water-drinking', and all the other
buildings were demolished in 1876.

WALLACE, Alfred Russel (1823–1913), Welsh,
naturalist
44 St Peter's Road, Croydon. *Greater London Council*
Travels in Amazonia (1848–52) and the Malay
Peninsula (1854–62) led Wallace, who lived here, to a
conception of evolution very similar to Darwin's
(q.v.). Their correspondence prompted Darwin to
publish his landmark book, and Darwin always
acknowledged the worth of Wallace's work.

**WILKS, Reverend
William**
(1843–1923),
English, cleric,
horticulturalist
**47 Shirley Church
Road, Shirley.**
London Borough of Croydon
Wilks, who lived here from 1879 to 1912, most
famously propagated the Shirley poppy. With its white
base, yellow or white stamens, anthers and pollen, and
no trace of black, it is now known worldwide and is
carved on Croydon's ceremonial mace. Wilks was
awarded the Royal Horticultural Society Victoria
Medal in 1912.

ZOLA, Émile
(1840–1902),
French, novelist
**Queen's Hotel,
122 Church Road,
SE19.** *English Heritage*
Zola lived here from
1898 to 1899. He
had fled France after
his famous letter to
the newspaper
L'Aurore headed
'*J'accuse*', written in
support of the Jewish
army officer Dreyfus, who was maliciously and falsely
accused of spying, brought official prosecution.
Pardoned after a year in London, he returned to
France a national hero. He was a pioneer of naturalism
in fiction, his works *Germinal* (1885), *La Terre* (1887)
and *La Débâcle* (1892) revealing a France not previously
accounted for in its literature.

EALING

On the western side of Greater London, the
London Borough of Ealing, once wholly in
Middlesex, is an amalgamation of the three
former municipal boroughs of Ealing, Southall
and Acton.

BALCON, Sir Michael (1896–1977), English, film
producer
Ealing Film Studios, Ealing Green, W5.
English Heritage
Sir Michael, who worked here from 1938 to 1956,
presided over the golden era of the studios, producing
a string of classic British comedies, including
Kind Hearts and Coronets and *Whisky Galore* (1949),
and *The Lavender Hill Mob* (1951). (See also Hackney
and Westminster 4.)

BLUMLEIN, Alan Dower (1903–42), English,
engineer, inventor
37 The Ridings, W5. *Greater London Council*
At the age of seven, Blumlein, who lived here,
presented his father with an invoice for repairing the
doorbell from 'Alan Blumlein Electrical Engineer'. He
went on to invent stereo (1931–3) and then designed

the in-flight radar system used by Bomber Command
during the Second World War. He was killed on board
a Halifax bomber during tests of a new radar
development.

BYRON, Lady Anne
(1792–1860), English,
educationalist
**Thames Valley
University, St
Mary's Road, W5.**
Ealing College
Lady Byron founded the
famous Co-operative School
on this site in 1834. She had
married Lord Byron in 1815, leaving after a year,
accusing him of insanity. Lord Byron was the first
person to have a heritage plaque erected (now
destroyed), and now has none, while his wife is here
remembered.

**CHAMBERS,
Dorothea Lambert**
(1878–1960), English,
tennis champion
**7 North Common
Road, W5.**
English Heritage
Chambers, who lived
here from 1887 to 1907,
was seven times Wimbledon Ladies Champion, and
winner of the gold medal at the London Olympics of
1908. She wrote *Tennis for Ladies* (1910), with advice
not only on technique but also on clothing. Her 1911

Wimbledon victory was a 6-0 6-0 whitewash. The only other person ever to win a Grand Slam title without dropping a game is Steffi Graf.

HAYNES, Arthur (1914–66), English, comedian
72 Gunnersbury Avenue, Ealing, W5.
Dead Comics Society
Haynes lived here from 1963 to 1966. *The Arthur Haynes Show* (1957–66), networked by ATV, was the most popular comedy series on television, featuring Haynes as a working-class tramp. In 1961 he appeared in the Royal Variety Show and was voted Television Personality of the Year.

JAMES, Sid (1913–76), South African, comic actor
35 Gunnersbury Avenue, Ealing, W5.
British Comedy Society
James, who lived here from 1956 to 1963, was born Joel Solomon Cohen, came to Britain in 1946 and never stopped working, in film, radio and television. Best remembered for nineteen 'Carry On' films, and a long association as foil to Tony Hancock (q.v.), he died on stage in Sunderland. (See also Richmond upon Thames.)

PERKIN, Sir William Henry (1838–1907), English, chemist
Oldfield Lane North, Greenford.
Royal Society of Chemistry
Local lore has it that the Grand Union Canal, running alongside, would change colour according to what was going on in the factory. In 1874 Perkin, under pressure from the rampant German chemical industry, sold up and retired a wealthy man. (See also Tower Hamlets.)

RICHARDS, Frank (1876–1961), English, children's story writer
Ealing Broadway Centre, Ealing, W5. *Private*
Frank Richards, the pen-name of Charles Hamilton, was born in a house on this site in 1876. He is in the *Guinness Book of Records* as the most prolific author of all time, penning an estimated 72.5 million words. Billy Bunter, 'the Fat Owl of the Remove', is his most enduring creation, and Bunter, according to George Orwell (q.v.), was 'famous wherever the Union Jack waves'.

YEAMES, W. F. (1835–1918), English, painter
8 Campbell Road, W7. *Ealing Museum Art and History Society*
Yeames lived here from 1894 to 1912. His famous painting *And When Did You Last See Your Father?* (1878) is one of the most popular in the Walker Art Gallery, Liverpool. He was a member of the St John's Wood clique, whose narrative art was popular but never critically acclaimed. He was elected a Royal Academician in 1878.

ENFIELD

On the northern edge of Greater London, once
wholly in Middlesex, the London Borough of
Enfield is an amalgamation of the three former
municipal boroughs of Southgate, Enfield and
Edmonton.

THE ANGEL
Angel Place, Fore Street, N18.
London Borough of Enfield
The plaque notes that this is the site of the Angel,
where the Stamford Hill Green Lanes Turnpike Trust
met from 1713 to 1826. This trust was concerned with
local road maintenance, financed by the levying of
tolls.

AYLWARD, Gladys
(1902–70), English,
missionary
**67 Cheddington
Road, N18.** *London
Borough of Enfield*
**Aylward School,
Windmill Road, N18.**
London Borough of Enfield
Aylward, who lived at the first
address and went to school at the second, spent her
savings in 1930 to travel to China, where she founded
a Christian mission called 'the Inn of the Eight
Happinesses'. Known eventually to the Chinese, after
initial distrust, as *Ai-Weh-Deh* ('Virtuous One'), her
work was the inspiration for the Hollywood film *The
Inn of the Sixth Happiness* (1958), starring Ingrid
Bergman.

BOOTH, William (1829–1912), English, Salvationist
33 Lancaster Avenue, Hadley Wood.
London Borough of Enfield
Booth, who lived here from 1903 until his death,
became a Methodist minister in 1844 and held his first
Christian Mission meeting in New Road, Stepney, in

1865. From this he evolved the worldwide Salvation
Army. (See also Tower Hamlets.)

**BOWLES, Edward
Augustus** (1865–1954),
English, gardener
**Myddleton House,
Bulls Cross.**
London Borough of Enfield
Bowles, who lived here,
was a self-taught enthusiast
of horticulture. His three
books, *My Garden in Spring*,
My Garden in Summer (both 1914) and *My Garden in
Autumn and Winter* (1915), have been reprinted several
times. There are forty different flower varieties named
after him, and there is a 'Bowles Corner' at the Royal
Horticultural Society Gardens at Wisley.

BRADSHAW, John (1863–1939), English, brewer,
philanthropist
Bourne Crescent, N14. *London Borough of Enfield*
Bradshaw, who lived in The Grange on this site from
the 1890s until his death, was a great benefactor of
Southgate. He was president and chairman of the
Taylor Walker brewery from 1906. Not given to many
public appearances, he was president and principal
supporter of the Southgate Reading Room and Library
from 1921 until his death and gave to a host of other
worthwhile local causes.

BRYDGES, James, third Duke of Chandos
(1731–89), English, courtier
14 The Green, N14. *London Borough of Camden*

The plaque records that this is the site of Minchenden House, demolished in 1853, home of the third Duke of Chandos. The Duke held various positions under George II and George III, such as Lord of the Royal Bedchamber, and for the last five years of his life he was Lord Steward of the Royal Household. His obituary noted that he was 'Unfeigned in his devotion, and his charity and benevolence were unbounded'.

CASH DISPENSER, World's first Barclays Bank, The Town, Enfield.
London Borough of Enfield

The world's first cash dispenser was installed here on 27 June 1967.

COWARD, Charles
(1905–76), English, rescuer of Jews
133 Chichester Road, N9.
English Heritage
Coward, who lived here from 1945 until his death, was elected one of 'the Righteous among the Nations', having a tree planted in his honour in the Avenue of Righteous Gentiles at Yad Vashem, the Holocaust memorial in Israel. He had been a prisoner of war at Auschwitz III, near the death camp Auschwitz II, and contrived to rescue some four hundred Jews. His story was told, spuriously, in the 1962 film *The Password is Courage*, starring Dirk Bogarde.

CRESSWELL, Henrietta
(1855–1931), English, writer, artist
16 Station Road, Winchmore Hill, N21.
Southgate District Civic Trust
Cresswell is best remembered for her elegiac book *Winchmore Hill: Memories of a Lost Village* (1912),

in which she vividly recalled the arrival of the navvies and the railway in 1869. She was also a book illustrator of, for example, *Alexis and His Flowers* (1891), written by her near-namesake Beatrix Creswell.

EDMONTON BOARD OF HEALTH
Church Street, N9. *London Borough of Enfield*
The plaque records that this was the site of the offices of the Edmonton Local Board of Health (1850–84).

ENFIELD CHASE
Mallinson House, 321 Chase Road, N14.
London Borough of Enfield
The plaque records that on this site stood the south gate to Enfield Chase, around which the hamlet of Southgate originally grew. Enfield Chase was a hunting ground, mentioned as early as 1154, in which local citizens had some common rights. It ceased to exist by an Act of Parliament of 1777, which divided the territory among various authorities, the king retaining ownership of approximately half.

HOOD, Thomas (1799–1845), English, poet
59 Vicar's Moor Lane, N21. *London Borough of Enfield*
Hood lived in Rose Cottage on this site from 1829 to 1835. He edited various literary magazines and was friends with the literati of his day, especially Lamb (q.v.) and de Quincey (q.v.). His most famous poem is 'The Song of the Shirt' (1843), a savage evocation of sweatshop conditions: 'Oh! God! that bread should be so dear, And flesh and blood so cheap!' (See also City, Westminster 1 and Westminster 4.)

HUNT, Leigh (1784–1859), English, poet, essayist
41–43 High Street, N14. *Southgate Civic Trust*
Hunt was born in a house on this site. As founding editor of *The Examiner* (1808–21), he was friends with Byron, Moore (q.v.), Shelley (q.v.) and Lamb (q.v.), championing the Romantics and publishing early works by Keats (q.v.). He was imprisoned with his brother from 1813 to 1815 for libelling the Prince Regent and lived abroad from 1822 to 1825 with Shelley and Byron. (See also Merton, Kensington & Chelsea 2, Hammersmith & Fulham and Camden 1.)

ICE WELLS
Redwood Close, N14. *London Borough of Enfield*
The plaque records that this is the site of the 'Ice Wells' which supplied ice to London in the nineteenth century. There is a grim picture of the job in James

Greenwood's *Low Life Deeps* (1881): 'The roads are alive with ice-getters, who with eager eyes and their blue noses peeping over the ridge of the ragged comforters in which their throats are enveloped, are hurrying to the ponds to see what sort of a crop King Frost has grown for them during the night.'

KEATS, John

(1795–1821), English, poet
Enfield Town Station booking hall, Enfield Town. *Private*
7 Keats Parade, Church Street, N9.
Edmonton Council

The first plaque records that this is the site of the school Keats attended, and the second that this is the site of the cottage in which Keats served his apprenticeship to Thomas Hammond, a surgeon. (See also City and Camden 1.)

LAKE, Sir James Winter (1742–1807), English, colonial pioneer
335 Firs Lane, N13. *London Borough of Enfield*
Sir James lived at Firs Hall, formerly on this site, all his life. He was deputy governor of the Hudson's Bay Company from 1782 to 1799, and governor from 1799 until his death. He was a patron of the arts, and a contemporary chronicler noted that he had 'the most extensive and choice collection of English portraits in the Kingdom'.

LAMB, Charles

(1775–1834), English, essayist
Clarendon Cottage, 85 Chase Side, Enfield Town. *Private*
89 Chase Side, Enfield Town. *Private*
Lamb's Cottage, Church Street, N9.
English Heritage
Lamb lived at the first address from 1827 to 1829, the second from 1829 to 1833, and the third for the last year of his life. Among his enduring work is *Tales from Shakespeare* (1807), written with his sister, Mary (see below), designed as an easy introduction to

the Bard for children. He wrote many essays under the pen-name of 'Elia', which were collected and published in two volumes (1823 and 1833). (See also City and Islington.)

LAMB, Mary (1764–1847), English, essayist
Lamb's Cottage, Church Street, N9.
English Heritage
Mary Lamb lived in her brother's care from 1796 onwards after an unfortunate episode in which, in a bout of insanity, she stabbed their mother to death. She repaid his devotion with loving collaboration on several works, including *Mrs Leicester's School* (1809), a book of children's stories of which she wrote the majority, and on *Tales from Shakespeare* (1807), where he handled the tragedies and she the comedies.

LAWRENCE,

Sir John (1811–79), English, colonial governor
Southgate House, Michenden School, High Street, N14. *Private*
Sir John, who lived here from 1861 to 1863, first went to India in 1829. Later, while working in the Punjab, he successfully prevented the spread of the 1857 Mutiny and led the troops which recaptured Delhi from the rebels. He was noted for his concern for the peasantry and his attempts to eradicate suttee, the practice of widows being put on their husbands' funeral pyres.

MARRYAT, Captain Frederick (1792–1848), English, novelist
470 Baker Street, Enfield Town.
London Borough of Enfield
Captain Marryat was educated at Holmwood on this site. Retiring from the Navy in 1830, he turned to novel-writing. Among his works are *Frank Mildmay* (1829), *Peter Simple* (1834) and *Mr Midshipman Easy* (1836), but his best-known book, still popular, is the children's story *Children of the New Forest* (1847). (See also Merton and Westminster 2.)

MYDDLETON, Sir Hugh (1560–1631), Welsh, engineer
Cunard Crescent/Bush Hill Road, N21.
London Borough of Enfield

Sir Hugh was a goldsmith, clothmaker, banker, mine owner and entrepreneur, but it is as a self-taught engineer that he is remembered; he was the driving force, while living here, behind the construction of the New River (1609–13), bringing fresh water from Ware in Hertfordshire to Islington. Much of the original 38 miles still wanders through North London.

PITT, William, the Elder (1708–78), English, Prime Minister
44 Merryhills Drive, Oakwood.
London Borough of Enfield
Pitt lived at South Lodge, near this site, prior to 1754. One of the towering figures in British political history, known as 'the Great Commoner', he was Prime Minister only from 1766 to 1768 but was the pivotal figure in British politics long before and after. It has been suggested that the history of Britain from the mid-1750s onwards was the history of Pitt. (See also Camden 1 and Westminster 4.)

SMITH, John Thomas (1766–1833), English, artist
314 Firs Lane, N13. *London Borough of Enfield*
Smith lived in Myrtle Cottage on this site from 1788 to 1795. He was invited to Edmonton by Sir James Winter Lake (see page 255) and was drawing master to the large Lake family. He illustrated a number of publications about London, including *The Antiquities of London and Its Environs* (1797), *The Ancient Topography of London* (1815) and *The Streets of London* (1815). Not surprisingly, he was known as 'Antiquity Smith'. In 1816 he was appointed Keeper of Prints at the British Museum, a post he held till his death.

SMITH, Stevie (1902–71), English, poet, novelist
1 Avondale Road, Palmers Green, N13.
English Heritage
Smith lived here from the age of three. Her three novels were well received, but she is best remembered for her seven volumes of poetry, which she read very well.

Her best-known poem is 'Not Waving but Drowning' (1957): 'I was much too far out all my life, and not waving but drowning.'

SOUTHGATE LOCAL GOVERNMENT
40 The Green, N14. *London Borough of Enfield*
The plaque notes that in 1881 this house became the first seat of local government in Southgate.

SOUTHGATE VILLAGE HALL
151 High Street, N14. *London Borough of Enfield*
This is the site of the former village hall, 'erected for the benefit of the Parish of Southgate in 1882'.

WAUGH, Reverend Benjamin (1839–1908), English, cleric
33 The Green, N14.
London Borough of Enfield
Waugh was living in a house on this site when in 1884 he founded the National Society for the Prevention of Cruelty to Children. The plaque says: 'The only voice which reached him was the cry of the child.' Having founded the society, he became its director from 1889 to 1905 and remained a consulting director thereafter. (See also Barnet and Greenwich.)

WHITAKER, Joseph (1820–95), English, publisher, bookseller
White Lodge, 68 Silver Street, Enfield Town.
English Heritage
Whitaker, who lived and died here, was apprenticed to a bookseller at the age of fourteen. In his thirties he set up on his own account, starting *The Bookseller* (still the trade's journal) in 1858, and in 1868 starting *Whitaker's Almanack*, an annual that still contains 'a vast amount of information'.

WILDE, Thomas, first Baron Truro (1782–1855), English, lawyer
2 Kelvin Avenue, N13. *London Borough of Enfield*
Wilde, who lived here, was a distinguished cross-examiner and was retained to defend Queen Caroline in 1820. Subsequently he became Solicitor General (1839–41), Attorney General (1841 and 1846), Chief Justice of the Common Pleas (1846–50) and Lord Chancellor (1850–2).

HARINGEY

In north London, the London Borough of
Haringey is an amalgamation of the three
former municipal boroughs of Hornsey, Wood
Green and Tottenham.

BARLOW, William
(1845–1934),
English,
crystallographer
**74–80 Muswell
Hill Broadway,
N10.** *London Borough
of Haringey*
Barlow may have
been the last great amateur in British science;
inheriting a fortune from his father, a speculative
builder, he was at leisure to pursue his interest in the
structure of crystals. He deduced that there were only
230 forms of symmetrical crystal arrangements,
known as space groups, and published his findings in
1894, unaware that Evgraf Federov in Russia and
Arthur Schönflies in Germany had separately reached
the same conclusions in 1891. A ridge on the moon,
Dorsa Barlow, is named in his memory.

BLAKELOCK, PC Keith (1945–85), English, police
officer
Muswell Hill Roundabout, N10.
Police Memorial Trust
On the night of 6 October 1985 there was fierce
rioting on the Broadwater Farm Estate in Tottenham.
In the course of the night, PC Blakelock, who was a
community police officer, not trained in riot duty,
tripped and was set upon with knives and machetes.
He was posthumously awarded the Queen's Police
Medal for Gallantry, and the police fundamentally
revised their strategies for handling riots. Unusually,
this memorial is set up in his usual area of patrol,
rather than where he was killed.

CHAPMAN, Colin
(1928–82), English,
sports-car designer
**7 Tottenham Lane,
N8.** *Club Lotus*
The plaque is situated
at the entrance to
what is now a Jewson
depot, next door to
the former Railway Hotel pub (now the Wishing Well),
where the landlord was Colin Chapman's father. Lotus
won the Formula 1 Constructors' Championship seven
times between 1963 and 1978, with cars driven by Jim
Clark and Graham Hill (q.v.). Lotus sports cars have
cult status with their owners.

COLLINS, W. J. (1856–1936), English, architect,
developer
14 Cranmore Way, N10. *London Borough of Haringey*
Collins lived here from 1902 to 1911. He was an
influential figure in the Arts and Crafts architecture of
the early twentieth century, particularly remembered
for the Rookfield Garden Estate at the foot of Muswell
Hill, where the generous amount of green space
echoes the more famous ambience of Hampstead
Garden Suburb. In 1912 he
moved to Southampton and
developed further suburbs
along the same lines.

DICKENS, Charles
(1812–70), English,
novelist
92 North Road, N6. *Private*

Dickens stayed here in 1832. Several characters in *David Copperfield* (1849–50) lived in this very area, including David's aunt, Betsey Trotwood, his old schoolmaster, Dr Strong, and Copperfield himself after his marriage to Dora. (See also Westminster 2, Westminster 4, Southwark and Camden 2.)

GERMAN INTERNEES
Alexandra Palace, N22.
Anglo-German Family History Society
This plaque is erected to the memory of over seventeen thousand German and other enemy aliens of military age interned at Alexandra Palace between 1914 and 1919.

HARVEY, Lilian (1906–68), German, actress
13 Weston Park, Crouch End, N8.
Private
'The Sweetest Girl in the World' was born here, daughter of an English mother and a German businessman father. She was a star of German cinema in both silent and talkie eras, but her four Hollywood films were not successful. She lost her German citizenship in 1943 after long-strained relations with the Gestapo, because of her continued contacts with Jewish friends. She lived in France after the war and had a successful singing career.

HEATH ROBINSON, William (1872–1944), English, artist, cartoonist
25 Southwood Avenue, N6. *London Borough of Haringey*
Heath Robinson, who lived here, has given his name to any elaborate, rickety piece of machinery; his drawings of fantastically complicated contraptions, tended by balding bespectacled boffins, involving great lengths of knotted string and multiple pulleys and levers to perform tasks such as 'removing a wart from the top of the head' have a special niche in the national consciousness. American readers may think of him as the British Rube Goldberg. (See also Harrow.)

HOUSMAN, A. E. (1859–1936), English, poet, classical scholar
17 North Road, Highgate, N6.
Greater London Council
Housman wrote his most famous work, the sixty-three poem cycle *A Shropshire Lad*, while living here. Amazingly, he had to publish it himself in 1896; it has never been out of print since and remains the cornerstone of his reputation as a great lyric poet. Housman thought of himself as a classical scholar first and a poet second, but posterity disagrees.

HOWARD, Luke (1772–1864), English, chemist, meteorologist
7 Bruce Grove, N17. *English Heritage*
Howard, 'Namer of Clouds' according to the plaque, lived and died here. In his monograph *The Modification of Clouds* (1803) he proposed a Latin classification of cloud types – cirrus, stratus, cumulus, and combinations thereof – which remains in use today.

KINGSLEY, Mary (1862–1900), English, traveller, ethnologist
22 Southwood Lane, Highgate, N6.
Greater London Council
Mary Kingsley lived here as a child. A niece of Charles Kingsley (q.v.), she travelled extensively in West Africa (1893–5) and published *Travels in West Africa* (1897) and *West African Studies* (1899), recounting her experiences. She died of fever while nursing in the Second Boer War.

MacDOWELL, Patrick (1799–1870), Irish, sculptor
34 Wood Lane, Highgate, N6. *Private*
MacDowell lived here for many years. Among his portrait works are both Pitt the Elder and Pitt the Younger (qq.v.) in the Palace of Westminster, and Turner (q.v.) in St Paul's. His last major work was *Europe*, one of the four great groups of figures around the Albert Memorial. He was elected a Royal Academician in 1846.

MATCHAM, Frank (1854–1920), English, theatre
architect
10 Haslemere Road, N8. *English Heritage*
Matcham, who lived here from 1895 to 1904,
designed over 150 theatres all over Britain, in London
including the Hackney Empire (1901), the Coliseum
(1904), the Palladium (1910) and the Victoria Palace
(1911). Noted for his exuberant interiors, he also
pioneered the use of cantilevered steel, enabling
balconies to be built without pillars, giving improved
sightlines for the rear stalls.

PRENTICE, Carswell (1891–1964), English,
inventor
118 Hillfield Avenue, Crouch End, N8.
Society for Promoting Historic Buildings
There is just a hint of subversion here; those of a
po-faced disposition should perhaps not read on.
Carswell Prentice did not exist and he did not invent
the supermarket trolley, nor did he stay here in 1932.
The 'Society' that erected the plaque is a front for a
guerrilla conspiracy to undermine the whole business
of orthodox *plaquerie*. However, not all their plaques
are spurious: see Vivian Stanshall, below.

SAVARKAR, Vinayak Damodar (1883–1966),
Indian, philosopher, politician
65 Cromwell Avenue, Highgate, N6.
Greater London Council
Savarkar, who lived here while studying law in
London, developed the Hindu nationalist political
ideology of *Hindutva* ('Hinduness'), a more extreme
line than that of the Indian National Congress. He was
sentenced to fifty years in prison in 1910 for agitation
but released in 1921, having promised, falsely, to give
up revolutionary activity. His last years were clouded
by accusations of involvement in Gandhi's
assassination; he was tried but cleared on grounds of
'insufficient evidence'.

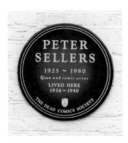

SELLERS, Peter
(1925–80), English,
actor, comedian
**10 Muswell Hill
Road, Highgate,
N6.** *Dead Comics Society*
Sellers, who lived
here from 1936 to
1940, first came to
fame on *The Goon*

Show (1951–9) (q.v.) and moved on to a prolific
film career, too often self-indulgent, including
The Ladykillers (1955), *I'm Alright Jack* (1959),
Dr Strangelove (1963) and the *Pink Panther* series.
His final unqualified triumph was his straight role
in his last but one film, *Being There* (1980).

STANSHALL, Vivian
(1943–95), English,
musician, humorist
**1 Hillfield Park,
N10.** *Society for the
Promotion of Historic
Buildings*
Musician, painter, singer,
songwriter, poet, raconteur
– Stanshall, who lived his last five
years here, is beyond ready characterisation. Often
called an eccentric, he hated the term, thinking it
implied he was putting on an act. Most famous for his
work with the Bonzo Dog Doo-Dah Band, his career
was clouded by alcohol but, like his friend Keith Moon
(q.v.), he was unrepentant, saying: 'If I had all the
money I've spent on drink – I'd spend it on drink.'

TAMBO, Adelaide
(1929–2007), South
African, politician
**51 Alexandra
Park Road, N10.**
*London Borough of
Haringey*
Adelaide Tambo lived
here with her husband,
Oliver (see below), from
1959 to 1990. They married in 1956 and she was
scarcely less famous in the anti-apartheid struggle than
her husband, being known with genuine affection as
'Mama Tambo' across South Africa.

TAMBO, Oliver (1917–93), South African, politician
51 Alexandra Park Road, N10.
London Borough of Haringey
Tambo lived here from 1959 to 1990. He had been
active in the African National Congress since the 1940s
and, when he was served with a five-year banning
order by the South African government in 1959, he
was sent abroad by the ANC to mobilise international
support for the anti-apartheid struggle. He was
President of the ANC from 1967 until his death.

TEGETMEIER, William Bernhard (1816–1912), English, naturalist
101 St James's Lane, N10. *London Borough of Haringey*
Tegetmeier lived here from 1858 to 1868. A difficult man to pin down, he kept bees, he was natural history editor of *The Field*, he developed the use of homing pigeons for military purposes, and he worked with Charles Darwin (q.v.) in his enquiries into variations in animals.

TELEVISION
Alexandra Palace, N22.
Greater London Council
The inaugural television service began with two systems alternating: Marconi/EMI, a team led by Alan Blumlein (q.v.) with 405 lines; and John Logie Baird (q.v.) with 240 lines. This alternation continued until February 1937, when the Baird system was discontinued. Transmission from 'Ally Pally', a nickname coined, it is said, by Gracie Fields (q.v.), continued till 1981.

WAKEFIELD, Priscilla (1751–1832), English, philanthropist
310 High Road, Tottenham, N15.
London Borough of Haringey
Wakefield lived in Ship Yard, near this site. She wrote numerous educational books for young people on a range of topics, founded a lying-in charity for women in 1791, and the first Frugality Bank, or Penny Bank, in 1798 on this site. In the same year she wrote *Reflections on the Present Condition of the Female Sex*, which places her in the front rank of early feminists, alongside Mary Wollstonecraft (q.v.).

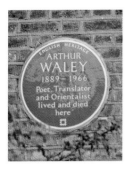

WALEY, Arthur
(1889–1966), English, orientalist, sinologist
50 Southwood Lane, Highgate, N6.
English Heritage
Waley lived and died here. While working at the British Museum (1913–29), he taught himself Chinese and Japanese and subsequently published numerous translations of oriental classics, aimed, he said, at 'people who do not ordinarily read poetry'. He never actually went to the Far East.

WILLIAMS, John (1796–1839), English, missionary
Cooke Estate, 316 Tottenham High Road, N15.
London Missionary Society
Williams was born near this site. He carried out successful missionary work in Tahiti, Samoa and Raratonga, but the New Hebrides in 1839 was new territory for him and the natives on Erromanga were in a vengeful mood after a bruising recent visit from a trading ship.

HARROW

Lying at the north-west corner of Greater London, the London Borough of Harrow was formed as an Urban District of Middlesex in 1934 and is the only London Borough to occupy the same borders as a single former district.

ATTLEE, Clement (1883–1967), English, Prime Minister
Heywood Court, London Road, Stanmore.
Harrow Heritage Trust
The plaque records that this was the site of Clement Attlee's family home. First elected to Parliament in 1922, Attlee became leader of the Labour Party in 1935. He was Churchill's Deputy Prime Minister in the wartime coalition government (1940–5), Prime Minister in the reforming Labour government of 1945–51, and Leader of the Opposition from 1951 to 1955. (See also Redbridge.)

BALLANTYNE, R. M. (1825–94), Scottish, novelist
Duneaves, Mount Park Road, Harrow.
Greater London Council
Ballantyne, 'author of books for boys' (says the plaque), lived here from 1886 until his death. After experiences in Canada as a young man between 1841 and 1848, he wrote over a hundred stories, where his narrative skill and the manly virtues of his heroes ensured his popularity well into the twentieth century. Among his best are *The Young Fur Traders* (1856),

The Coral Island (1857) and *Martin Rattler* (1858).

BEETON, Mrs Isabella (1836–65), English, cookery writer
513 Uxbridge Road, Hatch End.
Harrow Heritage Trust
Mrs Beeton's *Book of Household Management* (1861) was first issued in parts in her husband's publication *The Englishwoman's Domestic Magazine* in 1859–61. It begins without compromise: 'As with the Commander of an Army, or the leader of an enterprise, so it is with the mistress of a house.' Republished many times, it includes dicta such as 'a place for everything, and everything in its place'.

BRYDGES, James, first Duke of Chandos (1673–1744), English, aristocrat
St Lawrence's Church, Whitchurch Lane, Canons Park. *Harrow Heritage Trust*
Brydges, under whose patronage Handel (see page 263) played and composed here, was Paymaster General of the British Army during the War of the Spanish Succession (1701–14), from which he amassed a vast fortune, which he spent on building his house, Cannons, nearby, and on building this church. When he died, his son found the estate so encumbered by debt that Cannons was demolished and the contents were sold off in 1747.

FATAL MOTOR ACCIDENT, First Grove Hill, Harrow.

Borough of Harrow
'Take heed', says the plaque – this is the site of the first recorded fatal car accident. On 25 February 1899, demonstrating a wagonette to some friends, thirty-one-year-old engineer Edward Sewell was travelling down Grove Hill at a mere 14 mph when a wheel shed its rim. Sewell and his front-seat passenger died in hospital three days later.

GILBERT, W. S. (1836–1911), English, humorist, librettist
Grim's Dyke, Old Redding.
Harrow Heritage Trust / Greater London Council
Gilbert lived here from 1890 until his death by drowning in the lake while trying to save a young lady in difficulties. His collaboration with Sir Arthur Sullivan (1875–96) produced thirteen comic operas that are regularly performed to this day. They include *Trial by Jury*, *The Pirates of Penzance*, *Iolanthe*, *The Mikado*, *Ruddigore* and *The Yeomen of the Guard*. (See also Kensington & Chelsea 2.)

GOODALL, Frederick (1822–1904), English, painter
Grim's Dyke, Old Redding.
Harrow Heritage Trust / Greater London Council
Goodall had this house built for him by Richard Norman Shaw (q.v.) in 1872. He had begun by painting historical episodes such as *Cranmer at the Traitors' Gate* (1856) but had his greatest success with scenes from Egypt, which he visited in 1858–9 and 1870–2. He was a notable and generous host, which unfortunately meant that by the time of his death he was bankrupt. The house is now a hotel.

HANDEL, George Frederick (1685–1759), German, composer
St Lawrence's Church, Whitchurch Lane, Canons Park. *Harrow Heritage Trust*
Handel composed and played at this church in 1717–18. While here he wrote the oratorio *Esther*, the *Chandos Anthems* and *Acis and Galatea*. The organ of

1716 is by Gerard Smith, with a case carved by Grinling Gibbons; it was refurbished in 1994. (See also Westminster 3.)

HEATH ROBINSON, William (1872–1944), English, artist, humorist
75 Moss Lane, Pinner. *Greater London Council*
Heath Robinson, who lived here from 1913 to 1918, has given his name to any elaborate, rickety piece of machinery; his drawings of fantastically complicated contraptions, tended by balding bespectacled boffins, involving great lengths of knotted string and multiple pulleys and levers to perform tasks such as 'removing a wart from the top of the head', have a special niche in the national consciousness. (See also Haringey.)

SHAW, Richard Norman (1831–1912), Scottish, architect
Grim's Dyke, Old Redding.
Harrow Heritage Trust / Greater London Council
Shaw designed this house for the painter Frederick Goodall (see above) in 1872. It is now a luxury hotel. (See also Camden 1.)

SULLONIACAE
Brockley Hill, Stanmore.
Private
This is the site of the Roman pottery of Sulloniacae (AD *c.* 65–160). First identified in the 1850s, and the subject of several digs since 1937, this was a major production centre serving legions heading north and west along Watling Street. Remains of its products have been found throughout Britain.

WARE, Edwin M. (1888–1971), English, local historian
13 High Street, Pinner. *Private*
Ware, who lived here from 1912 to 1915, was parish clerk for thirty-two years. His great work as a local historian was the four-part *Pinner in the Vale* (1955–7), but he also wrote other works on, for example, Pinner's national schools. His home is now a Café Rouge.

HAVERING

At the north-east corner of Greater London,
once wholly in Essex, the London Borough of
Havering is an amalgamation of the former
municipal borough of Romford with the
Hornchurch urban district.

BLACKER BOMBARD

Station Lane, Hornchurch. *McCarthy & Stone*
The Blacker bombard was a cheap and simple anti-tank
weapon developed by Lieutenant Colonel Stewart
Blacker at the beginning of the Second World War.
It was widely issued to the Home Guard and the
emplacement here was designed to protect the
municipal buildings and RAF Hornchurch. It was
never fired in anger.

HAVERING PALACE

**St John the
Evangelist
Churchyard,
Havering-atte-
Bower.** *London
Borough of Havering*
Havering Palace had
a busy six-hundred-
year life, being the
official residence of
England's queens, as
well as seeing
conspiracy and the investiture of Richard II. It fell into
decay in Charles I's reign and was sold off during the
Commonwealth.

PILGRIM FERRY

Ferry Lane, Rainham. *London Borough of Havering*
Built to facilitate the travel of pilgrims to Canterbury,
the ferry survived until the late nineteenth century.
The plaque is erected on the river wall in one of the
least attractive locations in the metropolis.

REPTON, Humphry (1752–1818), English, landscape gardener

182 Main Road, Gidea Park. *Private*

Repton, who lived in a cottage on this site, was the last
great landscape gardener of the eighteenth century,
employed by the chief noblemen of the day. He
published a number of important treatises, including
Sketches and Hints on Landscape Gardening (1795),
*Observations on the Theory and Practice of Landscape
Gardening* (1803), *An Enquiry into the Changes of Taste in
Landscape Gardening* (1806) and *Fragments on the Theory
and Practice of Landscape Gardening* (1816). (See also
Redbridge.)

TE WHARE PUNI

67 Butts Green Road, Hornchurch. *Private*
Whare puni means 'warm house' or 'meeting house' in
Maori and clearly conveys the notion of a welcoming
home from home for the New Zealand troops
convalescing in the area during the First World War.

HILLINGDON

Lying on the western edge of Greater London, once wholly in Middlesex, the London Borough of Hillingdon is an amalgamation of the former municipal borough of Uxbridge with the three Urban districts of Hayes & Harlington, Ruislip-Northwood and Yiewsley & West Drayton.

DENLEY, John (d.1555), English, martyr
Windsor Street Garden, Uxbridge. *Private*
This plaque was erected in August 1955 to commemorate the burning at the stake opposite this spot in August 1555 of three English martyrs. John Denley is described as 'a gentleman from Maidstone' in Foxe's *Book of Martyrs*. Condemned at the consistory court of St Paul's on 1 July, he was burnt here on or about 28 August. He is said to have sung a psalm as the flames took hold.

GOSPEL TREE
Swakeleys Road, Ickenham. *W. S. Try (Builders)*
The plaque records: 'Here in medieval days beneath this holy oak or Gospel Tree came once a year the curate and people to invoke the divine blessing upon their forthcoming crops.' It was erected in 1950 when the area was being developed. It is thought the location had been chosen historically because it marked the boundaries of three parishes – Ickenham, Harefield and Uxbridge. The stone was re-carved in 2008.

ORWELL, George (1903–50), English, novelist, essayist
116–118 Church Road, Hayes.
Hayes Literary Society
It was during his time teaching here, a job he took simply to make ends meet, that Eric Blair used the *nom de plume* 'George Orwell' for the first time, with the publication of *Down and Out in Paris and London*.

PACKINGHAM, Patrick (1534–55), English, martyr
Windsor Street Garden, Uxbridge. *Private*
Packingham was another of the martyrs burned opposite this spot in August 1555 under the Marian persecution so zealously pursued by Edmund Bonner, bishop of London.

SMITH, Robert (d.1555), English, martyr
Windsor Street Garden, Uxbridge. *Private*
A clerk in the college at Windsor, Smith was examined several times by Edmund Bonner, John Dee and others to determine the nature of his heresy. Foxe reports in his *Book of Martyrs* that Smith, condemned to be burnt, 'sent his mother-in-law some nutmeg and his daughter some comfets [sweets]'.

WILBERFORCE, William (1759–1833), English, anti-slavery campaigner
The Chestnuts, Honeycroft Hill, Uxbridge.
London Borough of Hillingdon
Wilberforce lived here from 1824 to 1826. He is third only to Dickens and William Morris in the number of plaques put up in his memory. (See also Barnet, Lambeth, Kensington & Chelsea 2, Wandsworth and Merton)

HOUNSLOW

Lying at the south-west corner of Greater
London, once wholly in the County of
Middlesex, the London Borough of Hounslow
is an amalgamation of three former urban
districts: Brentford & Chiswick, Feltham, and
Heston & Isleworth.

BERESFORD, Jack (1899–1977), English, oarsman
19 Grove Park Gardens, Chiswick, W4.
English Heritage

Beresford, who lived here from 1903 to 1940, won
medals at five consecutive Olympic Games (1920–36)
and would have been favourite for the double sculls in
1940 if the Second World War had not intervened. His
record of three golds and two silvers has been
surpassed by Sir Steve Redgrave's five golds, but he
was undoubtedly the greatest oarsman in the world
between the wars.

FORSTER, E. M. (1879–1970), English, novelist
**9 Arlington Park Mansions, Sutton Lane,
Chiswick, W4.** *Greater London Council*
Forster lived here from 1939 to 1961. He was an
associate of the Bloomsbury Group (q.v.), and his
novels include *A Room with a View* (1908), *Howard's End*
(1910) and *A Passage to India* (1924), the last written

after several years in India, including some time as
secretary to the Maharajah of Dewas. He was awarded
the Order of Merit in 1969.

**GANDY, Joseph
Michael**
(1771–1843),
English, artist,
architect
**58 Grove Park
Terrace, Chiswick,
W4.** *English Heritage*
Gandy, described on
the plaque as an
'architectural
visionary', lived here from 1833 to 1838. His greatest
success was in his work with Sir John Soane, producing
perspective drawings of Soane's designs that made the
plans real for the clients. In his own architectural
practice he was a failure, reputedly a difficult
customer, refusing to compromise, and twice rescued
by Soane from debtors' prison. His 'vision' was
encapsulated in two articles written in 1821 on
The Philosophy of Architecture, but he was unable to
realise his dreams and died in an asylum, to which his
family committed him in 1839.

HITCH, Private Frederick, VC (1856–1913),
English, soldier
62 Cranbrook Road, Chiswick, W4.
English Heritage
Hitch, who lived and died here, was one of eleven
recipients of the Victoria Cross after the battle of
Rorke's Drift, on 22/23 January 1879. Severely

wounded in the shoulder early in the battle, he fought to keep the hospital working and supplied ammunition to his comrades at the defences. In later life he was a London cabbie, and there is a Fred Hitch award for gallantry by cab drivers. In the film *Zulu* he was portrayed by the actor James Booth.

HOGARTH, William (1697–1764), English, painter
Hogarth House, Hogarth Lane, Chiswick, W4.
County of Middlesex
Hogarth lived here from 1749 until his death.

He is best known for his satirical series depicting moral corruption, such as *The Rake's Progress* (c.1732) and *Marriage à la Mode* (1743–5). His mastery of human expression and characterisation is shown in many works, such as his portrait of Captain Thomas Coram (1740) and his study of his servants (1750–5). The house is now a museum.

LINDLEY, John (1799–1865), English, botanist
Bedford House, The Avenue, Chiswick, W4.
English Heritage
Lindley, who lived here from 1836 until his death, was assistant to Sir Joseph Banks (q.v.), and Professor of Botany in the University of London (1829–60). A pioneer in the cultivation of orchids, his works include *An Outline of the First Principles of Horticulture* (1832), *The Genera and Species of Orchidaceous Plants* (1835), *A Natural System of Botany* (1836) and *The Vegetable Kingdom* (1846).

PISSARRO, Lucien (1863–1944), French, painter, wood engraver
27 Stamford Brook Road, W6.
Greater London Council
The son of Camille Pissarro (q.v.), with whom he studied, he adopted the Impressionist and later Neo-Impressionist style. He settled in London in 1890 and founded the Eragny Press (1896), which was very influential on English book design. He was later one of the founders of the Camden Town Group with Bevan (q.v.) and Sickert (q.v.).

POPE, Alexander (1688–1744), English, poet, essayist

110 Chiswick Lane South, W4. *English Heritage*
Pope, who lived in this row from 1716 to 1719, was crippled from an early age, and largely self-educated, but he became one of the greatest English poets, a master of metre. Among his most familiar phrases are: 'To err is human; to forgive, divine' and 'Fools rush in where angels fear to tread'. (See also City.)

REYNOLDS, St Richard (c.1492–1535), English, monk
The Art Centre, Syon House, Isleworth. *Private*
Reynolds lived in these precincts. A Brigittine monk, he was the first person to refuse to take Henry VIII's oath of supremacy. For this he was hanged, drawn and quartered at Tyburn on 4 May 1535. He was canonised by Pope Paul VI in 1970 as one of the Forty Martyrs of England and Wales.

VAN GOGH, Vincent (1853–90), Dutch, painter
160 Twickenham Road, Isleworth. *Private*

Van Gogh lived here in 1876. At the time he was in the grip of a religious fervour, wanting 'to preach the gospel everywhere', and acted as an unpaid assistant to a nearby Methodist minister. He was not to take up painting until 1880. (See also Lambeth.)

YEATS, Jack Butler (1871–1957), Irish, painter
3 Blenheim Road, Chiswick, W4.
Bedford Park Society
Yeats, who lived here from 1888 to c.1900 with his father and brother (see

below), was the most important Irish artist of the twentieth century. He began with small illustrations and cartoons, including the first graphic strip version of *Sherlock Holmes* in 1894, but moved on after 1918 to vivid Irish landscapes with horses and travelling players.

YEATS, John Butler (1839–1922), Irish, painter
3 Blenheim Road, Chiswick, W4.
Bedford Park Society
Yeats was initially a lawyer but took up painting in 1867, studying at the Heatherley School of Art and the Slade. His vivid portraits of leading Irish figures, such as Countess Markiewitz and John O'Leary, were emblems of Irish nationalism. He wrote brilliant letters, collected and edited in 1946, which give a sparkling picture of Irish life.

YEATS, William Butler (1865–1939), Irish, poet, playwright
3 Blenheim Road, Chiswick, W4.
Bedford Park Society
A giant of English language literature of the twentieth century, Yeats was a key figure in the Irish literary revival as co-founder of the Abbey Theatre (1904) and was awarded the Nobel Prize in 1923. His lines speak for the age: 'Things fall apart, the centre cannot hold.' (See also Camden 2.)

ZOFFANY, Johann (1733–1810), German, painter
65 Strand-on-the-Green, Chiswick, W4.
Greater London Council

Zoffany, who lived here from 1790 until his death, was patronised by George III. He specialised in family portraits and was the first to depict royal groups informally, in a genre that he more or less invented and which came to be called 'conversation pieces'. He also painted the leading actors of the day in famous parts, such as *Garrick as Hamlet*. He was a founder member of the Royal Academy in 1769.

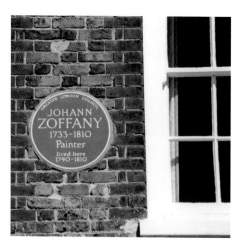

KINGSTON UPON THAMES

Lying at the south-west corner of Greater
London, and formerly wholly in Surrey, the
Royal Borough of Kingston upon Thames is an
amalgamation of three former municipal
boroughs: Surbiton, Malden & Coombe and
Kingston upon Thames. Several Saxon kings
were crowned here.

BENN, Sir Anthony (1569/70–1618), English,
lawyer
Norbiton Hall, Birkenhead Avenue, Norbiton.
Private
Sir Anthony is listed as one of four notable former
inhabitants of Norbiton Hall (see page 270), including
George Evelyn (see below), his uncle by marriage. He
bought the house from his father-in-law in 1605 and
lived there until his death. He was Recorder of
Kingston in 1610 and Recorder of London in 1617.

BESTALL, Alfred
(1892–1986), Welsh,
illustrator
**58 Cranes Park,
Surbiton.**
English Heritage
Bestall lived here from
1936 to 1966. His early work
included illustrations for Enid
Blyton (see below) and *Punch* and *Tatler* magazines.
But his rise to wider fame began when he took over
the writing and illustration of the *Rupert Bear* strip in
the *Daily Express* in 1935. He strengthened the story
lines and created a magic landscape, particularly
featured in the *Rupert Bear Annuals*, inspired by
Snowdonia, which he knew from his own childhood
family holidays. He retired from the *Express* in 1965.

BLYTON, Enid (1897–1968), English, children's
writer
207 Hook Road, Chessington. *English Heritage*
Blyton lived here from 1920 to 1924. With a steady
output of ten thousand words a day, she produced over

four hundred stories for children, the best-
remembered being the 'Famous Five' and 'Secret
Seven' series, and the 'Toyland' adventures of Noddy,
Big Ears and friends. (See also Bromley and
Southwark).

EISENHOWER, Dwight D. (1890–1969),
American, soldier, President
Warren Road, Coombe.
Royal Borough of Kingston-upon-Thames
Eisenhower lived in Telegraph Cottage, along Warren
Road, from 1942 to 1944. He commanded Allied
Forces in North Africa and Italy in 1942–3 and the
invasion of Europe in 1944–5. He resigned from the
army in 1952
and served two
terms as the
thirty-fourth
President of the
United States. In
his valedictory
speech he coined
the prophetic
phrase 'military-
industrial complex', and warned of the threat it posed.
(See also Westminster 3 and Westminster 4.)

EVELYN, George (1530–1603), English, gunpowder
maker
Norbiton Hall, Birkenhead Avenue, Norbiton.
Private
George Evelyn is credited as the first person to
manufacture gunpowder in Britain, having brought the
techniques over from Flanders. He was granted a

monopoly by Elizabeth I in 1565 and had his main mill at Long Ditton, though there is a reference to gunpowder being stored at Norbiton Hall in 1588. He was the grandfather of John Evelyn, the celebrated diarist and friend of Pepys.

LIVERPOOL, Mary, Countess of (d.1846), English
Norbiton Hall, Birkenhead Avenue, Norbiton.
Private
After the death of her husband, the second Earl of Liverpool, who had been Prime Minister (1812–27), the countess lived here from 1827 until her own death. She was his second wife, marrying him in 1822 after the death of his first wife, who had been one of her best friends.

MELBA, Dame Nellie (1861–1931), Australian, soprano
Coombe House, Devey Close, Coombe.
English Heritage
Dame Nellie, stage-name of Helen Porter Mitchell, lived here in 1906. She was the most famous soprano of all and first appeared at Covent Garden in 1888. The peach Melba dessert and Melba toast were named after her. She was not universally popular with her fellow-singers, who apparently had much to put up with from her.

MEREDITH, George (1828–1909), English, novelist
Buick House, London Road, Norbiton. *Private*
Meredith lived here from 1865 to 1868, completing his novels *Rhoda Fleming* and *Vittoria* in that time. In his old age he was highly regarded, Oscar Wilde (q.v.) saying of him: 'Ah, Meredith! Who can define him? His style is chaos illumined by flashes of lightning.' (See also Kensington & Chelsea 2.)

MUYBRIDGE, Eadweard (1830–1904), English, photographer
2 Liverpool Road, Kingston.
Royal Photographic Society / Olympus
Muybridge was born in Kingston and returned in 1894, living here in his cousin's house until his death. His fame comes from his career in the United States; in 1872, the wealthy American racehorse owner Leland Stanford wanted a question solved: did all four of a horse's hooves leave the ground during a gallop? He hired Muybridge, already a celebrated photographer of the American landscape, to prove it. With the crucial assistance of a railroad engineer, John D. Isaacs, who devised a trigger for the cameras, Muybridge was able to demonstrate that the hooves did indeed all leave the ground.

NORBITON HALL
Norbiton Hall, Birkenhead Avenue, Norbiton.
Private
Norbiton Hall is described on the plaque as dating from the sixteenth century but clearly had a complex building history, being described as 'new-built' in 1681. Its estates were gradually diminished by the coming of roads and railways and the general development of Kingston, and it was demolished in 1933 and the present flats, which also are called Norbiton Hall, were erected.

PICTON, Cesar (*c.*1755–1836), Senegalese, slave, coal merchant
52 High Street, Kingston. *Borough of Kingston*
Picton lived here from 1788 to 1807. Left money by various members of the Philipps family, he had obviously been more than a servant. The family wealth came from coal mines, and they were probably useful for his business in getting their well-to-do friends to buy his coal. He married a local girl and died a rich man.

TAVERNER, Richard (*c.*1505–75), English, religious reformer
Norbiton Hall, Birkenhead Avenue, Norbiton.
Private
Taverner lived here in the 1540s, while work was carried out on his main residence at Woodeaton. He is remembered for 'Taverner's Bible', a 1539 English translation. He was clearly something of a maverick – imprisoned by Henry VIII, restored to favour, and canny enough to survive Mary I and Elizabeth I.

V2 ROCKET
Corner of King's Road and Park Road, Kingston. *Borough of Kingston*
On 22 January 1945 at 2.35 p.m. the last V2 long-range rocket to hit Kingston fell near this spot, killing eight people and injuring 117 more. Thirty-three homes were destroyed and over two thousand others were damaged. This was the most severe incident in Kingston in the Second World War. In all 1,358 V2s were fired at London, killing 2,754 people. The only defence was to attack the launch sites. (For other Second World War damage sites, see City, Tower Hamlets, Newham and Lewisham.)

MERTON

Formerly wholly in Surrey, the London Borough of Merton is an amalgamation of two former municipal boroughs, Mitcham and Wimbledon, plus Merton & Morden Urban District.

BADEN-POWELL, Robert (1857–1941), English, army officer
Mill House, Windmill Road, SW19. *Private*
'BP', as he was universally known, wrote parts of his book *Scouting for Boys* while staying here in 1908. He was already a national hero since his defence of Mafeking (1899–1900) during the Boer War. He had begun to form ideas about a boys' movement and conducted an experimental camp on Brownsea Island in 1907. Thus the Scout Movement was born, followed in 1910 by the Girl Guides. Baden-Powell was made Chief Scout of the World in 1920. This house is now a museum. (See also Kensington & Chelsea 1.)

BELL, Robert (1564–1640), English, merchant adventurer
Eagle House, High Street, Wimbledon, SW19.
London Borough of Merton
Bell, who built this house in 1613, was a member of the Girdlers' Company and one of the earliest investors ('adventurers') in the East India Company. He rose rapidly through its ranks, but he acquired a reputation for dubious accounting and was eventually forced out under a cloud.

BUTLER, Josephine (1828–1906), English, suffragette
8 North View, Wimbledon Common, SW19.
English Heritage
Butler lived here from 1890 to 1893. She had been instrumental in the repeal of the Contagious Diseases Act in 1886 and devoted herself to campaigns about child prostitution, which led to the raising of the age of consent from thirteen to sixteen, and about the 'white slave traffic' on the Continent. She was also a leading member of the women's suffrage movement.

CHAIN, Sir Ernst (1906–79), German, scientist
9 North View, Wimbledon Common, SW19.
English Heritage
Sir Ernst lived here. He was a Jewish refugee from Nazism, coming to Britain in 1933. In 1939 he began working with Howard Florey and they discovered penicillin's therapeutic action and its chemical composition. It was Chain who worked out how to isolate and concentrate penicillin. For this research, Chain, Florey and Fleming (q.v.) received the Nobel Prize in 1945.

DOWDING, Air Chief Marshal Lord (1882–1970), English, air force officer
3 St Mary's Road, SW19. *English Heritage*
Lord Dowding lived here from 1941 to 1951. He had joined the Royal Flying Corps in 1918 and became commander-in-chief of Fighter Command in 1936, leading it through the Battle of Britain until November 1940, when he was removed in contentious circumstances. In the film

Battle of Britain (1969) he was played by Laurence Olivier, and Dowding, who watched the filming from a wheelchair, is said to have wept at the accuracy of Olivier's performance.

EAGLE HOUSE
High Street, Wimbledon, SW19.
London Borough of Merton
Eagle House, after an eventful life, is now an Islamic heritage foundation, home to a noted collection of art and manuscripts.

EVANS, Richardson (1846–1928), English, conservationist
The Keir, West Side Common, SW19.
Wimbledon Society
Evans, who lived here and is described on the plaque as a 'Protector of Natural Beauties', founded the John Evelyn Society, later renamed the Wimbledon Society, in 1903. He was also the founder (in 1893) and honorary secretary of the National Society for Checking the Abuses of Public Advertising, believing billboards were an insidious privatisation of the public domain. The society swam gallantly against the tide until the 1950s.

GORE, Spencer (1850–1906), English, tennis champion
Westside House, West Side Common, SW19.
London Borough of Merton
Gore, who was brought up here, was the first Wimbledon men's singles champion, in 1877, although apparently he would have preferred to have become a first-class cricketer with Surrey. A six-footer with a red beard, he sailed through the championship, dropping only two sets in four matches, to claim the prize of 12 guineas and a silver cup presented by *The Field*. He lost the next year's final and did not compete again.

GRAVES, Robert (1895–1985), English, novelist, poet
1 Lauriston Road, Wimbledon, SW19.
English Heritage

Graves was born here. He nearly died on the Somme, and his First World War memoir, *Goodbye to All That* (1929), is one of the greatest books from that war. His novels *I, Claudius* and *Claudius the God* (both 1934) were huge successes, and his *The Greek Myths* (1955) gave popular access to the classic stories.

HUNT, Leigh (1784–1859), English, poet, essayist
The Rose and Crown, High Street, SW19.
London Borough of Merton
The plaque claims that Hunt and Swinburne (see page 273) often used to meet here at the Rose and Crown, one of Wimbledon's oldest pubs, dating from the seventeenth century. This seems unlikely, as Swinburne was only twenty-two when Hunt died aged seventy-five. (See also Hammersmith & Fulham, Kensington & Chelsea 2, Camden 1 and Enfield.)

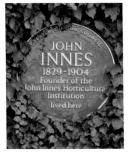

INNES, John (1829–1904), English, merchant, horticulturalist
Rutlish School, Watery Lane, Merton Park, SW20.
Greater London Council
Innes, who lived here, was a city merchant, lord of the manor of Merton, and developed Merton Park. He left funds to establish the Horticultural Research Institution, which has produced the many types of compost that bear his name.

JACKSON, Sir Thomas (1835–1924), English, architect
Eagle House, High Street, Wimbledon, SW19.
London Borough of Merton
Sir Thomas saved Eagle House from demolition in 1887 and lived here until his death, restoring the building to its original condition and removing various later additions. He had entered the office of Sir George Gilbert Scott (q.v.) in 1858 and went on to contribute significantly to the architecture of Oxford, including the Examination Schools, new buildings at Brasenose College, and the chapel and 'Bridge of Sighs' at Hertford College. Elected a Royal Academician in 1896, he was created a baronet, 'of Eagle House in Wimbledon in the County of Surrey', in 1913.

LYNDHURST, Lord (1772–1863), English, lawyer, politician
Westside House, West Side Common, SW19.
London Borough of Merton
Lyndhurst, who lived here, was born John Singleton Copley, son of the painter of the same name. He was known as 'the Flexible Tory' and was three times Lord Chancellor (1827–30, 1834–5 and 1841–6). During the agitation against the Corn Laws, he took a firm reactionary line until Peel, the party leader, signalled it was time to give in. He died without a male heir, so the title became extinct.

MARRYAT, Captain Frederick (1792–1848), English, naval officer, novelist
6 Woodhayes Road, SW19.
Wimbledon Society
This was Marryat's childhood home, from which he more than once attempted to run away to sea, eventually being allowed to join the Royal Navy at the age of fourteen as a midshipman on HMS *Imperieuse*, commanded by Lord Cochrane (q.v.), who inspired much of his fiction. (See also Westminster 2 and Enfield.)

NELSON, Horatio, Lord (1758–1805), English, admiral
Doel Close, Merton High Street, SW19.
London Borough of Merton

Nelson lived at Merton Place on this site with his lover, Emma Hamilton, from 1802. She had had his daughter Horatia in 1801 and, in the brief intervals between his duties at sea, they were apparently happily domesticated. After Nelson's death, Emma got into financial difficulties and the estate was sold off bit by bit, the house being demolished in 1823. (See also Westminster 3.)

RUTHERFORD, Dame Margaret (1892–1972), English, actress
4 Berkeley Place, SW19. *English Heritage*
Dame Margaret lived here from 1895 to 1920. She was a very popular character actress, tending to play well-bred if slightly daffy spinsters, as in four *Miss Marple* stories from the Agatha Christie series, and a memorable Miss Prism in *The Importance of Being Earnest* (1952). She won a best supporting actress Oscar in 1963 for her playing of the absent-minded Duchess of Brighton in *The VIPs*.

SCHOPENHAUER, Arthur (1788–1860), German, philosopher
Eagle House, High Street, SW19. *English Heritage*
Eagle House was from 1789 to 1805 'The Rev Mr Lancaster's Academy' and Schopenhauer lived and studied here for three months, July to September 1803, laying the foundations of his knowledge of English. Apparently he did not enjoy the experience, finding English formality not to his liking.

SWINBURNE, Algernon (1837–1909), English, poet
The Rose and Crown, High Street, SW19.
London Borough of Merton
The plaque claims, rather improbably, that Swinburne and Leigh Hunt (see above) 'often met here'; Swinburne was only twenty-two when Hunt died aged seventy-five. However, Swinburne was a regular in later life; apparently, after pictures of him drinking here were published in the *Pall Mall Gazette*, he took to slipping in by a side door and drinking in a private room. (See also Kensington & Chelsea 2 and Wandsworth.)

TOOKE, John Horne (1736–1812), English, cleric, politician
Chester House, Westside Common, SW19.
Wimbledon Society
Tooke lived here. A supporter of Wilkes, he formed the Constitutional Society in 1771, backing the American colonists. Tried and acquitted for high treason in 1794, he became an MP in 1799. His conversation is supposed to have rivalled that of Dr Johnson – but he had no Boswell.

TOYNBEE, Arnold (1852–83), English, economic
historian
Beech Holme, 49 Wimbledon Parkside, SW19.
English Heritage
Toynbee lived here with his father, Joseph (see below),
from 1854 to 1866. He broke his health working for
social improvement in the East End, and Toynbee Hall,
the first 'settlement', founded by Samuel Barnett
(q.v.) in 1884, is named in his memory. In his hugely
influential Oxford *Lectures on the Industrial Revolution*
(published posthumously in 1884), he coined the
phrase 'the Industrial Revolution'.

TOYNBEE, Joseph
(1815–66), English,
otologist
**Beech Holme, 49
Wimbledon
Parkside, SW19.**
English Heritage
Toynbee lived here with his
son Arnold (see above) from
1854 to 1866. In 1857 he became aural surgeon and
lecturer at St Mary's Hospital in Paddington, and while
there he wrote two pioneering works: *A Descriptive
Catalogue of Preparations Illustrative of the Diseases of the
Ear* (1857), and *The Diseases of the Ear: Their Nature,
Diagnosis and Treatment* (1860).

WILBERFORCE, William (1759–1833), English,
anti-slavery campaigner
**Lauriston House Stables, Southside Common,
SW19.** *Wimbledon Society*
Wilberforce lived in a house on this site from 1777 to
1786. These years were immediately prior to his taking
up the anti-slavery cause; inheritances had made him
independently wealthy, and his time at Cambridge
(1776–81) was given over to cards, gambling and late
night drinking. But in 1785 he underwent an
evangelical conversion, resolving to mend his ways and
involve himself with important issues, and in 1786 he
left this house to live in Westminster, near Parliament.
(See also Wandsworth, Lambeth, Barnet and
Kensington & Chelsea 2.)

NEWHAM

In East London, once wholly in Essex, the
London Borough of Newham is an
amalgamation of two former county boroughs,
West Ham and East Ham, plus North
Woolwich and a small part of Barking.

The site is now
occupied by a defunct
telephone exchange.
The most famous
former student of the
institute was the actor
Stanley Holloway.

GREENWOOD, Ron (1921–2006), English, football
manager
**West Ham United Football Stadium, Green
Street, E13.** *Sports Heritage*
Greenwood managed West Ham through a golden era
(1962–74), notable for their cultured football,
winning the FA Cup in 1964 and the European Cup
Winners' Cup the next year, with a team starring
Bobby Moore (see page 276), Geoff Hurst and Martin
Peters. He subsequently managed the England team
(1977–82).

**HOPKINS, Gerard
Manley** (1844–89),
English, poet
**Stratford Library,
The Grove, E15.**
Private
Hopkins was born and
lived his first eight

ABBEY ROAD DEPOT BOMBING
Abbey Road, Stratford, E15. *Private*
The Abbey Road municipal depot was being used as an
Air Raid Precautions centre during the Blitz. On
7 September 1940, the first night of the Blitz proper, it
suffered a direct hit and fifteen ARP wardens and
firemen were killed.

CARPENTERS' COMPANY'S INSTITUTE
Jupp Street, E15. *Carpenters' Company*

years at 87 The Grove nearby. The plaque carries four
lines from one of his most famous poems, 'The Wreck
of the Deutschland'. His reputation as a major poet is
almost entirely due to his friend Robert Bridges, who
published the first collected edition of Hopkins's poetry
in 1918. (See also Camden 1 and Wandsworth.)

LYALL, John (1940–2006), English, football manager
West Ham United Stadium, Green Street, E13.
Sports Heritage
A useful defender at West Ham until a knee injury ended his playing career at twenty-three, Lyall then rose through the coaching ranks to manage West Ham (1974–89), maintaining Ron Greenwood's (see page 275) cultured style and winning the FA Cup in 1975.

MACKAY, WPC Nina (1972–97), English, police officer
Arthingworth Street, E15. *Police Memorial Trust*
On 24 October 1997 WPC MacKay was with a team from 3 Area Territorial Support Group sent to arrest a man who had broken bail conditions. This was a specialist unit with body armour and CS spray. However, WPC MacKay, for some unknown reason, had removed her body armour before the raid took place and was fatally stabbed.

MOORE, Bobby (1941–93), English, footballer
West Ham United Stadium, Green Street, E13.
Sports Heritage
With 108 England caps, ninety as captain, Moore was the central figure in England's triumph in the Football World Cup of 1966. Pelé said he was 'the greatest defender I ever played against'. Scotland manager Jock Stein said: 'There ought to be a law against him, he knows what's happening twenty minutes before anyone else.'

THORNE, Will (1857–1946), English, trade unionist, politician
1 Lawrence Road, Upton Park, E13.
Greater London Council
Thorne, who lived here, began work at the age of six, which informed his later politics. He was more or less illiterate until Eleanor Marx (q.v.) helped him learn to read and write. As a member of H. M. Hyndman's (q.v.) Social Democratic Federation, he helped organise the London dock strike of 1889. In the same year he founded the National Union of Gasworkers and General Labourers and was its general secretary until amalgamation with the General & Municipal Workers in 1924. He was then general secretary of the GMW to 1934. He was one of the first Labour MPs and sat in the House from 1906 to 1945.

REDBRIDGE

At the north-east edge of Greater London, once wholly in Essex, the London Borough of Redbridge is an amalgamation of two former municipal boroughs, Ilford and Wanstead & Woodford, plus a small part of Dagenham and the south-east corner of Chigwell.

ATTLEE, Clement (1883–1967), English, Prime Minister
17 Monkhams Avenue, Woodford Green.
Greater London Council
This modest house was Attlee's London home from the 1920s until his death. He was first elected to Parliament in 1922 and became Leader of the Labour Party in 1935. He was Churchill's deputy prime minister in the wartime coalition government (1940–5) and Prime Minister in the reforming Labour government (1945–51), and then Leader of the Opposition (1951–5). In 2004 he was voted the greatest British Prime Minister of the twentieth century in a poll of professors organised by MORI.

BRADLEY, James (1693–1762), English, astronomer
Grove House, 2 Grove Park, Wanstead, E11.
London Borough of Redbridge
James Bradley, who served in Wanstead as curate to his uncle, a leading amateur astronomer, was elected a Fellow of the Royal Society in 1718 and was subsequently appointed the third Astronomer Royal (1742–62). His two critical discoveries were the aberration of light and the nutation of the earth's axis – in lay terms the 'wobble' as the earth spins.

FONTANNE, Lynn (1887–1983), English, actress
6 Station Terrace, Snakes Lane, Woodford.
London Borough of Redbridge
Lynn Fontanne, who was born and lived here until she was twenty-nine, was a major stage star in American theatre for over forty years. She and her husband, Alfred Lunt, whom she married in 1922, were the most acclaimed acting partnership in American theatre history. She never relinquished her British citizenship.

MANSBRIDGE, Albert (1876–1952), English, educationalist
198 Windsor Road, Ilford.
Greater London Council
Mansbridge, who lived here, was largely self-taught, attending university extension courses at King's College, London. Experience in the co-operative movement led him to found the Workers' Educational Association in 1903 and he was its first general secretary (1905–15). He also helped found similar bodies elsewhere in the world.

MORRIS, William (1834–96), English, poet, designer, socialist
Woodford Parish Church Memorial Hall, High Street, E11. *Private*

Morris lived from 1840 to 1847 in Woodford Hall, which formerly stood to the rear of this site. The house was demolished in 1900. (See also Hammersmith & Fulham, Camden 2, Hackney, Bexley, Waltham Forest and Westminster 3.)

PANKHURST, Sylvia (1882–1960), English, suffragette
Tamar Square Flats, Charteris Road, Woodford Green. *Private*
Sylvia Pankhurst lived in a house on this site from 1933 to 1956 with her common-law partner, Silvio Corio, an anti-fascist refugee from Mussolini's Italy. Their 'living in sin' was not generally approved locally. Together they campaigned, particularly about the Italian invasion of Ethiopia and, after Corio died in 1954, the emperor Haile Selassie invited Sylvia to live in Addis Ababa as his guest, which she did for the last four years of her life. (See also Tower Hamlets and Kensington & Chelsea 2.)

REPTON, Humphry (1752–1818), English, landscape gardener
Woodford County High School, High Road, Woodford. *Borough of Walthamstow*
Repton lost his fortune and became a professional landscape gardener, employed by the chief noblemen of the day. He worked here in 1794 on the grounds of Highams House, damming the River Ching to form a lake. He published a number of treatises, including *An Enquiry into the Changes of Taste in Landscape Gardening* (1806). The house is now Woodford County High School. (See also Havering.)

WALTERS, PC Phillip (1967–95), English, policeman
Empress Avenue, Ilford. *Police Memorial Trust*
Called to a disturbance at a house on the evening of 18 April 1995 in Empress Avenue, PC Walters was shot and fatally wounded as he attempted to arrest a 'Yardie' gangster. The man was subsequently sentenced to sixteen years' imprisonment for manslaughter.

RICHMOND UPON THAMES

At the south-west edge of Greater London,
once wholly in Surrey and Middlesex, the
London Borough of Richmond upon Thames is
an amalgamation of three former municipal
boroughs, Twickenham, Barnes and Richmond.

BAKER, Hylda
(1905–86), English,
comedienne
**Brinsworth House,
Staines Road,
Twickenham.**
Comic Heritage
Baker, who lived here in
retirement, first appeared on
stage at the age of ten. Her best-
known comic routine was with a tall silent man in
drag, of whom she confided to the audience: 'She
knows, you know.' She was famous for the television
sitcom *Nearest and Dearest* (1968–73) with Jimmy
Jewel (q.v.).

BEARD, John (*c.*1717–91), English, tenor
Hampton Branch Library, Rose Hill, Hampton.
English Heritage
Beard was an actor contemporary of Garrick (q.v.),
more noted as a tenor, especially in parts written for
him by Handel (q.v.). Losing his hearing, he retired to
Hampton and built this house in 1774.

CHADWICK, Sir Edwin (1801–90), English,
reformer
5 Montague Road, Richmond. *English Heritage*
Sir Edwin lived here. His *The Sanitary Condition of the
Labouring Population*, published at his own expense in
1842, was a key document in the history of Victorian
public health reforms. Successively a commissioner for
sewers and of the first Board of Health, he campaigned
to the end.

COOPER, Tommy
(1921–84), English,
comedian
**Teddington
Studios, Broom
Road, Teddington.**
Comic Heritage
Cooper, who worked
here over many years, was
one of the funniest men who ever
drew breath – a big, shambling, incompetent
magician, whose tricks were always going wrong, with
a stream of silly jokes and a red fez on his head. His
catchphrase was 'Just like that', when, for once, a trick
worked.

COWARD, Sir Noël (1899–1973), English, actor,
playwright
131 Waldegrave Road, Teddington.
English Heritage
Sir Noël was born here. Noted for his clipped, brittle,
sophisticated wit, he was hugely successful in the
1930s and 1940s. Among his successes were *Private
Lives* (1930), *Cavalcade* (1931), *Blithe Spirit* (1941) and
This Happy Breed (1943). He also produced films,
including *In Which We Serve* (1942) and *Brief Encounter*
(1945). (See also Sutton and Westminster 4.)

DE LA MARE, Walter (1873–1956), English, poet
**Southend House, Montpelier Row,
Twickenham.** *English Heritage*
De la Mare lived here from 1940 until his death. He is
best known for his verses and short stories for
children, including the celebrated *Memoirs of a Midget*

(1921), which explored the world of the minute Miss M. He loved childhood, fantasy and mystery, often with a strain of melancholy. He was made a Companion of Honour in 1948 and awarded the Order of Merit in 1953. (See also Bromley.)

DE VALOIS, Dame Ninette (1898–2001), Irish, ballet dancer
14 The Terrace, Barnes, SW13.
English Heritage
Dame Ninette lived here from 1962 to 1982. Born Edris Stannus, she changed her name in 1921 and retired from dancing with Diaghilev's *Ballets Russes* in 1926. She was engaged by Lilian Baylis (q.v.) from 1928 as director of the Sadler's Wells company, which evolved into the Royal Ballet. She also founded the Royal Ballet School and, having a stern appearance, was universally known as 'Madame', which is how she would sometimes sign letters.

ESPINOSA, Edouard (1871–1950), Spanish, ballet teacher
Woolborough House, 39 Lonsdale Road, SW13.
British Ballet Organisation
Espinosa was born in Moscow, where his father Léon was working with the ballet master Petipa. This house became the family home in 1913, and from 1930 the headquarters of the British Ballet Organisation, which has trained dancers such as Phyllis Bedells and Ninette de Valois (see above) and whose motto is 'Dance for all'. There are two plaques, one on the main house, the other on a studio extension built in 1933.

EVERETT, Kenny (1944–95), English, disc jockey, comedian
Teddington Studios, Broom Road, Teddington.
Comic Heritage
Everett, who worked here many times, was born Maurice Cole in Liverpool. His broadcasting career began on pirate radio, graduating to BBC radio and then television. His shows, whether as disc jockey or comedic lord of misrule, were characterised by inspired lunacy – 'all done', as he used to say, 'in the *best possible* taste'.

EWART, William (1798–1869), English, reformer, politician
Hampton Branch Library, Rose Hill, Hampton.
English Heritage
Ewart, who lived here in John Beard's (see page 279) old house, sat for forty years in the House of Commons and was the first person to propose the erection of official plaques to mark the former homes of distinguished people. (See also Westminster 4.)

FARADAY, Michael (1791–1867), English, scientist
Faraday House, Hampton Court Road, Hampton. *Private*

Faraday lived here from 1858 until his death. His experiments with electricity led to the invention of the dynamo, the transformer and the electric motor. He was Professor of Chemistry at the Royal Institute from 1833 and is regarded as one of the greatest experimenters of all time. (See also Southwark and Westminster 2.)

FIELDING, Henry (1707–54), English, novelist, lawyer
Milbourne House, Barnes Green, SW13.
Greater London Council
Fielding, who lived here (it is thought) from 1750 to 1752, was one of the most engaging characters of the eighteenth century. His early satirical plays, now forgotten, directly caused the passing of the 1737 Licensing Act, which decreed that only government-approved plays could be put on. He thereafter turned to novels and his most famous, *Tom Jones* (1749), remains popular to this day. He was a justice of the peace and London's chief magistrate. He and his half-brother, John, founded the Bow Street Runners, the forerunners of today's Metropolitan Police. (See also Westminster 4.)

FREEMAN, Alan 'Fluff' (1927–2006), Australian, disc jockey
Brinsworth House, Staines Road, Twickenham.
Music Heritage
Freeman, who lived here in retirement, began his European career as a locum on Radio Luxembourg in 1959, moving to the BBC in 1961, and having a long association with shows such as *Pick of the Pops*, *Top of the Pops* and *Juke Box Jury*. With his signature catchphrase 'Greetings, pop pickers!', he became a genuinely loved, if slightly comic, figure, and John Peel gave him the accolade: 'Fluff was the greatest out-and-out disc jockey of them all.'

GARRICK, David (1717–79), English, actor-manager
Garrick's Villa, Hampton Court Road, Hampton.
Greater London Council
Garrick, whose country house this was from 1754 until his death, was the greatest actor of the eighteenth century. (See also Westminster 4 for his main entry.)

GODFREE, 'Kitty' (1896–1992), English, tennis champion
55 York Avenue, Mortlake, SW14. *English Heritage*
Kathleen ('Kitty') Godfree (née McKane) lived here from 1936 until her death. She was twice Wimbledon ladies' singles champion (1924 and 1926) and winner of five Olympic medals at tennis (1920 and 1924). She and her husband, Leslie, are the only married couple so far to win the Wimbledon mixed doubles title (1926). She was also nine times All-England badminton champion.

GREATHEAD, James Henry (1844–96), South African, engineer
3 St Mary's Grove, Barnes, SW13. *English Heritage*
Greathead, who lived here from 1885 to 1889, made the tunnel under the Thames for the world's first underground railway, completed in 1869, with a boring machine of his own design. The 'Greathead shield' was used on several other tunnels and he was largely responsible for the boring and excavation of the early London tube system.

HANCOCK, Tony (1924–68), English, comedian, actor
Teddington Studios, Broom Road, Teddington.
Comic Heritage
Hancock worked here regularly. He is remembered for his lugubrious, pretentious misfit, resident of 'Railway Cuttings, East Cheam', in *Hancock's Half Hour*, on radio (1954–6) and on television (1956–61), with scripts by Galton and Simpson. Some of the lines are very memorable, such as when Hancock, appealing to fellow members of a jury in 'Henry Fonda' mode, declaimed: 'What about Magna Carta? Did she die in vain?' An alcoholic, he killed himself in 1968. (See also Barnet.)

HANDL, Irene (1901–87), English, comic actress
Teddington Studios, Broom Road, Teddington.
Comic Heritage

Handl, who worked here regularly, did not take up acting until the age of thirty-six. She became a much-loved dotty character actress, rarely starring, always engaging. Her films included *I'm Alright Jack* (1959), *The Rebel* (1961) and *The Private Life of Sherlock Holmes* (1970). She starred on television in *For the Love of Ada* (1970–1) and wrote a successful novel, *The Sioux* (1965).

HILL, Benny (1925–92), English, comedian
Teddington Studios, Broom Road, Teddington.
Comic Heritage
Hill worked here regularly. His fame rests on the worldwide success

of *The Benny Hill Show* (1969–89), denounced by the new wave of comedians as 'dirty old man' humour built round Hill's lecherous relationship with 'Hill's Angels', a nubile bunch of scantily clad lovelies who spent a lot of time chasing or being chased by Benny in speeded-up motion. He did not recover from the attacks and his abrupt dismissal by Thames Television. (See also Kensington & Chelsea 2.)

HIRD, Dame Thora (1911–2003), English, actress
Brinsworth House, Staines Road, Twickenham.
Comic Heritage
Dame Thora, who lived here in retirement, became a national treasure through her appearances on television in *Meet the Wife* (1963–6) and *Last of the Summer Wine* (1986–2003), in both playing a termagant far removed from her deeply Christian real self. She also won two BAFTA awards for monologues in Alan Bennett's *Talking Heads* series.

HOGARTH PRESS
Hogarth House, 34 Paradise Road, Richmond.
Greater London Council
The Hogarth Press was founded in this house by Leonard and Virginia Woolf (see page 285) in 1917. The policy of the Press was to publish new and experimental work by writers such as T. S. Eliot (q.v.), along with translations of important foreign writers such as Gorky, Chekhov, Rilke and Svevo (q.v.). Since 1947 it has been an imprint within the Chatto & Windus group.

HOLST, Gustav
(1874–1934), English, composer
10 The Terrace, Barnes, SW13. *Private*
Holst lived here from 1908 to 1913. Though he wrote in all genres of music, his most famous and enduring work is *The Planets Suite* (1917). A friend of Ralph Vaughan Williams (q.v.), he shared his interest in English folk music. His Swedish name came from his great-grandfather. (See also Hammersmith & Fulham.)

HUGHES, Arthur (1832–1915), English, painter, illustrator
22 Kew Green, Kew. *English Heritage*
Hughes, who lived and died here, was a Pre-Raphaelite noted for his glowing colours and delicate draughtsmanship. His most famous paintings are *Ophelia* (1853), *April Love* (1856) and *A Long Engagement* (1859). He was also a prolific illustrator for Tennyson (q.v.), Christina Rossetti (q.v.) and others. (See also Sutton.)

JAMES, Sid (1913–76), South African, comic actor
Teddington Studios, Broom Road, Teddington.
Comic Heritage
James worked here regularly. Born Joel Solomon Cohen, he came to Britain in 1946 and never stopped working, in film, radio and television. He is best remembered for nineteen 'Carry On' films and a long association with Tony Hancock (q.v.). He died on stage in Sunderland.

JOHNSON, Dame Celia (1908–82), English, actress
46 Richmond Hill, Richmond.
English Heritage
Dame Celia was born here and lived here until 1924. After the Royal Academy of Dramatic Art, she had a distinguished stage career and appeared in several films but is remembered especially for *Brief Encounter* (1946), playing opposite Trevor Howard, for which she earned her only Oscar nomination.

KAY, Louise (1889–1943), Australian, actress, singer
Woolborough House, 39 Lonsdale Road, SW13.
British Ballet Organisation
Born Eve Louise Kelland, she married Edouard Espinosa (see page 280) after a career as an actress and singer, and they founded the British Ballet Organisation here in 1930. She also founded *The Dancer* magazine in 1928.

LABOUCHÈRE, Henry (1831–1912), English, journalist, politician
Pope's Villa, 19 Cross Deep, Twickenham.
English Heritage

Labouchère lived here from 1881 to 1903. After a period in the diplomatic service, he was twice a Liberal MP. While out of Parliament he worked for the *Daily News*, achieving fame for his witty dispatches from Paris during the siege of 1870, and later founded a weekly called *Truth*, which was regularly sued for libel.

LODGE, David (1921–2003), English, character actor
8 Sydney Road, Richmond. *Comic Heritage*
Lodge, who lived here, appeared in over one hundred films between 1954 and 1989, invariably as a heavy, often a comic heavy. He thought himself too ugly for romantic roles and was content to be a foil to his friends Peter Sellers (q.v.) and Spike Milligan (q.v.), with whom he worked on the *Q* series of television programmes.

MORECAMBE, Eric (1926–84), English, comedian
Teddington Studios, Broom Road, Teddington.
Comic Heritage
After ten unforgettable years with the BBC, Morecambe and Wise were tempted away to Thames Television here, and their show continued, slightly less successfully, for another five years (1978–83). (See also Barnet.)

NEWMAN, Cardinal John Henry (1801–90), English, cleric
Grey Court, Ham Street, Ham.
Greater London Council
Newman spent some of his early years here. He was ordained into the Anglican church in 1824 and converted to Catholicism in 1845. His *Apologia Pro Vita Sua* (1864) was an exploration of his spiritual evolution and is recognised as a theological and literary classic. He became a cardinal in 1879. (See also Camden 2 and City.)

NIXON, David (1919–78), English, magician
Teddington Studios, Broom Road, Teddington.
Comic Heritage

Nixon, who worked here regularly, was a genial magician who first appeared on stage in 1941 but is best remembered for being a panellist on the television quiz show *What's My Line?* from 1954 to 1963. He also famously hosted the edition of *This Is Your Life* where the subject was the show's regular host, Eamonn Andrews.

O'HIGGINS, Bernardo (1778–1842), Chilean, soldier, politician
Clarence House, 2 The Vineyard, Richmond.
English Heritage
O'Higgins, who lived and studied here, was the illegitimate son of an Irishman serving the Spanish. One of the commanders in the Chilean War of Independence (1810–17), he became first leader of the independent country (1817–23). Deposed by a reactionary coup, he spent the rest of his life in exile in Peru.

PISSARRO, Camille (1831–1903), French, painter
Kew Green and Gloucester Road, Kew. *Private*
Pissarro stayed in a house on this site in 1892. He was a prolific artist who experimented with several different styles, notably Pointillism. One of the most important yet underrated of the Impressionists, and the only one of them to exhibit in all eight Impressionist salons, he made several visits to England. (See also Croydon.)

SCHWITTERS, Kurt (1887–1948), German, painter
39 Westmoreland Road, Barnes, SW13.
Greater London Council
Schwitters, who lived here from 1942 to 1945, was the founder of the Hanover branch of the Dada movement. He adopted collage (which he called *Merz*) as his preferred technique, deploying all kinds of found objects, later in large three-dimensional constructions, most of which were destroyed. He was forced to leave Germany in 1937, when his work was featured in a Nazi exhibition called Entartete Kunst ('degenerate art').

SIDHU, PC Kulwant (1975–99), English, police officer
Mereway Road, Twickenham. *Police Memorial Trust*
On the night of Monday 25 October 1999 PC Sidhu was pursuing two suspected burglars across the roof of commercial premises here when he fell to his death through a glass panel.

TENNYSON, Alfred, Lord (1809–92), English, poet
15 Montpelier Row, Twickenham. *Private*

Tennyson lived here from 1851 to 1853. He had been made Poet Laureate in 1850 and married the same year. His son, Hallam, was born here in 1852. However, he began to find that Twickenham was too close to London and the stream of callers was becoming oppressive, so he moved to the Isle of Wight. Doyen of Victorian poets, he had, according to T. S. Eliot (q.v.), 'the finest ear of any English poet since Milton'. (See also Westminster 4.)

THOMSON, James (1700–48), Scottish, poet, playwright
The Royal Hospital, Kew Foot Road, Richmond. *English Heritage*
Thomson lived here from 1739 until his death, his house now incorporated into the hospital. He was the author of 'The Seasons' (1726–30), one of the most perennially popular of English poems, and the lyrics for 'Rule Britannia!' (1740), which earned him a pension from the Prince of Wales.

TURNER, Joseph Mallord William (1775–1851), English, painter
40 Sandycoombe Road, St Margarets.
Greater London Council
Turner designed this house as a country retreat, with advice from his friend Sir John Soane, in 1811. It has been altered since he sold it in 1826. He used it as a base for his painting along the Thames valley. (See also Kensington & Chelsea 2, Westminster 2 and Westminster 4.)

WALPOLE, Horace (1717–97), English, novelist, man of letters
Strawberry Hill House, Waldegrave Road, Twickenham. *Private*
Walpole was the youngest son of Sir Robert Walpole (q.v.) and became fourth Earl of Orford on the death of his brother in 1791. Strawberry Hill House, his 'little Gothic Castle', was a life work; between 1747

and 1792 he doubled the size of a modest 1698 cottage into the finest example of Georgian Gothic in England. Over four thousand of his letters have been published, his main correspondents being Sir Horace Mann and Madame du Deffand. He coined the word 'serendipity'. (See also Westminster 4.)

WARRISS, Ben (1909–93), English, comedian
Brinsworth House, Staines Road, Twickenham.
Comic Heritage
Warriss, who lived here in retirement and died here,
first went on stage in 1930 and quickly formed a
comedy partnership (1934–66) with his cousin
Jimmy Jewel (q.v.), which included seven Royal
Variety Shows, a long-running radio show, *Up The Pole*,
in the 1940s, and twelve successive summer seasons at
Blackpool. They split up in 1966, Warriss continuing
solo, while Jewel moved into television sitcom.

WINTERS, Bernie (1932–91), English, comedian
Teddington Studios, Broom Road, Teddington.
Comic Heritage
Winters worked here regularly. Born Bernard
Weinstein, he formed a comedy duo with his older
brother, Mike. They were very successful from the
1950s, having their own television series (1965–73),
but broke up acrimoniously. Bernie went on to solo
success, often accompanied by his St Bernard,
Schnorbitz.

WOOLF, Leonard
(1880–1969),
English, novelist,
reformer
**Hogarth House,
34 Paradise Road,
Richmond.**
*Greater London
Council*
Woolf lived here
with his wife,
Virginia (see page
282), from 1915 to
1924, and together
they founded the
Hogarth Press here
in 1917 (see above). Woolf is somewhat overshadowed
by his wife, but worth remembering for his devotion
to social progress and international understanding, on
which he wrote extensively, despite the demands of a
stressful marriage.

WOOLF, Virginia (1882–1941), English, novelist
Hogarth House, 34 Paradise Road, Richmond.
Greater London Council
The Hogarth Press (see page 282) was founded here in
part as therapy for Virginia's regular bouts of mental

illness. While living here, she wrote her first three
novels, *The Voyage Out* (1915), *Night and Day* (1919)
and *Jacob's Room* (1922). (See also Camden 2.)

WORTH, Harry
(1917–89), English,
comedian
**Teddington
Studios, Broom
Road, Teddington.**
Comic Heritage
Worth, who worked
here regularly, was born
Harry Illingworth, first
appearing in London at the Windmill Theatre in 1947.
His comedy persona, of a genial bumbling middle-class
northerner who drove everyone mad, was suited to
television and he had successful series on both the
BBC and ITV between 1959 and 1980.

WREN, Sir Christopher
(1632–1723), English,
architect
**Old Court House,
Hampton Court
Green.** *English Heritage*
Wren lived in this house
intermittently from 1668
until his death, splitting his
time with his London residences.
It is thought he may have remodelled the place in
1706. He was working here on various amendments
and refurbishments to Hampton Court for Charles II
and successive monarchs to Queen Anne. He is the
pre-eminent figure in the history of British
architecture – designer of St Paul's Cathedral and fifty
other London churches, and of the Royal Exchange,
the Greenwich Observatory, the Sheldonian Theatre in
Oxford and many more. (See also Southwark.)

SUTTON

On the southern edge of Greater London, once wholly in Surrey, the London Borough of Sutton is an amalgamation of two former municipal boroughs, Sutton & Cheam and Beddington & Wallington, plus Carshalton Urban District.

ALCOCK, George Edgar (1902–75), English, conservationist
Corner of Christchurch Park and Brighton Road, Sutton. *Private*
A founding figure in the local conservation struggle, Alcock, who lived in Christchurch Park, fought almost alone to save the beeches that line the street. This led to the foundation of the Sutton and Cheam Society in 1959, of which he was the leading light almost until his death.

ANNE BOLEYN'S WELL
All Saints' Churchyard, High Street, Carshalton. *Borough of Sutton*
According to a not very plausible tradition, Anne Boleyn's horse kicked at a stone at this spot and a well sprang forth. It dried up in the 1920s and its site is now covered by Church Hill.

COWARD, Sir Noël (1899–1973), English, actor, playwright
56 Lenham Road, Sutton. *Borough of Sutton*

Sir Noël lived in Lenham Road from 1906 to 1909. His first public appearance on stage was on 23 July 1907 in a concert at Sutton Public Hall when he was eight years old. (See also Westminster 4 and Richmond.)

GILPIN, William (1724–1804), English, cleric, teacher
Tabor Court, High Street, Cheam.
Borough of Sutton
Gilpin was one of the first people to develop the idea of the Picturesque, which he defined in his 1768 *Essay on Prints* as 'that kind of beauty which is agreeable in a picture'.

HONEYWOOD
Honeywood Walk, Carshalton. *London Borough of Sutton*
This house was built in 1885 by a London merchant, John Pattinson Kirk (1836–1913), who made further alterations and additions in 1896 and 1903. Sold by his daughter to Carshalton Urban District Council in 1939, it is now Sutton's local museum.

HUGHES, Arthur (1832–1915), English, painter, illustrator
284 London Road, Wallington. *Borough of Sutton*

Hughes lived here from 1876 to 1891 and added the studio that can be seen to the right of the house. An associate of the Pre-Raphaelites, Hughes was a prolific artist and illustrator. The plaque mentions his most famous painting, *April Love* (1856), which now hangs in Tate Britain. (See also Richmond.)

PEAKE, Mervyn (1911–68), English, novelist, illustrator, poet
Surrey Court, 55 Woodcote Road, Wallington.
Borough of Sutton
Peake lived on this site twice, from 1922 to 1932 and again from 1952 to 1962. He is remembered above all for the *Gormenghast* trio of novels, intended as the start of something longer, an ambition thwarted by his declining health. (See also Kensington & Chelsea 2.)

ROWLAND, E. C. H. (1883–1955), English, music-hall singer
Times 2 Shopping Centre, High Street, Sutton.
Borough of Sutton
Rowland managed the Surrey County (later the Gaumont) cinema on this site after the First World War. As Reg Rowland, he had previously been a music-hall star, particularly associated with the mildly bawdy song, popular with the troops, 'Mademoiselle from Armentières', with its 'French' refrain, 'Hinky dinky parley voo'.

SUTHERLAND, Graham (1903–80), English, painter
Four Winds, Upland Road, Sutton.
Borough of Sutton
Sutherland lived here from 1922 to 1924. He was a major twentieth-century artist, whose work ranged from landscape to portraits of the great and famous, notably including Somerset Maugham (q.v.). He is perhaps best remembered for his portrait of Winston Churchill (q.v.), which was presented to the great man by the House of Commons in 1954. It was destroyed shortly afterwards by Lady Churchill because she hated it.

TATE, Harry (1872–1940), Scottish, music-hall comedian
27 Camden Road, Sutton. *Borough of Sutton*
Tate, stage-name of Ronald Hutchinson, lived at Camden House, near this site, from 1920 to 1931. He made his debut in 1895, initially as an impressionist, 'doing' the likes of Dan Leno (q.v.). Later, in his own comedy act, his catchphrases such as 'How's your father?' and 'I *don't* think' were universally popular in the 1930s. Thought to be the first owner of a personalised car number plate, T8, he died as a result of injuries received in the Blitz.

WALL, Thomas (1846–1930), English, entrepreneur, philanthropist
12 Worcester Road, Sutton. *Borough of Sutton*
25 Worcester Road, Sutton. *Borough of Sutton*
The business, trading in sausages, pork pies and ice cream, was founded by Richard Wall in St James's in 1786. Thomas Wall, his grandson, who lived at both addresses, took it to national prominence and in 1920 founded the Thomas Wall Trust, which is active to this day in the fields of adult education, social action and the protection of open spaces.

WELLS, H. G. (1866–1946), English, novelist
25 Langley Park Road, Sutton.
Borough of Sutton
Wells lived here in 1893–4 and later, after a spell in London, nearby in Worcester Park, which appeared as 'Morningside Park' in his novel *Ann Veronica* (1909). He was a prolific writer in several genres; his science fiction earned him a reputation as a prophet; his social realist novels remain vivid slices of lower middle-class life; and his didactic works, such as *The Outline of History* (1920), show him to have been a great teacher. (See also Bromley and Westminster 1.)

WHITE, William Hale (1831–1913), English, novelist
Honeywood, Honeywood Walk, Carshalton.
Borough of Sutton
19 Park Hill, Carshalton.
Greater London Council
White lived at Wandle Cottage on the site of the first address in 1864–5 and built the house at the second address in 1868, living there until his death. After abandoning training for the church, he worked as a civil servant in the Admiralty. His novels, written under the pseudonym Mark Rutherford, include *The Autobiography of MR* (1881) and *MR's Deliverance* (1885), the latter described by George Orwell (q.v.) as 'one of the best novels in English'.

WALTHAM FOREST

Lying at the northern edge of Greater London,
once wholly in Essex, the London Borough of
Waltham Forest is an amalgamation of three
former Municipal Boroughs: Chingford, Leyton
and Walthamstow.

BLAKE, Peter (b.1932), English, artist
**Waltham Forest College, Forest Road,
Walthamstow, E17.** *Private*
Blake is listed among the former students at the art
school here, which was built in 1938. He is the leading
figure in the British pop art movement, best known to
a wider public for his creation of the cover of the
Beatles' LP, *Sergeant Pepper's Lonely Hearts Club Band*, in
1967.

BREMER, Frederick (1872–1941), English,
engineer
1 Connaught Road, Walthamstow, E17. *Private*
In a small workshop in the garden of this house,
between 1892 and
1894, Fred Bremer
and Tom Bates
constructed
the first
British car
powered by an
internal
combustion engine. In
1931 Bremer presented the car to the Vestry House
Museum, where it can be seen to this day.

CHURCH COMMON
Former Sorting Office, 7–8 Vestry Road, E17.
Borough of Walthamstow
The plaque records that the playground opposite was
part of Bury Field or Church Common and was
enclosed in 1850. It was one of three commons in the
borough before the Enclosure Act and is by law to
remain an open space.

COGAN'S ACADEMY, Reverend
Billet Road, E17. *Borough of Walthamstow*
On this site stood Essex Hall, where the Reverend
Eliezer Cogan's (1762–1855) Academy offered a
classical education to the sons of gentlemen from 1802
to 1828, its most famous old boy being Benjamin
Disraeli (see page 289). The school closed on Cogan's
retirement.

CORNWELL, Jack, VC (1900–16), English, boy
sailor
Clyde Place, Leyton, E10. *Private*
Adjacent to this site stood Clyde Cottage, Cornwell's
birthplace. He is the youngest ever recipient of the
Victoria Cross, awarded for his bravery at the Battle of
Jutland in 1916. 'Mortally wounded early in the
action, Boy 1st Class John Travers Cornwell remained
standing alone in a most exposed position quietly
awaiting orders, until the end of the action, with the
gun's crew dead and wounded around him.'

CRADDOCK, Fanny (1909–94), English, cookery
writer
Fairwood Court, Fairlop Road, E11.
Craddock was born Phyllis Pechey in Apthorp House,
which stood on this site until 1930.
She had television
success in the late
1950s, assisted
by her partner
Johnnie
Craddock
(whose name
she took long

before they married in 1977). It was a double act in which he acted slightly drunk and she, all frills and bows, was in total command.

DISRAELI, Benjamin (1804–81), English, Prime Minister
Billet Road, E17. *Borough of Walthamstow*
The Reverend Cogan's Academy (see page 288) welcomed Disraeli in 1817. Although he had recently been baptised into the Anglican church, his name suggested Jewish origins, he looked foreign and he liked reading – all grounds for conflict with his fellow pupils. He was expelled for fighting in 1821. (See also City, Westminster 3 and Camden 2.)

DURY, Ian (1942–2000), English, pop star
Waltham Forest College, Forest Road, Walthamstow, E17. *Private*
Dury is among those listed as former students of the art school here. He did not pursue a career in art because, he said, 'I got good enough to realise that I wasn't going to be very good'. As singer-songwriter, his only number one hit (with the Blockheads) was the memorable 'Hit Me with Your Rhythm Stick'.

EDWARDS, Sir George (1908–2003), English, aircraft designer
499 Hale End Road, Hale End, E4. *Private*
Sir George was born here, above his father's toy shop. In 1945 he became chief designer at Vickers-Armstrong, and later managing director, being responsible for a long string of successful designs, including the Viking, Viscount, Valiant, Vanguard and VC-10, as well as the TSR2 (always referred to as 'ill-fated'). When Vickers merged with BAC, he became executive director and led the British Concorde team.

THE GREAT HOUSE 536–542 High Road, Leyton, E10. *Leyton Urban District Ratepayers' Association*
The Great House formerly stood here. Built *c.*1700 by Sir Fisher Tench (see page 292) in the Wren style, it was sold to developers in 1881 and eventually demolished in 1905. A clock, saved from the house before demolition, is incorporated into the tower of St Mary's Church. Strype described it in 1720:

'The magnificent and beautiful Seat and Habitation of Sir Fisher Tench, Bart., adorned with large and most delightful Gardens, Plantations, Walks, Groves, Mounts, Summer-Houses, and pleasant Canals, stored with Fish and Fowl, and curious Vistoes for Prospect.'

GREENAWAY, Peter (b.1942), Welsh, film director
Waltham Forest College, Forest Road, Walthamstow, E17. *Private*
Greenaway, a former student of the art school here, is heavily influenced in his film style by Renaissance painting; see, for example, his *The Draughtsman's Contract* (1982) and *The Cook, The Thief, His Wife and Her Lover* (1989). His unique work has gathered him a small but devout following.

HALEX FACTORY Jubilee Avenue, Highams Park, E4.
Plastics Historical Society
The plaque records that on this site stood the Halex factory of the British Xylonite Company from 1897 to 1971. The company was founded by Daniel Spill in 1869, after Alexander Parkes's (q.v.) Parkesine Company had failed. In its time in Highams Park it had a virtual monopoly of the manufacture of table tennis balls, among a host of other plastic products.

HILTON, James (1900–54), English, novelist
16 College Road, Walthamstow, E17. *Private*
42 Oak Hill Gardens, Woodford Green.
English Heritage
Hilton lived at the first address from 1906 to 1921 and attended Sir George Monoux Grammar School nearby. While subsequently living at the second address, he wrote two of his most successful novels, *Lost Horizon* (1933), which introduced the Tibetan utopia of Shangri-La, and *Goodbye Mr Chips* (1934), with the central character based on his own schoolmaster father. Moving to Hollywood, he won an Oscar in 1942 for work on the screenplay of *Mrs Miniver*.

HITCHCOCK, Alfred (1899–1980), English, film director
517 Leytonstone High Road, E11.
London Borough of Waltham Forest
Hitchcock, who was born in a house near this site,

is one of the handful of film directors whose name comes above the title. After early success in England, he moved to Hollywood in 1940 and directed a string of high-tension films, including *Strangers on a Train* (1952), *Vertigo* (1959) and *Psycho* (1963). (See also Kensington & Chelsea 2 and Hackney)

KENNEDY, Lena (1914–86), English, novelist
8 Wellington Road, Leyton, E10. *Private*
Kennedy lived and worked in this house for many years. She described her literary inspiration plainly: 'I used to work in a factory and the girls used to yell their bedroom secrets at one another, so I used to write them down and send them off under an assumed name and get £75 for them... When I was fifty-six, I couldn't work any more and I decided to write a book.' Her first novel, *Maggie*, was published when she was sixty-five, and she went on to produce another thirteen.

KING, Sergeant Alan (1950–91), English, police officer
Higham Hill Road, E17. *Police Memorial Trust*
On 29 November 1991 Sergeant King tackled two burglars, one of whom stabbed him eight times in a violent struggle. Sergeant King was posthumously awarded the Queen's Commendation for Brave Conduct.

LAWRENCE, T. E. (1888–1935), Welsh, soldier, philosopher
Pole Hill, Chingford, E4. *Private*
The plaque records that Lawrence, 'Lawrence of Arabia', owned 18 acres at the top of Pole Hill, where he intended building a house with his friend Vyvyan

Richards and to print fine books, including his own *Seven Pillars of Wisdom*. That plan was never realised and in 1930 Lawrence gave the land to the Corporation of London. (See also Westminster 4.)

LEA BRIDGE STADIUM
Rigg Approach, Leyton, E10. *Private*
The stadium, which formerly stood on this site, was the home of Lea Bridge Speedway team (1928–38) and of Clapton Orient Football Club (1930–7). The football team moved to Brisbane Road and is now Leyton Orient. Lea Bridge stadium was considered unsafe, and pitch invasions were frequent. It proved unsatisfactory for the Orient as it was too far from their main East End fan base. The site is now a dreary industrial estate.

LLOYD, Edward (1815–90), English, publisher
William Morris Gallery, Forest Road, E17.
Borough of Walthamstow
Lloyd, who shares this plaque with William Morris (see page 291), lived here from 1857 to 1885. As well as selling books and publishing cheap popular literature, he issued *Lloyd's Weekly London Newspaper* from 1842 and bought the *News Chronicle* in 1876.

MACKENZIE, Sir Morell (1837–92), English, physician
742 High Road, Leytonstone, E11.
Leyton Urban District Ratepayers' Association
Sir Morell was born here. A pioneer of laryngology in the United Kingdom, he founded the world's first throat hospital in Golden Square, Soho, in 1865 and was knighted in 1887. (See also Westminster 3.)

MANZE'S PIE AND MASH SHOP
76 High Street, Walthamstow, E17.
London Borough of Waltham Forest
Originally from Ravello in Italy, the Manze family came to England in 1878, founding eventually fourteen pie and mash shops around London. This branch was built in 1929 by Luigi Manze. A locally listed building, it was refurbished in 2004 under the Strategic Street Properties Refurbishment/Heritage Economic Regeneration programme in partnership with English Heritage.

MONOUX, George (1477–1543), English, draper, philanthropist
41 Billet Road, E17. *Borough of Walthamstow*
This is the site of Moones, where Monoux lived. Originally from Bristol, where he was mayor in 1501–2, he came to London shortly afterwards, becoming master of the Drapers' Company. He settled in Walthamstow, where he founded a school and almshouses, and served as mayor of London in 1514.

MORRIS, William (1834–96), English, designer, poet, socialist
Fire Station, Forest Road, E17.
Borough of Walthamstow
William Morris Gallery, Forest Road, E17.
Borough of Walthamstow

The plaque at the fire station records that directly opposite stood Elm House (demolished in 1898) in extensive grounds, which was Morris's birthplace on 24 March 1834. At the second address, the plaque records that Morris lived here through his teens (1848–56). This house was until 2008 run as a museum devoted to Morris and his work but was shut by Waltham Forest Council to save money. (See also Redbridge, Westminster 3, Bexley, Hackney, Camden 2 and Hammersmith & Fulham.)

OLIVER, Thomas (1740–1803), English, plantation owner
536–542 High Road, Leyton, E10.
Leyton Urban District Ratepayers' Association
This was the site of the Great House (see page 289), where Oliver lived until his death. His fortune derived from extensive family plantations in Antigua, where he was born. He carried on his merchant business in Mark Lane in the City and this was his country retreat.

PLAATJE, Solomon T. (1876–1932), South African, politician
25 Carnarvon Road, Leyton, E10.
Greater London Council
Solomon Tshekisho Plaatje, who lived here, was a founder member and first general secretary of the South African Native National Congress (later the African National Congress) in 1912. The next year he came to England as part of a delegation protesting against the Native Land Act. He spoke seven languages and translated Shakespeare into Tswana. He was the first black South African to publish a novel in English.

RICHMOND, Lieutenant Colonel Vincent C. (1893–1930), English, aircraft designer
24 Silverdale Road, Hale End, E4. *Private*
Richmond lived here as a boy and attended the nearby Selwyn Avenue School. He designed the R101 airship, the largest man-made object ever to fly, at Cardington near Bedford, and was one of fifty-four people on board for the maiden voyage to India. On 5 October 1930, in bad weather, seven hours into the journey, the ship crashed into a hillside at Beauvais in northern France. There were only eight survivors. The whole airship programme was shelved indefinitely.

ROE, Alliott Verdon (1877–1958), English, aircraft designer
Walthamstow Marshes Railway Viaduct, E17.
Greater London Council
The plaque records that under these arches Roe assembled his first aircraft, the Avro No. 1 triplane, and made the first flight in an all-British machine from these marshes in 1909. In 1910 he founded A. V. Roe Aviation, which became Saunders Roe in the 1920s. Their most famous plane was the Lancaster, the great bomber of the Second World War, of which seven thousand were built.

RUSSELL, Ken (b.1927), English, film director
Waltham Forest College, Forest Road, E17.
Private
Russell is one of several former students at the art school here who are mentioned on this plaque. Beginning with a startling series of arts documentaries as the *enfant terrible* of the BBC in the 1960s, Russell exploded on to the feature film scene with *Women in Love* (1969), *The Boy Friend* (1971) and *Tommy* (1975), but eventually his urge to untrammelled zaniness wore out its welcome.

SMITH, Rodney (1860–1947), English, preacher
Mill Plain, Oak Hill Gardens, Woodford Green.
Private

Born here in a gipsy caravan, 'Gipsy' Rodney Smith was spotted in his teens by William Booth (q.v.) and went on to preach to congregations of thousands all round the world. 'I didn't go through your colleges and seminaries. They wouldn't have me … but I have been to the feet of Jesus where the only true scholarship is learned.'

TENCH, Sir Fisher (*c*.1673–1736), English, politician
536–542 High Road, Leyton E10.
Leyton Urban District Ratepayers' Association

Sir Fisher built the Great House (see page 289) on this site around 1700. He was created a baronet in 1715 and was Whig MP for Southwark from 1713 to 1722. The baronetcy became extinct after his son died without issue.

WALTHAM FOREST COLLEGE
Forest Road, Walthamstow, E17. *Private*
Built in 1938, designed by the Essex County Architect, John Stuart, the college was the *alma mater* of various well-known members of the artistic community (see Peter Blake, Ian Dury, Peter Greenaway and Ken Russell, above).

WATCH HOUSE, Walthamstow
Vestry House Museum, Vestry Road, E17.
Borough of Walthamstow
Here stood the old watch house or 'cage', erected in 1765 and removed in 1912. (For other watch houses, see Camden 1 and Hackney.)

WIGRAM, Sir Robert
(1744–1830), English, merchant, politician
Walthamstow House, Shernhall Street, E17.
Borough of Walthamstow
Sir Robert, High Sheriff of Essex, lived here from 1782 until his death. He entered Parliament in 1802 and was created a baronet in 1805. He ran a fleet of East Indiamen, one of which was named *Walthamstow*. Trading with Bengal, Madras and Bombay, he was one of the major drug importers of the day.

WISEMAN, Cardinal Nicholas (1802–65), Irish, prelate
Etloe House, 180 Church Road, E10.
Leyton Urban District Ratepayers' Association
Wiseman lived here from 1858 to 1864. The Roman Catholic hierarchy was re-established in Britain in 1850, not without controversy, with Wiseman as the first Cardinal Archbishop of Westminster, and his tactful handling of English sensitivities was critical in the process. Archbishop until his death, he was mourned by a large turn-out of all faiths at Kensal Green, 'amid such tokens of public interest, and almost of sorrow, as do not often mark the funerals even of our most illustrious dead', wrote *The Times*.

INDEX